Popular cinema in Brazil, 1930–2001

STEPHANIE DENNISON and LISA SHAW

D0209460

Manchester University Press

Manchester and New York

distributed exclusively in the USA by Palgrave

Published by Manchester University Press
Oxford Road, Manchester M13 9NR, UK
and Room 400, 175 Fifth Avenue, New York, NY 10010, USA
www.manchesteruniversitypress.co.uk

Distributed exclusively in the USA by
Palgrave, 175 Fifth Avenue, New York,
NY 10010, USA

Distributed exclusively in Canada by
UBC Press, University of British Columbia, 2029 West Mall,
Vancouver, BC, Canada V6T 1Z2

British Library Cataloguing-in-Publication Data
A catalogue record for this book is available from the British Library

Library of Congress Cataloging-in-Publication Data applied for

ISBN   0 7190 6498 8 *hardback*
          0 7190 6499 6 *paperback*

First published 2004

13 12 11 10 09 08 07 06 05 04   10 9 8 7 6 5 4 3 2 1

Typeset in Minion
by Graphicraft Limited, Hong Kong
Printed in Great Britain
by CPI, Bath

Popular cinema in Brazil, 1930–2001

Published in our
centenary year
❧ **2004** ❧
MANCHESTER
UNIVERSITY
PRESS

For Anna and Caroline

Contents

List of figures

Acknowledgements

This book is the culmination of a long period of research that would not have been possible without the financial support and encouragement of the University of Leeds, England. A study of this nature has naturally required extensive field work in Brazil, which has been facilitated by the British Academy and the Arts and Humanities Research Board, who have generously funded study leave and several research visits overseas.

We would like to thank the following scholars who have kindly offered invaluable insights during the preparation of this book and comments on the manuscript, often at very short notice and with characteristic enthusiasm and professionalism: Randal Johnson, Lúcia Nagib, John Gledson, Anny Brooksbank Jones, Maite Conde and Diana Holmes.

We would also like to express our gratitude to Ismail Xavier, João Luiz Vieira, Fernão Ramos, Alice Gonzaga, Luiz Carlos Lacerda, Buza Ferraz and Júlio César Miranda, whose approachability and generosity of time and materials have greatly facilitated our research and enhanced this book. Thanks are also due to Hernani Heffner and Maurício Sales at the film archive of the Museum of Modern Art, Rio de Janeiro, and to the staff of the Cinemateca Brasileira in São Paulo, who helped us to locate and view rare movies and related ephemera.

The editorial staff at Manchester University Press have been unfailingly helpful and good humoured, and for this we are particularly grateful.

Finally, we would like to thank the following friends in Brazil, who have supported us in a variety of ways since the inception of this project in 1996: Elmar Pereira de Mello and Hilda White Rössle de Mello, Fernando and Gustavo Caldeira Barbosa, Maria Helena da Silveira Caldeira, Carmen and Eduardo Caldeira de Barros, Antenor José Pereira Neto, Martha and Paulo Schmidt, Marcelo Caldeira Barbosa and family, Jayme Marinho de Albuquerque Jr, Geraldo Lanna Filho† and Fernando Monteiro de Barros.

Preface

In writing this book our aim has been to study the movements, trends and traditions that have characterised commercially successful cinema in Brazil since the advent of sound. We have tried where possible to include a discussion of individual films that have made the greatest impact at the box-office over the last seventy years or so. Lamentably few films made in the 1930s and 1940s have survived, which has obliged us to rely more heavily on written sources, such as newspaper reviews, in Chapter 2 and Chapter 3. For films made after 1960 we have tended to focus in particular on those that dialogue with the *chanchada* tradition.

The titles of films are given in the original Portuguese, with an English translation provided by the authors in parenthesis the first time the title appears in a given chapter. Subsequently the title is given in Portuguese alone within each chapter. The filmography provides a list of all films cited, together with a translation of their title. Production details are given in the filmography only when these are referred to in the main text because of their particular relevance. Where Brazilian films have been exhibited abroad under a translated title, the latter is given in italics.

Citations from film scripts are given in Portuguese with an English translation provided in parenthesis in the main text. Quotations from secondary sources written in Portuguese are only provided in English translation, as indicated in the endnote references.

Introduction

This book provides a chronological study of popular cinema in Brazil since the introduction of sound at the beginning of the 1930s. Its prime object is to show that the Brazilian films that have appealed most successfully to popular audiences since then have engaged with intrinsically home-grown cultural forms, dating back to the nineteenth century, such as Brazil's version of music hall, the travelling circus, radio shows, carnival and, more recently, comedy television. As Ruben George Oliven says: 'the peculiarity of Brazilian society lies precisely in its capacity to take on those aspects of modernity that are of interest to it and to transform them into something suited to its own needs, in which the modern interacts with the traditional'.[1] Cinema took root in Latin America at the turn of the nineteenth century, but unlike in Europe or North America, it was essentially just a 'sign of the new', a foreign import rather than an indigenous consequence of internal industrialisation and urbanisation. In the words of Vivian Schelling: 'images of the experience of modernity circulated within the sphere of culture without equivalent processes of socio-economic modernisation . . . Cinema created the desire to have access to modernity, the centre of which was elsewhere, but also, crucially, suggested the possibility of a home-grown version, accessible through locally available means.'[2] We begin our study with a brief discussion of how we understand the term 'popular cinema' particularly within a Latin American context, drawing on the work of some of the most influential cultural theorists who have written about the region.

Defining the 'popular' in the Latin American context

In their study of popular culture in Latin America, William Rowe and Vivian Schelling identify three different versions of popular culture in the continent.[3] First is popular culture seen as authentically rural, threatened by industrialisation and the modern culture industry; second, popular culture as a variant of mass culture, trying to copy the cultural forms of advanced capitalist nations; third, popular culture as the culture of the oppressed, subaltern classes, in which their imaginary, ideal future is created. In Rowe and Schelling's view all these categories combine and intermingle in Latin America, and certainly our analysis of popular Brazilian cinema will apply elements of both the second and third definitions. They also draw a distinction between popular and mass culture: the former shares neither the audience nor the popularity (in raw numerical terms) of the latter, despite the fact that neither remains entirely distinct from the other. The traditional duality between 'popular' or 'low' and 'high' culture is dangerous, they argue, since it can lead on to other assumed, symmetrically polarised oppositions that have highly pejorative implications for popular culture, such as 'vulgar' versus 'polite' and 'impure' versus 'pure'.[4] In this book, we have made every effort to avoid falling into the trap of such subjective hierarchies in our descriptions of films and their reception. We recognise that, from its beginnings, Brazilian sound cinema has attempted to tap into the tastes of the masses. Our focus in this volume is on films that have intentionally engaged with 'low-brow' cultural products, whose origins lie in pre-industrial traditions, and which have been enjoyed by wide sectors of the population, chiefly at the lower end of the social hierarchy. Consequently, when we talk about popular cinema in this book, we are usually referring to films that have been commercially successful, 'popular' in a straightforward numerical sense.[5]

Since the establishment of sound cinema in the early 1930s, at least until the 1980s, popular film has provided a space for the expression of the cultural values of Brazil's lower classes.[6] Inspired in part by the work of Jesús Martín Barbero, we view popular Brazilian cinema from the perspective of popular experiences that provide access to different forms of cultural expression, rather than as simply mass manipulation.[7] The films analysed for this study are, we argue, direct descendants of other shared cultural experiences, rather than the agents of the destruction of a more 'genuine' popular culture. Our approach is thus one of anthropological tracing, focusing on the way film uses cultural practices that exist prior to or outside the mass media. In other words, we are interested in mediations with established cultural traditions, such as the influence of the music hall tradition and circus on popular film. These links with the past, and with a different kind of popular culture, are discussed at some length, particularly in Chapter 1.

Approaches to Brazilian cultural production

In terms of national identity, Renato Ortiz has argued that Brazilians are relatively sure of what they are not, but struggle to agree on a definition of what they are. One of the most enduring definitions of and approaches to

Brazilian culture is that which Ortiz describes as the contradiction between appearance and essence, between being and not being, or, to put it another way, the difference between theory and practice.[8] This, he believes, is a result of Brazil's third-world status. Disagreement over what Brazilians are, is linked to the hackneyed but nevertheless useful notion of 'two Brazils': the modern, urban, middle-class, sophisticated Brazil of cities like Rio de Janeiro and São Paulo, and its impoverished rural (and urban) flip-side, backward and poor. This book is informed by the theoretical frameworks provided by Ortiz and other critics, who have expressed similar opinions on Brazilian society in different contexts. These include such frameworks as those of Antonio Candido and his dialectic of *malandragem* (a counter-cultural ethos discussed in Chapter 1), Roberto Schwarz and his 'misplaced ideas', and influential film critic Paulo Emílio Salles Gomes and his theory of cultural underdevelopment. Historian and literary critic Roberto Schwarz's thesis of 'misplaced ideas' focuses on the fact that Brazilian intellectuals were busy importing liberal ideologies from Europe in the nineteenth century, even though the Brazilian economy and society were, until 1888, based on the incompatible practice of slavery.[9] As a result of this clash between theory and reality, there is in Brazil a sense that ideas and cultural practices that are appropriated from outside are somehow 'out of place', and that the legacy of slavery and paternalism means that when such foreign ideas are appropriated, they are often 'negotiated' first. (For evidence of this in the form of the so-called Brazilian *jeitinho* or 'string-pulling', see Chapter 1.) Salles Gomes' essay 'Cinema: a trajectory within underdevelopment', first published in 1973, argued, along similar lines, that:

> We [Brazilians] are neither Europeans nor North Americans. Lacking an original culture, nothing is foreign to us because everything is. The painful construction of ourselves develops within the rarefied dialectic of not being and being someone else. Brazilian film participates in this mechanism and alters it through our creative incapacity for copying.[10]

The notions of imitation and of contradiction between appearance and essence in Brazilian society and culture are reminiscent of the theories of Mikhail Bakhtin, who argues that in the world of carnival, where all hierarchies are abolished, participants are made aware that established authority and truth are relative.[11] It is this point that we find most useful in our analysis of the development of popular cinema in Brazil, which we see as often being carnivalesque in nature. Those critics who have been inspired by but have toned down Bakhtin's theories because of his at times nostalgic, utopian and populist vision of society's rank and file, have also informed our work, such as film critic Robert Stam and Brazilian anthropologist Roberto DaMatta. For example, DaMatta acknowledges the degree to which festivity is often 'licensed release' or dependent on permission and organisation from above, but he also 'praises its deep modelling of a different, pleasurable and communal ideal "of the people", even if that ideal cannot immediately be acted upon'.[12]

Modernity and hybridity in Latin America

Ana M. López writes that the fact that the cinema experienced by Latin Americans was and continues to be predominantly foreign is 'of tremendous significance for the complex development of indigenous forms, always caught in a hybrid dialectic of invention and imitation'.[13] As will be shown throughout this book, Brazilian popular film has been characterised by its engagement with imported cinema, above all that of Hollywood, resulting in both purely mimetic and parodic appropriations of the latter's stock paradigms. Latin American cultural forms have perennially been involved in complex negotiations with foreign models and the demands of 'Westernisation', giving rise to what has been called cultural *mestizaje/mestiçagem* (literally 'racial mixing' in Spanish and Portuguese respectively), or cultural hybridity. With the advent of modernity this process intensified, and as López says, 'we could argue that the cinema was one of the principal tools through which the desire for and imitation of the foreign became paradoxically identified as a national characteristic shared by many Latin American nations.'[14]

In *Hybrid Cultures: Strategies for Entering and Leaving Modernity*, the anthropologist Néstor García Canclini argues that the dependency theory model which opposes cultural imperialism to national popular cultures is inadequate to understand current power relations in Latin America.[15] We contend that this has been true of Brazil since the 1930s, as the country intensified its entry into modernity. From the onset of the era of the talkies, Brazilian popular film has entered into a dialectical relationship with Hollywood. By re-appropriating the Hollywood persona of Carmen Miranda, for example, the *chanchadas* or popular musical comedies of the 1950s 'dehierarchise', to use Canclini's terminology, the established asymmetry between the centre (Hollywood) and the periphery (Brazilian film).[16]

Canclini's work on 'deterritorialisation' and intercultural movements across the US–Mexican border is particularly useful in the context of Latin American re-workings of Hollywood paradigms. He analyses hybrid and simulated cultural products in the context of the border experience in cities like Tijuana, and argues that the home-grown version becomes a resource for defining identity, whereby the 'authentic' becomes relativised. Tijuana-based periodicals, for example, re-work definitions of identity and culture from the starting point of the border experience, becoming a voice for a generation who grew up exposed to both Mexican and US culture. Metaphorically, the border experience applies to the Brazilian audiences of Brazilian popular film since 1930, who have continuously been exposed to both domestic movies and the Hollywood imports. These audiences, like the inhabitants of the physical frontier land with the USA, experience two cinematic worlds.[17] The Brazilian *chanchada*, for example, celebrates the migration of the *baiana* and the inter-cultural crossings that she has made, and Brazilian audiences are content to celebrate her hybrid identity, the 'authenticity' of which is immaterial. Canclini argues that popular sectors in Latin America deal with ideological oppression today by 'incorporating and positively valuing elements produced outside of their own group (criteria of prestige, hierarchies, designs, and functions of objects)'.[18] In the same way, popular cinema in Brazil has traditionally re-appropriated Hollywood paradigms, usually in parodic form, particularly by ironically re-working stereotypical visions of Brazil and the rest of Latin America.

Popular Brazilian cinema has thus been characterised by its recourse to hybridity, and by its interplay with pre-modern cultural forms and ideals, and with contemporary media. The following comments by José de Souza Martins are particularly relevant to our reading of popular film in Brazil:

> In the Latin American and, in particular, the Brazilian case, the critical element within modernity is generated by cultural 'hybridity', by the conjunction of past and present, the finished and the unfinished. It arises out of the recourse to traditionalism and conservatism, which questions modern social reality and the concepts which are part of it and mediate it.[19]

Of course cinema was not the only medium to adopt such a strategy in Brazil. De Souza Martins cites the example of *sertaneja* music.[20] He writes:

> It was from the beginning a biting critique of the most representative elements of modernity in the city, as well as a means of comprehending it – a musical genre which combined elements from the old travelling circus and the new possibilities offered by records and the radio. It was a genre which emerged on the point of the decisive emergence of the contours of modernity in Brazil, in contrast with the rural and traditional world that was crumbling away.[21]

Insistent mockery of urban elites, irreverent humour and nostalgia for an idealised bucolic past would define popular film in Brazil through the decades. It remorselessly pokes fun at the modern, exposing the contradictions and failings of modernity, as experienced in Brazil, with a critical laugh. As de Souza Martins concludes in relation to cultural production as a whole, 'this critical laugh is contained precisely in, and born out of, the disjointed and grotesque juncture between what is actually modern and what is not; in the forced co-existence of mismatched relationships, cultures juxtaposed and thereby disfigured.'[22]

Cinematic endeavour within Latin America has always been bound up with notions of national self-definition. As Renato Ortiz and Carlos Monsiváis contend, the media as a whole have played a leading role in consolidating national identities within the continent.[23] In Brazil, popular cinema has acted as a source of collective identification in a modern, increasingly urban world in which the secular nation-state has replaced religion, village or region as the 'imagined community', to use Benedict Anderson's now famous phrase.[24] But the notion of self-definition conveyed in popular film has been characterised by comic self-deprecation, and by highlighting the very distinctive paradoxical nature of modernity in Brazil, and the incongruities of the lives of ordinary people, often uprooted and marginalised. The perception of the self in relation to the nation and the State has proved to be an enduring preoccupation for filmmakers.

A note on statistics

Although no official records of box-office receipts for the 1930–66 period exist, the Brazilian press's coverage of the long-awaited launches of domestic films, and the proliferation of magazines devoted to describing the lifestyles of the public's screen heroes and heroines give ample evidence of their popularity, particularly that of the *chanchada*. In the film magazine *Cinelândia* in April 1957, Zenaide Andréa wrote in relation to two examples of this tradition: 'Box-office records have been broken by some of the latest Brazilian films. *Metido a bacana* (A Cut Above the Rest) grossed more than nine million *cruzeiros* in just two weeks. *Garotas e samba* (Girls and Samba) took seven million, also in the first couple of weeks.'[25] Cinema entrance fees in Brazil were the seventh cheapest in Latin America in 1952 and Brazil enjoyed a place in the top ten when it came to the number of cinema halls and the size of audiences.[26] By the 1950s cinema theatres had sprung up all over Brazil, in every large town or city, far outnumbering today's equivalents, which increasingly tend to be out-of-town multiplexes.

It is considerably easier to gauge the success of national films released after 1966 when the National Cinema Institute (INC) was set up (later to be replaced by Embrafilme, until its demise in 1990). From then on box-office statistics for national and foreign films began to be more systematically and reliably published.[27] Although in many instances these figures were still open to manipulation by the owners of cinema theatres, distributors and producers alike, they give us a good idea of how individual films fared with the public at the time of their release. More recently, Maria do Rosário Caetano set about compiling a list of the fifty most watched Brazilian films.[28] In order to compare the box-office results of films released before the INC was set up with those released up until 1990, she interviewed industry professionals, and in particular directors and those involved in production companies, and their relatives and descendants.[29] Although only four films released before

1966 make their way into her new top fifty (two early Mazzaropi films, together with *O ébrio* (The Drunkard, 1946) and the award-winning *O cangaceiro* (*The Bandit*, 1953)), it is clear from the statements gathered that, had better statistics been available, many *chanchadas*, and in particular *Nem Sansão, nem Dalila* (Neither Samson, Nor Delilah, 1954), would likely have dominated the upper echelons of the chart.[30]

One criterion for judging the success of (recent) national films with a national audience which Maria do Rosário Caetano does not take into consideration, but for which some useful statistics are available and will occasionally be used in this study, is how films have fared on television. A number have been shown on prime-time networked television over the last few years, and bearing in mind that forty million spectators have been known to tune into the TV Globo network in the evenings, this would arguably make them the most watched Brazilian films.[31]

Notes

1 Ruben George Oliven, 'Brazil: the modern in the tropics', in Vivian Schelling (ed.), *Through the Kaleidoscope: The Experience of Modernity in Latin America* (London and New York: Verso, 2000), p. 70.

2 Vivian Schelling, 'Introduction: reflections on the experience of modernity in Latin America', in Schelling (ed.), *Through the Kaleidoscope*, pp. 24–5.

3 William Rowe and Vivian Schelling, *Memory and Modernity: Popular Culture in Latin America* (London, Verso, 1991), pp. 2–3.

4 *Ibid.*, pp. 2–10, pp. 193–6.

5 Renato Ortiz has said that this notion of the 'popular' arose as a consequence of the emergence of the culture industry and a market of symbolic national goods in Brazil since the 1970s. Renato Ortiz, 'Popular culture, modernity and nation', in Schelling (ed.), *Through the Kaleidoscope*, p. 138. In our study, however, we have applied this definition retrospectively and have found that in relation to cinematic production pre-dating the 1970s it is not mutually exclusive with the idea of the 'popular' as something linked to the traditional cultural forms of the lower classes.

6 Since then, as Renato Ortiz has argued, the 'popular' in Brazil has ceased to be first and foremost linked to the traditional culture of the popular classes or the project of popular liberation, but instead to the products of the culture industry. See Renato Ortiz, *A moderna tradição brasileira* (São Paulo: Brasiliense, 1988).

7 See, for example, Jesús Martín Barbero, *Communication, Culture and Hegemony: From the Media to Mediations* (London: Sage, 1993).

8 Ortiz, 'Popular culture, modernity and nation', pp. 127–8.

9 See, for example, Roberto Schwarz, 'Misplaced ideas: literature and society in late-nineteenth-century Brazil', in *Misplaced Ideas: Essays on Brazilian Culture* (London and New York: Verso, 1992). Ruben George Oliven does not agree entirely with Schwarz's thesis. Oliven argues that slavery was not incompatible with economic liberalism in Brazil, since slaves were viewed by the elites as commodities to be

used and exchanged like any others. He goes on to say, 'strictly speaking, nothing is ever "in place" – everything leaves one place and enters another, where it is adapted to the interests of different groups and changing circumstances. Cultural borrowing is a constant in any culture.' Oliven, 'Brazil: the modern in the tropics', p. 55.

10 Paulo Emílio Salles Gomes, 'Cinema: a trajectory within underdevelopment', in Randal Johnson and Robert Stam (eds), *Brazilian Cinema* (New York: Columbia University Press, 1995), p. 245.

11 Quoted in Peter Stallybrass and Allon White, *The Politics and Poetics of Transgression* (Ithaca: Cornell University Press, 1986), p. 6.

12 *Ibid.*, p. 18.

13 Ana M. López, '"A train of shadows": early cinema and modernity in Latin America', in Schelling (ed.), *Through the Kaleidoscope*, p. 151.

14 *Ibid.*, p. 167.

15 Néstor García Canclini, *Hybrid Cultures: Strategies for Entering and Leaving Modernity* (Minneapolis and London: University of Minnesota Press, 1995), p. 229.

16 See Chapter 4.

17 Canclini, *Hybrid Cultures*, p. 238.

18 *Ibid.*, p. 260.

19 José de Souza Martins, 'The hesitations of the modern and the contradictions of modernity in Brazil', in Schelling (ed.), *Through the Kaleidoscope*, p. 251.

20 *Sertaneja* music, which emerged in São Paulo at the end of the 1920s and was popularised throughout Brazil in the 1940s and 1950s by the North Eastern singer-songwriter-accordionist Luiz Gonzaga, is an urban musical genre rooted in rural, backlands traditions. It is sometimes referred to as the Brazilian equivalent of country and western music.

21 Martins, 'The hesitations of the modern and the contradictions of modernity in Brazil', p. 255.

22 *Ibid.*, p. 257.

23 Ortiz, *A moderna tradição brasileira*, and Carlos Monsiváis, in *Contratexto*, 3 (July 1988).

24 Benedict Anderson, *Imagined Communities: Reflections on the Origin and Spread of Nationalism* (London and New York: Verso, 1983).

25 *Cinelândia*, April 1957, p. 69, quoted in Rosângela de Oliveira Dias, *O mundo como chanchada: cinema e imaginário das classes populares na década de 50* (Rio de Janeiro: Relume-Dumará, 1993), p. 14.

26 Dias, *O mundo como chanchada*, p. 15.

27 See for example the top twenty films released between 1970 and 1984 listed in *Cinejornal* 6 (Rio de Janeiro: Embrafilme, 1986).

28 Maria do Rosário Caetano, 'As maiores bilheterias do cinema nacional', *Revista de Cinema*, www.revistadecinema.com.br (accessed April 2002).

29 Certain journalists and researchers have compiled box-office takings for films released since 1990, since such statistics are still not systematically collated by the state.

30 Caetano, 'As maiores bilheterias do cinema nacional'.

31 For example, *Guerra de Canudos* (*Battle of Canudos*, 1997), *Central do Brasil* (*Central Station*, 1998) and *O auto da compadecida* (*A Dog's Will*, 2000).

1

The cultural origins of popular cinema in Brazil

Brazilian popular cinema, at least until the 1980s, can be seen as a direct descendant of other shared cultural experiences. Just as a line can be traced from British music hall, via saucy picture postcards, radio comedy and holidays at the seaside to the *Carry On* films with their contemporary references, so too is it possible to read the special intimacy which popular films in Brazil achieved with their audiences as a celluloid continuation of the culturally respectable traditions of the *teatro de revista*, Brazil's version of music hall, for example.[1]

The legacy of the *teatro de revista*

The *teatro de revista*, Brazil's home-grown version of music hall, which had taken shape by the 1880s and continued to flourish in the period that concerns us, between the 1920s and 1940s, has proved to have been the most enduring influence on popular cinema, and particularly the *chanchada* or musical comedy film.[2] The evolution of the *teatro de revista* in many ways pre-empted that of popular film, as both relied heavily on circus humour, socio-political critique and musical numbers. Like the *chanchada*, the *teatro de revista* was a particularly *carioca* (Rio de Janeiro-based) phenomenon.[3]

Both theatrical revues (*revistas*) and the *chanchada* featured music of African origin within an eclectic mix of imported and home-grown styles, including US fox-trots, ragtimes and shimmies, Portuguese *fados*, Argentine tangos, the lambeth-walk, the rumba and bolero, Afro-Brazilian rhythms (*maxixes, lundus*), regional music from the North and North East of Brazil and the *sertão* or rural backlands, and the light classical work of Carlos Gomes and Offenbach. In both popular theatre and popular film, satirical commentary and music took precedence over choreography, although both gave centre stage to scantily clad dancing girls. In the pre-1920s *revistas* dance routines were largely improvised, and as in the *chanchada* they were rarely integrated into the action, but served merely as an interlude, often at the beginning or the end of the show, or as an ensemble piece to showcase the talents of a given star or stars. Saucy humour and glimpses of bare flesh similarly characterised both popular entertainment forms.

Carnival provided the *teatro de revista* with enduring subject matter, and was often combined with political satire. From the 1910s the *revista carnavalesca* (carnival revue) came into its own. Launched a few months before carnival, in the 1930s it vied with the talking cinema as the mouthpiece for promoting the music destined for the annual celebration. The inversions so intrinsic to carnival were reflected in the title of the 1915 *revista De pernas pro ar* (Topsy-Turvy), which featured the tenor Vicente Celestino, who would go on to star in one of the biggest box-office successes before 1960, *O ébrio* (The Drunkard, 1946).

Many stars such as Dercy Gonçalves, Oscarito and Ankito made the transition from the stage to the screen.[4] Oscarito, who had earned his stripes in the circus, made his first stage performance in the *revista Calma, Gegê* (Keep Calm, Gegê (a common nickname for Getúlio Vargas)) of 1932. Carmen Miranda also trod the boards, and the *teatro de revista*, like popular film later, incorporated performances of contemporary songs by well-known singers to lend weight to the production.

The typical themes of the comic sketches in the *teatro de revista* were to resurface throughout the *chanchada* tradition. Criticism of authority, and even of individual politicians, was rife, providing an outlet for the resentments of the disadvantaged theatre audiences, who were encouraged to laugh in the face of adversity. Salvyano Cavalcanti de Paiva argues that the *teatro de revista* represented a mechanism for those on society's lower rungs to vent their anger towards the dominant class.[5] He argues that its success during an era that witnessed the consolidation of capitalism and the relentless expansion of consumer society was no coincidence.[6] The first of the *revistas de ano* (revues of the year), as they were first called, premiered in 1859. At the end of each year, they provided good-humoured commentary on political events, and focused on daily life through a comic lens. Like the early *chanchadas* of the 1930s and 1940s, they referred to everyday problems with which the audience could identify, such as faulty telephone connections, the failings of public transport and dirty streets. Artur Azevedo's revue *O Rio de Janeiro em 1877* (Rio de Janeiro in 1877), for example, poked fun at the stupidity of the police force and politicians, and highlighted problems faced by ordinary people during the previous year, ranging from flooding in the then capital and the terrible drought which afflicted the North East in that year, to the yellow fever epidemic which was a regular summer occurrence in the city. Written by the most prolific and highly regarded popular playwright of the time, who dominated the tradition for thirty years, this production also tackled the theme of *malandragem* (living by one's wits), described in more detail below, in the form of trickster dentists with no qualifications.

Music hall's irreverent attacks on the establishment took the form of comic impersonations of Mussolini and Hitler, and of Brazilian authority figures, such as President Getúlio Vargas (1930–45), Luís Carlos Prestes, the Communist leader released from prison in 1945, and President Eurico Gaspar Dutra (1946–51). In the revue *Música, maestro!* (Music, Maestro!, 1940), for example, Pedro Dias wore a mask of Vargas's face. In cinema, the *chanchadas* poked fun at authority at both a local and national level. In the parodic *chanchada Nem Sansão, nem Dalila* (Neither Samson, Nor Delilah, 1954), to quote one example, satirical references to Brazilian politics in the first half of the twentieth century abound, as Samson imitates the mannerisms, voice and oratorical techniques of President Vargas. The building of the new capital city, Brasília, is also made fun of in other examples of this genre, as is its champion, President Juscelino Kubitschek (1956–61). Mockery of the 'other' within the *teatro de revista* and the *chanchada* took the form of comic attacks on Brazil's own 'outsiders'. These included the stereotypically dimwitted Portuguese immigrants, with their distinctive accent, often played by Portuguese actors.

Both the *teatro de revista* and popular film articulated the seductive powers of modernity and city life, but equally lamented the loss of tradition, thus reflecting the city–countryside dialectic that was central to modernity debates in Latin America as a whole, and not least Brazil. In both media, the culture clash between rural and urban lifestyles is symbolised by the arrival of the illiterate hick, known as the *caipira*, in the big city, where he has to contend with modern modes of transport and decipher everyday *carioca* speech, when his own version of Portuguese is full of grammatical errors. In the *revista Abacaxi* (Pineapple, 1893), for example, the actor João Colás played a character referred to simply as 'o caipira do Ceará', literally 'the hick from Ceará', a drought-ridden state in Brazil's North East. In *O meu boi morreu* (My Ox Has Died, 1916), an identical character from Ceará arrives in Rio and is overwhelmed by the marvels and pitfalls of city life; he is finally reassured that his rural existence, however humble, is infinitely preferable. This character became synonymous with the Jeca, who appeared in the eponymous revue *Jeca Tatu* (1919). As Cavalcanti de Paiva writes of this stock character, 'Via his caricatured "Brazilianness", he was enthusiastically received by an audience engulfed by mass culture.'[7] The figure of *Tatu* (literally an armadillo) would resurface periodically in popular theatre, such as in *Tatu subiu no pau* (Tatu Learns to Climb, 1923), which stressed the morality and grass-roots wisdom of the simple country dweller. The largely uneducated audience could identify with this character, as well as laugh at him.

Jeca was also the character played by the actor/director Amácio Mazzaropi in all the films he starred in after 1958, allowing him to appeal to and be instantly recognised by his audiences. His screen persona was a composite of the *caipira*, the European (especially Italian) immigrant, and the *caboclo*, a term which denotes mixed European and Indian ancestry but which is often synonymous with the mixed-race rural poor from the North East of Brazil. Mazzaropi's films were particularly successful in the city and state of São Paulo, in the interior of the country and the North East of Brazil, which suggests that audiences flocked to see his films at least partly because they identified with the character Jeca. The figure of Jeca represents the oppressed and marginalised rural poor who moved to the cities in search of work. The Jeca played by Mazzaropi (whose performance was based on Genésio Arruda's *jeca* from the *teatro de revista* and silent movies)[8] either still lived in the countryside or tried to hold on to his traditional way of life in the town or city.

The stereotypes of the urban landscape that provided the stock characters of the *teatro de revista* were to dominate popular film from the 1930s onwards, ranging from the uneducated migrant to the indolent civil servant, from the wily *mulata* (mixed-race woman of African and white European descent) and wide-boy *malandro* or spiv, to the Portuguese immigrant.[9] Furthermore, the stylised, white-skinned *baiana* (the caricature of the Afro-Brazilian female street vendors of the city of Salvador), pretending to be black, that would become synonymous with Carmen Miranda's screen persona and later with that of Eliana Macedo in the *chanchadas* of the 1950s, emerged from the *teatro de revista*. In *Tim-tim por tim-tim* (Down to the last T) of 1892, for example, the Spanish actress Pepa Ruiz appeared resplendent in the *baiana* costume.[10] The stock type of the *mulatinha sestrosa* or devious mixed-race beauty was similarly established via popular theatre, but was often played by a white actress who had darkened her face with make-up. One such was the pale-skinned Lia Binatti, of Italian and German ancestry, who often took this role in the 1920s. White males such as João Martins in *Diz isso cantando* (Say It Singing, 1930), also blackened their faces, clearly taking their lead from Al Jolson in *The Jazz Singer* (1927). As in the *chanchada*, Afro-Brazilian performers were relegated to supporting roles; indeed in *Pirão de areia* (Sand Soup, 1926), Rosa Negra was billed as dancing with eight 'black-girls'. Inspired by the Cotton Club of Harlem and the cabaret shows of Paris, Brazilian theatres began to showcase the dancing skills of the Afro-Brazilian inhabitants of Rio's shantytowns, which also provided the setting for a number of productions.

The theme of shifting identities in a period of immense social change is also common to popular theatre and popular film. A recurrent feature of both is that of parodic imitations of foreign stars, such as the actress Sarah

Bernhardt (in the theatre revue *Abacaxi*, 1893) and singer Josephine Baker (in the theatre revue *Guerra ao mosquito* (War on Flies), 1929). One of the most memorable examples within the *chanchada* tradition was Norma Benguel's impersonation of French screen icon Brigitte Bardot in *O homem do sputnik* (Sputnik Man, 1960). Sarah Bernhardt makes a more recent appearance in Miguel Faria Jr's neo-*chanchada* from 1999, *O xangô de Baker Street* (*Xango from Baker Street*), set in the days of Sherlock Holmes.

The *chanchada*'s fascination with cross-dressing can also be traced back to the *teatro de revista. A mulher-homem!* (The Woman-Man!, 1886), for example, took its lead from a true-life case of a man who gained employment in domestic service by dressing as a woman, only to become front-page news. Similarly, in the revue *Silêncio, Rio!* (Shut up, Rio!, 1941) five well-known female artists were impersonated by male stars.

The impact of circus on popular film

The twentieth-century 'theatre-circus' *circo-teatro*, *circo-pavilhão* or *circo mambembe* developed in the second half of the nineteenth century from the traditional circus with its origins in Renaissance Europe, partly inspired by developments in the circus in Argentina at the same time. In most cases these small and inexpensively run circuses functioned like travelling variety shows, with their clowns, magic acts, plenty of musical interludes and the staging of one-act plays, often set to music.[11] In Rio de Janeiro, the sketch shows and mini-plays that they included were filled with typically *carioca* figures. These circuses kept diversifying throughout the twentieth century, in order to survive competition from radio, cinema and later, television. Despite the proliferation of television sets in Brazil, there were between 100 and 150 *circos-teatros* in the suburbs of São Paulo in 1980.[12] This was possible because, in the words of José Magnani: 'the circus does not compete with the mass media but instead seeks to integrate the media into its very structure and repertoire.'[13]

The shows described by Magnani in his useful book on popular culture in the poor neighbourhoods surrounding São Paulo in the early 1980s include lengthy interviews with contestants for prizes offered in between acts, dancing competitions, groups playing samba and North Eastern music, as well as pop hits from television and the radio. The guaranteed success of such a format was and continues to be evident in the popularity of the weekend television staple in Brazil, the so-called *programa de auditório* or variety show, which also has its roots in popular theatre and the circus, and which was made popular on television by Sílvio Santos, whose personal style of locution (for example, the ingratiating presentation and frequent interviews with members of the audience in which he repeats their answers by way of confirmation) in turn influenced the *animadores* or ringmasters in the circuses.[14]

Circus audiences were free to voice their opinions during the performance (talking loudly, booing and heckling actors depicting greedy landowners, and so on), all of which went some way to creating a sense of community spectatorship. They could even influence the performances, as long as they did not show disrespect for the artists themselves.[15] The social practice of attending the *circo-teatro* inspired audience behaviour at the cinema, and this should be borne in mind when considering issues of spectatorship in the context of popular cinema in Brazil. In fact, popular cinema around the world has often been watched in ways that challenge the notion of hegemonic brainwashing *en masse* argued by many postmodern theorists, for example. In an article on the attraction of popular films in post-war Italy, Christopher Wagstaff describes a context very similar to the reception of films by Mazzaropi, for example, which will be discussed in Chapter 6.[16] He recounts how the spectators were nearly always men, who would go to their nearest cinema (or the only cinema in the area) at a set time. They would rarely seek to find out in advance what film was showing, would not necessarily arrive at the beginning of the film, and would talk to friends during the show whenever they felt like it (unless something on screen drew their attention). People would come and go and change seats throughout the screening.

In the *circo-teatro*, this sense of audience participation is reinforced on a practical level by the help offered by the local population, and children in particular, in setting up the circus tent. Most of the circus members were from poor neighbourhoods similar to those where they performed. Those who were 'discovered' in the circus and went on to become radio, television and film stars, often returned to their communities and made guest appearances in these small circuses, in much the same way that they would appear on Sílvio Santos's television programme, for example.

One of the most significant elements of the circus in Brazil, and one which is very important for popular cinema, was the clown, who in the late nineteenth century played a pivotal role in the development of circus theatre.[17] The so-called *palhaço-ator* or actor-clown is regarded as being unique to Brazil. These clowns are also considered responsible for increasing the importance of music in the circus, often by setting plays to music or singing slightly rude *modinhas*, a popular sentimental song style, presumably under pressure of competition from the increasingly popular music hall in cities such as Rio de Janeiro.[18] A number of successful *palhaços-atores* at the turn of the century went on to have careers in the music industry, thus reinforcing the link between clowning, singing and musicality. Eduardo Sebastião das Neves was one such *palhaço-ator* who found success as a musical performer.[19] Like many singing clowns, he was black and he had *ginga* or swing, considered essential in black entertainers for successful comic performances.[20] Another example, who although not from the circus may well have been influenced by these popular clowns, was the black North Eastern singer Jackson do Pandeiro (1919–82), who was noted for his crazy dance steps and humorous facial expressions while he sang. Within popular cinema, four such 'clowns' are Mazzaropi (who would also burst into song in his films), Oscarito and Grande Otelo (the well-known double act of the Atlântida *chanchadas*, both renowned for their facial expressions),[21] and Mussum, the black member of the Trapalhões, to be discussed in Chapter 6, who combines a background in music (samba) with, again, humour based on facial expressions.[22]

The legacy of the circus can be seen throughout the *chanchada* tradition, in the form of slapstick humour, and particularly physical knockabout, falls and chase sequences. The 'clowns' of popular film are a source of both amusement and identification for the audience, and their gags play on the public's fears of physical and social maladjustment. As Alan Dale writes: 'the slapstick hero's skill at deploying his paradoxically acrobatic clumsiness is central to his status as an Everyman ... It's one of our comic rituals because it's common – it happens to everyone.'[23] As in the United States, in Brazil this low-brow form of physical comedy grew directly out of the clowning characteristic of both live popular theatre and circus acts, and drew on the established skills of their performers. This popular cultural legacy is openly acknowledged in the opening scene of the *chanchada Sai de baixo* (Look Out!, 1956), which takes the form of a revue show. Between a performance by a comic male singer and that of the well-known female accordion player Adelaide Chiozzo, is sandwiched a clownish circus act in which an Afro-Brazilian strong man is knocked to the floor by a malodorous shoe belonging to a pale-skinned weakling.[24]

Fight scenes and the most common structural device in slapstick movies, chases, both feature heavily in the *chanchada*. In *Aviso aos navegantes* (Calling All Sailors, 1950) a cat-fight breaks out on the dance floor of an ocean liner, as the well-heeled passengers look on like the extra-diegetic audience, and later Oscarito's character is chased around the ship by the villain of the piece. The climax of this film is a long fight sequence that involves all the main protagonists, both male and female, and from which the four anti-heroes emerge victorious, reassuring audiences of the triumph of the small man, even in the face of evil deeds and crimes perpetrated by the villain, in this case a devious master of hypnosis. Similarly, in *Sai de baixo!* a brawl breaks out at the military base, much to the delight of the female onlookers, who like the real-life audience are transfixed by the acrobatics and smashing of furniture. An extension of the carnivalesque chaos of the chase features in *A grande vedete* (The Great Star, 1958), when poisonous snakes escape from a crate backstage at a theatre, causing pandemonium among both the performers on stage and the audience members. In true slapstick tradition, the protagonist, Jeanette, is bitten on the bottom.

The films of Mazzaropi are filled with stylised fight sequences that are not always played for laughs, which invariably take place in bars, with barmen ducking behind the counter, as in all good Westerns. Likewise, the Trapalhões films are full of such fight scenes, although the troupe tends to rely more on slapstick humour in these sequences. After all, physical knockabout is the comic mainstay of this quartet, whose humour is supposedly aimed more at children than adults. Unsurprisingly, many *pornochanchadas* (the soft-core porn comedies to be discussed in Chapter 6) also include Benny Hill-style high-camp chase and fight sequences. For example, in *Histórias que nossas babás não contavam* (Stories Our Nannies Never Told Us, 1979), an erotic spoof of *Snow White and the Seven Dwarves*, an effete outlaw is chased and deliberately allows himself to be caught by Costinha, his pursuer, declaring: 'É a lei da selva. Matou, tem que comer!' (It's the law of the jungle: you must eat what you kill) – the verb for 'to eat' being a well-known expression in Portuguese meaning to have sex. Such double entendres form part of a tradition of verbal slapstick in popular film, which encompasses puns, nonsequiturs and outrageous metaphors.

Carnival and popular film

Popular cinema in Brazil has often engaged with elements of the nation's most famous and pervasive festival, carnival. In Brazil some form of pre-Lenten celebration has existed since the mid-sixteenth century, after the arrival of the Portuguese colonisers in 1500. The early carnivals in Brazil were based on a popular festival known as *entrudo*, a tradition that originated in the Azores and became popular in Portugal in the fifteenth and sixteenth centuries. Associated with riotous antics and pranks, the *entrudo* was outlawed in Brazil in 1853, and finally died out at the beginning of the 1900s. In the first years of the twentieth century three separate carnivals were held in Rio de Janeiro: firstly, that of the poor, largely Afro-Brazilian population, in the central Praça Onze district of the city, secondly, that of the middle classes in the Avenida Central (now the Avenida Rio Branco), and thirdly, that of the wealthy, white elite, which centred on lavish costume balls. By the 1920s the annual event had become associated with two musical rhythms, the carnival march (*marcha* or *marchinha*), of bourgeois origin and inspired by Portuguese marches that were taken to Brazil with music hall, and the samba, believed to have grown out of the percussion-based *batuques* and *lundus* performed by African slaves on rural plantations.[25]

Carnival settings and songs on screen
During the silent era carnival was the focus of much interest among Brazilian filmmakers, and it has been estimated that between 1906 and the arrival of

the talkies in the early 1930s around fifty shorts were produced using footage from the annual celebrations in Rio.[26] The advent of sound led to the production of films about the annual carnival celebrations, the first of which, *A voz do carnaval* (The Voice of Carnival), appeared in 1933. This film was part documentary and incorporated real-life footage from the Rio carnival of that year. The *chanchada* genre grew out of these early carnival films, and was born in 1935 when the Rio-based Cinédia studios launched the famous musical *Alô, alô, Brasil!* (Hello, Hello, Brazil!). Taking their lead from the *teatro de revista*, Cinédia realised that films featuring songs destined for the annual carnival celebrations and competitions offered mass appeal and huge commercial potential. *Alô, alô, Brasil!* established the trend for using radio artists to sing and dance in front of the cameras and to perform the most popular songs of the moment in the run-up to carnival.

In 1949 the payment of copyright dues was enforced with increased rigour, with the result that *chanchadas* no longer relied exclusively on recognisable carnival sambas and *marchinhas*, preferring instead to incorporate a much more diverse array of diegetic music. For example, jazz is performed at a high-society cocktail party in the film *Samba em Brasília* (Samba in Brasília, 1960), in contrast to the percussion-based *samba de morro* (literally 'shantytown samba') performed by the inhabitants of a neighbouring shantytown, and in *Metido a bacana* (A Cut Above the Rest, 1957) carnival sambas and *marchinhas* are performed alongside rock and roll numbers. The plot of this *chanchada* centres on the spectacular costume balls of Rio's carnival. The opening credits appear over footage of the street processions, and, as the visiting foreign prince declares: 'o carnaval no Brasil é o maior' (Carnival in Brazil is the greatest). He invites his lowly Afro-Brazilian footman, played by Grande Otelo, to join him in the celebrations with the cry of 'Vamos cair na farra!' (Let's party!), illustrating how for the duration of the carnival Brazil becomes a true racial and social democracy.

The carnival metaphor on screen

> The carnivalesque principle abolishes hierarchies, levels social classes, and creates another life free from conventional rules and restrictions. In carnival, all that is marginalized and excluded – the mad, the scandalous, the aleatory – takes over the center in a liberating explosion of otherness. The principle of the material body – hunger, thirst, defecation, copulation – becomes a positively corrosive force, and festive laughter enjoys a symbolic victory over death, over all that is held sacred, over all that oppresses and restricts.[27]

Bakhtin's understanding of the carnival tradition has been applied to the Brazilian variant of this pre-Lenten revelry by cultural anthropologist Roberto DaMatta.[28] He has focused on how the normal rules that govern social interaction, such as racial and social hierarchies, are suspended for the duration of carnival, and replaced by a total overturning of convention and irreverence towards authority. He writes of the carnival parades: 'what catches our attention in these marches is the reversal effected between the marcher (a poor person, usually a black or mulatto man or woman) and the figure they represent in the parade (a noble, a king, a mythological figure); and we also note the participation of society as a whole, whether as judge or rooter.'[29] He adds that 'the universality and homogeneity of Carnival serve precisely to reinforce, and compensate on another plane, the particularism, hierarchy, and inequality of Brazilian everyday life'.[30] In popular film the trope of carnival would eventually replace the overt promotion of carnival music, and carnivalesque elements permeated the *chanchada* of the 1940s and 1950s in particular, as discussed in Chapters 3 and 4.

Within Brazilian popular film, the legacy of the carnivalesque manifests itself in irreverent parody and the upending of norms of good taste and propriety. The tradition of conscious and ironic imitation emerged in early sound film. As with later examples of this cinematic trend, Luiz de Barros's 1931 comedy, *O babão* (The Idiot), capitalised on the popularity of a Hollywood movie, Ramon Novarro's *The Pagan*, which was literally translated as *O Pagão* in Brazil. The title of Barros's parodic film referred to the main character, a naive hillbilly by the name of Zé Babão, played by Genésio Arruda, the archetypal *caipira* of several forerunners of the *chanchada*. His farcical rendition of a pastiche of 'Pagan Love Song', with his pronounced rural accent and attire of undergarments, is often cited as the high-point of the movie and provided a hilarious comic contrast with the seductive tones of the Latin heart-throb in the Hollywood original. Parody has been a recurrent feature of popular film in Brazil, whether directed at imported cultural products and their underlying associations or at high-brow art forms, which are farcically debunked in the true spirit of bacchanalian revelry. The *chanchada De vento em popa* (Wind in the Sails, 1957), for example, which comically attacks the USA's preoccupation with the Cold War via references to the atom bomb, culminates in a typical celebratory finale, in which Oscarito, in a parody of Elvis, performs a pastiche of a rock and roll number. Tellingly, two thugs have been sent to the airport to send a virtual namesake of the American star, one Melvis Prestes back to the USA. Brazil does not need to import its musical icons and the *chanchada* humorously undermines North America's cultural imperialism.

Foreign films were an obvious target for parodic treatment, which allowed Brazilian filmmakers to poke fun at the glossy originals, share in their success and yet also admit to their own creative limitations. *Matar ou correr* (Kill or Run, 1954) was a self-confessed parody of the Western *High Noon* of 1952, released in Brazil with the title *Matar ou morrer* (Kill or Die). *Nem Sansão, nem Dalila* loosely took as its basic premise Cecile B. de Mille's *Samson and*

Delilah (1949), and the Biblical epic in general.[31] As well as being a parody of a Western, *Matar ou correr* venerates and vindicates the counter-cultural lifestyle of *malandragem*, one of the poles of popular Brazilian identity in this era, discussed in more detail below. This ethos is personified in the characters of the cowardly sheriff and his sidekick, who make their livings by cheating people with fake medicines before turning a stroke of luck to their advantage. Typically of the *chanchada*, the two hustling *malandros* or loveable rogues find themselves in positions of power by a quirk of fate in a classic case of carnivalesque role reversal. These parodic comedies of the 1950s support Roberto Schwarz's view that parody of dominant cultural forms is inevitable in a country where culture is an import product, and that it can be used to counter the incursions of the hegemonic power.[32] As we shall see, many of the films produced by Mazzaropi and the Trapalhões team humorously relied in part on Hollywood models, but as in the case of some of the more familiar *pornochanchadas*, parody was often limited in these films to comic re-workings of the titles of successful US movies.

Popular film in Brazil is littered with examples of carnivalesque inversions of societal norms and established hierarchies. A stock plot device in the *chanchada* is that of mistaken identity, a classic case of carnivalesque *troca* or exchange, which permits characters from very different social backgrounds to assume each other's position in the world, albeit for a limited period of time akin to the suspension of the normal rules of society during carnival. In *Metido a bacana*, for example, the comic actor Ankito plays two roles, Anacleto, the prince of the fictitious Araquelândia (who on his arrival in Brazil is asked about his romance with Rita Hayworth, in a topical allusion to Ali Khan), and Hilário, a lowly popcorn seller. Set during carnival in Rio, this film sees the Arabian prince deliberately take on the identity of his uneducated doppelgänger so that he can enjoy the delights of the annual celebrations. Hilário, meanwhile, struggles to adopt the social skills of a visiting dignitary during his stay at the embassy. Nevertheless, when the film draws to a close and everyday social codes are restored, just as in the aftermath of carnival, Hilário's girlfriend is keen to take him back, rejecting the amorous advances of the wealthy royal. Similarly, Carlos Diegues's *über*-carnivalesque *Xica da Silva* (*Xica*, 1976), itself based on the theme of a Rio carnival parade, depicted the colourful eponymous heroine swapping her place in the *senzala* or slave-quarters for the *casa-grande* or big house in eighteenth-century Brazil.

One way in which this motif of *troca* or exchange is seen in more recent films is in story lines that bring two different social or cultural types together, in what could be seen as a carnivalesque suspension of normal societal rules.[33] Walter Salles's *Central do Brasil* (*Central Station*, 1998) brings the south of the country into potentially uncomfortable contact with the North, when Dora the schoolteacher takes young Josué to the impoverished North East in search of his father. Salles's 1999 feature *O primeiro dia* (*Midnight*), set on the eve of the millennium, temporarily and accidentally brings together a middle-class woman and a hardened criminal who has been let out of jail for the night to commit a murder. Vinícius Mainardi's *16-0-60* (*Sixteen-Oh-Sixty*) from 1995, a clever black comedy which made little commercial impact in Brazil due to its limited release, deals with what happens when the very rich and the very poor are forced to live under the same roof, and how they feed off and eventually destroy each other. This same idea of the bringing together of two social extremes under the one roof is pursued in Beto Brant's feature film, *O invasor* (*The Trespasser*, 2001), in which a seedy hired assassin gradually worms his way into São Paulo's upper-middle-class society through his relationship with a reckless teenage girl.

Jokes premised on the overturning of established racial hierarchies, a central theme of Rio's carnival processions, abound in popular film. In the *chanchada Aviso aos navegantes*, for example, we see a well-dressed, white Argentine woman passionately bidding farewell to a lover at the dockside in Buenos Aires. The camera then cuts to the object of her affections, the aptly named Bagunça (Trash), a ship's cook played by Grande Otelo, often described as a physical caricature of blackness, who here exaggerates his comic persona with his bulging eyes. For once he has a white love-interest, presumably deemed respectable because she is an 'exotic' foreigner. He also turns the tables on society's norms, by forcing the white stowaway (Oscarito) to be his domestic servant on board ship. This is an archetypal case of the blurring of boundaries and the one-up-manship of the slippery *malandro* figure or spiv, as is reinforced by the fact that Grande Otelo's character is dressed in a white suit and black shirt, the typical garb of the Afro-Brazilian hustler, whose arrogant swagger the black actor also adopts here. Likewise, in *O xangô de Baker Street*, racial categories are transcended when Sherlock Holmes's sidekick Dr Watson, on a visit to Brazil, tries to blend in with the natives by wearing a pair of flat leather sandals and a leather cowboy hat – the typical garb of the lowly *caipira*. Brazilian cultural history is humorously rewritten in this scene when it is revealed that it was in fact the archetypal Englishman, Dr Watson who inadvertently invented Brazil's most popular alcoholic beverage, *caipirinha*.

The comic actor, Oscarito, who starred in countless *chanchadas* in the 1940s and 1950s, often appeared in drag, yet another illustration of carnivalesque inversions of the norm. In *Aviso aos navegantes* he passes himself off as a Spanish American rumba performer, who dances, sings and flashes 'her' thighs on a cruise ship. In these roles Oscarito can usefully be compared to his contemporary, the Mexican comic actor, Mario Moreno, better known as Cantinflas, who also often cross-dressed in his films. Part of the strategy to turn the world upside down, their frequent transgressions of gender roles on screen articulated a discourse of ambivalent masculinity, discussed at length in Chapter 4. In Bruno Barreto's box-office record-breaking *Dona Flor e seus dois maridos* (*Dona Flor and Her Two Husbands*, 1976) husband number one memorably drops dead while cross-dressed as a *baiana* and dancing with a *mulata* during a street carnival.[34] In the true spirit of carnival, the 'high' and the 'low' change places within popular film, and recognised cultural and aesthetic hierarchies are overturned. In the comedy film *A dupla do barulho* (The Terrible Twosome), Oscarito plays the clownish Tonico, who drunkenly attributes one of his own ludicrous aphorisms to the German philosopher Schopenhauer. In this same film we are reminded that this irreverence towards high culture was a feature of the *teatro de revista*. In a montage of scenes that recreate the early music hall career of Tonico and Tião (played by Grande Otelo), we see Oscarito, dressed as Hamlet, in a blonde wig and clutching a skull. He asks 'To be or not to be' in exaggeratedly poor English, only to provide an answer in colloquial Portuguese that refers to a contemporary advertising slogan. Such playing with the notion of the perceived superiority of European cultures continues to be a staple of popular film and much television comedy in Brazil: in particular, poor pronunciation of English words is often made fun of. *O xangô de Baker Street* successfully translates this preoccupation on to the big screen.

Malandragem and *jeitinho*: challenges to the established order

Malandragem and the interrelated concept of *jeitinho* are two unofficial tenets of Brazilian identity. The figure of the *malandro* or hustler has been explored at length by the literary critic Antonio Candido and the social anthropologist Roberto DaMatta.[35] The former traces the development of the literary representation of this rogue figure back to Manuel Antônio de Almeida's novel *Memórias de um sargento de milícias* (Memoirs of a Militia Sergeant), published in 1853–54. Candido also maintains that aspects of the counter-cultural lifestyle of *malandragem* can be identified in the work of the seventeenth-century poet Gregório de Matos, and that the pragmatic, picaresque *malandro* was epitomised by the eponymous hero of Mário de Andrade's modernist novel *Macunaíma* (1928). Such figures are not unique to Brazilian culture, and it is no coincidence that the Cuban literary imagination should have produced the *curro* (who appears in the nineteenth-century novel *Cecilia Valdés*, by Cirilo Villaverde), and the characters of Nicolás Guillén's poetry of the 1930s, who like the *malandro*, typically wore two-tone shoes. Both former slavocracies, Cuba and Brazil created mythical black figures who spurned manual labour, too closely associated with the institution of slavery, and took on the system, becoming the popular heroes of the marginalised. The *malandro*, however, is closely linked to other characters from Brazilian folklore, such as Pedro Malasartes, a country dweller who lives by cheating his boss and compensating for his lack of power with his homespun wisdom. DaMatta says that Pedro is 'a personage who characteristically knows how to transform every disadvantage into an advantage, an ability which is the sign of any good rogue (*malandro*) and all good roguery (*malandragem*).'[36]

The *malandro* is often described as *jeitinho* incarnate. The concept of *jeito* or *jeitinho* refers to a way of subverting authority, evading the law, or using one's contacts for personal advantage. Although similar mechanisms exist throughout the world, in Brazil the *jeitinho* has become an accepted feature of everyday life, which helps to eliminate hierarchies of ethnicity, gender or class. As Lívia Neves de H. Barbosa says, 'the *jeitinho* is a flexible way of dealing with the surprises of daily life, a way of humanising the rules that takes into account the moral equality and social inequalities of persons in the society . . . In short, the *jeitinho* works as an equalising ritual.'[37] She continues: 'As a symbol of national identity, the *jeitinho brasileiro* focuses an entire way of perceiving Brazil and Brazilians. It also emphasizes the side of Brazilian society that privileges the *human* and *natural* aspects of social reality over the legal, political and institutional ones.'[38]

The *chanchada* of the 1950s reflected the capitalist fervour and consumerism of the decade, but it implicitly derided both in favour of the counter-cultural values of *malandragem* or *jeitinho*. The anti-heroes of these films often come into money or gain access to a life of luxury, but this is never by dint of hard toil, rather by a stroke of luck or a slightly underhand or illegal ruse. In Cinedistri's *O camelô da rua Larga* (The Street Vendor of Larga Street, 1958), Zé Trindade plays Vicente, a loveable rogue who has no qualms about admitting that he is waiting for his aunt to die so he can get his hands on his inheritance. Vicente is the *camelô* or illegal street vendor of the film's title, who earns his living by selling his wares out of a suitcase and is constantly on the run from the police. Although his girlfriend constantly implores him to find a decent job, he prefers his precarious existence, proudly declaring 'Sou vigarista mas sou honesto!' (I'm a conman but I'm honest!). By a characteristic stroke of good fortune and in a classic case of *troca* or inversion, he picks up someone else's suitcase by mistake, which just so happens to be crammed with counterfeit bank notes.

The popularity of many commercially successful films from the late 1960s and 1970s hinged on the presence of loveable but lazy rogues, and it is likely that these characters appealed to audiences, at least in part because their work-shyness and petty criminality went against everything that the military dictatorship (1964–85) stood for. An obvious example of this is Joaquim Pedro de Andrade's popular *chanchada*-inspired film version of the novel *Macunaíma* from 1969, featuring one of Brazilian culture's best-known slothful anti-heroes. In the same vein, Hugo Carvana directed and starred in the comedy *Vai trabalhar, vagabundo* (Go and Get a Job, You Lout) in 1973 as an inveterate *malandro* incapable of leading a decent life, while Ruy Guerra's 1985 *Ópera do malandro* (*Malandro*), based on Chico Buarque's musical of the same name, followed the shady machinations of a classic *malandro* from President Vargas's New State (1937–45) in order to pillory the post-1964 dictatorship.

Film critic and scholar José Carlos Avellar's views on spectatorship and national identity in relation to the *pornochanchada* are relevant in the context of this notion of transgression. Avellar describes the short government propaganda films that cinema theatres were obliged to show before feature films in the 1970s.[39] These films invariably sought to put across an image of order, progress, national pride and community spirit, and were in sharp contrast to the chaos, individualism, debauchery and *malandragem* of the *pornochanchadas* that often followed them: 'The sloppy narration of the *pornochanchada* belied the image of progress, edification, civilization, good manners, unity and common effort of the community as a whole that the authorities sought to create.'[40]

The placing of these well-made advertisements for the dictatorship produced 'aberrant readings' in the audience, or readings which went against the grain of the discourse, and what Marilena Chauí would define as popular resistance, characterised by a refusal to react to the state in the way the state expected.[41] Audiences, in the true spirit of *malandragem*, would boo and heckle during these advertisements, and would then settle down to watch images that quickly debunked the pompous and clearly erroneous notions that the government promoted of the state of development of the nation at that time. Nearly every Brazilian film that was successful in the 1970s featured social inversions of one kind or another that contrasted with these government-sponsored short features.[42]

Radio and popular film

José Carlos Avellar argues that the *chanchada* occupied an intermediate space between Brazilian radio and American cinema. He describes the *chanchada* as follows:

> Sophisticated radio: the performers remained motionless in front of the camera, as if they were facing an invisible microphone, and recited their words thinking only about the clarity of their diction, since all the important information was relayed via the script. It was via their words (and only via the words themselves, not even how they were delivered) that the story developed. The characters explained what was happening in the scenes and kept the audience informed just like in a radio programme, as if sounds were the only means at their disposal to communicate with the spectator.[43]

Many of the stars of popular cinema had forged their careers and fame on the radio, whether as singers, musicians or comic actors. The musical comedy films of the 1930s, 1940s and 1950s likewise shared their audiences with the *programas de auditório* or variety shows, broadcast by all the major radio stations, described by José Ramos Tinhorão as follows: 'a uniquely Brazilian type of show . . . a mixture of radio programme, music concert, music hall show, circus and neighbourhood party, that even featured prize draws'.[44] These variety shows, in the true sense of the word, which aired on weekend afternoons, mirrored popular film by incorporating an eclectic musical repertoire, ranging from regional styles to radio crooners, together with comic interludes and magic acts. The live audiences were attracted by the chance to participate in show business, however peripherally. These radio shows energetically fostered notions of stardom, encouraging audiences to swear allegiance to their favourite female singer, whether Emilinha Borba, Marlene or Ângela Maria, who competed to be crowned the 'queen of radio' on a yearly basis; many of these 'queens' would later appear in cameo roles in popular films. As Bryan McCann writes: 'these programs sacrificed musical refinement in favor of a noisy ambiance of festivity and delirium. Musically, they nourished the ascendance of the slow, melodramatic Mexican bolero and its Brazilian counterpart, the *samba-canção*.'[45]

The state-run Rádio Nacional dominated Brazil's airwaves, taking these intrinsically *carioca* shows to all four corners of the nation.[46] As Tinhorão argues, the Brazilian population's fascination with these programmes lay both in their artistic merits and in the attraction of the idealised federal capital of Rio de Janeiro, particularly for the inhabitants of Brazil's less developed regions, who were eager to taste modernity.[47] Like popular film, radio thus provided a source of communal identification for a largely illiterate or semi-literate public.[47] Both media encouraged audience participation and inter-action, using specialist magazines to engender a sense of familiarity with the 'stars' by giving details of their lives.[48]

Radio stations broadcast plays in the evenings, known generically as *rádio-teatro* (literally radio-theatre), which later developed into the *radionovela* or radio soap opera, and provided serious competition for music hall. They became very popular with the public in the 1930s and 1940s. From 1941 onwards, with the airing of the soap *Em busca da felicidade* (In Search of Happiness), written by the Cuban Leandro Blanco, Rádio Nacional gradually began to devote more and more airtime to soap operas. By 1945, radio-theatre occupied 14.3 per cent of Rádio Nacional's programming, slightly more than variety shows.[49] Between 1943 and 1945 the station broadcast 116 radio soaps, and a total of 2,985 episodes.[50] Strong parallels can be drawn between the plots and performance style of these productions, and those of popular film, as outlined by Avellar above. As the heyday of the radio soaps was drawing to a close in the mid-1940s, the *chanchada*, an observant understudy, was waiting in the wings.

The style of humour in radio shows had a very definite impact on that of popular film. Rádio Nacional broadcast comedy shows such as 'Alma do sertão' (Soul of the Backlands), together with 'Jararaca e Ratinho' and 'Alvarenga e Ranchinho', both of which were titled after the comic double acts that starred in them. These duos would later appear in musical comedy films, alongside other comedians who made their names on radio, like Zé Trindade. Pre-empting a characteristic feature of the *chanchada*, a North Eastern motif featured in various radio shows such as 'Alma do sertão'. As former radio presenter Renato Murce writes: 'this programme transmitted the true soul of our *caboclo*, almost always ignorant, illiterate, but full of qualities that I wanted to foreground, such as quickwittedness, cunning, persistence in fighting adversity . . . I incorporated a variety of topics. Poetry, customs, legends, sayings, the medicinal remedies of the *sertão* (which vary from region to region), everything was broadcast over the radio and shared with our listeners.'[51]

Responding to demographic shifts brought about by internal migration, the music of Brazil's North East was incorporated into the play-lists of the stations of the developed Centre South in the 1940s, as it would later be in the musical comedy films of the 1950s. The *baião* style thus became the rage throughout Brazil, thanks to the radio performances of the accordionist Luiz Gonzaga and his band – the *Cangaceiros* or Bandits, and recordings by the likes of Emilinha Borba, or Carmélia Alves – crowned 'the queen of *baião*' in 1950.[52]

Concluding remarks

The intention of this chapter was to map the key sites of mediation between popular cinema and wider cultural traditions in Brazil. Whether elements of long-standing popular memory, such as the counter-cultural ethos of *malandragem*, or the media of the time, such as the radio, the various influences on popular film that have been examined here serve to establish the shared cultural repertoire of film audiences in Brazil.[53] We will endeavour to show in the subsequent chapters how these cultural matrices or common currency of popular culture have shaped tastes among the cinema-going public since the consolidation of sound cinema in the early 1930s.

Notes

1 Andy Medhurst describes the important reference points of the *Carry On* films as almost entirely extra-cinematic aspects of working-class leisure culture, such as

music hall, circus, and radio comedy. Andy Medhurst, 'Carry On Camp', *Sight and Sound*, August 1992. Brazilian popular cinema draws on identical 'low-brow' cultural markers.

2 *Chanchada* is the term used to refer to a particular tradition of comedy film that features interludes of music and dance, and which grew out of the so-called 'filmes cantantes' or sung films of the silent era. It is often described as the only truly Brazilian cinematic genre. Agreeing on a precise definition of what constitutes a *chanchada* has proved to be a source of preoccupation for both critics and the tradition's most important directors. In the words of J. B. Tanko, director of the self-proclaimed *chanchada*, *Sai de baixo* (Look Out!, 1956): 'To define what a *chanchada* is I have to begin by defining what a comedy is, namely a drama with a comic solution. The protagonists are realistic, they have character. But there is another type of funny film that features stock types rather than characters, and relies on exaggeration. This is the *chanchada*. In the *chanchada* the characters are not realistic, they are superficial caricatures, and the crudest methods are used to make the audience laugh' (unmarked press cutting from the film archive of the Museum of Modern Art, Rio de Janeiro, 'J. B. Tanko passou a vida fazendo filmes. Mas só agora está enriquecendo', our translation). Jean Claude Bernardet's definition of the term encompasses a much wider variety of films: 'I think that *chanchada* is the general name that is given to all comedies, and musical comedies, with popular appeal, made in Brazil between 1900 and 1960, more or less, which featured stars like Oscarito. But there has never been a definition of what constitutes a *chanchada*' (interview with Jean Claude Bernardet, *Cinema*, 3, February 1974, our translation). He continues: 'But it was only from 1929 onwards, with the film *Os otários*, that the musical film appeared, with singers and jokes – that is when people really began to talk about *chanchadas*.' (He is referring here to the first Brazilian talkie, *Acabaram-se os otários* (No More Suckers, 1929).) As João Luiz Vieira says, 'The printed advertisements for *Acabaram-se os otários* reveal the basic formulae of the emerging genre, promising the public an array of "songs, *modinhas*, jokes and puns"' (João Luiz Vieira, 'Hegemony and Resistance: Parody and Carnival in Brazilian Cinema', PhD dissertation, New York University, 1984, p. 59). Vieira divides the history of the *chanchada* into two distinct phases, each with certain formal and thematic qualities. He writes: 'the first phase runs through the thirties and mid forties, when *chanchada* presented elementary and schematic plots, with single sketches and jokes expanded into entire sequences, alternating with more or less autonomous musical numbers. The ecstatic direct presentation of production numbers gave spectators the impression that they were seated in front of the stage of a vaudeville theater. The second phase is marked by the consolidation of the Atlântida Film Studios, founded in 1941, as the major producer of *chanchada* for the next twenty years. With Atlântida, *chanchada* offered more complex narratives no longer centered on the traditional backstage plots and introducing new elements such as gangsters and suspense. As musical production numbers became more varied and heterogeneous, the filmmakers began to exploit a broader repertory of camera movement and lighting techniques.' (*Ibid.*, pp. 59–60).

3 For a more detailed analysis of the *teatro de revista* see Salvyano Cavalcanti de Paiva, *Viva o rebolado!: Vida e morte do teatro de revista brasileiro* (Rio de Janeiro: Editora Nova Fronteira, 1991).

4 Procópio Ferreira, Francisco Alves, Mesquitinha (Olímpio Bastos), Genésio Arruda, Violeta Ferraz, Sônia Mamede, Grande Otelo, Catalano, Heloísa Helena, Renata Fronzi, the radio singers Marlene and Ângela Maria, Chocolate, Elvira Pagã, and the duo Jararaca and Ratinho also began their careers in music hall and later appeared on cinema screens.

5 Cavalcanti de Paiva, *Viva o rebolado!*, pp. 23–4, p. 9.

6 *Ibid.*, p. 33.

7 *Ibid.*, p. 197 (our translation).

8 For example, *Vocação irresistível* (Irresistible Vocation, 1924). Arruda starred in three of Mazzaropi's early films from the 1960s.

9 Civil servants went on strike in several cities, including Rio and São Paulo, in 1934, giving ample ammunition for more jokes about their legendary laziness. Their miserable salaries were also often alluded to in music hall.

10 Cavalcanti de Paiva, *Viva o rebolado!*, p. 107.

11 Inspiration for the inclusion of these plays in the circus programme may well have come from the *entremez*, the tradition of short comic plays set to music which had been brought over from Portugal to Brazil in the first half of the nineteenth century.

12 José Guilherme Cantor Magnani, *Festa no pedaço: cultura popular e lazer na cidade* (São Paulo: Brasiliense, 1984), p. 23.

13 *Ibid.*, p. 166 (our translation).

14 Sílvio Santos (Senor Abravanel) famously started out as a street trader before making the move to television via radio. He is now one of the most influential media figures in Brazil and the owner of the commercial television network based in São Paulo, SBT. Santos was not the first television variety show host: he was pre-dated by Chacrinha (José Abelardo Barbosa de Medeiros, 1916–88), who moved from radio to television in 1956 and used a different style of presentation, which placed a certain emphasis on humiliating members of the audience. The roots of the *programa de auditório* are discussed in more detail below in the section 'Radio and popular film'.

15 Magnani, *Festa no pedaço*, p. 23.

16 Christopher Wagstaff, 'A forkful of Westerns: industry, audiences and the Italian Western', in Richard Dyer and Susan Hayward (eds), *Popular European Cinema* (London and New York: Routledge, 1992), p. 253.

17 José Ramos Tinhorão, 'Circo brasileiro: o local no universal', in Antonio Herculano Lopes (ed.), *Entre Europa e África: A invenção do carioca* (Rio de Janeiro: Topbooks/ Edições Casa de Rui Barbosa, 2000), p. 194.

18 One of the most important influences on modern popular music in Brazil, the *modinha* enjoyed success in the nineteenth century. Based on the arias of European opera, it came to symbolise a blending of high and low art, or a reinvention of erudite music for the masses.

19 Tinhorão, 'Circo brasileiro', p. 206.

20 The term *ginga* also refers to the confident swagger of the *malandro* spiv, an icon of popular identity in Brazil that will be discussed later in this chapter.

21 See Chapters 3 and 4.

22 When Oscarito was young he appeared in a circus act alongside the black clown, Benjamin de Oliveira. According to the *Enciclopédia do cinema brasileiro* the shape of Oscarito's mouth, accentuated by his full cheeks and his nose, was highly reminiscent of a typical clown's mask: Fernão Ramos and Luiz Felipe Miranda (eds), *Enciclopédia do cinema brasileiro* (São Paulo: Senac, 2000), p. 408.

23 Alan Dale, *Slapstick in American Movies* (Minneapolis and London: University of Minnesota Press, 2000), pp. 14–15.

24 A number of popular films are set, at least partly, in circuses, including Mazzaropi's first celluloid outing, *Sai da Frente* (Get Out of My Way) of 1952, one of the Trapalhões's most successful films, *Os saltimbancos Trapalhões* (The Acrobatic Trapalhões), and Carlos Diegues's memorable *Bye bye Brasil* (*Bye Bye Brazil*) of 1979.

25 For more information on these musical genres, see Chris McGowan and Ricardo Pessanha, *The Brazilian Sound: Samba, Bossa Nova and the Popular Music of Brazil* (Philadelphia: Temple University Press, 1998).

26 Sérgio Augusto, *Este mundo é um pandeiro: a chanchada de Getúlio a JK* (São Paulo: Companhia das Letras, 1993), p. 88.

27 Robert Stam, *Subversive Pleasures: Bakhtin, Cultural Criticism and Film* (Baltimore and London: Johns Hopkins University Press, 1989), p. 86.

28 Roberto DaMatta, *Carnivals, Rogues, and Heroes: An Interpretation of the Brazilian Dilemma* (Notre Dame and London: University of Notre Dame Press, 1991).

29 *Ibid.*, p. 38.

30 *Ibid.*, pp. 43–4.

31 The titles of popular theatrical revues also played on those of Hollywood movies. The 1940 revue *E o Bento levou* (literally And Bento Took It), for example, parodied the title of *E o vento levou* (literally, And the Wind Took It, the Portuguese translation of *Gone with the Wind*).

32 Roberto Schwarz, *Misplaced Ideas: Essays on Brazilian Culture* (London and New York: Verso, 1992), p. 40.

33 See Stephanie Dennison, 'A meeting of two worlds: recent trends in Brazilian cinema', *Journal of Iberian and Latin American Studies*, 6:2, 2000.

34 The issue of cross-dressing crops up in two significant films from 1985: Hector Babenco's *O beijo da mulher aranha* (*Kiss of the Spider Woman*) and Ruy Guerra's *Ópera do malandro* (*Malandro*).

35 See Antonio Candido de Mello e Souza, 'Dialectic of Malandroism', in *On Literature and Society* (tr. Howard Becker), (Princeton: Princeton University Press, 1995) and DaMatta, *Carnivals, Rogues, and Heroes*.

36 *Ibid.*, p. 218.

37 Lívia Neves de H. Barbosa, 'The Brazilian *jeitinho*: an exercise in national identity', in David J. Hess and Roberto A. DaMatta (eds), *The Brazilian Puzzle: Culture on the Borderlands of the Western World* (New York: Columbia University Press, 1995), pp. 40–1.

38 *Ibid.*, p. 46.
39 Jose Carlos Avellar, 'Teoria da relatividade', in *Anos 70: Cinema* (Rio de Janeiro: Europa Empresa Gráfica Editora, 1979), pp. 71–7.
40 *Ibid.*, p. 69 (our translation).
41 Marilena Chauí, *Conformismo e resistência: cultura popular no Brasil* (São Paulo: Brasiliense, 1986), p. 66.
42 As discussed in Chapter 3, the Vargas regime (1930–45) made the screening of state-sponsored newsreels compulsory in Brazil's cinema theatres. The favourable images of the regime and its representatives were subsequently undermined by the irreverent discourse of the *chanchadas* that followed as the main feature.
43 José Carlos Avellar, 'A chanchada', *Jornal do Brasil*, no date – unmarked newspaper clipping from Museum of Modern Art film archive, Rio de Janeiro, published on the death of the *chanchada* director Watson Macedo (our translation).
44 José Ramos Tinhorão, 'Nos anos de ouro dos auditórios', *Jornal do Brasil*, 1 May 1977 (our translation).
45 Bryan McCann, 'The invention of tradition on Brazilian radio', *The Brazil Reader: History, Culture, Politics* (London: Latin America Bureau, 1999), p. 479. This type of music would resurface in the *chanchada*.
46 Rádio Nacional was founded in 1936 and set about contracting the leading lights of Rio and São Paulo's entertainment world, such as the presenter Almirante and the singers Emilinha Borba, Ângela Maria, Cauby Peixoto and Black Out/ Blecaute. In 1940 Rádio Nacional was placed under government control and thus became the premier station in Brazil for over twenty years. The importance of radio in the lives of Brazilians living in remote communities has notably been portrayed in Andrucha Waddington's acclaimed film *Eu, tu, eles* (*Me, You, Them*, 1999).
47 Tinhorão estimates that at the beginning of the 1950s there were some fifty such programmes broadcast by Rio's radio stations alone, but by the mid-point of the decade they were increasingly being replaced by disc jockeys and hit parades. It is likely that radio audiences were also increasingly drawn away towards popular film. Tinhorão, 'Nos anos de ouro dos auditórios'.
47 The importance of local radio in the lives of *favela* inhabitants is the focus of Helvécio Ratton's 2002 film *Uma onda no ar* (*Something In the Air*) and supplies the backdrop to Carlos Diegues's *Orfeu* (Orpheus, 1999).
48 A variety of magazines dedicated to the world of radio were on the market in the 1920s, 1930s and 1940s, including *Sintonia, A voz do rádio* and *Revista do rádio*. Likewise, many titles on the subject of cinema were readily available, such as *Cena muda* and *Cinearte*. The latter publication is discussed at length in Chapter 2. The Rádio Cruzeiro do Sul station was the first to air a talent show (*programa de calouros*), in 1935, recorded before a live audience, a format that would be copied by Brazil's plethora of radio stations from then on, and which launched the careers of many stars.
49 Renato Murce, *Bastidores do radio: fragmentos do radio de ontem e de hoje* (Rio de Janeiro: Imago, 1976), p. 54.
50 *Ibid.*, p. 51.

51 Luiz Carlos Saroldi and Sonia Virginia Moreira, *Rádio Nacional: o Brasil em sintonia* (Rio de Janeiro: Martins Fontes/Funarte, 1984), p. 54 (our translation).
52 Rádio Nacional broadcast a show called 'No mundo do baião' (In the World of *baião*).
53 Just as in the case of popular theatre and the radio, the relationship between television and Brazilian popular cinema has been a very significant one ever since television's appearance in Brazil in the 1950s. Its pervasive influence will be commented on in Chapters 6, 7 and 8.

2

The 1930s

Introduction

In 1930 the political landscape of Brazil experienced a seismic shift. The revolution that brought Getúlio Vargas to power that year ushered in a period of sweeping economic, social and cultural changes that would irrevocably shape the identity of the nation. In 1937 Vargas tightened his political grip with the establishment of his authoritarian *Estado Novo* or New State, which took much of its inspiration from Mussolini's Italy and its nomenclature from Salazar's autocratic regime in Portugal. The birth of industrialisation and the creation of a work ethic, rewarded by a nascent welfare system, coincided with continued attempts to integrate former Afro-Brazilian slaves and their descendants, as well as European immigrant workers, into mainstream society. The forging of a national consciousness was thus a central concern of the Vargas regime, until its overthrow in 1945. The administration sought to create a coherent image of Brazil both internally and abroad, in response to the need for national integration and to the challenges posed by Brazil's increasingly multiethnic demographic profile. A unifying identity was essential, particularly given the vast size of the nation and the importance of regional politics and identities.

The 1930s witnessed the rise of the radio, the record industry and the talking cinema. Popular culture as a whole became the focus of the attentions of Vargas's propaganda-mongers, and a delicate balancing act of co-option and censorship was employed to enlist the support of popular musicians and artists in the construction of a nation-conscious mythology. The fledgling Brazilian film industry was seen as an important facet of the regime's powerful propaganda machine, and the cinema was viewed as an instrument of national unity that could engender a sense of *brasilidade* or 'Brazilianness'. Thus the government commissioned the filming of Rio's annual carnival celebrations, of which it had taken direct control, to be shown both at home and abroad.

As Randal Johnson writes in relation to film: 'Industrialization was seen, at least rhetorically, as a means to a pedagogical and patriotic end.'[1] Decree 21,240 of 4 April 1932 centralised all censorship duties, created a tax to be levied on all films shown in Brazil, and most importantly, established the principle that the government could set aside a percentage of screen time for domestic films. On 30 June 1934 Vargas addressed the Association of Brazilian Film Producers (*Associação Cinematográfica de Produtores Brasileiros*), of which he was named honorary president, and stated: 'the cinema will be the book of luminous images in which our coastal and rural populations will learn to love Brazil, increasing confidence in the Fatherland. For the mass of illiterates, it will be the most perfect, the easiest, and the most impressive pedagogical tool.'[2] He concluded his speech by highlighting the role of film in the formation of the Brazilian nation:

> Combining the cinema with radio and the rational cultivation of sports, the government will complete an articulated system of mental, moral, and hygienic education, endowing Brazil with the indispensable tools for the development of an enterprising, hardy, and virile people. And the people that comes into being in this way will be worthy of the enviable heritage it receives.[3]

Yet, as João Luiz Vieira argues, the Vargas regime was more interested in the educational and patriotic potential of cinema than in the development of a film industry.[4] Gustavo Capanema, head of the Ministry of Education and Health between 1934 and 1945, and other high-ranking officials kept up with developments in European cinema, 'where "educational" film had become an important part of education and civic nationalism in totalitarian and democratic regimes'.[5] In response to Capanema's fears that the unchecked growth of commercial film threatened to erode moral and educational standards, on 13 January 1937 Vargas created the National Institute of Educational Cinema (INCE), one of a series of initiatives aimed at co-opting popular performers and artists.[6] The INCE survived for almost thirty years and produced or acquired hundreds of educational films for free distribution to schools and cultural institutions. As Daryle Williams writes:

> Educational film was entirely consistent with the cult of personality and the cult of the state promoted by the Estado Novo regime. The INCE also produced patriotic dramatic films, including the classic *O descobrimento do Brasil* (The Discovery of Brazil, 1937), which brought together the talents of pioneer filmmaker Humberto Mauro and modernist composer Heitor Villa-Lobos in a cinematic recreation of Pero Vaz de Caminha's narrative of the momentous encounter between Pedro Álvarez Cabral and the Tupi in April 1500. The resonance of these dramatic releases was undoubtedly enhanced by official cultural nationalism.[7]

State-promoted documentaries were filmed throughout the 1930s, largely to meet the requirements of the quota system, and ensured regular work for

actors and technical staff. They thus complemented the employment possibilities created by the production of full-length feature films by the three
Rio-based studios, namely Cinédia, Brasil Vita Filme and Sonofilmes. The
director Humberto Mauro, who worked with both Cinédia and Brasil Vita
Filme, made a major contribution to the development of the film industry
in Brazil via the production of documentaries, including some of feature
length.[8] After the establishment of the authoritarian *Estado Novo* in 1937,
Adhemar Gonzaga's Cinédia was at the forefront of the production of
newsreels. Thanks to the zeal of the inspectors of the Press and Propaganda
Department (*Departamento de Imprensa e Propaganda*, henceforth referred
to by its well-known acronym, DIP), who enforced screenings of newsreel
journals, in 1940 Cinédia exhibited more newsreels in São Paulo than the
government itself.[9]

A decree-law of 30 September 1939 raised the screen quota for Brazilian
films to one full-length feature film and one short per year in every cinema
theatre, casino and sporting association in the land. The same legislation
also introduced procedures for film censorship and made compulsory the
insertion of propaganda messages supplied by the DIP at the beginning or
end of all film programmes. (The quota system was, in fact, unnecessary
since several films were being produced each year in this period by all the
main Brazilian studios.)[10] The regime, however, did nothing to prevent or
even hinder the mass importation of foreign films, even lowering the tariff
on imported products.

Vargas saw Brazilian films as a source of national pride, and during his
presidential visit to Argentina in 1935, the musical comedy *Carioca maravilhosa*
(Marvellous Girl from Rio), a co-production from Cinédia and Régia Film,
was screened in Buenos Aires, prior to its premiere in Brazil. Under his
direction, the DIP promoted the production of films that valorised the natural
beauty of Brazil, key historical events and the achievements of the regime.
Keen to enhance the nation's image abroad, the legislation introduced in
1939 prohibited the export of films that gave an unfavourable view of the
country or posed a threat to national security.[11] Cinema was also employed
to enhance the image of the regime back home. In 1939, for example, the
Hammann Filme studios produced a film version of the theatrical revue
Joujoux e balangandans (Knick-knacks and Trinkets), staged at Rio de Janeiro's
Municipal Theatre to raise funds for the charity work of the President's wife,
Darcy Vargas. On 1 December 1939 Brazil's first lady attended the premiere
of the film version, which publicised the benevolent dimension of the State
to a far wider audience.

On balance the Vargas regime provided only token assistance for the film
industry, and curtailed its freedom with the help of the censors of the powerful
and omnipresent DIP. As Silvana Goulart writes, 'the DIP participated in

every stage of film production, promoting, rewarding and punishing, censoring, registering, licensing and, finally, supervising the exhibition of the end product.'[12] (As discussed below, the first initiatives of the sound era relied upon private capital and the profits, however meagre, generated by popular film genres, as producers realised that they could not survive on 'quality' pictures alone.) Catherine Benamou argues that throughout the 1930s popular Brazilian cinema (and more specifically the *chanchada* tradition, discussed in more detail below) was in synchrony, at least nominally, with the cultural policies of the central state apparatus.[13] Nevertheless, the tradition of comedy films that emerged in the course of this decade would also introduce a note of light-hearted irreverence and traces of an emerging counter-cultural discourse.

The arrival of the talkies in Brazil brought with it a mood of euphoria among filmmakers, who rather naively believed that incomprehensible foreign languages would spell the demise of imported films and finally herald the age of domestic productions.[14] This prompted a wave of musical films that relied on the talent and popularity of established stars of the *teatro de revista*, popular music and especially the radio, and combined carnival songs with comic dialogues that everyone could understand. As João Luiz Vieira writes with regard to the advent of sound: 'Prevented from competing with the fascination of deliberately seductive techniques, Brazilian cinema turned to a format which, despite being based on more or less similar ideas, differed from the foreign films precisely in terms of its own national characteristics, such as language and culture.'[15] These Brazilian musicals sought to tap into the public's fascination with Hollywood glamour and movie stars, and it has been argued that Brazilians made sense of these unsophisticated home-grown replicas via their prior knowledge of the US originals on which they were loosely based.[16]

Brazilian audiences crowded into cinema halls to watch both the glossy imports from the USA and the pale domestic imitations that came to be known as *chanchadas*. In spite of their commercial success, the *chanchadas* of the 1930s were ridiculed by the critics for their technical inferiority and were dismissed as an apologetic response to the flooding of the Brazilian market by Hollywood movies. In this decade film critics used the term *chanchada* in a pejorative sense to imply poor quality, yet these films became ingrained in popular consciousness. As Johnson and Stam write: 'Although they fostered an idealized and inconsequential image of Brazilians, crystallized in a perpetually playful Rio de Janeiro, the *chanchadas* had the virtue of establishing an authentic link between Brazilians and their cinema.'[17] This chapter will trace the birth and early evolution of the *chanchada* and challenge the traditional interpretation of these films as highly derivative and ruthlessly commercial. It will explore the ambivalent and often self-parodic images of national identity that these films conveyed, and examine their oppositional stance in relation to Hollywood's representations of *brasilidade/latinidad* ('Latinness') in the context of President Roosevelt's 'Good Neighbour Policy' towards the Latin American continent.

Carnival, Carmen Miranda and the birth of the *chanchada*

The first Brazilian sound films tended to draw their inspiration from the US musical revues that inundated the domestic market from 1929 onwards, the year in which MGM's *Broadway Melody*, the screen's first musical, was shown in Brazil, complete with primitive subtitles. This film inspired the first commercially successful Brazilian talkie, *Coisas nossas* (Our Things), of 1931, produced and directed by a shrewd American record company executive, Wallace Downey, a film which established the interaction between the cinema and popular music.[18] An advertisement for the film that appeared in *Cinearte* magazine on 2 December 1931 reflects the patriotic pride associated with the production of domestic cinema: 'Our customs, our music, our songs, our artists! A Brazilian film, a talkie, a musical, made here in Brazil.' The press made much of the fact that President Vargas himself went to see *Coisas nossas*, which in spite of the involvement of North American capital, was heralded as a national triumph, and prompted the departure of various Brazilian cineastes for Hollywood, where they researched the innovative techniques of the sound era. Although *Coisas nossas* was made in São Paulo, where it broke all box-office records, and its grand finale featured establishing shots of the city's high-rise skyline that clearly aimed to evoke associations with Manhattan, Rio de Janeiro was soon to take over as the capital of both the burgeoning music and film industries in the 1930s. The then federal capital was to witness the coming together of popular song and cinema, a union that would ensure the survival and future success of Brazilian film.

Brazil's most famous annual celebration, carnival, was to provide a central focus for early film production, dating back to the silent era. The first sound documentary on this popular theme, *O carnaval cantado de 1933 no Rio de Janeiro* (The 1933 Rio de Janeiro Carnival in Song), was screened on Ash Wednesday 1933, and combined footage of carnival processions and costume balls with scenes of musicians, including a young Carmen Miranda, performing in the studio. Such carnival documentaries, alongside *Coisas nossas*, paved the way for a series of fiction films, such as *A voz do carnaval* (The Voice of Carnival, 1933) from the Rio-based Cinédia studios, directed by Adhemar Gonzaga and Humberto Mauro, and released in the run-up to carnival. This combined real-life footage of carnival processions recorded live in the streets of Rio, with a fictitious plot line shot in the studio. It featured the well-known comedian Palitos in the role of King Momo, who arrives by ship in Rio and goes in search of the city's legendary pre-Lenten celebration. The soundtrack was provided by some of the leading lights of the Rio popular music scene, such as Noel Rosa and Lamartine Babo, and included a range of carnival *marchas* or marches and sambas, performed by the likes of Carmen Miranda, in her second screen appearance. *A voz do carnaval* was well received both in Brazil and in Paris, where it was shown on the initiative of the French Ambassador to Brazil. A review of the film in the magazine *Cinearte* stated: 'The first talkie from the Cinédia studios is worthy of mention. At the end of the day it has its merits and artistic qualities, despite being a carnival documentary film.'[19]

As the decade wore on the promotion of carnival music became the raison d'être for most films, which were released in the run-up to the annual celebration and found a ready-made cast of actors and performers amongst Brazil's radio stars, whose established fame and popularity represented a huge box-office draw. The *chanchada* genre grew out of these early carnival films, and the formula was established in 1935 when the Cinédia and Waldow Filmes studios teamed up to produce their first co-production, *Alô, alô, Brasil!* (Hello, Hello, Brazil!), which was released just in time for carnival and featured radio artists performing the most popular songs of the moment on screen.[20] After premiering at the Cinema Alhambra in Rio on 4 February 1935, this film was shown there for a further three weeks and various reviews comment on the crowds that clamoured to see it.[21] Headed by Wallace Downey, Waldow Filmes built on the success of *Coisas nossas* by drawing on the mass appeal and huge commercial potential offered by films that featured songs destined for the annual carnival celebrations and competitions. Cinédia's founder, Adhemar Gonzaga, on the other hand, insisted the name of his studio did not appear in the credits of *Alô, alô, Brasil!*, such was his disdain for this overtly commercial venture. This film was made up of a series of loosely connected scenes created with the sole intention of allowing the up-and-coming star Carmen Miranda, her sister Aurora, and a host of other popular composers, to sing a selection of hit carnival *marchas*. Taking its lead from the *teatro de revista*, *Alô, alô, Brasil!* featured three comperes or masters of ceremonies, namely Mesquitinha, Jorge Murad and Barbosa Júnior. The film benefited from the Movietone recording equipment brought from the USA by Downey, with which sound could be recorded directly on to film, as opposed to the Vitaphone system previously used in Brazil, which recorded sound on to discs. The inhabitants of the big cities of Brazil, who had begun to swarm into the radio studios to watch live performances and talent contests being recorded, now provided a ready-made viewing public for these musical films.

Alô. Alô. Carnaval! (Hello, Hello, Carnival!), discussed in more detail below, has been called 'a carbon copy of the first Metro musicals (or revue-films)'.[22]

This follow-up to *Alô, alô, Brasil!* was first screened on 20 January 1936 at the Cinema Alhambra in Rio de Janeiro, and remained in exhibition for the whole of the month, breaking all previous box-office records. Like its fore-runner, it featured a selection of hit songs destined for the forthcoming carnival, including a memorable rendition by Carmen Miranda and her sister Aurora of the song 'Cantoras do rádio' (Radio Singers), written by the popular composers Braguinha and Alberto Ribeiro. The titles of these first two proto-*chanchadas* clearly reflect the close links between the radio and early talking cinema in Brazil, since *alô, alô* was the greeting used by radio presenters at the beginning of their shows. Furthermore, the plot of *Alô, alô, Brasil!* was based around an avid radio fan who falls in love with a female radio singer. Although by the end of the 1930s the backstage device was being supplanted in Hollywood by less stereotypical motives for song and dance,[23] its adoption by Brazilian filmmakers was to continue until the end of the 1950s, and in the *chanchada* the revue aspect was to retain its struc-tural prominence long after it was eliminated from the US musical.

Estudantes (Students) of 1935, another co-production from Waldow and Cinédia, directed by Downey and based on a script by musicians João de Barro and Alberto Ribeiro, was set in a university student residence. In this film Carmen Miranda played a promising young radio star called Mimi, who was in love with a student played by the crooner Mário Reis, and for the first time she acted out a role as well as singing. Two other students, played by Mesquitinha and Barbosa Júnior, vie for her affections, giving rise to a wealth of comic incidents. Shot in just one week, *Estudantes* premiered at Rio's Cinema Alhambra on 8 July 1935, where it was shown for a further two weeks. Although the film's soundtrack featured well-known carnival *marchas* and sambas, it was not designed to tie in with the annual celebrations, but rather was an example of so-called 'mid-year' productions (*de meio de ano*), the premieres of which were often timed to coincide with the 'festas juninas' or popular Catholic festivals held in June. Inspired by the success of the film vehicles for carnival music, other 'mid-year' musicals were simply intended to promote the radio and record industries. *Estudantes* featured musical numbers associated with the popular religious celebrations, and the song 'Cadê Mimi?' (Where's Mimi?), performed by Mário Reis as he serenades Carmen Miranda's character. This song subsequently became a huge hit throughout Brazil. In spite of its success at the box-office, *Estudantes* received mixed reviews. An anonymous P. de L., writing for the Rio newspaper *O Globo* on 25 June 1935, called it a retrograde step in relation to *Alô, alô, Brasil!*, whereas Alfredo Sade, writing in the Rio-based publication *A Batalha* in July 1935, argued that *Estudantes* was a far superior film. He praised the quality of the photography and the sound in what he termed this 'very Brazilian musical comedy'. Another anonymous review by a certain A. F. in the newspaper *Diário Português* of July 1935 argued that *Estudantes*'s greatest value was its spontaneity and the promise that it and its young creators represented for the future of the cinema industry in Brazil.[24] This potential was to be more fully realised in Cinédia's next production, *Alô. Alô. Carnaval!*

Alô. Alô. Carnaval!: a landmark in popular film

A detailed analysis of *Alô. Alô. Carnaval!* is essential to understand the origins of popular cinema in Brazil. It is invariably described as the genesis of the Atlântida *chanchadas* of the 1940s and 1950s. The use of Rio's carnival celebrations and their accompanying music, together with the backstage plot, were to become two distinctive elements of the *chanchada*. Directed by one of the pioneers of Brazilian cinema, Adhemar Gonzaga, and shot in Cinédia's studios, *Alô. Alô. Carnaval!* took the same formula as that used in Gonzaga's earlier carnival musicals, namely *A voz do carnaval*, *Alô, alô, Brasil!* and *Estudantes*, but reflected his more ambitious artistic vision. (Wallace Downey initially collaborated in the project, undertaking the purchase of the latest equipment in the USA to shoot a section of the film in colour, on Gonzaga's initiative. Downey subsequently abandoned the project, but went on to use the new technology for a colour sequence in his film *João Ninguém* (Johnny Nobody, 1937).)

Under the working title of *O Grande Cassino* (The Grand Casino), shooting began on 14 October 1935. Gonzaga used the 'one shot, one cut' technique for the musical sequences, using two static cameras, and later a third, in order to ensure that the film, later renamed *Alô. Alô. Carnaval!*, was ready in time for the run-up to carnival. The sound was recorded live, with microphones hidden in strategically positioned props, such as bunches of bananas and flowers, and the film made pioneering use in Brazil of the play-back technique in two scenes in which artists mimed to pre-recorded soundtracks. Improvisation was the order of the day, and there are tales of rather wooden extras being given copious amounts of whiskey to improve their dancing skills. In the words of the singer Heloísa Helena, who appeared in the film: 'The consequences are there for all to see: everybody dancing in a different direction, in total chaos.'[25] Costumes for the film were largely left to the devices of the performers. Carmen Miranda drew on her experience in dressmaking and millinery to design many of them herself, such as the lamé trouser suit she wore (see figure 1), and when the actor, Jaime Costa appeared in drag, he wore a dress borrowed from Adhemar Gonzaga's sister-in-law. Since the stars of the film enjoyed hectic radio careers, the film was generally shot in the early hours of the morning, after their radio work had ended for the day. There was little time for rehearsals, since filming began in October for a January release.

1 A young Carmen Miranda (right) and her sister, Aurora (left), in *Alô. Alô. Carnaval!* (1936).

Alô. Alô. Carnaval! was an unprecedented success, a fact which Gonzaga himself explained as follows: 'The idea was to showcase the great singers of the era, true idols, at a time when television had not been invented and the general public were unable to go to casino shows. At the same time . . . the public wanted the hits they heard on the radio. This was the key to the film's success.'[26] As soon as the film left the laboratory it was rushed to a preview screening at midnight on 15 January 1936 at Rio's Cinema Alhambra. It was there that it opened to the public on 20 January, and in São Paulo it also premiered at the Alhambra on 3 February. In both cities *Alô. Alô. Carnaval!* was shown for four weeks, a record in its day, and recouped its production costs during its first week's screening in the city of Rio alone. The confidence of the exhibitor, Francisco Serrador, had been well placed; he had made a personal visit to the Cinédia studios to pick up the first copy.[27] In Gonzaga's words: 'Serrador knew a future hit when he saw one, and believed in our group.'[28] The film cost approximately 120 *contos de réis* to produce, with a quarter of this amount spent on the musical performers, and in the first year after its release it took more than 315 *contos de réis* at the box-office. This represented a box-office record that was only broken in the 1930s by *Bonequinha de seda* (Little Silk Doll, 1936) and *Banana da terra* (Banana of the Land, 1939).[29]

Alô. Alô. Carnaval! was equally well received by the critics in Brazil; a review in the *Folha da Manhã* stated: 'In terms of the revue genre, we can safely say that this is the best example ever produced in Brazil. The recording is good, as are the sets, the costumes are better than most, and the performances are almost faultless. The well-crafted dialogues are entertaining and never monotonous.'[30] The modern and rather daring trouser suits worn by Carmen Miranda and her sister Aurora, and the art deco sets designed by the well-known cartoonist J. Carlos and Emílio Casalegno (see figure 1), reflect the influence of the modernist aesthetic that made its way from Europe to Hollywood in the 1920s and 1930s after the International Exhibition of Modern Industrial and Decorative Arts, held in Paris in 1925. Cinédia not only emulated the Hollywood studios' embracing of *le style moderne* in production design and mise-en-scène, but also adopted an art deco stylised palm tree as the studio emblem, designed by J. Carlos in 1934.[31]

The reviewer for the USA's *Variety* magazine (12 February 1936), accustomed to Hollywood's exacting standards, was perhaps unsurprisingly much more scathing in his assessment of the Brazilian film:

Poor photography was to be expected, owing to the inexperience of Brazilian technicians. However, it is still hard to believe that after two years of serious production, actors' features are frequently unrecognizable through misplaced lighting. Camera immobility spoils the picture throughout, resulting in stars of top-spot qualities missing the full effect of their numbers through long range.

Producers seemed over-concerned with filming the scenery and setting, though this consideration was hardly needed. It would have been better to have given the undivided attention of the camera to each singer, the women especially being mostly lookers . . . These production defects, resulting from lack of experience and poor equipment of the producers, were to be expected and might be excused. What definitely marks the pic as bad are faults in the smaller details of setting and dress. A man's dress collar that is too low, a misfit white mess-jacket, a gentleman singing as if he had an acute attack of indigestion, a male singer standing too close to a vine of cherry-blossom, a close-up showing a trace of perspiration. Things like that.[32]

In spite of its flimsy plot, modest sets and static camera work, *Alô. Alô. Carnaval!* represents a watershed in Brazilian popular film. It would be unfair to compare its technical and artistic merits with those of Hollywood, given the relative underdevelopment of the Brazilian cinema industry in the 1930s. The rigid nature of the performances and camera work in early musicals such as *Alô. Alô. Carnaval!* can partially be excused as a legacy of radio and the constraints imposed by the equipment available in Brazil. A damning review of this film by a certain P. R. Browne in the Brazilian *Veja* magazine, 25 September 1974, written to coincide with its re-release, describes it as follows: 'an inert camera in front of a stage where bad actors move around like pitiful puppets'.[33] In each musical number the sound takes precedence over the choreography and the stage direction. The camera rarely moves, remaining fixed above the performers. Close-up shots of the latter are rare, and tellingly they tend to focus on Carmen Miranda in the finale, implicitly acknowledging her star status.[34] They are supplemented with close-ups of members of the diegetic audience. Thus the experience of viewing this film is akin to belonging to the audience of a *teatro de revista* revue, and occasionally glancing at your neighbour. Only Carmen Miranda succeeds in bringing alive the art deco cardboard sets with her natural exuberance during the performance of the song 'Cantoras do rádio'.[35] Other musical numbers in the film included the *marchinhas* 'Pierrô Apaixonado' (Pierrot in Love) by Noel Rosa and Heitor dos Prazeres, sung by Joel and Gaúcho, and 'Querido Adão' (Dear Adam) by Benedito Lacerda and Osvaldo Santiago, performed by Carmen Miranda. Noel Rosa's 'Palpite Infeliz' (Unhappy Hunch) was due to be performed by the female singer Araci de Almeida, but neither appeared in the film due to an altercation in the studios between Rosa and the singer Francisco Alves.[36] As João Luiz Vieira writes, 'the musical numbers were the film's forte. A veritable constellation of male and female stars from the radio and the theatre of the era performed songs that have become, as years have gone by, true classics of Brazilian popular music.'[37]

The plot of *Alô. Alô. Carnaval!*, which served to link the various musical segments together, was written by the popular musicians João de Barro and

Alberto Ribeiro, and clearly took its inspiration from the backstage plots of Hollywood, typified by Mervyn LeRoy's *Goldiggers of 1933*, which portrayed artists endeavouring to stage a Broadway production. The Brazilian film centres on two writers called Tomé and Prata, played by Barbosa Júnior and Pinto Filho, who are trying to find a backer for their revue entitled 'Banana da Terra' (Banana of the Land). Their show is finally staged in a casino thanks to an impresario, played by Jaime Costa, who reluctantly has to accept their offer in order to replace an act from France who have failed to show up. The Brazilian replacement proves to be a flop. *Alô. Alô. Carnaval!* established many of the conventions of the *chanchada*, such as self-deprecating humour and comic contrasts between sophisticated foreign imports, such as the absent French performers, and the less glamorous realities with which Brazil has to make do, such as the second-rate, local performers and the ironically named Cassino Mosca Azul (Blue Fly Casino). When obliged to resort to staging the amateurish Brazilian revue show, the impresario exclaims 'Salve o teatro nacional!' (Three cheers for national cinema!), another tongue-in-cheek comment on Brazilian culture on the part of the film's creators. The contemporary fascination with foreign languages, particularly English, both in elite circles and as a reflection of the pervasiveness of Hollywood imports, is parodied in the same sequence. The impresario overhears one of the budding showmen say, in the true spirit of *malandragem*, 'Vamos tirar proveito da "situation"' (Let's take advantage of the situation), and there ensues an exchange that combines a nonsensical mix of English, Spanish and French. Two male performers mimic this linguistic trend by referring in English to 'girls' and 'boys', the latter a homophone for the Portuguese word for oxen. In the same vein, the film includes a scene in which the Brazilian characters exaggerate the pronunciation of the English names of supposedly sophisticated cocktails. According to the critic and filmmaker Gustavo Dahl, 'the overt mockery of everything that is foreign (from the European theatrical company that is imprisoned for fraudulent dealings to the sophisticated pronunciations of the names of exotic cocktails) results in an anti-imperialist stance, in a tangible, prosaic and good-humoured assertion of the superiority of our tropical culture over an imported one.'[38] Comic linguistic acrobatics of this kind would prove to be a recurrent feature of the *chanchada*, as is exemplified in Chapter 4.

Parody of elite culture in *Alô. Alô. Carnaval!*, another lynch pin of the *chanchada*, takes the form of an irreverent performance by Barbosa Júnior of the 'Canção do aventureiro' (Song of the Adventurer) from the Brazilian Carlos Gomes's ultra-patriotic opera *O Guarani* (The Guarani Indian). Poking fun in Hollywood's direction, an act in the 'show-within-the-film' features young school children singing a risqué song, with one of them caught in close-up with a finger up his nose, but more tellingly another dancing badly at the front of the stage in a comic skit on Shirley Temple. Parody is combined with transgression and the overturning of norms in a humorous scene in which a serenade from Franz Liszt's *Liebesträume* is 'performed' by the impresario. Dressed as a woman (the missing classical singer), and miming to the falsetto voice of Brazil's most popular singer of the era, Francisco Alves, Jaime Costa hams up his performance. He uses a fan to look coy as he slowly bursts out of his dress and one of his 'breasts' pops (to the delight of even today's audiences when a re-mastered copy of the film was exhibited in Rio de Janeiro in the summer of 2002). Cross-dressing, a recurrent motif of the *teatro de revista*, carnival and the *chanchada*, is also adopted by female performers in various show numbers in *Alô. Alô. Carnaval!*, who appear dressed as sailors or harlequins.

This trailblazing film venerates the ethos of *malandragem*, personified by the two protagonists, who are ready to use every trick in the book to gain an inroad into the world of show business. They are street-wise chancers, who put their drinks bill on a non-existent tab at the casino, chat up female patrons who are well out of their league, and are constantly on the cadge for money, even to pay their bus fare home. To pay for the expensive drinks ordered by their lady friends, they place a bet at the gaming tables, only to lose virtually everything. Down to their last five *mil-réis*, the Brazilian currency of the day, they decide to place their bet wherever it lands on the table, which happens to be in the box of gratuities for the waiters. In exchange for helping the impresario out of his tight spot they oblige him to pay off their debts, including seven months' rent and their slate at the butcher's. The *malandro* persona is equally evoked in the self-consciously tongue-in-cheek stage performances, such as those of the double-act Joel and Gaúcho, who appear in dapper white suits (in contrast to the black attire of their backing performers), with slicked back hair and spivvy moustaches. Many of the carnival songs performed in the film also deal with the popular theme of *malandragem*.

Oscarito, a music hall comedian who would go on to become one of the stars of the Atlântida *chanchadas* in the 1940s and 1950s, appears in *Alô. Alô. Carnaval!* as a drunk who is enjoying a winning streak at the casino (see figure 2). Although his is a minor role, Oscarito's comic persona and small man's gullibility are established (he is taken in by the two protagonists' ludicrous sob story and gives them his money). Tomé and Prata celebrate their con trick with the phrase 'Viva trouxa desconhecido!' (Three cheers for the gullible stranger!), a reference to Oscarito's character, the archetypal *otário* or sucker, the antithesis of the *malandro* hustler in Brazilian popular culture. As the *chanchada* evolved in the 1940s and 1950s, such down-trodden anti-heroes would take centre stage as the champions of popular identity in a constant battle with authority and devious, urbane strangers. Many of these characters would be played by Oscarito, with whom low-brow audiences

2   A young Oscarito (centre) in a scene at the casino in *Alô. Alô. Carnaval!* (1936).

could easily identify. In the *chanchadas* of the 1940s and 1950s the latter were encouraged to feel better about themselves by laughing at Brazil's own 'outsiders', particularly the Portuguese immigrant community, thus maintaining a music hall tradition. Similarly, in *Alô. Alô. Carnaval!* a musical number targets Brazil's Portuguese 'discoverers', laughing at the former colonial power in typically irreverent fashion. The film also incorporates a performance by a stand-up comedian, who cracks ethnic jokes that target the stereotypical features and speech of *turcos*, literally 'Turks', but the term used widely to refer to Brazil's Syrio-Lebanese community.[39]

With the release of *Alô. Alô. Carnaval!* the paradigms of the *chanchada* tradition were definitively established. As Orlando L. Fassoni writes: 'the film gave rise to the genre that, afterwards, the Atlântida studios would take charge of developing with all its paraphernalia of comics, feathers, sets, and songs: the *chanchada*, a genre that is inextricably bound up with Brazilian identity.'[40] Many critics refer to *Alô. Alô. Carnaval!* as encapsulating the authentic spirit of the *carioca* or inhabitant of Rio de Janeiro. Gustavo Dahl sees this 'under-developed musical' (vis-à-vis Hollywood super-productions), the roots of which are firmly buried in the *teatro de revista*, as 'profoundly original, modern and

Brazilian'. He adds that the film's lack of pretension and self-deprecation would prove to be fundamental characteristics of the Brazilian musical comedy, establishing the *chanchada* as a unique genre.[41] Adhemar Gonzaga's daughter, Alice, has perhaps best summed up the film's legacy:

> The major contribution of *Alô. Alô. Carnaval!* is that it established the basic narrative for a popular Brazilian cinema – that later became known as the *chanchada* – the elements of which were successfully combined for the first time in this film by Adhemar Gonzaga. It did not simply use elements from the radio or the *teatro de revista*, as had already been done in *Coisas nossas* and *Alô, alô, Brasil!*, but mixed up these elements with a satirical perspective, drawing on the relationship between Brazilian and foreign culture.[42]

Adhemar Gonzaga, *Cinearte* magazine and the Cinédia studio

Prior to founding the Cinédia studio in 1930, Adhemar Gonzaga tried his hand as an actor, appearing on cinema screens in Brazil in 1920 in the twenty-minute short *Convém martelar* (Keep Trying), an advertisement for a pharmaceutical product. In 1933 he went on to play a small part in the RKO 'Good Neighbour' musical *Flying Down to Rio*, released in the year that Roosevelt took office. Gonzaga's career as a director began during the silent era, and he is remembered for the classic *Barro humano* (Human Mud) of 1928, a resounding success in Brazil both at the box-office and in the opinions of the critics.[43] He began writing about the cinema in the magazine *Palcos e Telas* in 1920, and later wrote film reviews for *Rio Jornal* and *Para Todos*. To the latter magazine he contributed a regular section entitled 'Filmagem Brasileira' (Brazilian Film), in which he reported on and championed domestic production, as he went on to do in *Cinearte* magazine. Tellingly his first article for the film magazine *Cena Muda* (8 September 1942) was entitled 'Minha Campanha Favorita: O Cinema Brasileiro' (My Favourite Campaign: Brazilian Cinema).

Gonzaga was the co-founder, with Mário Behring, of the film magazine *Cinearte*, which ran from 1926 until 1942, and was modelled on the US magazine *Photoplay*, in terms of both its format and content. It catered for female readers in particular, featuring stills of North American stars supplied by the Hollywood studios alongside photos of Brazilian actors in virtually identical poses. *Cinearte* defined itself as 'the natural intermediary between the Brazilian market and the North American producer' but it always maintained an interest in Brazilian film, and constantly campaigned in favour of national cinema. As Ismail Xavier writes, 'In the eyes of its creators, *Cinearte*'s stance was progressive and patriotic. Its oft-repeated slogan – "a country's progress is gauged by the number of its cinema theatres" – highlights the idea that, striving for the development of the cinema industry, this magazine would be doing a great service to the nation.'[44] The magazine featured reports from various regional correspondents in Brazil, giving a false impression of thriving national film production. It clearly depicted the consumption of cinema as synonymous with modernity.

By filling its pages with copious photographic images of stars from both home and abroad, together with details of their lifestyles, *Cinearte* provided vital support for the creation of a 'star system' in Brazil.[45] From virtually nothing, this magazine endeavoured to create an image of Brazilian cinema and its stars, via film reviews, publicity stills and gossip columns. It was distributed in several other Latin American countries, as well as Portugal, and became the biggest selling cinema magazine in the whole of the Latin American continent. *Cinearte* clearly aimed to attract a mass market, as well as proving to be a formative influence on many of the future key players in Brazilian cinema. Its fourth edition, dedicated to the recently deceased Rudolph Valentino, sold out in Brazil, cementing the future success of the magazine. Gonzaga took his creation with him to Hollywood, where it was advertised at the Twentieth Century-Fox studio and sold well. The magazine even had a permanent correspondent in Hollywood. Gonzaga's visits to the USA, in 1927, 1929, 1932, and 1935, served to strengthen his contacts with producers, actors and technical staff, and he wrote several reports on his trips for *Cinearte*. He assimilated the technical know-how of Hollywood, as well as visiting studios in Argentina and Europe, and assisted Orson Welles in his filmmaking adventure in Brazil in 1942. Nevertheless, Gonzaga was fiercely patriotic, and defended Brazilian cinema to the hilt. *Cinearte*'s slogan was 'Todo filme brasileiro deve ser visto' (All Brazilian films must be seen), and the magazine had a section dedicated to amateur filmmaking in an effort to foster creativity.

The Cinédia studio (initially called Cinearte Studio, to tie in with the magazine) was established in 1930 in the Rio district of São Cristóvão, where it was in operation until 1951. In 1956 the studio relocated to Jacarepaguá, on the outskirts of the city of Rio. It was the first Brazilian studio to model itself on the Hollywood system, filming simultaneously on different sound stages, using state-of-the-art equipment and Max Factor make-up flown in from Hollywood, and employing technicians and staff on a permanent con-tract.[46] Cinédia was thus the first to organise film production on an industrial basis, continually creating advertising material and three weekly film journals (*O Cinédia Jornal*, *Globo Atualidades* and *Cinédia Revista*), using its own artists and controlling the distribution of its productions. The importance of Cinédia to the evolution of the film industry in Brazil cannot be under-estimated. As Gilberto Souto writes: 'Cinédia represents one of the most solid foundations of Brazilian cinema today. A cinema that is now dynamic but which would perhaps not even exist were it not for Cinédia, which functioned as a breeding ground, a hive of activity, and a training camp for countless professionals across the film industry.'[47] Gonzaga became the director of the Association of Brazilian Film Producers in 1932. His slogan was 'cinema é fazer o público sentir, participar' (cinema should make the public feel, participate), and although he did not abandon more artistic films with serious story lines completely, the carnival film, or light, unpretentious comedy became the mainstay of Cinédia's production.

In spite of the huge success of *Alô. Alô. Carnaval!* among popular audiences, Cinédia went out on a limb with its next production, *Bonequinha de seda* (Little Silk Doll, 1936), a musical cum romantic comedy directed by Oduvaldo Vianna. Its star was Gilda de Abreu in the role of Marilda, a beautiful young woman who pretends to be French and recently arrived in Brazil. Pre-empting the Atlântida *chanchadas* of the 1940s and 1950s with its comic critique of the status afforded to foreign cultural products in elite circles and its self-referential humour, the film centres on Marilda's social success. Her refined manners and style are deemed to be proof that she cannot be Brazilian.[48] *Bonequinha de seda* premiered on 26 October 1936 at the Palácio Teatro cinema in Rio and proved to be a hit, remaining in exhibition for five weeks. Such was its success that Cinédia resolved to diversify its production to include other romantic comedies, such as *Maridinho de luxo* (Upmarket Hubbie, 1938) and musicals, not necessarily linked to carnival, like *O samba da Vida* (The Samba of Life, 1937).

O samba da vida, starring Jaime Costa and Heloísa Helena, both of whom had appeared in *Alô. Alô. Carnaval!*, was directed by Luiz de Barros, whose 1929 *Acabaram-se os otários* (No More Suckers), was the first Brazilian sound film and a precursor of the *chanchada*.[49] The plot, adapted from the *teatro de revista*, involves a thief and his accomplice who break into a mansion and subsequently find themselves catapulted into positions of power and prestige, in a classic case of carnivalesque inversion. Such cases of mistaken identity and ensuing role reversal were to resurface throughout the *chanchadas* of the 1940s and 1950s. Similarly, this film pre-empted the *chanchadas* of the following two decades by venerating the counter-cultural lifestyle of *malandragem*, as evidenced in the following dialogue exchanged by Jaime Costa's character and the other burglar, played by Manuelino Teixeira:

> Jaime Costa: 'Meu pai, quando eu era pequeno, me dizia: "Meu filho, na vida só há duas espécies de homens, os que furtam e os que se deixam furtar. Os que furtam comem todos os dias. Os outros . . ." O que você pretende fazer?' (When I was little my father used to say to me: 'Son, in life there are just two types of men, those who steal and those who are stolen from. Those who steal eat every day. The others . . .' What do you intend to do?)
>
> Manuelino Teixeira: 'É lógico . . . eu quero comer todos os dias . . . (That's easy . . . I want to eat every day)

Released in October and therefore not intended to promote carnival music, *O samba da vida* had a generally mediocre soundtrack in spite of its title, but received some critical acclaim.[50] A review by Mário Nunes for the *Jornal do Brasil* stated:

> *O samba da vida* is a comic story, told with simplicity, to which have been added very well chosen fantasy sequences, pretexts for a little bit of song and music. The photography is good, on the whole, and the sound is clear but still displays highs and lows. The performers, although slightly wooden, have moments when they shine. The direction has endeavoured to avoid theatricality and to incorporate sophisticated camera angles, and in general is well done. The montage, in turn, deserves a great deal of praise, as it is elegant and tastefully executed.[51]

Cine Magazine chose to review *O samba da vida* on more than one occasion, praising the film's surprisingly grandiose sets, irresistible dancing girls, subtle comedy and, in particular, the performance given by the 'star', Heloísa Helena.[52]

Throughout the 1930s Cinédia's commercial success was built on a tried-and-tested formula: Wallace Downey and Gonzaga as directors of musical comedy productions scripted by the duo of popular composers, João de Barro and Alberto Ribeiro. Given that Gonzaga and other producers derived little benefit from the state initiatives ostensibly designed to foster the cinema industry, the production of *chanchadas* staved off bankruptcy and the limited profits made could periodically be channelled into more ambitious and less economically viable projects, such as a historical drama (*O descobrimento do Brasil*, 1937), a semi-documentary (*Aruanã*, 1938, about the Javahés indigenous tribe), and a literary adaptation (*Pureza* (Purity), 1940). In spite of the huge financial losses incurred in the making of the stylistically ambitious part-sound feature film *Ganga bruta* (Brutal Gang), directed by Humberto Mauro in 1933, Cinédia persisted in learning the hard way that high-brow cinema was expensive to produce and did not necessarily recoup its costs at the box-office.[53]

Brasil Vita Filme and Sonofilmes studios

In addition to the Cinédia studio, Rio de Janeiro was home to the two other major production companies in operation in Brazil in the 1930s, namely Brasil Vita Filme, founded in 1934, and Waldow Filme (renamed Sonofilmes in 1937).[54] All three were interlinked, with Humberto Mauro directing features for both Cinédia and Brasil Vita Filme, and Wallace Downey's Waldow Filme working with Adhemar Gonzaga's Cinédia on co-productions, such as *Alô, alô, Brasil!*, *Estudantes* and *Alô. Alô. Carnaval!*

In 1935 Carmen Santos's Brasil Vita Filme released its first production, *Favela dos meus amores* (Shantytown of My Loves), in which Santos, a screen idol from the silent era, also starred, alongside the well-known crooner Sílvio Caldas and the comic actor Jaime Costa. Directed by Humberto Mauro, the film was a tremendous box-office success and was re-released at the beginning of the 1940s. The plot centred on two young men, just returned from a trip to Paris, who decide to open a nightclub in a Rio shantytown. A love story develops, in which one of them falls for a teacher from the *favela*, played by Carmen Santos, and the plot is interspersed with melancholy sambas sung by Caldas, such as 'Arrependimento' (Repentance). By all accounts Mauro's direction displayed moments of brilliance, as comic scenes and sentimental moments were incorporated into a dramatic story, which culminated in the funeral of a popular composer, played by Armando Louzada.[55] As Mauro said of his film, 'I simply grabbed life in the favelas as it was. I documented it.'[56] According to the critic Alex Viany, the originality of *Favela dos meus amores* lay in its pioneering use of the *morro* or hillside shantytown as its setting. He refers to it as 'the first Rio-made film to make use of one of the most tragic, exuberant and musical aspects of life in Brazil's capital: the shantytown . . . an immensely important milestone, not only because it represents the most serious legacy of the early years of sound film, but also because of its popular dimension, that paved the way for Brazilian filmmakers'.[57] A review of the film by the novelist Jorge Amado heaped praise upon it:

> What Humberto managed to extract from the shantytown (absolutely amazing photography) as a motive for human emotion is simply extraordinary. The physiognomy of the great legendary shantytown is not disfigured in this film. On the contrary, Humberto Mauro has preserved the essential quality of the location, its miserable reality, and yet has created something of beauty. The blacks and mixed-race women that propel the film along prove to be, above all else, admirable performers. They display a striking naturalness as if the camera were invisible to them. The photographic effects achieved on the streets of the shantytown are finer than anyone could have expected. Praise should also be given to the presence of the samba schools, the *maxixe* danced in the cabaret club, and all the excellent music in the film. The sound is also good, and only a relatively small number of words are unintelligible.[58]

The positive reception, both critical and commercial, of *Favela dos meus amores* may in large part have been due to the film's ground-breaking realism, achieved via the use of location shooting, non-professional actors and a soundtrack that featured the authentic percussion-based music of Rio's carnival parades. (As John King writes: 'Mauro broke a taboo by treating the *favelas* not as a site of urban depravity, but rather as a vibrant cultural entity, the cradle of samba.')[59] It effectively combined these realistic elements with the trusted staples of the musical/romantic comedy formula.

The follow-up from Brasil Vita Filme, *Cidade-mulher* (City-Woman) of 1936, a celebration of the city of Rio de Janeiro, took the form of a mid-year 'backstage' tale, likewise directed by Humberto Mauro and starring Carmen Santos. Her screen romance with Mário Salberry was once again interspersed with comic interludes provided by Jaime Costa and Sara Nobre, and the plot hinged on the staging of a revue show at the Beira-Mar casino. The show-within-the-film provided the perfect excuse for the inclusion of musical numbers composed especially for the film (a first in Brazil) by popular song-writers Noel Rosa and Assis Valente. Rosa's compositions focused on typical scenes and characters from the city of Rio, such as 'Tarzan, o filho do alfaiate' (Tarzan, the Tailor's Son). This song made fun of the contemporary fashion for large shoulder pads in men's jackets and the muscular posturing of the Hollywood Tarzan, Johnny Weissmuller, at one and the same time. (The Atlântida *chanchadas* of the 1940s and 1950s would similarly mock the tastes of the elite and undermine the screen idols of Hollywood). *Cidade-mulher* also featured the household names Orlando Silva and Raul Roulien (one of the stars of RKO's *Flying Down to Rio* of 1933), who performed an improvised fox-trot. Perhaps because of the return to a more formulaic setting and plot, *Cidade-mulher* did not prove as successful as *Favela dos meus amores*. Henceforth Carmen Santos's productions would take the form of 'quality' feature films, such as *Argila* (Clay, 1940) and the historical reconstruction *Inconfidência mineira* (Conspiracy in Minas Gerais, 1948), which took many years to complete, leaving the musical comedy genre behind. For Wallace Downey's Waldow Filme/Sonofilmes, however, the *chanchada* would remain the staple diet.

Alô. Alô. Carnaval! would prove to be the last co-production between Cinédia and Wallace Downey. From then on the latter would work alone as Waldow Filme/Sonofilmes, using his own team of actors and actresses, technical staff and script writers. The success of this studio was due in large part to their awareness of the limitations of the Brazilian market and their modest aspirations. From 1937 onwards they unashamedly produced annual carnival musicals, along with only a handful of documentaries, together with an equally regular output of 'mid-year' productions, particularly comedies based on popular theatrical works.[60] In 1937 Downey released the comedy *João Ninguém*, which included the pioneering use of colour film in Brazil during a dream sequence. The plot of the film, for which the comic actor Mesquitinha made his directorial debut, was co-authored by João de Barro and Alberto Ribeiro (Cinédia's trusted scriptwriting team), and the script was written by Rui Costa. João Luiz Vieira argues that this film was in many ways a precursor of Atlântida's *chanchadas* of the 1950s in that the screen romance involved a hero, a girl-next-door or *mocinha*, and a villain, and the diegetic music was not drawn directly from carnival rhythms.[61] Mesquitinha plays the hero, a popular composer who writes a song as a birthday gift for his girlfriend, who happens to work at a record company. The hero asks a young boy from a boarding house, played by Grande Otelo, another future star of Atlântida's productions, to take the song to her, but en route he is knocked down and the piece of music is found by someone else (in a classic case of *troca* or exchange, as examined in relation to the *chanchadas* of the 1940s in Chapter 3). Mesquitinha's character ends up in jail, where he hears his song being performed on the radio.[62] Vieira argues that *João Ninguém* and *Favela dos meus amores* were perhaps 'genuine attempts to represent the characteristic aspects of life in Rio de Janeiro in this era, capturing the typical temperament and attitude to life of the city's inhabitants'.[63]

Bananas and *baianas*

In 1939 Sonofilmes released the musical comedy *Banana da terra* (Banana of the Land), which like many of its film musical predecessors, belonged to the tradition of carnival films that included hit songs and were released just before the annual celebrations.[64] According to the *Jornal do Brasil* newspaper, *Banana da terra* was to premiere on 10 February at the MGM-owned cinemas in Rio and São Paulo, the Pedro II cinema in Petrópolis, in the state of Rio de Janeiro, and the Guarani cinema in Salvador, Bahia, as well as in Recife, Porto Alegre and Ribeirão Preto.[65] Negotiations were also underway to show the film in the state capitals Curitiba and Belo Horizonte. Thanks to the links between Alberto Byington Jr, Wallace Downey's associate, and Hollywood, this Sonofilmes production was distributed by MGM in Brazil, and consequently premiered in the luxurious Metro Passeio cinema in Rio.[66] *Banana da terra* proved to be a great commercial success and to markedly influence the *chanchada* tradition, not least by combining self-deprecating humour with a tongue-in-cheek critique of Hollywood clichés.

The plot of *Banana da terra*, first and foremost a construct to link together the various musical numbers, revolved around the imaginary Pacific island of Bananolândia, an allegorical tropical paradise, which was faced with the problem of a surplus of bananas. In this self-parodic comedy Brazil adopts the reflected identity of the exotic island of plenty. (The last emperor of Brazil, Pedro II, had, after all, been nicknamed Pedro Banana by the press and the ordinary people, and Brazil was represented by a bunch of bananas in the allegorical theatre revue *Caiu do galho!* (It Fell off the Branch!) of 1939). The film's story line toys with the stereotypical notion of Brazil as both an underdeveloped banana republic and a fertile Eden. It is surely no coincidence that João de Barro, one of the film's scriptwriters, was the co-author of the 1938 carnival *marchinha* 'Yes, nós temos bananas' (Yes, We Have Bananas), along with Alberto Ribeiro. This carnival *marchinha* took its lead from the 1923 song 'Yes, We Have No Bananas', made famous by the comedian Eddie Cantor, and stole the show in the 1938 carnival. Its lyrics are a light-hearted attack on the clichéd view of Latin America held by the United States, and both of its composers would incorporate similar comic critiques into their film scripts:

Yes, nós temos bananas (Yes, we've got bananas)
Bananas pra dar e vender (Bananas to give away and to sell)
Banana, menina, (Bananas, young lady,)
Tem vitamina (Are full of vitamins)
Banana engorda e faz crescer. (Bananas fatten you up and make you grow.)

Vai para a França o café (Coffee goes off to France)
Pois é (Sure enough)
Para o Japão o algodão (And cotton to Japan)
Pois não (Of course)
Pro mundo inteiro (To the whole world)
'Home' ou mulher (For men or women)
Bananas para quem quiser. (There are bananas for anyone who wants them.)[67]

In *Banana da terra* the actor Oscarito plays a man in charge of a publicity campaign for bananas who decides to kidnap the queen of Bananolândia, played by Dircinha Batista. She is taken to Rio and promptly falls in love with a character played by Aloísio de Oliveira, a member of Carmen Miranda's backing group, the Bando da Lua. The action unfolds in the glamorous realm of Rio's radio stations and casinos, thus providing the perfect pretext for the inclusion of a variety of musical numbers. These included 'A Jardineira' (The Gardener) by Benedito Lacerda and Humberto Porto, sung by Orlando Silva, which proved to be the carnival smash of the 1939 celebrations, and 'Sei que é covardia' (I know It's Cowardice) by Ataúlfo Alves and Claudionor Cruz.

Banana da terra is best remembered for Carmen Miranda's rendition of the Dorival Caymmi song 'O que é que a baiana tem?' (What is it about the *baiana*?), dressed in the *baiana* costume, in keeping with the song's lyrics. It is said that the composer went to Miranda's house where he taught her the lyrics and suggested appropriate gestures and inflections for her performance.[68] The *baiana* outfit, with its characteristic turban, frills and beads, was adapted from that of the black street vendors of Salvador da Bahia, and was already a popular choice of fancy dress for carnival among both men and women. White-skinned *baianas* like Miranda permeated Brazil's music hall tradition, and doubtless featured heavily in the first carnival documentaries. But it was Miranda who made the look her own and used it to launch her international career as the embodiment of a pan-Latin American identity.[69] *Banana da terra* was to be Miranda's last Brazilian film; it was when performing its hit song 'O que é que a baiana tem?' at Rio's Urca casino that she was 'discovered' by the show business impresario Lee Schubert and taken to Broadway, and subsequently to Hollywood.[70]

Concluding remarks

There can be no doubt that musical comedies designed to tap into the city's carnival celebrations were the most reliable source of income for the Rio-based film studios of the 1930s. They were relatively cheap to make and were virtually guaranteed box-office success. Often timed to premiere in the run-up to carnival, they were usually filmed on the tightest of schedules, but the record goes to Cinédia's *Tererê não resolve* (Chatting Gets You Nowhere, 1938), directed by Luiz de Barros, which was filmed in just seven days. Once again mistaken identity provided the excuse for comic mayhem in the midst of carnival, as two wives, both dressed in domino costumes, went in search of their respective husbands, who had thrown themselves headlong into the celebrations. In his autobiography Luiz de Barros is keen to distinguish between the comedy films and the *chanchadas* that he directed. He terms *Maridinho de luxo*, for example, a 'comédia fina' ('sophisticated comedy') and not a *chanchada*.[71] The following quotation from this influential director's memoirs partially reveals his own understanding of what the term *chanchada* implied: 'I filmed *E o circo chegou* (And the Circus Arrived, 1940), a comedy, not a *chanchada*, since it did not contain any nonsense, any clowning around, any exaggeration.'[72] Paramount distributed this film throughout Brazil but its *chanchada* label seems to have irritated Barros. As he continues: 'this comedy, performed in an unexaggerated style, featuring perfectly human characters, is one of those that are considered to be *chanchadas* by some critics'.[73] Defining precisely what constitutes a *chanchada* is clearly problematic, and the term's generic possibilities will be examined in greater depth in Chapters 3 and 4.

During the 1930s the key elements of popular cinema were established that would feed directly into the fledgling *chanchada* tradition as it took shape in the latter half of the decade. The legacies of popular theatre and the circus, not least in the performers who made the transition from these domains to film, such as Oscarito, would continue to be much in evidence in the 1940s and beyond. The fascination with the backstage plot would also endure, finding obvious motives for song and dance and escapist settings in Rio's expanding pleasure industry, particularly the nightclub and casino. The *chanchada*'s engagement, both purely mimetic and sometimes parodic, with Hollywood's generic models in the 1940s and 1950s, was established in countless films from the 1930s, as was the tradition's penchant for comic juxtapositions, especially between the local and the 'exotic', and ensuing self-deprecating humour. The theme of mistaken identity and the motifs of transgression and inversion, particularly of established boundaries of good taste, propriety and hierarchy, had already begun to characterise popular cinema by the end of the 1930s. Finally, with the creation of magazines such as *Cinearte*, the assembling of a 'star machine' was underway, and would be subject to further expansion in the 1940s under the auspices of the Atlântida studio, as will be examined in Chapter 3.

Notes

1 Randal Johnson, *The Film Industry in Brazil: Culture and the State* (Pittsburgh: University of Pittsburgh Press, 1987) p. 51.
2 *Ibid.*, p. 47.
3 Quoted by Anita Simis, 'Movies and moviemakers under Vargas', *Latin American Perspectives*, 29:1 (2002), p. 108.
4 João Luiz Vieira, 'A chanchada e o cinema carioca (1930–1955)', in Fernão Ramos (ed.), *História do cinema brasileiro* (São Paulo: Art Editora, 1987), p. 144.
5 Daryle Williams, *Culture Wars in Brazil: The First Vargas Regime, 1930–1945* (Durham and London: Duke University Press) p. 71.
6 *Ibid.*, p. 71.
7 *Ibid.*, p. 72.
8 Simis, 'Movies and moviemakers under Vargas', p. 113.
9 *Ibid.*, p. 111.
10 Vieira, 'A chanchada e o cinema carioca (1930–1955)', p. 152.
11 Silvana Goulart, *Sob a verdade oficial: ideologia, propaganda e censura no Estado Novo* (São Paulo: Marco Zero, 1990), p. 52.
12 *Ibid.*, p. 52 (our translation).
13 Catherine Benamou, 'Orson Welles's Transcultural Cinema: An Historical/ Textual Reconstruction of the Suspended Film, *It's All True*, 1941–1993', PhD dissertation, New York University, 1997, p. 371.
14 Of course this did not prove to be the case. As John King writes: 'Hollywood did not fade into the background and the Brazilian public soon adapted to the sub-titling of North American films. Brazilian cinema resumed its marginal place in the market and the number of features fell from seventeen in 1931 to seven in 1936 and 1939.' John King, *Magical Reels: A History of Cinema in Latin America* (London and New York: Verso, 1990), p. 56.
15 Vieira, 'A chanchada e o cinema carioca (1930–1955)', p. 141 (our translation).
16 Nicolau Sevcenko, 'Brazilian Follies: The Casting, Broadcasting and Consump-tion of Images of Brazil on Both Sides of the Continent, 1930–50', paper given at the *Ways of Working in Latin American Cultural Studies* conference, King's College London, April 1995.
17 Randal Johnson and Robert Stam (eds), *Brazilian Cinema* (New York: Columbia University Press, 1995), p. 27.
18 It featured the popular musicians Noel Rosa, João de Barro, Alvinho, Henrique Brito and Almirante, dressed in the typical attire of the rural North East.
19 *Cinearte*, 1 May 1933 (our translation).
20 In 1934 a theatrical revue was performed in Rio de Janeiro entitled *Alô . . . alô . . . Rio?* (Hello, Hello, Rio?), which dealt with the impact of the telephone, the public's obsession with the radio, and other new fads.

21 Reviews of this film included the following: 'It delights audiences and is making money' (*Revista do Exhibidor* (February 1935) (our translation)) and 'The public have flocked to see it' (*Gazeta de Notícias* (19 March 1935) (our translation)).

22 Sérgio Augusto, *Este mundo é um pandeiro: a chanchada de Getúlio a JK* (São Paulo: Companhia das Letras, 1993), p. 92 (our translation).

23 Rick Altman, *The American Film Musical* (Bloomington and Indianapolis: Indiana University Press, 1987), p. 234.

24 These three reviews are cited in Alice Gonzaga, *50 anos de Cinédia* (Rio de Janeiro: Record, 1987), p. 46.

25 Unmarked newspaper cutting from the Museum of Modern Art film archive, Rio de Janeiro (our translation).

26 *Jornal do Brasil*, 23 November 1973 (our translation).

27 In 1922 Serrador began building the Cinelândia area of downtown Rio de Janeiro, where the city's cinema theatres were constructed, on the site of the former Ajuda convent.

28 Unmarked newspaper cutting from the Museum of Modern Art film archive, Rio de Janeiro (our translation).

29 Statistics taken from the press book for *Alô. Alô. Carnaval!*, published on the release of the restored version of the film in 2002, kindly supplied by Adhemar Gonzaga's daughter, Alice Gonzaga, the current director of Cinédia.

30 *Folha da Manhã*, 15 February 1936 (our translation).

31 The term 'Copacabana Style' was used to refer to the architectural features that emerged in Rio, particularly in the Copacabana district of the city, in the late 1920s and early 1930s, inspired by North American art deco. This daring style combined chrome and decorative themes reminiscent of modern machinery, speed and energy. It made its impact on the design of movie theatres in the Cinelândia district of Rio, frequented by the same fashionable set, as well as on the aesthetics of moviemaking.

32 *Alô. Alô. Carnaval!* was reviewed for *Variety* in Rio de Janeiro on 23 January 1936, and mistakenly referred to as 'in Spanish'. In the course of the research for this book it was sometimes necessary to consult US sources such as *Variety*, which not surprisingly judge Brazilian film by Hollywood's very exacting standards. Much of the irony of the film would have been lost on this reviewer, such as the references to *malandragem* and parodies of 'high culture'. According to the press book published when a restored version of the film was released in 2002, one or two of the technical failings pointed out by critics may well have been deliberate. It is said that the cinematographer, Edgar Brasil, who disliked the handsome singer Francisco Alves, intentionally over-lit shots of him, quite literally casting him in a less flattering light. Information taken from the press book for *Alô. Alô. Carnaval!*, published on the release of the restored version of the film in 2002.

33 (Our translation). *Alô. Alô. Carnaval!* was re-released in 1974 and was hugely popular, perhaps because it was during a self-consciously nationalist period, under the military dictatorship.

34 The press book for *Alô. Alô. Carnaval!*, published on the release of the restored version of the film in 2002, explains that in the original 1936 version of the film,

the final musical number was 'Manhãs de sol' (Sunny Mornings), sung by Francisco Alves. When the film was re-released in 1974 Adhemar Gonzaga replaced this number with 'Cantoras do rádio' performed by Carmen and Aurora Miranda. In the restored version released in 2002 Alice Gonzaga decided to maintain the order chosen by her father in 1974.

35 Moacir Fenelon, one of the founders of the Atlântida studio, discussed in more detail in Chapter 3, was responsible for the sound.

36 In his memoirs, Almirante claims that Almeida refused to perform the song in the film since she was to do so while hanging out washing on the set of the backyard of a humble dwelling. Almirante (H. F. Domingues), *No tempo de Noel Rosa* (Rio de Janeiro: Francisco Alves, 1977), p. 161.

37 Vieira, 'A chanchada e o cinema carioca (1930–1955)', p. 146 (our translation).

38 Gustavo Dahl, *Alô, alô, carnaval: banana da terra vale ouro!*, [n.p.], 19 February 1975 (our translation).

39 Such jokes were premised on the assumption that *turcos* were mean with their money, and drew on the fact that in this era money lenders, travelling salesmen and loan sharks were predominantly European immigrants but collectively known as *judeus* (Jews) or *turcos* (Turks).

40 'Adhemar Gonzaga, o homem de "Alô, Alô, Carnaval"', *Folha de São Paulo*, 1 February 1978 (our translation).

41 *Ibid.*

42 Interview with Alice Gonzaga from the press book for *Alô. Alô. Carnaval!*, published on the release of the restored version of the film in 2002.

43 *Barro humano* told the story of a rich boy who falls in love with a poor girl from a shantytown, and the film caused a scandal in its day for featuring scenes of a Rio *favela*, some of which had to be cut from the film.

44 Ismail Xavier, 'O sonho da indústria: a criação de imagem em *Cinearte*', *Sétima arte: um culto moderno* (São Paulo: Perspectiva – Secretaria da Cultura, Ciência e Tecnologia do Estado de São Paulo, 1978), p. 176 (our translation).

45 Vieira, 'A chanchada e o cinema carioca (1930–1955)', p. 132.

46 *Ibid.*, p. 135.

47 'Gonzaga um pioneiro', *Filme Cultura*, 8 March 1968, p. 11 (our translation). The Cinédia studio produced shorts, including propaganda films in support of the Vargas regime, such as *Assinatura do decreto do 'Salário Mínimo' por Getúlio Vargas* (Signing of the 'Minimum Wage' Decree by Getúlio Vargas, 1 May 1938). Oddly enough, the first film that Gonzaga directed after Cinédia's move to Jacarepaguá was entitled *Salário mínimo* (Minimum Wage, 1970).

48 *Bonequinha de seda* was also the first Brazilian film to use the technique of rear projection, in a scene in a moving automobile, and it incorporated crane shots.

49 Posters advertising *Acabaram-se os otários* promised a succession of 'songs, *modinhas*, jokes and word play', the basic ingredients to win over popular audiences (our translation). It proved to be a box-office hit, and remained in exhibition for seventy-six days in the city of Rio de Janeiro. Afrânio M. Catani and José I. de Melo Souza, *A chanchada no cinema brasileiro* (São Paulo: Brasiliense, 1983), p. 10.

50 In his autobiography, Luiz de Barros explains how he built a primitive wooden crane in order to achieve a tracking shot of Heloísa Helena descending a staircase from her bedroom to the front door of her mansion. Luiz de Barros, *Minhas memórias de cineasta* (Rio de Janeiro: Artenova, 1978), p. 134.

51 *Jornal do Brasil*, 26 October 1937 (our translation).

52 *Cine Magazine*, 49 (May 1937), and 53 (September 1937).

53 Randal Johnson and Robert Stam write that *Ganga bruta*, 'deeply impressed the future Cinema Novo directors who saw it at a 1961 Retrospective. The film creatively melds the cinematic styles of expressionism and Soviet montage in a story about a man who kills his bride on the honeymoon and then attempts to rebuild his life.' Johnson and Stam (eds), *Brazilian Cinema*, p. 26.

54 As John King says, 'Outside the three main production companies, other individuals and companies made the occasional feature, usually without any financial success or critical acclaim, although Raul Roulien, a Brazilian actor returning from Hollywood in the mid thirties, did manage to direct several features' (King, *Magical Reels*, p. 56).

55 *Ibid.*, p. 145.

56 Carlos Roberto de Sousa, *Jornal do Brasil*, 14 May 1977. Quoted in Johnson and Stam (eds), *Brazilian Cinema*, p. 26.

57 Alex Viany, *Introdução ao cinema brasileiro* (Rio de Janeiro: Revan, 1993), p. 80 (our translation). As João Luiz Vieira points out, the shantytown would go on to provide the setting for the first production from the Atlântida studios, *Moleque Tião* (Street Kid Tião, 1943), and Nelson Pereira dos Santos's *Rio, 40 graus* (Rio, 40 Degrees, 1955), among other notable examples. Vieira, 'A chanchada e o cinema carioca (1930–1955)', p. 181.

58 Jorge Amado, 'Favela dos meus amores', *Boletim de Ariel*, s. d., p. 30 (our translation).

59 King, *Magical Reels*, p. 56.

60 Vieira, 'A chanchada e o cinema carioca (1930–1955)', p. 151.

61 *Ibid.*, pp. 148–9.

62 The plot pre-empted that of Nelson Pereira dos Santos's *Rio, Zona Norte* (Rio, North Zone, 1957), a film that is referred to in more detail in Chapter 4.

63 Vieira, 'A chanchada e o cinema carioca (1930–1955)', p. 149.

64 *Banana da terra* formed part of a trilogy, linked only by their fruity titles, produced by the Sonofilmes studio, and was followed by *Laranja da China* (Orange from China) in 1940 and *Abacaxi azul* (Blue Pineapple) in 1944, both discussed in more detail in Chapter 3.

65 *Jornal do Brasil*, 4 February 1939.

66 This cinema theatre, which opened in September 1936, revolutionised film exhibition in Rio, with its air conditioning and comfortable leather seats. See Vieira, 'A chanchada e o cinema carioca (1930–1955)', p. 150.

67 It is equally no coincidence that the film *Banana da terra* shares its title with the stage show around which the plot of *Alô. Alô. Carnaval!* revolved, since both scripts were penned by João de Barro, although in this later film he teamed up with Mário Lago, another musician, and not Alberto Ribeiro.

68 *Banana da terra* was to have featured two songs by Ari Barroso, performed by
    Carmen Miranda, but Barroso fell out with Wallace Downey over payment. They
    were replaced by Caymmi's 'O que é que a baiana tem?' and the *marcha* 'Pirulito'
    by João de Barro and Alberto Ribeiro, performed in duet by Miranda and
    Almirante, both in blackface.

69 The white actress Heloísa Helena actually stole Miranda's thunder by appearing
    on screen as a *baiana* in 1936 in *Alô. Alô. Carnaval!* She recalls, 'Gustavo Dória
    designed a *baiana* costume all in satin, with a velvet skirt in varying shades of
    green. Really pretty.' Unmarked newspaper cutting from the Museum of Modern
    Art film archive, Rio de Janeiro (our translation).

70 It is commonly believed that Miranda took Brazil's unofficial 'national costume'
    to Hollywood in 1939, where it was reproduced in various musicals such as
    Twentieth Century-Fox's *The Gang's All Here* (1943). However, versions of the
    same characteristic outfit are worn by the resident dancers in a Rio casino in
    RKO's *Flying Down to Rio* (1933), made several years before Carmen first wore
    the outfit on screen. As will be explored in Chapter 4, the celluloid *baiana* would
    move back and forth between Brazil and Hollywood both as an emblematic motif
    of national self-definition and as a symbol of a generic 'Latino' identity.

71 Barros, *Minhas memórias de cineasta*, p.136. This film starred Fada Santoro, one
    of the future stars of the *chanchada* tradition, the music hall comedian Mesquitinha,
    as well as the tenor Cândido Botelho.

72 *Ibid.*, p. 139 (our translation).

73 *Ibid.*, p. 140 (our translation). Similar efforts were made by certain filmmakers
    in the 1970s to assert the differences between the *pornochanchada* and erotic
    comedies, as examined in Chapter 6.

3

The 1940s

Introduction

The first half of the 1940s witnessed a continuation of Vargas's quest for economic expansion based on the creation of a dignified workforce, rewarded for its efforts by improvements in the welfare system. National integration remained at the top of his political agenda, and in 1944 the regime's Press and Propaganda Department (DIP) hosted the so-called 'Congress on Brazilian Identity' (*Congresso de Brasilidade*), in an effort to foster a heightened sense of belonging among the nation's far-flung and heterogeneous population. The cult of the self-styled 'Father of the poor', as Vargas liked to be known, was reinforced by the introduction of 'President's Day' (*Dia do Presidente*) in 1942, when radio stations, schools, newspapers, recreational clubs and professional institutions were obliged to explicitly heap praise on their leader and celebrate the nation-state. Film magazines were likewise required to praise the president for his ostensible support of the cinema industry. As the publication *Cinema* stated in May 1941: 'President Vargas breathed life into our national film industry. We must keep this flame alive so as not to disappoint the man to whom Brazil owes not only the admiration of its own people, but also of the world.'[1] With the introduction of decree-law 4,064 on 29 January 1942, the regime created the National Film Council (*Conselho Nacional de Cinematografia*), within the DIP, headed by the latter's director general, Lourival Fontes. This law effectively gave the DIP the authority to increase the screen quota for Brazilian films, but as Randal Johnson writes: 'Such a provision reflected the increasing power and ideological nature of the propaganda arm of Vargas's *Estado Novo*, incorporating instruments of mass communication such as radio and cinema into the corporative policies of the regime.'[2]

The Rio-based Cinédia studio was heavily involved in the production of newsreels, and by September 1944 it had completed 426 issues of its *Cinédia*

Jornal, in addition to accepting a government commission for the production of the first 127 issues of the government's *Cine Jornal Brasileiro,* which
first appeared in late 1938.[3] From December 1939 onwards, however, the
DIP had begun to contract its own cameramen, many of them enticed away
from Cinédia, chiefly to produce the *Cine Jornal Brasileiro.* Newsreels were
shown before every feature film throughout the nation on a daily basis, with
some even exhibited abroad, and they primarily featured recordings of official
events and the supposedly joyous reception of the public spectators. As Daryle
Williams writes:

> The *Cine Jornal* offered carefully crafted, optimistic visions of Brazil and its
> progress under Vargas rule. The newsreels glossed over the details of Vargas-era
> public policy, letting seductive images and orchestration develop the visual
> textures of state-sponsored political culture. These newsreels were important
> venues through which culture managers showed to Brazil's movie-going
> audiences that their nation was indeed in the throes of dynamic political and
> administrative modernization, economic diversification and cultural renewal.
> The newsreels imagined the fruits of modernization without a hint of conflict
> within the state or in society. Compulsory screenings certainly helped to
> guarantee that movie-goers were exposed to an imagined Brazil that contained
> no conflict, no misery, no setbacks, and no culture wars, even if this was a
> fiction of a repressive regime.[4]

The DIP's film releases represented the majority of films produced in Brazil
in this period, when domestic production averaged just 7.6 feature-length
films per year, as opposed to nearly four hundred imported releases.[5] By
all accounts these newsreels were often met with the booing and hisses of
the cinema audience,[6] who would have subsequently delighted in the ironic
juxtaposition of state-sponsored, self-congratulatory propaganda and the
counter-cultural messages of popular film, particularly the irreverent attitudes towards authority conveyed by a typical *chanchada,* discussed in more
detail below. The *Cine Jornal Brasileiro* promoted Vargas as a charismatic
and powerful leader, a persona that would be remorselessly undermined by
the anti-establishment discourse of the *chanchada.*

Under Vargas's direction the DIP had to control the image of the regime
that was disseminated by the cinema. The head of the cinema division of the
DIP, Henrique Pongetti, when called upon to film a luncheon for Vargas and
high-ranking officials from the armed forces, was required to cut a sequence
in which the president could be seen chewing on a toothpick. As Pongetti put
it, 'my job was to avoid a scene from a *chanchada* in a serious documentary'.[7]
In line with the rigid censorship restrictions imposed on the cinema, throughout the remaining years of Vargas's dictatorship all theatre and radio scripts,
public lectures and films had to be submitted to the censors of the DIP in
order to receive prior approval before being disseminated to the public. Any

actor caught improvising by an official of the censorship board could have received a prison sentence.[8]

In the run-up to the Second World War, the Vargas regime had openly sided with the Fascist dictators of Germany and Italy. With the outbreak of the conflict in Europe, however, Brazil, with its Fascist-style *Estado Novo*, commercial ties with Germany, sizeable immigrant communities from Italy and Germany, and strategic geo-political location, became the focus of the attention of both the Axis and the Allies. The ensuing intensification of the USA's 'Good Neighbour Policy' towards the Latin American continent relied heavily on Hollywood's products, and the Vargas regime was more than happy to endorse the imported visions of *brasilidade* that appeared on the silver screen. Intrinsically Brazilian musical genres and their accompanying dances, such as the samba and the maxixe, were projected back to Brazilian audiences in cinema halls all over the nation, but in a highly diluted and pastiched form. In spite of the best efforts of Nelson Rockefeller's Office of the Co-ordinator of Inter-American Affairs (CIAA), images of a mythical Brazilian utopia were blurred with those of oriental origin, and in a sense Hollywood reinvented Brazil/Latin America, which became a historically frozen paradise, that offered an escape from Depression-hit North America and subsequently war-torn Europe. Hollywood's 'Latin America' became merely a collection of confused motifs and rhythms, yet although ordinary Brazilians were perplexed by what they saw on the screen, Vargas's propaganda machine gained a useful tool with which to homogenise Brazilian identity. What is so fascinating about these often ludicrous, hybrid visions of the continent is that when they were projected back there they altered the way Brazilians, at any rate, began to portray themselves. Gradually the Brazilian film industry absorbed these images and re-worked them in the *chanchada*.

The 'Good Neighbour Policy' paid off, and in August 1942 Brazil declared war on the Axis in response to torpedo attacks on Brazilian shipping off the North Eastern coast, and more importantly, perhaps, in exchange for a twenty million dollar loan from the Export-Import Bank of the USA to build the Volta Redonda steelworks in Brazil. Brazil's involvement in the world conflict would ultimately lead to Vargas's downfall in 1945, since the *Estado Novo* was an anachronism in a post-war climate where democracy had triumphed over totalitarianism. Ousted from power by the military, Vargas was succeeded in the presidency by General Dutra (1946–51). In the latter half of the 1940s the USA's popular cultural presence in Brazil was consolidated. Dutra dipped into Brazil's foreign currency reserves and opened up the country to mass imports of consumer goods, such as Quaker Oats, Ovaltine, Ray-Ban sunglasses, cosmetics and the latest fashions, in an effort to combat a rate of inflation that had risen as a consequence of the nation's involvement in the Second World War. The new president consolidated the position of the cinema within Brazilian society, not least by introducing tax incentives for Brazilian film companies on 11 August 1949. By 1945 there were 1,317 cinema theatres in Brazil, but just five years later this number had increased to 3,033.[9] The so-called *poeiras*, literally 'dust cinemas', offered the poor a cheap form of entertainment with few frills.

By the end of the 1940s Brazilians were beginning to lose their agrarian vocation, and manufactured goods accounted for 20 per cent of gross domestic product. Migration from the countryside to the cities increased and a new social class emerged in the form of the urban masses. The city of São Paulo, for example, with only 270,000 inhabitants at the beginning of the twentieth century, encompassed a population of over two and a half million by 1950, the result of successive waves of national and foreign immigration.[10] The power of the rural oligarchies was gradually eroded as individual states lost their autonomy and a national internal market was constructed along with an integrated highway system.[11] The themes of progress and modernity naturally became central to political discourse, but equally to popular film, which intensified its focus on the modern metropolis as the site of national identity, and its appeal to the new uprooted social groups.

Atlântida Cinematográfica and the consolidation of the *chanchada* tradition

The Rio-based film production company, Atlântida Cinematográfica was founded in 1941 by Moacir Fenelon, Alinor Azevedo and José Carlos Burle, and in its patriotic mission statement the studio declared its ambition to create a cinema capable of providing 'indisputable services to national greatness'.[12] Atlântida set out to establish a national cinema industry and to reach a level of production comparable with that achieved in the USA. It also aimed to represent real life on screen, and to introduce an element of social commentary into its films. The studio's first production, *Moleque Tião* (Street Kid Tião), was based on the life story of the comic actor Grande Otelo (Sebastião Bernardes de Souza Prata). Its release in 1943 coincided with a period of optimism within the Brazilian film industry, since the Second World War had interrupted the flow of European movies, allowing more breathing space and screen time for Brazilian producers.[13] *Moleque Tião* proved to be a success, and was followed up in 1943 by *É proibido sonhar* (Dreaming is Forbidden), another film on a serious social theme that nevertheless was both a critical and commercial flop. Consequently Atlântida soon bowed to commercial pressures. To satisfy the mass market the studio started to channel its efforts into carnival musicals, developing the comedic dimension of the tried-and-trusted formula of such proto-*chanchadas* as *Alô. Alô. Carnaval!* (Hello, Hello, Carnival!, 1936). *Tristezas não pagam dívidas* (Sadness Won't

Pay Your Debts, 1944) and *Não adianta chorar* (It's No Good Crying, 1945), were the first two comedy films produced by Atlântida, and their titles unwittingly reflected the inviability of making movies with more sober story lines. Both successfully modelled themselves on the 'radio-broadcast' musicals of the previous decade. *Tristezas não pagam dívidas*, which was screened for 139 consecutive days, was also the first film to combine the comic talents of Grande Otelo and Oscarito, both stars of the *teatro de revista*, who went on to star together in thirteen of Atlântida's *chanchadas*. These included the equally successful *Não adianta chorar*, screened for an uninterrupted period of 137 days.[14] Atlântida would dominate film production in Rio de Janeiro for the next fifteen years, particularly after 1947 when Luiz Severiano Ribeiro became the majority shareholder. The owner of a national chain of cinema theatres, Ribeiro was able to ensure the all-important widespread distribution of Atlântida's output and thus give the foreign films that continued to flood the market a run for their money via the strategy of vertical integration. Smaller production companies, such as the São Paulo-based Cinedistri studio, where the director J. B. Tanko made his name, would release copy-cat *chanchadas* throughout the 1940s and 1950s, but found it difficult to hold their own alongside what Sérgio Augusto terms 'the tropical MGM'.[15]

In the 1940s and 1950s *chanchadas* were exhibited in Brazil's major cities, particularly Rio de Janeiro and São Paulo, but also in the towns of the interior and at improvised open-air screenings in rural areas. The latest films were publicised via large colour posters displayed on billboards and via newspaper articles and advertisements. Film magazines such as *A Cena Muda*, *Revista Cinelândia* and *Cine-repórter* played a major part in generating a star system in Brazil, by including features on and interviews with the *chanchada*'s stars, who became household names all over the country. Many of them went on tours of the countryside with their own stage shows, often in the wake of the first screening of their latest film. (As João Luiz Vieira explains, their income ironically did not come primarily from their work in films but from such live circus and theatre performances around the country.[16] As in the USA, the star system within popular theatre provided a model for the film industry.) Although box-office figures for this era are at best sketchy, the tradition's popular appeal is evidenced in press reports. *Este mundo é um pandeiro* (This World Is a Tambourine, 1946) established Atlântida's dominance, remaining in exhibition for several weeks at a time when only foreign films enjoyed such a privilege.[17] The proliferation of magazines devoted to telling fans about the lifestyles of the stars equally testifies to the reception of home-grown popular film. With the rise of Atlântida and the fostering of a star system, the performers who looked down from the silver screen were now film stars in their own right in contrast to the cross-over artists from the radio who characterised film production in the 1930s. *Chanchadas* were cheap to produce, relying on low production values and salaries (actors were often asked to provide their own costumes), and tight shooting schedules, and they often recovered their costs from the premieres in the cities of Rio de Janeiro and São Paulo alone. The price of cinema tickets in Brazil was relatively low throughout the 1940s, movie theatres were plentiful, and thus the audience numbers swelled. The high illiteracy rate in Brazil in the 1940s undoubtedly contributed to the *chanchada*'s success in relation to subtitled Hollywood imports.

Protagonists and plots

Atlântida released a series of *chanchadas* in the 1940s that were produced on a shoestring and yet held great appeal for both children and adults. These musical comedies were specifically aimed at a popular audience, whose life experiences they tapped into. As Ney Costa Santos Filho writes: 'At a time when US films dominated the market in Brazil, the *chanchada* accustomed audiences to hearing their own language and seeing on the screen types with whom, for better or for worse, they could identify.'[18] These films incorporated actors and popular performers, many from humble origins themselves, who had established careers in music hall, the radio or the circus. They featured characters that used colloquial language and slang expressions in which the audience members would also be well versed. The audience could identify with the stock types portrayed on screen, ranging from the faceless, idle, petty bureaucrat to the alienated newcomer to the city. As João Luiz Vieira and Robert Stam say of the *chanchada*: 'Brazilian culture and popular desire infiltrated the genre; the on-screen presence of marginal characters drawn from daily urban life paralleled the physical incorporation of the urban masses into the movie theatres themselves.'[19]

The *chanchada* typically centred on a character's social advancement, often by a twist of fate, but thus reassured audiences about the likelihood of making it in the city. One of the main comic stars of the tradition, Oscarito, epitomised the man in the street, who struggled to come to terms with modern times and urban lifestyles. Useful comparisons can be drawn between him and the Mexican film star, Mario Moreno, better known as Cantinflas, and even Charlie Chaplin, particularly in terms of their popular reception. As Jeffrey Pilcher writes: 'Cantinflas and the Tramp both represented the human debris of industrialization, rootless migrants to the big city who survived by their wits in a bewildering and coldhearted environment. Both were masters of physical comedy and possessed an innate geniality that elicited sympathy for their underdog status.'[20] Oscarito's characters are archetypal *malandros*, anti-heroes of modest means who somehow manage to turn their lives around by pure chance. The son of Spanish immigrants and born into a travelling circus, Oscarito clearly drew on his own life experiences. In an interview for the Museum of Image and Sound in Rio in 1968, he said: 'I had to get by in life like a *malandro*. I've always been very Brazilian.'[21]

The *chanchadas* of the 1940s tended to be filmed against the clock and to follow a schematic plot line. The director Carlos Manga has identified four basic stages in the archetypal *chanchada* plot: firstly, a young man or woman becomes embroiled in a sticky situation, secondly, a comic character tries to protect him or her, thirdly, the villain gains the upper hand, and finally, the villain is defeated.[22] The well-known comic double act of Oscarito and Grande Otelo ensured huge popular appeal. They both starred in the paradigmatic Atlântida *chanchada Carnaval no fogo* (Carnival on Fire) of 1949, which like numerous examples of the genre revolved around carnivalesque inversions, more specifically changes of identity, and followed the formulaic story line to the letter. It has been argued that the very predictability of popular film, far from being detrimental, guarantees continued box-office success. Audiences become familiar with the standard format and are thus repeatedly willing to revisit it without fear of disappointment.[23]

Music

The archetypal Atlântida *chanchadas* of the 1940s and 1950s contained some ten to twelve musical interludes, commonly in the form of stage shows in a theatre or night club, which could be logically inserted into a backstage plot. Carnival sambas and *marchas* were performed in the *chanchada* alongside an increasingly eclectic mix of imported and regional rhythms, such as the Mexican bolero and the North Eastern *baião*, reflecting changing audience tastes moulded by the radio.[24] In keeping with the tacit conventions of the *chanchada* established by the '*alô, alô*' musicals of the 1930s, in turn inspired by the early backstage musicals of Hollywood, these intervals of music and dance continued to occupy pauses in the narrative, and the lyrics of the songs performed rarely alluded to any aspect of the story line or characterisation.

Atlântida's *chanchadas* tapped in to the audience's familiarity with popular song in other ways. In the film *É com este que eu vou* (I'll Go with This One), of 1948, for example, the names of the two protagonists, Amélia and Oscar, were undoubtedly inspired by two famous sambas that entered the con- sciousness of the masses via carnival. In the film an abandoned woman (Amélia) has much in common with the eponymous heroine of Ataúlfo Alves's carnival hit 'Ai, que saudades da Amélia' (Oh, How I Miss Amélia), of 1941. Likewise, the film's errant husband/beggar (Oscar) is a text-book *otário* or loser, just like his namesake from the popular samba 'A mulher do seu Oscar' (Oscar's Good Lady), co-written by Ataúlfo Alves and Wilson Batista in 1940.

Carnaval no fogo was to represent a landmark in the development of the *chanchada*, in that for the first time the plot took precedence over the musical numbers incorporated into the film, which were not carnival songs.[25] A review in the newspaper *O Globo* of 8 February 1950 even went so far as to state, '*Carnaval no fogo*, from the Atlântida studios, is better than the majority of North American musicals that have been shown recently in Rio. For the first time, we have produced a film in which the story overshadows the musical elements.'[26] It is no coincidence that 1949 saw a perceptible shift in the role of carnival music within the cinema, since it was in that year that copyright laws were tightened significantly, and the performance of carnival songs was increasingly restricted by legislation and the payment of copyright charges. Even the most popular songs could not be performed in dance halls, on the radio, or in the cinema, without proper authorisation.

Carnivalesque somersaults

The *chanchadas* of the 1940s overturned established hierarchies of social norms or aesthetic standards in a spirit of carnivalesque irreverence, giving status to popular culture, particularly music, and ridiculing examples of elite culture, usually in the form of parody or pastiche. As the *chanchada* gradually lost its close associations with carnival music in the late 1940s and early 1950s, the inversions so intrinsic to carnival became central to this cinematic genre. Gender bending, the subversion of racial stereotypes and prejudices, and the elevation of the status of the popular at the expense of the pillars of erudite or hegemonic culture characterised much of Atlântida's production in this era. (The actor Oscarito's propensity for dressing as a woman on the screen was even commented on in the press.)

In Atlântida's prototype *chanchada Este mundo é um pandeiro* (1946) Oscarito performed a parody of the fox-trot 'Put the Blame on Mame', made famous by Rita Hayworth in the film *Gilda* of the previous year. The diminutive and very black actor Grande Otelo succeeded in disguising himself as a white man in *E o mundo se diverte* (And the World Has Fun, 1948) by answering a phone and describing himself to the woman on the other end of the line as follows: 'tall, neither fat nor thin, narrow nose, thin lips'. When asked if he is 'moreno' (dark), he replies that he is more on the fair side. As Robert Stam comments, 'the "gag" is premised on the self-rejection engendered by the "ideology of whitening".'[27] In a later scene, a camera explodes in the faces of Grande Otelo and his white sidekick, Oscarito. The latter is covered with black soot whereas the former is dusted with white powder, as both confront the extra-diegetic audience in a visual joke that overturns racial distinctions. Society's ethnic prejudices are, however, endorsed in this film, when a middle-class white character condescendingly says to the lowly stage-hand, played by Grande Otelo: 'Não sei como uma cabeça tão preta pode ter um pensamento tão claro' (I don't know how such a black head can have such clear [also literally 'pale'] thoughts). (The issue of racism in the *chanchada* is discussed more extensively in Chapter 4). Erudite culture is ridiculed in *E o mundo se diverte*, in a scene in which the voices of male concert singers are replaced by those of their female counterparts and vice versa, another example of *troca* or exchange. In the same film, this carnivalesque plot device also takes the form of the switching of x-rays belonging to two very different patients, one a dying man, the other in the prime of his life.[28]

Two paradigmatic *chanchadas* from the late 1940s

A close analysis of two musical comedies from the end of the decade, namely *E o mundo se diverte* and *O caçula do barulho* (The Topsy-Turvy Kid, 1949), will highlight conventions that would come to dominate or characterise the *chanchadas* of the 1950s. In *E o mundo se diverte* authority is challenged by disenfranchised characters, such as when the stage-hand played by Grande Otelo strikes a match for his cigar on a sign that states: 'É proibido fumar' (Smoking is prohibited). This film's backstage plot permits the easy inclusion of musical numbers set in theatres, nightclubs and radio stations. Modernity and the glamour of the capital city are celebrated in the form of shots of the stunning curve of Copacabana beach, backed by high-rise buildings, and aerial shots from Corcovado mountain. The failings of technology are humorously revealed when the results of two x-ray examinations are switched, but new modes of transport allow for greater physical and social mobility. Nevertheless, traditional sites of pleasure for the masses are valorised, such as the *teatro de revista*, carnival processions, and fairgrounds. The latter provide the setting for a memorable musical number in which the well-known singers and accordion players, Adelaide Chiozzo and Luiz Gonzaga perform against a backdrop of a big wheel, a merry-go-round, sideshows and crowds clutching balloons. Mockery of the supposed First World takes the form of a lethal cocktail concocted and named 'atomic bomb' by Oscarito's character. Alcohol is used to undermine the position of society's elite, as a prim French ballet teacher is led astray. The impact of Hollywood models on the *chanchada* is obvious in the musical numbers in *E o mundo se diverte*. These include a poor man's recreation of a Busby Berkeley-style kaleidoscope dance sequence of fourteen women dressed as belly dancers (filmed slightly from the side, from the top of a diegetic staircase, so not quite an aerial shot). Hollywood's preoccupation with 'Latino' themes in the 1940s is echoed in performances of flamenco and other Spanish-language songs by artists dressed as Mexicans in stereotypical sombreros and ponchos. Eliana Macedo's performance in this *chanchada* of the popular song 'No tabuleiro da baiana' (On the *Baiana*'s Tray) is highly reminiscent of Aurora Miranda's rendition of another Ari Barroso samba ('Os quindins de Yayá' – Missy's Coconut Cakes) in Walt Disney's partially animated feature *The Three Caballeros* (1945). Finally, *E o mundo se diverte* is characteristic of the *chanchada* tradition as a whole in that it provides a rather stylised and sanitised vision of Afro-Brazilian culture, and marginalises its creators. Displays by black dancers of the martial art/dance form *capoeira*, created by African slaves, are restricted to backdrops for a performance of a samba song by the very white-skinned Eliana Macedo. In this scene she wears the *baiana* costume made famous by Carmen Miranda in Hollywood but that would equally become her own trademark.

The *baiana* persona takes pride of place in the opening dance sequence of Atlântida's *O caçula do barulho*, wielding a basket of fruit alongside a male dancer dressed as a toreador, once again reflecting the pervasive influence of Hollywood's 'Latino' motif. (Oscarito's character also dons a fruit-laden head-dress, not unlike those worn by Carmen Miranda in Hollywood, when helping a starlet to pack her bags later in the film, perhaps poking fun at the stereotypical depiction of Brazilian identity in the USA.) Also set behind the scenes of a theatre, where Grande Otelo's character is a meek and poorly treated cleaner, this *chanchada* displays, perhaps unwittingly, the racism inherent in contemporary society. When the white Oscarito's character tries to trick his way into the theatre by pretending that one of the workers there is his aunt, he is caught out when the woman in question arrives and is quite plainly Afro-Brazilian. This visual joke is accompanied by another comic line from Oscarito that plays on racial distinctions and their social implications. When asked to woo a starlet's maid in order to gain access to the former's home, he becomes horrified when he spies a matronly, black woman through his binoculars and exclaims: 'Puxa! Nunca vi preta tão preta!' (Gosh! I've never seen such a black black woman!) Later, the villain of the piece curses Grande Otelo's character, with the presumably commonplace phrase 'Maldito negro!' (Damn black man!)

Two constants of the *chanchada* tradition of the 1950s were fight scenes and chase sequences, both of which are pre-empted in *O caçula do barulho*. The opening musical number is abruptly followed by a bar brawl and subsequent chase, viewed with appreciation by the diegetic spectators. Towards the end of the film another backstage punch-up spills over on to the stage, inviting both the diegetic and extra-diegetic audiences to look on. The threats of violence posed by urban life are further reflected when the villain uses a revolver to deal with a cleaner who overhears his criminal plot. The novelty of the urban metropolis is, nevertheless, celebrated, with drawn-out shots of car-filled avenues at night and vehicles speeding through spot-lit road tunnels to the strains of exhilarating extra-diegetic music.

The concept of identity is characteristically central to this *chanchada*. Here identities are not switched but are revealed by a material object, in this case a cigarette lighter. Similarly, in *Carnaval no fogo*, the hero, Ricardo, played by Anselmo Duarte, finds a cigarette case belonging to a gangster named Anjo (Angel). By using the silver case Ricardo is identified by other hoods as their leader, in a classic case of mistaken identity. In an era of dramatic shifts in the organisation of society, it is no coincidence that these popular films gave importance to a given character's ability to change or adapt his/her identity to best deal with the changing environment. This recurrent theme is symptomatic of the identity crisis that was experienced by many of those in the audience, particularly rural-urban migrants and the mixed-race descendants of African slaves.

As in countless examples of the *chanchada* tradition, Oscarito plays an emasculated coward, who is afraid of life and more importantly women, in *O caçula do barulho*. This parody of masculinity can be seen when he hides in a barrel during a bar brawl, and later when he cowers on top of a wardrobe to evade the amorous advances of a formidable Afro-Brazilian maid. The loss of confidence brought on by displacement and alienation is reflected in the behaviour of the male anti-heroes of the *chanchadas* of the late 1940s. As discussed in Chapter 4, such characters would continue to provide a source of humour and popular identification for the marginalised men in the audience throughout the 1950s.

Atlântida's *E o mundo se diverte* and *O caçula do barulho* together provided the prototype for the studio's productions throughout the 1950s. These two films maintained the key elements of the first-phase *chanchadas* of the 1930s and early 1940s, namely a backstage plot, visible legacies from the *teatro de revista* and carnival traditions, imitation of Hollywood musicals, and depictions of Afro-Brazilian culture that went hand in hand with the marginalisation of its creators. But these two films also introduced a range of additional themes and devices that would come to define the *chanchada* over the following decade: an anti-establishment discourse, parodic engagement with Hollywood paradigms, a celebration of modernity tempered with comic references to the fallibility of technology, fight sequences (a more sophisticated form of circus slapstick), shifting identities, and effeminised masculinity.

The Sonofilmes and Cinédia studios in the 1940s

Although Atlântida dominated film production in Brazil throughout the 1940s, Sonofilmes and Cinédia continued to offer some competition, concentrating production on the *chanchada* genre. Hot on the heels of the box-office smash *Banana da terra* (Banana of the Land, 1939), Sonofilmes released *Laranja da China* (Orange from China, 1940), and this cinematic trilogy (linked only by their 'fruity' titles) was completed in 1944 with the premiere of *Abacaxi azul* (Blue Pineapple).[29] As their titles suggest, these films critically reworked the 'tutti frutti' image of Brazil/Latin America created by Hollywood in the Roosevelt era, that was personified by Carmen Miranda herself, and her fruit-piled turbans, in a host of US movies. This trilogy was undoubtedly influenced by the composite representations of 'Latino' identity that Hollywood disseminated under the auspices of the 'Good Neighbour Policy'. It tellingly re-used the clip of Miranda, dressed as a *baiana*, performing 'O que é que a *baiana* tem?' from *Banana da terra*, now that she had departed to pursue her career in the USA. However, such hackneyed imagery was not simply rehashed for an ingenuous domestic market, but rather was appropriated by Brazilian filmmakers, and given an ironic slant. In *Laranja da China*, for example, one of the many popular songs performed was the ultrapatriotic samba by Ari Barroso, 'Aquarela do Brasil' (Watercolour of Brazil).[30] Yet, this popular song, so representative of national pride, was sung in Spanish in the film by the Mexican performer, Pedro Vargas, in a rendition that was reportedly *cucarachíssima* or exaggeratedly 'Latino'.[31] By subverting the symbolic force of this unofficial national anthem, this Brazilian musical poked fun at the nation-building ideology of the Vargas regime. It likewise made a tongue-in-cheek allusion to the blurring of geographic borders and, more specifically, the linguistic confusions that resulted when Hollywood first started to portray Spanish America and Brazil.[32]

Laranja da China featured a selection of characters that would resurface time and again in the Atlântida *chanchadas* of the 1950s. These included a mad scientist, Professor Salchich (a name that sounds suspiciously like the word for 'sausage' in Portuguese and thus comically undermines this authority figure), and his crazy servant, Boneco de Piche, played by Grande Otelo. This name, literally 'Tar Doll', was an obvious reference to the black actor's skin colour, but it also played on the title of a popular song, 'Boneca de Piche' (Female Tar Doll), written by Ari Barroso and performed by Carmen Miranda at the official 'Popular Music Day' celebrations in Rio in 1939. Such visual gags premised on Brazil's ethnic diversity, and more often than not using Afro-Brazilians as the butt of the joke, would prove to be a mainstay of the *chanchada* tradition. The latter's veneration of popular culture, particularly music, at the expense of erudite genres, is similarly presaged in *Laranja da China*, when Professor Sausage inoculates some rabbits with the 'samba microbe'.

Abacaxi azul was a co-production from Sonofilmes and Cinédia and was directed by Wallace Downey. Filmed between 11 November and 23 December 1943, this satirical musical comedy premiered in Rio on 14 February 1944. Timed to coincide with carnival it included a typical selection of popular songs and artists. A review by the acclaimed filmmaker Humberto Mauro for *Cena Muda* magazine praised various aspects of the film:

The film's photography is reasonable, clean, and the sound is great. Downey's recording equipment is one of the best examples, if not the best, seen in Brazil. The musical numbers are all very well recorded, well performed and entertaining, on the whole. The film also contains very humorous sections . . . *Abacaxi azul* is a patchwork quilt, but . . . fortunately, within it there are small pieces of cloth that are of excellent quality. I have watched countless North American films that are all made up of a single piece of cloth, but . . . unfortunately, that cloth is of very poor quality.[33]

The term *abacaxi*, literally a pineapple, was used by film critics in this era and beyond to refer disparagingly to poor-quality films, as an alternative to the label of *chanchada*, the pejorative connotations of which gradually subsided. This final instalment of the 'tutti frutti' trilogy thus not only poked fun at the clichéd view of Brazil, as endorsed in particular by Hollywood during the 'Good Neighbour Policy' era, but also made fun of itself and the aesthetic and technical limitations of the Brazilian film industry. As its title reveals, this film had modest aspirations, as is confirmed by the critic Sérgio Augusto: 'The most notable merit of *Abacaxi azul*, aside from humorously acknowledging its own "inferiority", was that it stimulated the wit of the normally dull critic of the *O Globo* newspaper, who began his diatribe with the following pithy comment: "Why it's called blue, nobody knows. But there's no doubt about the rest of its title".'[34]

The plot of the 1943 Cinédia production *Samba em Berlim* (Samba in Berlin), directed by Luiz de Barros, follows some *caipiras* or hicks, who go to the capital city in search of a young woman who has sent them a photograph. The character of the hillbilly, bewildered by his encounter with the big city, was to reappear throughout the *chanchada* tradition, as discussed at length in Chapter 4, and in the films of Mazzaropi, as examined in Chapter 6, but its origins can be traced back to the *teatro de revista* and silent film.[35] *Samba em Berlim* starred a host of performers who would go on to prominence in the *chanchadas* of the 1950s, such as Grande Otelo, Catalano and Dercy Gonçalves, in addition to the music hall comedian Mesquitinha and the well-known crooner Francisco Alves. This film also featured a parodic reference to another star of the screen, Carmen Miranda, in Alice Vianna's mimicry of Miranda's hit 'Baianinha' (Little Girl from Bahia). (Such intertextual allusions would characterise the *chanchadas* of the 1950s, as discussed in Chapter 4.) *Samba em Berlim* made fun of Hitler, by now Brazil's enemy, but the film suffered at the hands of the censors as a result of a stage set that featured a cartoon likeness of Stalin in a boat, and this scene was cut.[36] Produced to a very tight schedule (filming began on 23 January 1943 and finished on 16 February of the same year), this musical comedy premiered on 22 February in Rio. As Adhemar Gonzaga, its producer, said: 'The film was very successful and helped Cinédia out, since it had been through a difficult period due to the war. Exhibitors wanted lots of copies but this demand could not be met because there was not enough raw material available, so-called positive, to make the copies.'[37] The critics were not as complimentary, with one commenting: '*Samba em Berlim* is nothing more than a Cinédia musical that allows the public to get to know or to reacquaint themselves with performers from the world of radio and casino shows. Performers who have been put into a film without intelligence or direction, merely to be there, giving the impression of a badly put together show full of artists who are obliged to feature in it, no matter what.'[38] The musical numbers in this film included the samba 'Praça Onze' (11th Square), a reference to Rio's original samba stronghold, by Herivelto Martins and Grande Otelo. As its director, Luiz de Barros says in his memoirs: 'Forgive me for saying so but this was an entertaining *chanchada*, that was very successful, like all *chanchadas*, in spite of the ill will of the critics.'[39]

The comedies of Luiz de Barros

Hitler and the international conflict provided the point of departure for another Cinédia *chanchada*, *Berlim na Batucada* (Berlin to the Samba Beat), which was directed by Luiz de Barros and premiered on 7 February 1944, proving much more successful at the box-office than *Abacaxi azul*. This musical featured a *malandro* by the name of Zé Carioca, played by Procópio Ferreira, and a rotund American tourist who had come to Rio in search of carnival, played by Delorges Caminha. Clearly this film engaged satirically with the 'Good Neighbour Policy' initiatives of Hollywood and the Co-ordinator of Inter-American Affairs (CIAA) more specifically Walt Disney's creation, Zé Carioca, a *malandro* parrot who embodied Brazil and appeared in *Saludos Amigos* (1943) and later in *The Three Caballeros* (1945), and the USA's 'cultural ambassador' to Latin America, Orson Welles.[40] The musical sequences of this film, performed by the likes of Francisco Alves in the role of a typical shantytown *malandro*, were interspersed with comic sketches such as an imaginary dialogue with Hitler. For the first time in a Brazilian film, an actor, in this case Silvino Neto, was shown on screen in three different roles simultaneously, but most critics were more impressed by the quality of the sambas recorded on location and the musical finale.

In his biography, *Minhas memórias de cineasta*, Luiz de Barros attests to the purely materialistic motives behind his decision to make *chanchadas*: 'Those that I made at carnival time, when those films generated the most money, were produced out of absolute commercial necessity, given that they were a great source of income.'[41] He says of *Berlim na batucada*: 'it fulfilled its mission very well in provoking hearty laughter and making money.'[42] He became aware of the public's preference for comic films after the great success of his film *Augusto Anibal quer casar!* (Augusto Anibal Wants a Wife!, 1923), a silent precursor of the *chanchada*, which starred a transvestite by the name of Darwin. Basking in the limelight generated by *Berlim na batucada*, Barros directed *Corações sem piloto* (Hearts without a Driver, 1944) for Cinédia. This comedy featured the radio singers Marlene and Marion, and the Afro-Brazilian actor Chocolate. The latter and Marlene also starred alongside the country-music duo Jararaca and Ratinho in Cinédia's *chanchada* *Pif-Paf* (Card Game) of 1945, directed by Adhemar Gonzaga and Luiz de Barros. Barros directed the literary adaptation, *O cortiço* (The Tenement, 1946) for Cinédia, which starred the Afro-Brazilian actor Colé in the role of a *malandro* who stabs a man, but the director was soon obliged to return to the money-making formula of the *chanchada*. He thus went on to direct *Caídos do céu* (Fallen from the Sky, 1946) for Cinédia, starring Linda Batista, Dercy Gonçalves and her side-kick Walter D'Avila, the Afro-Brazilian *sambista* Ataúlfo Alves, Violeta Ferraz and Chocolate, and the songwriter Herivelto Martins, who composed songs for the soundtrack. As Barros says, 'It was a very funny *chanchada* and served its purpose perfectly in cinema theatres.'[43]

In 1947 Carmen Santos called on the services of Luiz de Barros to direct *O malandro e a granfina* (The Spiv and the Lady) for her Brasil Vita Filme studio. This film was to be the screen debut of the comic actor Zé Trindade, who played a prisoner who cracked jokes from behind bars. Trindade would later be a key player in the comic line-up of the *chanchadas* of the 1950s. Barros then went on to direct the musical *Fogo na canjica* (Fire in the Soup), the plot of which was merely the pretext for the inclusion of musical numbers performed by big names, as Barros himself admits.[44] For the carnival of 1948 Barros was called upon to shoot a *chanchada* in just ten days. The end result was *Esta é fina!* (She's a Good One!), which featured the music hall star Mesquitinha, and a host of popular musicians, such as Aracy de Almeida, Marlene, the Trio de Ouro and the country-music duo Joel and Gaúcho.[45] Scenes were filmed in the grill-room and on the terrace at the swanky Copacabana Palace, the hotel that would become the iconic setting for countless encounters between rich and poor and carnivalesque inversions in the Atlântida *chanchadas*, from the 1949 hit *Carnaval no fogo* onwards. Barros is at pains to distinguish between comedies and *chanchadas* in his repertoire. He stresses that *Está com tudo* (You've Got It All) falls into the former category. The distinction for Barros seems to be that *chanchadas* took comedy to extremes. In 1949 he directed a film scripted and produced by his son Victor entitled *Eu quero é movimento* (What I Want Is Action). Barros senior describes it as: 'a very funny film that could be classed as a *chanchada* because of its exaggerated style'.[46] A slapstick scene in which two characters smeared each other's faces with butter, eggs and flour was adored by the public but reviled by the critics. As Barros writes in his memoirs: 'when it was shown in cinemas it made the audience really laugh, which proves that the general public still loves this kind of scene, although it was panned by my journalist chums'.[47] *Eu quero é movimento* relied on visual humour, such as the smashing of bottles (actually made of wax) over people's heads. The fight scene, often slapstick, would become a staple of the *chanchada* tradition in the 1950s.

The *chanchada*'s fascination with the possibilities for carnivalesque inversions of norms, and its fixation with the hick who arrives in the big city, are both pre-empted in Luiz de Barros's *Prá lá de boa* (Top Notch, 1949). The story centres on a middle-aged woman from the sticks who comes to Rio to visit her married daughter. On her second day in the capital city she leaves her daughter's house and fails to return, causing great concern. The family contacts the police, fearing the worst, in a reflection of the real-life anxieties experienced by displaced migrants, with which many in the audience could no doubt identify. Suddenly, the door bursts open and in strides the girl's mother, transformed by her contact with modernity and the high-life (more specifically a beauty salon and a skilful dressmaker), with a clutch of male admirers in her wake.

Popular melodrama: *O ébrio*

Surprisingly one of the biggest home-grown box-office successes in Brazil during the 1940s did not adhere to the conventions of the *chanchada*. Indeed *O ébrio* (The Drunkard, 1946) had more in common with the socially committed films that Atlântida experimented with at the beginning of the decade, only to reject in favour of the musical comedy. Co-produced by Adhemar Gonzaga at Cinédia and the film's director, the former actress, songwriter and singer Gilda de Abreu, *O ébrio* was a hugely popular melodrama of which five hundred copies were made, breaking all records in Brazil.[48] According to José Ramos Tinhorão this film 'discovered a formula for appealing to the excessive romanticism of the popular classes'.[49] It was shown throughout the nation and has continued to appeal to wide audiences ever since. João Luiz Vieira calls it 'Cinédia's most well-known film and one of the greatest successes of Brazilian cinema' and the quintessential Brazilian moralistic melodrama.[50] *O ébrio* was well received by the critics, but as Viera writes, 'the film's consecration stems from the public, who watched this melodrama time and again in the state capitals and throughout the countryside until very recently'.[51]

Gilda de Abreu, and her husband Vicente Celestino, who starred as the film's protagonist Dr Gilberto Silva, had their own production company that staged light operas in Rio theatres. Abreu also performed as both a singer and actress on the radio and in films such as *Bonequinha de seda* (Little Silk Doll, 1936), a hit as far afield as Buenos Aires, in addition to writing and adapting novels, plays and musical numbers. *O ébrio* was an adaptation of a successful play penned by Celestino, which in turn had been based on one of his musical compositions, recorded on 7 August 1936 by RCA and an immediate and long-standing hit. The play proved to be equally successful when performed at Rio's Carlos Gomes theatre, and this prompted Adhemar Gonzaga to invite Gilda de Abreu to adapt, script and direct a screen version of it.

As its title suggests, *O ébrio* deals with the topic of alcoholism, as well as that of adultery, and is clearly a morality tale. It recounts the story of a poor man, Gilberto Silva, the son of a bankrupt land owner, who is abandoned by his family but taken in by the Catholic Church. Keen to repay the Church for its charity, Gilberto hears a talent show on the radio and decides to enter. His talent is discovered and he becomes rich enough to train as a doctor, a profession that he exercises with dedication. He marries a flirtatious nurse named Marieta, who falls for the flattery and cunning ways of her husband's cousin, José. Deceived into believing that her husband is having an affair, Marieta runs off with the womanising José. Heartbroken, Gilberto goes in search of her, to no avail. When he hears a drunken beggar say 'eu bebo só para esquecer' (I drink just to forget) and then witnesses him being run over by a passing car, Gilberto decides to adopt the down-and-out's identity so that he too can drink himself into oblivion. In the closing scenes of the film, Gilberto, drunk in a down-market bar, is asked by a curious customer to tell his life story, at which point he grabs a guitar and breaks into the title song, on which the film was based. Those present and even passers-by are mesmerised and visibly moved. After singing about 'aquela ingrata que eu amava e que me abandonou' (that ungrateful woman whom I loved and who abandoned me), his errant wife enters the bar, herself now living on the streets. He proceeds to forgive her for her actions but there is no happy ending.

It is interesting to note the points of convergence between this didactic melodrama and the fun-loving, irreverent *chanchada*. In both cases the radio provides the pretext for the insertion of musical numbers and we see the impact of the medium on the tastes and pastimes of the masses. In *O ébrio* there are several shots of the enthusiastic audiences applauding Gilberto's performances in the talent shows that are broadcast over the airwaves, and of switchboard girls at the radio station being inundated with calls in response. More significantly, the motif of *troca* or exchange, a recurrent one in the *chanchada* tradition and intrinsic to the carnivalesque inversions of many films produced at Atlântida in the late 1940s and 1950s, appears in *O ébrio*. Most obviously, Gilberto takes on the identity of the tramp, and the wily José steals a medal from honest, God-fearing Gilberto's pocket in order to put into operation his plan to deceive Marieta. Finally, as the film draws to a close a punch-up breaks out in the seedy bar, ironically called 'Café da Paz'

(Peace Café), involving mulatto *malandros*. Such fight scenes were common in the *chanchada* and their appeal to popular audiences stemmed from the slapstick traditions of circus. Perhaps most importantly, the unprecedented success of *O ébrio* across Brazil pointed to a burgeoning demand for popular film outside the big cities. As José Ramos Tinhorão writes:

> Vicente Celestino's success among the general public, not only in the cities but also in the countryside, served to indicate that new socio-economic conditions were paving the way for new means of communication in rural areas, and for cinema aimed at the popular classes. In fact the era of modern, production-line films, for rapid consumption by an undemanding audience, was about to begin. The era of the *chanchada* had arrived.[52]

The moral of the story of *O ébrio* is self-evident, as the audience confronts the human tragedies provoked by both the sin of adultery and the vice of alcoholism. After the success of the film Gilda de Abreu went on to script and direct *Pinguinho de gente* (Tiny Tot, 1949), but this romantic melodrama did not elicit the same popular response. In 1951 Abreu set up her own production company, Pro-Arte, in order to make *Coração materno* (Maternal Heart) in the same year. In both these later films the female protagonists, Matilde and Ruth respectively, are condemned to a life of celibacy for their involvement in love triangles.[53] As Munerato and Darcy de Oliveira write, 'no man suffers additional punishment for having lost in amorous dispute. And it is the punishment of "evil actions" committed by women that regulates and "normalizes" the happiness of the couples. The destruction of triangles and the sanctioning of the couple is the rule in all the films . . . In the films of Gilda de Abreu, the triangle has to be undone in order for the misunderstandings to be cleared up.'[54] In melodrama love serves to reconcile class differences, as can be seen in Gilda de Abreu's trilogy, whereas in comedy film fortunes are turned around via carnivalesque role reversals based on chance. Poor but pretty girls, like Marieta in *O ébrio* and Maria Lúcia in *Pinguinho de gente*, marry rich men, and the poor orphan Carlos in *Coração materno* wins over the heart of the aristocratic Violeta.

Concluding remarks

The popular appeal of films as diverse as the sentimental *O ébrio* and the irreverent comedy *Laranja da China* can be explained by their engagement with easily identifiable popular songs performed by artists who were equally well known from their established careers in the radio and music hall.[55] *O ébrio*'s landslide success at the box-office was unexpected, given that Brazil, unlike, for example, Mexico, did not have an established tradition of popular melodrama. A consequence of its seductive blend of a morality tale and the glamorous world of radio and popular music (echoing the '*alô, alô*' musicals of the 1930s), *O ébrio*'s widespread appeal pointed to the burgeoning demand for films which spoke to popular audiences. The film's soundtrack undoubtedly contributed to its success, given that melodrama relies heavily on musical accompaniment to highlight emotion within a dramatic narrative. The film contained many of the 'primary attributes' of melodrama identified by Buckland, namely the perspective of the victim, moral conflicts, twists and reversals, chance events and encounters, secrets and dramatic knots which complicate the plot.[56] Coincidentally, all of these elements, albeit in a comic context, also came to characterise the archetypal *chanchada*.

With the release of the *chanchada Carnaval no fogo* in 1949, Atlântida proved that it could successfully combine the musical comedy formula with Hollywood-inspired sophistication, namely suspense, underworld intrigue and romance. From then on the twists and turns of a typical *chanchada* plot would rely on accidental changes of fortune, usually involving one of society's marginalised outsiders, who would subsequently be propelled into an alien environment and faced with an array of moral dilemmas. *Carnaval no fogo* established the careers of many future screen stars, such as Eliana Macedo and Anselmo Duarte, who, as the archetypal girl-next-door and heartthrob respectively, would help to mix romance with comic capers, all to the strains of a contemporary soundtrack, throughout the 1950s. The *chanchadas* from the Atlântida studio were thus poised to dominate the market for domestic films for the next decade.

Notes

1 *Cinema*, 45 (May 1941), p. 2.
2 Randal Johnson, *The Film Industry in Brazil: Culture and the State* (Pittsburgh: University of Pittsburgh Press, 1987), p. 57.
3 Anita Simis, 'Movies and moviemakers under Vargas', *Latin American Perspectives*, 29:1 (January 2002), p. 111.
4 Daryle Williams, *Culture Wars in Brazil: The First Vargas Regime, 1930–1945* (Durham and London: Duke University Press, 2001), pp. 84–5.
5 *Ibid.*, p. 84.
6 Mário Audrá Jr, *Cinematográfica Maristela: memórias de um produtor* (São Paulo: Silver Hawk, 1997), p. 151.
7 Quoted by Heloísa Paulo, *Estado Novo e propaganda em Portugal e no Brasil: o SPN/SNI e o DIP* (Coimbra: Minerva, 1994), p. 146 (our translation).
8 *Ibid.*, p. 155.
9 Sérgio Augusto, 'Watson Macedo, o rei da chanchada detestava fazer rir', *Filme Cultura*, 41–2 (May 1983), p. 32.
10 Nicolau Sevcenko, 'Peregrinations, visions and the city: from Canudos to Brasília, the backlands become the city and the city becomes the backlands', in Vivian

Schelling (ed.), *Through the Kaleidoscope: The Experience of Modernity in Latin America* (London and New York: Verso, 2000), p. 99.

11 Ruben George Oliven, 'Brazil: the modern in the Tropics', in Schelling (ed.), *Through the Kaleidoscope*, p. 63.

12 Sérgio Augusto, *Este mundo é um pandeiro: a chanchada de Getúlio a JK* (São Paulo: Companhia das Letras, 1993), p. 104 (our translation).

13 Jorge A. Schnitman, *Film Industries in Latin America: Dependency and Development* (Norwood: Ablex, 1984), p. 56.

14 Statistics cited in Afrânio M. Catani and José I. de Melo Souza, *A chanchada no cinema brasileiro* (São Paulo: Brasiliense, 1983), p. 42.

15 Augusto, *Este mundo é um pandeiro*, p. 14. Other examples of Atlântida's competitors in this era included the producers Herbert Richers, Watson Macedo, Flama Produtora (*Tudo azul* (All Blue, 1951)), and Luiz de Barros. In addition to many *chanchadas*, Barros directed the doomed biopic, *O rei do samba* (The King of Samba, 1952), based on the life of the samba composer and pianist Sinhô. In the same vein, São Paulo's up-market Vera Cruz studio produced the musical melodrama *Tico-Tico no fubá* (Tico-Tico Bird in the Corn Meal, 1952), directed by Adolfo Celi, which told the life story of the composer Zequinha de Abreu.

16 João Luiz Vieira, 'Hegemony and Resistance: Parody and Carnival in Brazilian Cinema', PhD dissertation, New York University, 1984, p. 67.

17 Angela Belmiro Fontes, 'A chanchada por um drama', *Correio da manhã*, 18 July 1971.

18 'Chanchada carioca e populismo', *Cine-Olho*, 1 (November 1976) (our translation).

19 Robert Stam and João Luiz Vieira, 'Parody and Marginality: The Case of Brazilian Cinema', *Framework*, 28 (1985), p. 26.

20 Jeffrey M. Pilcher, *Cantinflas and the Chaos of Mexican Modernity* (Wilmington: SR Books, 2001), p. xv.

21 Our translation.

22 Augusto, *Este mundo é um pandeiro*, p. 15.

23 For further discussion of this idea see Andy Medhurst, 'Carry On Camp', *Sight and Sound*, August 1992.

24 The soundtracks of *chanchadas* were orchestrated by a group of talented musicians of Italian descent, such as Enrico Simonetti, Léo Peracchi, and especially Lirio Panicalli, Alexandre Gnatalli and Radamés Gnatalli. For more information on the rise of the *baião* style see Chapter 4.

25 *Carnaval no fogo* harked back to the *alô, alô* musicals of the 1930s, in that it featured several famous radio singers, whose careers had been established at the Rádio Nacional station.

26 Augusto, *Este mundo é um pandeiro*, p. 52 (our translation).

27 Robert Stam, *Tropical Multiculturalism: A Comparative History of Race in Brazilian Cinema and Culture* (Durham and London: Duke University Press, 1997), p. 95.

28 Such inversions have been interpreted as a reflection of the pervasive influence of the carnival tradition in Brazil, but can also be seen as a legacy of Hollywood. The veneration of the popular, at the expense of the classical or erudite, was also an established feature of the Hollywood musical, which grew out of the 'opera versus

swing' plots of a series of musicals produced by Joe Pasternak at MGM in the 1940s. See Jane Feuer, *The Hollywood Musical* (Basingstoke and London: The Macmillan Press/BFI Cinema Series, 1993), pp. 55–6.

29 *Laranja da China* (literally a type of orange found in Brazil) was also the title of a theatre revue of 1929 that included a sketch that caricatured Getúlio Vargas, the former Chancellor of the Exchequer and then state governor of Rio Grande do Sul. It also featured the Argentine comic actor, Palitos dressed in drag as Napoleon's Josephine.

30 This samba begins: 'Brasil/Meu Brasil brasileiro/Meu mulato inzoneiro/Vou cantarte nos meus versos' (Brazil/ My Brazilian Brazil/ My devious mulatto/ I'm going to sing about you in my songs).

31 Augusto, *Este mundo é um pandeiro*, p. 96.

32 See Sérgio Augusto, 'Hollywood Looks at Brazil: From Carmen Miranda to *Moonraker*', in Randal Johnson and Robert Stam (eds), *Brazilian Cinema* (New York: Columbia University Press, 1995).

33 *Cena Muda*, 15 February 1944 (our translation).

34 Quoted in Augusto, *Este mundo é um pandeiro*, p. 99 (our translation).

35 For example, the silent film *Nhô Anastácio chegou de viagem* (Mr. Anastácio Arrived From a Trip, 1908) portrayed a yokel, played by the singer and acrobat José Gonçalves Leonardo, who visited Rio and fell in love with a singer, at least until his wife arrived in the big city in search of him. Such story lines were not unique to Brazilian film, as pointed out in the *Enciclopédia do cinema brasileiro*, which cites the 1903 US film *Rube and Mandy at Coney Island* as an example. Fernão Ramos and Luiz Felipe Miranda (eds), *Enciclopédia do cinema brasileiro* (São Paulo: SENAC, 2000), p. 117.

36 In 1941 there were disturbances in the city of Rio as German and Italian-owned premises came under attack. The bohemian hang-out, Bar Adolfo, on the Rua da Carioca, was forced to change its name to Bar Luiz. Hitler and Mussolini were caricatured in the *teatro de revista*, in shows such as *Fora do eixo* (Outside the Axis, 1942).

37 Quoted in Alice Gonzaga, *50 anos de Cinédia* (Rio de Janeiro: Editora Record, 1987), p. 102 (our translation).

38 *A Noite*, 24 February 1943 (our translation).

39 Luiz de Barros, *Minhas memórias de cineasta* (Rio de Janeiro: Artenova, 1978), p. 143 (our translation).

40 Orson Welles visited Brazil in 1942 to begin work on *It's All True*, the ill-fated film project in which Luiz de Barros was also involved. The Vargas regime clearly saw this as an opportunity to attract North American tourists to Brazil with dollars to spend. For the 'Carnival' section of the film Welles's team were strongly discouraged from filming in Rio's shantytowns by the Brazilian secret police, and elements of the conservative press in Rio, as well as RKO executives, objected to Welles's foregrounding of black and mixed-race Brazil in his recreation of carnival. Barros provided the decorations for a carnival ball filmed by Welles, and then went on to poke fun at him in *Berlim na batucada*.

41 Barros, *Minhas memórias de cineasta*, p. 53 (our translation).

42 *Ibid.*, p. 144 (our translation).

43 *Ibid.*, p. 152 (our translation).

44 *Ibid.*, p. 156.

45 According to Barros, this film, shot in just ten days, made eight times more money than his literary adaptation *O cortiço. Ibid.*, p. 244.

46 *Ibid.*, p. 159 (our translation).

47 *Ibid.*, p. 160 (our translation).

48 Johnson and Stam (eds), *Brazilian Cinema*, p. 27.

49 José Ramos Tinhorão, *Música popular: teatro e cinema* (Petrópolis: Vozes, 1972), p. 259 (our translation).

50 João Luiz Vieira, 'A chanchada e o cinema carioca (1930–1955)', in *História do cinema brasileiro*, Fernão Ramos (ed.) (São Paulo: Art Editora, 1987), p. 157 (our translation).

51 *Ibid.*, p. 158 (our translation). In a reflection of the enduring appeal of *O ébrio* throughout Brazil, it is the only film that is shown by the travelling projectionist in the backlands of Brazil's North East in Caros Diegues's *Bye Bye Brazil* (1979), set in the late 1970s, and discussed in more detail in Chapter 7.

52 Tinhorão, *Música popular: teatro e cinema*, pp. 259–60 (our translation).

53 See Elice Munerato and Maria Helena Darcy de Oliveira, 'When women film' in Johnson and Stam (eds), *Brazilian Cinema*.

54 *Ibid.*, p. 346.

55 The unrivalled success of the 1910 silent movie *Paz e amor* (Peace and Love), a light-hearted critique of national politics and social mores, among the elite of Rio de Janeiro, was also due in large part to its title song, promoted incessantly by the Edison music company. This film pre-empted the *chanchada*, with its use of music, socio-political critique, puns, parody and carnivalesque inversions, the latter exemplified by a caricature of then president Nilo Peçanha dressed as a fictitious king named Olin I, an anagram that leaves no doubt as to the intended allusion.

56 Warren Buckland, *Film Studies* (London: Hodder and Stoughton, 1998), p. 81.

4

The 1950s

Introduction

The 1950s were ushered in with the official opening of the Maracanã football stadium in Rio, where the Brazilian squad was to lose the final of the World Cup to Uruguay in 1950. In spite of this body blow to national pride, the 1950s are remembered as a period of optimism based on economic expansion. Getúlio Vargas, who returned to the presidency by democratic vote in 1950, continued to pin the nation's hopes on industrialisation, creating the state oil company, Petrobrás and the National Bank for Economic Development (*Banco Nacional de Desenvolvimento Econômico*). Expectations were high but so was the inflation rate, making it increasingly difficult for Vargas to deliver on his campaign promises. One of the more memorable consequences of his social legislation was the creation of a plethora of bureaucratic jobs and a civil service underpinned by nepotism and widespread corruption.

Following Vargas's suicide while in office in August 1954, the election of President Juscelino Kubitschek (1956–61) restored Brazil's faith in its future. JK or Jusça, as he was affectionately known, promised 'fifty years' progress in five', based on the large-scale expansion of industrial output and the development of heavy industry. For a time it also seemed that Brazil's new-found wealth would be more evenly distributed among the population, as in 1956 the minimum wage was raised by 60 per cent. JK's policy of developmental nationalism gave foreign firms special incentives to invest in Brazil, and for the decade as a whole, Brazil's per capita real growth was approximately three times that of the rest of Latin America.[1] Brasília, the futuristic, purpose-built capital city, the creation of which had been written into the constitution of 1891, but which became JK's personal crusade, is a lasting reminder of the vitality and self-belief of the 1950s. The inauguration of the symbolic new capital in 1960 represented the high point of Kubitschek's modernising policy.

Migration from rural to urban areas peaked in the 1950s, particularly from Brazil's arid North East, which experienced severe droughts in 1951, 1953 and 1958. The countryside and its inhabitants had been neglected during the Vargas years, with the consequence that Brazil's industrial centres were now confronted with an influx of impoverished migrants, attracted by the economic boom, which masked widespread under-employment in the service sector. These poorly educated, displaced newcomers, who hoped to gain access to both the goods and the messages produced by modernity, were drawn to the cinema theatres of the cities, where they had much in common with the other members of the audience as well as the characters on screen.

In 1952 Vargas introduced the so-called 'eight for one' law, which made it compulsory for all cinema theatres in Brazil to show at least one Brazilian film for every eight foreign ones. In the 1950s it was common practice to buy a ticket for the cinema without even knowing which film was showing, particularly in São Paulo, where the cinema and football were the principal forms of mass entertainment.[2] As Mário Audrá Jr writes: 'With the price of a cinema ticket fixed at ten *cruzeiros* for years on end, in 1954 this figure corresponded to about US$0.25 and film importers were already threatening to cease all imports, since the box-office income obtained barely covered the cost of the copies and advertising.'[3] In this favourable climate, the appeal of the home-grown *chanchada* endured throughout the 1950s. Carlos Manga's *Colégio de brotos* (College of Chicks, 1956), for example, attracted a quarter of a million viewers in the first week it was shown, a record that was not broken until 1975.[4] In the film magazine *Cinelândia* (April 1957), Zenaide Andréa wrote, 'Box-office records have been smashed by some recent Brazilian films. *Metido a bacana* (A Cut above the Rest) took, in just two weeks, more than nine million *cruzeiros*. *Garotas e samba* (Girls and Samba) took seven million, also as soon as it was released.'[5] The *chanchada* played on the audience's feelings of alienation in the big city and encouraged them to identify with the characters and predicaments presented on screen. These Brazilian films were naturally favoured by the semi-literate or illiterate masses over subtitled imports. (It is no coincidence that in *Minervina vem aí* (Here Comes Minervina, 1959) the likeable but unsophisticated eponymous heroine, a one-time domestic servant, has to ask her new, socially superior husband whether her name is spelled with the letter 'm', when signing the marriage register.)[6] For the studios, the economic imperative continued to influence production decisions and schedules throughout the 1950s. Atlântida, for example, contracted the director Luiz de Barros, with a view to teaching its own directors, such as Carlos Manga, how to shoot on a tighter schedule. Barros thus went on to direct *Malandros em quarta dimensão* (Malandros in the Fourth Dimension, 1954), for Atlântida in just eighteen days.

Anti-establishment discourses in popular film

Malandragem and *jeitinho*: reactions to capitalism and consumerism
The ethos of *malandragem* permeated the *chanchada* tradition throughout
the 1950s, offering a personalised and informal way of dealing with the problems that modernity presented to the marginalised in daily life. This survival
strategy is embodied in the leading lady of *De vento em popa* (Wind in the
Sails, 1957), Mara, an archetypal *virador* or 'table-turner', who stows away
on an ocean liner in order to break into show business. Oscarito also plays a
stowaway on a cruise ship, keen to get home to Rio in time for carnival, in
Aviso aos navegantes (Calling All Sailors, 1950). In this film Cléia, played by
Eliana Macedo, explicitly says she will 'dar um jeito' (pull a fast one) in order
for him to gain access to a party on board. Characters from the lower rungs
of the social ladder are ultimately rewarded by a stroke of good fortune, such
as the uneducated popcorn seller in *Metido a bacana* (1957), whose chance
physical similarity to a foreign prince turns his life around and ultimately
earns him five hundred thousand *cruzeiros* with which to buy his own grocer's
shop. The *chanchada* offered a temporary answer to the inadequacies of
real-life Brazilian society via the survival strategy of *malandragem*, in keeping
with Richard Dyer's definition of entertainment as the offer of 'something
better' to escape into.[7]

The policy of developmentalism espoused by Kubitschek is rejected in
these films by humble characters that would undoubtedly benefit little from
it. Similarly, the ultimate emblem of the era, the new capital city, Brasília, is
made fun of in the *chanchada*. In *O camelô da Rua Larga* (The Street Vendor
of Larga Street, 1958), the long-suffering girlfriend of the illegal street vendor
chides him with the line 'Arruma uma tanga e vai para Brasília!' (Get your-
self a loincloth and go to Brasília), a place supposedly overrun by Indians
(hence the loincloth reference) and thus a highly unsuitable location for the
future federal capital.[8] The *chanchada* tradition articulated an implicit disdain
for gainful employment, inferring that ordinary people were exploited by the
government's work ethic for little reward. Audiences were thus reminded of
their economic predicament but reassured that they were not alone. In *O
camelô da Rua Larga*, for example, a shopkeeper makes it clear to a customer
that she cannot have any credit, and in the opening scene of this *chanchada*
the itinerant salesman lectures his punters on the country's high rate of
inflation. Poverty exists in both the countryside and the city; in *O homem
do sputnik* (Sputnik Man, 1959) hillbillies comment that they own nothing
worth stealing, and in *Treze cadeiras* (Thirteen Chairs, 1957) two shopkeepers
remark that they have only one hen for a thief to pinch. The audience is
constantly reminded that material wealth is no match for the solidarity of the
poor. In *Rico ri à toa* (The Rich Can Afford to Laugh, 1957) the former taxi

driver turned millionaire, Zé (an everyman figure, as his name, Joe, suggests) cannot spend his inherited fortune fast enough and enthusiastically declares to a group of his old friends, 'Como é bom ser pobre' (It's so good to be poor).

Conspicuous and vulgar consumption is, however, applauded on screen, in a satirical response to the aspirational living of the late 1950s and the consumerism promoted in Hollywood movies of this era.[9] In *Rico ri à toa*, on hearing of their new-found fortune, Zé's ambitious wife declares 'Nós estamos ricos! Vamos morar no bairro mais chique da cidade' (We're rich! We're going to live in the most chic district of the city), and proceeds to buy a mansion in the upmarket neighbourhood of Ipanema, where she hosts *soirées* for high society. In the same vein, in *Esse milhão é meu* (That Million is Mine, 1958), the wife and mother-in-law of Felismino Tinoco, a lowly civil servant played by Oscarito, make a long list of items that they are going to buy with the one million *cruzeiros* that he has won. As well as a fur coat and hi-fi system, their list topically includes a plot of land in Brasília, another comic swipe at Kubitschek's purpose-built capital. The mythical 'million' that transforms the recipient's reality beyond recognition, however temporarily, also features in the *chanchada Treze cadeiras*, in which a poor barber named Bonifácio Boaventura, who hails from the sticks, inherits a million *cruzeiros* from a deceased aunt. His luck is reflected in his surname, Goodfortune, as is that of the protagonist of *O homem do sputnik*, one Sr Fortuna or Mr Fortune. *Treze cadeiras* also includes a parody of the fashion-show sequence that featured in many Hollywood movies of the 1950s, such as *Lovely to Look At* (1952) and *How to Marry a Millionaire* (1953), reflecting North America's consumer economy.

Attitudes to authority

The *chanchadas* of the 1950s repeatedly poked fun at the state and its representatives. The political regime and public administration are criticised via references to the mundane problems of everyday life, such as price rises, power cuts, unreliable public transport, petty bureaucracy, and an incompetent police force. In *O camelô da Rua Larga* a musical number entitled 'O que é que Copacabana tem?' (What is it about Copacabana?), performed on a stage set that depicts the elite at play on these famous sands, ends with the refrain 'água que é bom não tem' (clean water it doesn't have). This musical interlude is cleverly juxtaposed with a street scene in which poor women are washing clothes and complaining about a shortage of water. In the same vein, a musical number from *Aviso aos navegantes*, sung by Emilinha Borba, repeats the refrain 'Tomara que chova' (I hope it rains [so that there is water to wash with]). Other films explicitly ridicule Brazil's political leaders, such as *Nem Sansão, nem Dalila* (Neither Samson, Nor Delilah, 1954), in which the people of Gaza are only required to work one day per year, on the so-called 'Dia do Trabalho' (Day of Work). This is a humorous dig at Vargas's attempts to galvanise the Brazilian work force and dramatically increase economic development, and his introduction of various official commemorations, such as the 'Dia do Trabalhador' (Workers' Day). Like Vargas, the Brazilian Samson uses radio broadcasters to disseminate his propaganda and introduces censorship.[10] It is no coincidence that written on the wall behind him are the words: 'Votai em Sansão – um homem de ação' (Vote for Samson – a man of action) for one of President Vargas's popular nicknames was 'o homem de ação' (the man of action).[11]

Given Vargas's legacy of a cumbersome bureaucracy staffed by countless faceless pen-pushers, it is no coincidence that the *barnabé* or idle civil servant, the butt of many a joke in the *teatro de revista*, should resurface in several *chanchadas* from the 1950s, such as *Barnabé, tu és meu* (Civil Servant, You're Mine, 1951), and *Esse milhão é meu*. In the latter, the poorly paid, work-shy government employee, who lives off his father-in-law, wins a prize of a million *cruzeiros* and a week's holiday for managing not to miss a day's work in one week. His equally indolent boss is a thinly veiled caricature of Getúlio Vargas, who informs an employee that he will be going on vacation for a month to the south of Brazil (Vargas came from the southern state of Rio Grande do Sul). In *O homem do sputnik*, all but one of the government officials are on an extended coffee break at the fictitious DPI (Departamento de Pesquisas Interplanetárias – Department of Interplanetary Research), clearly a tongue-in-cheek allusion to the *Estado Novo*'s DIP, the all-powerful Press and Propaganda Department. The fact that the name of the villain in *Esse milhão é meu* is Juscelino would have raised a smile in cinema halls throughout Brazil in 1958. The fearsome wife of the diminutive adulterer in *Garotas e samba* (Girls and Samba, 1957) also just happens to be called Jocelina (virtually the female equivalent of the President's given name). Senseless, time-wasting red tape is also depicted in the first film to showcase the talents of the comedian Amácio Mazzaropi, entitled *Sai da frente* (Get Out of My Way, 1952). Playing the archetypal *caipira*, Mazzaropi fruitlessly seeks assistance in various government offices, where he is told to join 'a fila para entrar na fila para encher os questionários' (the queue to join the queue to fill in the forms), as a portrait of Getúlio Vargas gazes down on him from the wall. In a later scene Vargas is impersonated by a passer-by who takes charge following a traffic accident. He addresses the crowd as 'trabalhadores' (workers), and imitating the speech of the then President he states: 'O Brasil espera que cada um cumpra com o seu dever' (Brazil hopes that everyone will do their duty), a well-known government slogan.[12] Those in positions of authority are often treated with suspicion by less educated characters, in a reflection of the mistrust commonly felt by migrant workers in the big city. In *Rico ri à toa*, for example, Zé, the epitome of the humble man in the street, voices such fears: 'Quanto mais elegante, mais vigarista' (The more well-dressed you are, the more likely you're a con man). His concerns prove to be legitimate when a bank clerk is exposed as a bank robber.

Undermining the elite

Brazil's elite is the object of ridicule in the *chanchadas* of the 1950s, and audiences are encouraged to recognise the folly of social climbing. These films ultimately instil a sense of pride in ordinary people and implicitly promote good-humoured acceptance of the class system. In *Samba em Brasília* (Samba in Brasília, 1960), for example, high-society is mercilessly mocked when the upper-crust character Eugênia, played by Heloísa Helena, resorts to the Afro-Brazilian cult practice of *macumba*, with the help of her domestic servant Teresinha, in order to win a place on a 'best dressed' list. Sérgio Augusto comments that a recurrent motif in the *chanchada* was that of a member of the social elite opening his/her home to a gossip columnist to gain greater exposure.[13] In *Rico ri à toa* the nouveau-riche wife of Zé donates money to farcical charities to get her name in the papers, and in *O homem do sputnik* three 'ladies who lunch' boast of their so-called 'Movimento da Pipoca' (Popcorn Movement), which aims to provide all Latin American children with free popcorn. The professional classes are equally a target for mockery, as in *De vento em popa* when the doctor on board the cruise liner is still crippled by seasickness after thirty years at sea. The lowly ship's waiter, played by Oscarito, offers him a popular remedy, comically undermining the skills of the highly educated. In the same vein, in *Aviso aos navegantes* Oscarito pretends to be the ship's doctor, and spouts pseudo-medical nonsense while examining a female patient's cleavage at close quarters. Journalists are also often subject to ridicule, such as the local reporter in *Pistoleiro bossa nova* (Bossa Nova Gunman, 1960), set in the one-horse town of Desespero, who represents the newspaper *A Voz do Desespero* (literally 'The Voice of Despair'). The *chanchadas* thus got their own back on the relentless savaging that they received from film critics in the press.

The dialogues of these comedy films repeatedly used language as a marker of social class, and the penchant of social climbers for using foreign words, especially Anglicisms, is remorselessly made fun of. In *Samba em Brasília*, Eugênia brags that she is going to host 'uma big party', while in *O homem do sputnik* a socialite invites her guests to join her in her 'parlour room' for 'dinner'. In *Treze cadeiras* a provincial gold-digger pretends to be a sophisticated French woman, but her use of the phrase 'avec plaisir' falls on deaf ears when the lowly barber Bonifácio, played by Oscarito, replies 'não sei inglês' (I don't speak English). Foreign brand names are also regularly brought into the dialogue, such as in the latter film when Bonifácio pretends to be a chauffeur for a member of Rio's elite. He tells the negligée-clad It-girl that her lover has a new 'Chevrolé' (Chevrolet), to which she replies that it was supposed to be a 'Jaguar'.[14] Class distinctions are reinforced by jokes premised on the linguistic features of speech in the *chanchada*; in *Aviso aos navegantes* the lowly Oscarito respectfully addresses the female star of the theatrical troupe as 'minha senhora' (my lady), and she dutifully explains to her social inferior what the term 'hipótese' (hypothesis) means. The audience is encouraged to laugh at his and their own ignorance when he uses the term inappropriately, having failed to grasp its meaning.

Comic attacks on the 'other'

Irreverence towards foreigners, particularly North Americans, and their cultural clichés was an intrinsic feature of the *chanchada*, and formed part of the tradition's up-ending of established hierarchies. The popular nickname for sex symbol Brigitte Bardot (BB) is comically alluded to in *O camelô da Rua Larga*, in which Dona Bebê is a bossy, larger-than-life fishwife. In *De vento em popa* Elvis Presley is transformed into Melvis Prestes (whose surname means 'ready' in Portuguese, but more importantly was shared by the former Brazilian Communist Party leader, Luís Carlos Prestes, and Vargas's rival for the presidency of Brazil, Júlio Prestes, also a former governor of the state of Rio Grande do Sul, like Vargas himself). The *chanchada* played on the public's prior knowledge of First-World movies and delighted in undermining their conventions, while at the same time poking fun at Brazil and its relative inferiority.[15]

The late 1950s were characterised by a growth in anti-capitalist sentiment in Brazil. In 1958 the International Monetary Fund set out the conditions for a new loan package, and in 1959 the vice-president, João Goulart blamed Brazil's economic woes on the excessive profits creamed off by foreign companies.[16] *O homem do sputnik* was produced in the context of the Brazilian government's increasingly tense relationship with the International Monetary Fund, which was trying to force Brazil to adopt much more restrictive economic policies, a period that culminated in Kubitschek's controversial decision to sever links with the IMF in June 1959. The plot of this *chanchada* revolves around a sputnik satellite, found in the backyard of a humble yokel, named Anastácio, played by Oscarito.[17] On hearing of his find, representatives from the USSR, France and the USA are dispatched to Brazil and use any means in their power to acquire the satellite, which ultimately turns out to be nothing more than a weather vane that has fallen off the roof of a local church. This film makes fun of consumerism and the supposed First World's ignorance of 'underdeveloped' nations, and paints an unflattering picture of the infantile superpowers locked in the futile and costly space race and Cold War. One of the Americans boasts 'Nós somos sempre os primeiros' (We are

always first), and cannot accept the injustice of the sputnik having fallen
to earth in a country like Brazil. The clichéd, patchy knowledge that the
Americans have of Brazil is clearly derived from the ostensible cultural
exchange of the Roosevelt era, and the 'Good Neighbour Policy' is ridiculed
explicitly. The French are stereotyped as sex maniacs who refer to Brazil as
the land of Pelé. Their secret weapon is a Brigitte Bardot clone called BB,
played by Norma Benguel, whom they send to Brazil. Obvious references to
the Iron Curtain are farcically debunked when Anastácio is caught flirting with
BB behind a real curtain, and when an American spy declares: 'Meu governo
garante que tudo que está por trás da cortina é mentira' (My government
guarantees that everything behind the curtain is a lie). The film ends with
the representatives of the three superpowers crowding around a well where
they believe the satellite to be hidden, each claiming 'é nossa' (it's ours) and
playing out their imperial pretensions in farcical circumstances. The ingenuous
yokel, Anastácio, ironically comments: 'Até parece a Liga das Nações!' (It's a
bit like the League of Nations!) The humiliation of the representatives of
foreign capital by ordinary folk no doubt delighted Brazilian filmgoers, at a
time when their political leadership was standing up to the IMF.

Debunking 'high culture'

The debunking of hegemonic culture permeates the *chanchadas* of the 1950s.
In *De vento em popa*, for example, the down-to-earth former stowaway, Mara,
interrupts when a woman is practising her scales with her Italian music
teacher, by declaring in a mock Italian accent that it is 'música de porcaria'
(rubbish music). She later warns the pair not to perform any 'gemido de
frango morrendo' (dying chicken screeching). The urban elite's supposed
appreciation of modern art, particularly trends imported from Europe, is
ridiculed in the *chanchada Pintando o sete* (Painting the Town Red, 1959), in
which Oscarito's character, Catito, a circus clown and archetypal *malandro*,
masquerades as an abstract artist named Paul Picanssô (an obvious comic
allusion to Pablo Picasso, see figure 3). Pretentious social climbers are duped
into paying an exorbitant price for his hastily created work, and once again
Rio's 'high society' is mercilessly made fun of, to the delight of the more
humble characters on screen.

  Carnaval Atlântida (Atlântida Carnival, 1952) hinges on the battle between
the popular and the erudite, and the backstage plot revolves around the
production of an epic movie about Helen of Troy. In spite of the best efforts
of the fictitious producer, which include contracting as technical advisor a
professor of Greek mythology named Xenofontes (played by Oscarito), the
production of a historical epic on Brazilian soil proves impossible and only
a carnival musical is a viable option. Ultimately, Xenofontes succumbs to the
bewitching rhythms of popular music, losing all composure when learning to

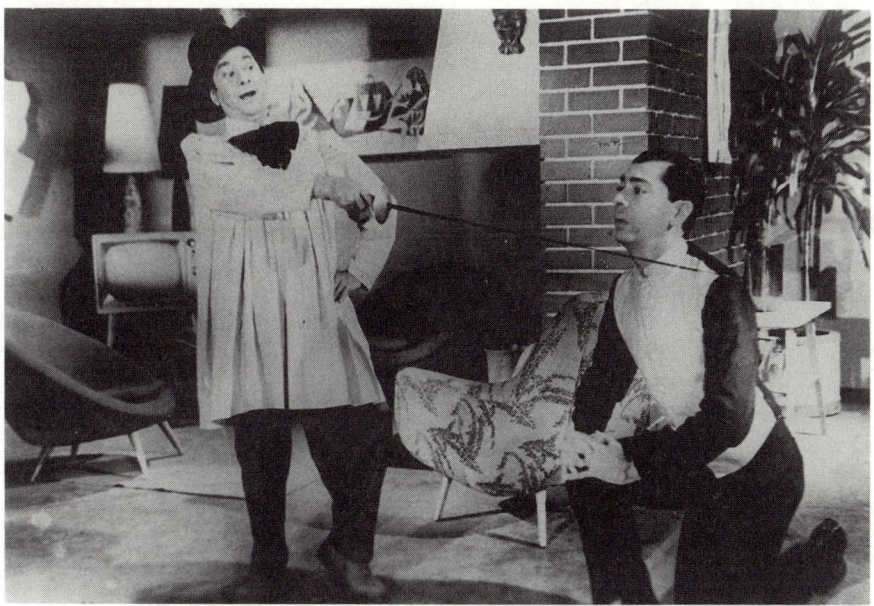

3   Oscarito (left) in the role of Paul Picanssô in the Atlântida *chanchada, Pintando o sete* (1959).

dance the mambo with the Cuban actress Maria Antonieta Pons. The ultimate defeat of classical music by popular song occurs when two humble studio cleaners, played by Grande Otelo and Colé, watch a scene on the set of a Greek garden in which Helen of Troy is entertained by the strains of a harp. The two onlookers make fun of the choice of music and in their minds the scene is transformed into a carnival celebration, in which the famous Afro-Brazilian singer Blecaute, dressed in a toga, performs the lively and risqué carnival hit, 'Dona Cegonha' (Mrs Stork), accompanied by Grande Otelo, who trips over his toga.[18] João Luiz Vieira argues that this *chanchada* also intentionally pokes fun at the absurd pretensions of the high-brow Vera Cruz studio, based in São Paulo, which looked down its nose at the popular productions made in the rival city of Rio de Janeiro.[19]

Migration, modernity and social upheaval

Sites of identification for the displaced
The *chanchadas* of the 1950s were predicated on the attraction of identification and self-recognition. They appealed to the mass audience's experiences of the dualities of modern life, reflecting the irreconcilable divide between the city and the countryside, the former embodying modernity and the latter tradition.

Rural and urban life clash head-on in these films, typically as a consequence of a poor migrant's arrival in the big city and the sense of confusion that he or she experiences. This theme naturally appealed to real-life migrants in the audience, including the millions who fled from the impoverished, drought-stricken North East in the 1950s. It has been estimated that in 1950 about 10 per cent of Brazilians were living outside their home state.[20] Nancy Wanderley's fiery temper and marked North Eastern accent in *Quem roubou meu samba?* (Who Stole My Samba?, 1958) prompts a by-stander to ask 'O que é que a baiana tem?' (literally, what is it about the girl from Bahia? – a comic reference to the title of Dorival Caymmi's famous samba which featured in the film *Banana da terra* of 1939), to which Iolanda retorts 'Sou pernambucana!' (I'm from Pernambuco! – another state in Brazil's North East). Wanderley's characters were regularly referred to as 'essa pernambucana' (that woman from Pernambuco), such as in *O camelô da Rua Larga*, no doubt striking a chord with many of the migrants in the cinema audience. The latter are reassured that economic advancement and social acceptance are attainable by the fact that the millionaire played by Zé Trindade in *Garotas e samba*, who now enjoys the Rio nightlife to the full, hails from Bahia in the North East, and perhaps more importantly by the apparent ordinariness of Brazil's screen stars.[21]

In *Samba em Brasília* Wanderley plays a cook who takes pride in the North Eastern musical and dance form *bumba-meu-boi*, but nevertheless soon learns how to dance samba. Clichés of North Eastern identity are evoked in the *chanchada*, most strikingly the mythical figures of Lampião and Maria Bonita, the legendary *cangaceiro* or bandit and his lover, who appear in a wax works museum in *Treze cadeiras* alongside the caption 'jagunço e jagunça' (male and female bandits).[22] Similarly, in *De vento em popa*, Oscarito (Chico) and Sônia Mamede (Mara) perform on stage to the North Eastern rhythms of *música sertaneja* or country music, dressed as stereotypical *cangaceiros*, and the opening musical number of *Aviso aos navegantes* is a North Eastern *baião*, as one of the characters spells out for the benefit of the audience ('Grande baião!' – Great *baião*!) The latter film stars the well-known accordionist Adelaide Chiozzo, whose brand of popular music held particular appeal for North Easterners. The diegetic soundtrack of *Rico ri à toa* tellingly caters for all regional affiliations in the audience, and ranges from the percussion-based *batucada*, the preserve of the shantytowns and poorer quarters of Rio de Janeiro, to a song performed by a duo in the style of the *repentista* improvisers, accordion music and *baião*, all of which are inextricably linked to the popular culture of Brazil's North East.[23]

Countless poorly educated, ingenuous yokels find themselves in sticky situations in the urban settings of the *chanhcada*. The action of both *O homem do sputnik* and *Treze cadeiras* begins in a backward but tranquil rural Brazil,

fittingly symbolised by a passing donkey. In both films Oscarito plays a
hillbilly character who is drawn to the big city of Rio; in *O homem do sputnik*
his character, Anastácio sets off to Brazil's then capital to make his fortune
with his 'sputnik satellite' and in *Treze cadeiras* the lowly barber that he
plays, Bonifácio goes in search of an unexpected inheritance. Both of these
characters feel disorientated on arrival in the city, where Anastácio does not
know how to behave in a bank, and Bonifácio is unable to do basic calcula-
tions in a furniture shop and unwittingly buys the wrong lot at an auction.[24]
The bucolic emblem of the ambling mule contrasts markedly with the
crammed buses and trams that rattle past in the big city. The train is usually
associated with the movement of migrants to the city in the *chanchada* and
scenes at railway stations are characterised by the optimism and excitement
of the characters concerned. In *A dupla do barulho* (The Terrible Twosome,
1953) we see Tonico and Tião end their music hall tour of the interior on a
train that pulls into Central Station in Rio, with its instantly recognisable
white, art deco clock tower. On arrival in the capital, the eager protagonists
look totally bewildered, as they spin around trying to take it all in.[25]

A crisis of identity

The *chanchadas* of the 1950s articulated both the excitement of a world in
flux and the cultural anxieties and sense of loss that the inherent transforma-
tions entailed. Both newcomers to the city and uninitiated locals experience
an identity crisis when confronted by the rampant modernity of the big city.
In *Esse milhão é meu*, for example, Oscarito's character, a humble civil servant,
is nearly knocked down by a bus. This physical joke would have struck a chord
with faceless migrants in the audience. As Alan Dale writes: 'the slapstick
hero's skill at deploying his paradoxically acrobatic clumsiness is central to
his status as an Everyman.'[26] Furthermore, many migrants were reportedly
fearful of being killed in an accident in the city and remaining unidentified.[27]
As the hick Bonifácio anxiously points out on his arrival in Rio in *Treze
cadeiras*: 'Eu não conheço ninguém aqui' (I don't know anybody here).

Longing for your homeland, however impoverished, is shown to be perfectly
natural and acceptable. In *De vento em popa*, for example, the ship's waiter,
played by Oscarito, wistfully and inappropriately likens the operatic voice of
one of the passengers to the whistle of the train that passes through his 'terra'
(homeland). In *Aviso aos navegantes*, while on tour in cosmopolitan Buenos
Aires, the lowly music hall star Frederico, played by Oscarito, lists all the
things he misses in Rio de Janeiro, exclaiming 'Eu quero voltar para minha
terra' (I want to go back to my land), namely the down-market district of
Madureira. His patriotic longing is echoed by the star of the show Cléia
(Eliana), who cannot wait to get back to the Brazilian capital for carnival,
in spite of the array of establishing shots of the Argentine capital's bustling,

neon-lit streets. As she says, 'Gosto muito de Buenos Aires mas não posso ficar longe do carnaval' (I love Buenos Aires but I cannot be far away from carnival). In keeping with the *chanchada* tradition as a whole, *Aviso aos navegantes* celebrates patriotism at a local level, as is echoed in the musical sequences. In one example Jorge Goulart sings of his encounters with foreign women overseas but extols the virtues of girls from Copacabana ('Eu quero uma sereia de Copacabana' – I want a mermaid from Copacabana), who appear in bikinis and wielding beach balls on the stage set. In this film's final number, performed just as the ship is pulling into Guanabara bay, a crooner sings a classic *samba-exaltação* or overtly patriotic samba, entitled 'Meu Brasil' (My Brazil) against the backdrop of a stage set of Sugar Loaf Mountain. As he fondly sings of 'minha terra brasileira' (my Brazilian land), he is joined on stage by a host of *baianas* and *malandros*, the traditional cinematic icons of Brazilian identity.[28]

The crisis of identity provoked by industrialisation, urbanisation and modernisation continued to be reflected in the *chanchadas* of the 1950s via the adoption of a new persona by characters on the bottom rung of the social ladder, like their audiences. The stowaway played by Oscarito in *Aviso aos navegantes* succeeds in passing himself off as a foreign prince with the aid of a white tuxedo and someone else's passport in order to gain access to a swanky party on board ship. Later in this film he convincingly pretends to be a doctor of medicine and even a Spanish American female dancer and singer. The message seems to be that anything is possible with a liberal dose of *malandragem* or *jeitinho*, and Brazil's social hierarchy, that judges and ranks people solely on their physical appearance, is implicitly ridiculed and undermined. When we first see Oscarito (Agapito) in *Colégio de brotos*, he is dressed as a university don and is delivering a lecture. It is only when he is interrupted by an officious secretary that his true status is revealed; he is a lowly cleaner, forced to wear a uniform reminiscent of that of a prison convict. When he cheats his way into an audition at a radio station, he is introduced as a high-ranking university official and a great writer. At the end of the film we are told that as a reward for his efforts in catching a thief, both of these falsehoods will, in fact, come true, and he turns the tables on the snooty secretary by ordering her to clean the toilets.

Maintaining the tradition established in the *chanchadas* of the 1940s, cases of mistaken identity often provide a way of changing one's station in life, such as Ankito's character in the spoof Western, *Pistoleiro bossa nova*. This nervous wreck, and one-time illegal popcorn vendor, happens to be a dead-ringer for the fearsome gunman of the town where he fortuitously ends up. He thus earns the respect of the inhabitants and the affections of a femme fatale by shooting several villains and injuring another with a stray snooker ball, all of which are totally fluke occurrences. Likewise, it only takes a wig and distinctive false moustache to transform the circus clown, Catito, played by Oscarito in *Pintando o sete*, into the illustrious European artist, Paul Picanssô, who bears a striking physical resemblance to Salvador Dalí rather than to his virtual namesake, Pablo Picasso. The *chanchadas* of the 1950s explored the ambiguity of identity within Brazil's social hierarchy, particularly by having disenfranchised anti-heroes transformed into authority figures and truly heroic figures. Rather than giving an unrealistic message about social mobility, the elasticity of identity was central to the carnivalesque, topsy-turvy world of these films, in which normality was always ultimately re-established. Such social fluidity reassured poor audiences that in truth there was little to distinguish them from their more fortunate, well-heeled compatriots.

The big city on screen

In the 1950s the overwhelming majority of rural-urban migrants settled in the city of Rio de Janeiro, the home of the Atlântida studio, who not unsurprisingly chose the then capital, particularly its up-market, beach-front districts, as the setting for its films.[29] *Chanchadas* were typically set in luxury hotels, glamorous night-spots, ocean liners (*De vento em popa; Aviso aos navegantes*), radio stations (*Garotas e samba* and *Colégio de brotos*), record companies (*Quem roubou meu samba?*), television studios (*Absolutamente certo!* (Absolutely Right!, 1957) and *Vai, que é mole* (Go On, It's Easy, 1960)) and other pleasure-oriented locales frequented by society's elite or associated with the world of show business. This screen world was far removed from the daily experiences of typical cinema-goers, since most migrants lived in makeshift shacks in the emerging Baixada Fluminense area on the outskirts of Rio, without basic services like running water, electricity or sanitation. Any familiarity with the bourgeois milieu depicted in the *chanchada* would only have been gained when journeying to their place of work, perhaps as domestic servants for the elite or street sellers in the so-called 'informal sector'.[30]

Establishing shots of the city's streets and easily recognisable locations, such as the curve of Copacabana beach, compensate for the audience's social exclusion by equipping them with a visual literacy in relation to their adoptive home and allowing them to dream of bettering their lot in life. In *A grande vedete*, for example, the audience can accompany the characters as they retire to the terrace of a nightclub to take in the breathtaking views of Botafogo bay and Sugar Loaf Mountain. As the has-been star comments, 'A cidade é muito grande' (the city is very big), reassuring the spectators that their impressions are shared by everyone, even members of the elite.

In addition to enhancing the spatial awareness of their audiences, the *chanchadas* emphasise the freedom of movement permitted by modern modes of transport, including the aeroplane (which even Oscarito travels in to get to

Hollywood in the final scenes of *Pintando o sete*), but particularly the automobile, such as an ultra-trendy bubble car in *Absolutamente certo!*, and the motor scooter favoured by the younger generation. Access to glamorous, bourgeois districts is facilitated by Rio's spot-lit road tunnels, updated at the end of the 1940s.[31] Ubiquitous shots of the façade of the Copacabana Palace hotel, in real life favoured by the super-rich and internationally famous, symbolise modernity and the mythical glamour of Rio throughout the *chanchada* tradition. Furthermore, the suspension of reality and social mores in the alien environment of the luxury hotel, the elite nightclub, the cruise ship or sophisticated casino allowed the provincial and marginalised characters on screen and the real-life audience temporarily to taste modernity and its attendant freedoms.

Modern times

Modernity is depicted with mixed feelings in popular film from the 1950s. On the one hand, the advances of the decade are celebrated, but on the other, the uninitiated poor are constantly challenged by their encounter with modernity, and ultimately remain unimpressed. *Samba em Brasília*, as its title would suggest, takes pride in the new futuristic capital city, inaugurated in 1960, the year this film was released. References to the city, however, are fleeting, such as the casual shot of a cover of *Manchete* magazine displaying the name Brasília, and a passing reference to the members of parliament who have not yet left Rio for the new capital. In fact, *Samba em Brasília* simply takes its title from that of a song performed in the film.[32] The domestic servant, Teresinha sings this samba at a high-society party on a stage set that reproduces in silhouette the most recognisable buildings of the federal capital, designed by Oscar Niemeyer, such as the cathedral, and the congress building in the Praça dos Três Poderes (Square of Three Powers). The simplistic lyrics praise Brazil's president and express a faith in the future: 'Brasil que trabalha/ Brasil de amanhã . . . Retrato do Brasil/ Brasil de JK' (Brazil that works hard/ The Brazil of tomorrow . . . Portrait of Brazil/ The Brazil of JK). Stylised construction workers, known as *candangos*, dance alongside performers of *capoeira* on the roof of the reproductions of government buildings.

In *Samba em Brasília* the latest technology and access to consumer society are symbolised by the electric food mixer that Teresinha uses in the course of her work as a cook at the home of a socialite. As she exclaims, 'Lá no morro não tem disso' (We don't have these things in the shantytown). She does not know how to operate this latest gadget and so enlists the help of the son of her bourgeois employer. They omit to replace the lid and are both covered in flour, much to their hilarity. Technology hinders those who are not equipped to negotiate it, just as it does the opposite of what it should, such as in *Garotas e samba* when the telephone hinders communication by simply confusing the poor Portuguese butcher.[33] The increased presence of technology in modern, urban life is emblematised by the huge time machine that transports Oscarito's character, Horácio, from Rio in the 1950s to Gaza in ancient times in *Nem Sansão, nem Dalila*. Likewise, *Colégio de brotos* features an over-sized, portable sauna, from which only the arrogant occupant's head is visible, as he smokes a cigar, speaks on the telephone, and more tellingly, looks a fool.[34]

The *chanchadas* of the 1950s incorporated contrasting decorative styles in their sets and props in order to encapsulate the clash of cultures and values brought about by migration and modernisation. Scenes of a shantytown with its wooden shacks, unpaved roads and communal outdoor washtubs are juxtaposed with shots of the up-market home of a socialite in *Samba em Brasília*. Inhabitants of the *favela* work as domestic servants in an ultra-modern white fitted kitchen, complete with king-size fridge and a range of household appliances, straight out of the American dream. But such consumer riches do not outweigh the sense of community and values of the shantytown, to which the heroine, Teresinha, ultimately returns. The Niemeyer-inspired neoteric architecture of the 1950s is drawn in opposition to traditional styles of buildings and furnishings, providing a fitting metaphor for the everyday contradictions provoked by rural-urban migration. In *Treze cadeiras* a marble-lined hallway and modern elevator lead Oscarito's character to the home of a well-heeled lady who spends her time gossiping on a large white telephone against a backdrop of a huge television set. Her environment could not differ more from the crumbling mansion that he has inherited from his deceased aunt. In the closing scenes of this film he returns to his abode to discover that it is being demolished, presumably to make way for another multi-storey apartment block like the one that has already been erected next door. Contemplating the onslaught of modernisation, dressed in a tattered suit, Oscarito's character is a Chaplinesque figure here, who sees his reflection in a shop window alongside that of the frenetic transport of the city. Down and out, he steals food from a nearby market, but he remains true to his simple, homely values and returns the articles. In the *chanchada* the humble characters ultimately remain unimpressed by their taste of modernity and the high life. The value system of the audience is by extension applauded and reinforced.[35]

Useful parallels can be drawn between the depiction of fledgling modernity in these Brazilian films and in those starring Oscarito's Mexican counterpart, Mario Moreno, better known as Cantinflas. Both figures emerged from the fissures within their respective national cultures that separated country from city, tradition from modernity. Both came to represent the small man dwarfed by his encounter with modern, city life, and synonymous with inarticulate inferiority. In the *chanchada Esse milhão é meu*, for example, the USA's preoccupation with winning the Cold War is referred to in a light-hearted fashion, when one of the characters jokes that his car 'anda mais que o sputnik' (goes faster than the sputnik). The character Felismino, played by Oscarito, then jokingly suggests he should try selling it to the Americans. The car in question, however, is an old banger, that only after much cajoling manages to jerk into motion, prompting the passengers to laugh heartily. It is no coincidence that in the 1943 Mexican film *Romeo y Julieta* (Romeo and Juliet), Cantinflas, in his typical *pelado* guise, drives a similarly rickety car that only starts up when he kicks it and which no one believes is a taxi. It can only travel down hill and when Cantinflas's character inspects its engine he pulls out a cat and assorted items of rubbish. Anti-heroes like those played by Oscarito and Cantinflas poke fun at their community's relative backwardness and at the same time celebrate the clash between the First- and Third-World elements of everyday life. In both cases the clapped-out cars act as symbols of what modernity means in Brazil and Mexico in this era.[36]

Humour and popular identification in the *chanchada*

Laughing at yourself

The humour of the *chanchadas* of the 1950s maintains a long-standing tradition of self-deprecation in Brazilian popular film, and the screen characters encourage the members of the audience to laugh at themselves and the difficulties they encounter in their daily lives. The films delight in the cultural anomalies of contemporary urban Brazil, where vestiges of rural life and backwardness co-exist with the trappings of the First World. In *O camelô da Rua Larga* a pistol-toting villain is overpowered with the aid of a simple rolling pin and the cultural clash between the 'exotic' and the local is encapsulated when, in a sophisticated nightclub restaurant, a Brazilian customer rejects the extensive list of imported gastronomic delights in favour of 'uma feijoada completa' (a complete *feijoada* – Brazil's national dish of black beans and pork, whose origins lie in the slave quarters of the country's colonial plantations), adding the colloquial request 'com dois ovos a cavalo!' (with two eggs on top!). In the same vein, in *Treze cadeiras* Bonifácio Boaventura seeks to drown his sorrows after a disastrous date and opts for a bottle of *cachaça* (cheap fire-water made from sugar cane) costing just fifty *cruzeiros* in preference to the cheapest imported cognac sold in the bar, declaring 'Vai ser uma bebedeira patriótica!' (It's going to be a patriotic booze-up!).

The down-market, unglamorous nature of life in Brazil/Rio, especially when juxtaposed with the 'exotic' images of reality disseminated by Hollywood, is a source of comic pride. Obvious ironic contrasts can be drawn between *Garotas e samba* (like all *chanchadas* shot in black and white) and the movie on which it was loosely based, *How to Marry a Millionaire* (shot in glorious Technicolor). The three female protagonists of this *chanchada* live in an overcrowded boarding house, worlds apart from the Manhattan apartment that is the residence of their alter-egos in the Hollywood film. *Garotas e samba* delights in creating comic oppositions between aspects of Brazilian life and Hollywood glitz. For example, one of the female leads pretends to telephone the 'Banco Internacional' (International Bank) but is connected, instead, to a butcher's shop (the 'Açougue Buenos Aires' – Buenos Aires [literally, good airs] Butcher's, a comic name in itself). Furthermore, the only millionaire to appear in this Brazilian film is the owner of the biggest factory of 'aparelhos sanitários' (toilet appliances) in Latin America, and thus no match for the oil barons of *How to Marry a Millionaire*.

Laughing at the 'other'

For generations the Portuguese immigrant community in Brazil has been the butt of many 'ethnic' jokes. As Jerry Palmer writes, such 'jokes, told through-out the Western world, conventionally link the butt with the character traits of stupidity or stinginess . . . any group will do as the butt, provided it can plausibly be regarded as outside the "mainstream" of the culture in question . . . '[37] In *O homem do sputnik* a simple-minded, rotund Portuguese hick, referred to as Seu Manuel, or less politely as a 'portuga', openly admits to this well-worn stereotype ('E depois nós é quem somos os burros!' – And then they go and call us asses!), in an exaggerated accent. Similarly, in *Minervina vem aí*, the outspoken eponymous heroine rebukes the unwanted advances of a Portuguese baker, whom she also refers to rudely as a 'portuga', by declaring 'Quem gosta de português é bacalhau' (Only codfish like the Portuguese) in a comic allusion to the Portuguese national dish. Likewise, the Jews of São Paulo are caricatured as avaricious and Italian female immi-grants as flighty in Vera Cruz's comedy, *Sai da frente*.

In the *chanchada* comic impersonations of foreigners focus on caricatures of their speech, and the marked Portuguese accent of the inhabitants of Brazil's former colonial power is repeatedly called on to raise a smile. Similarly, in *Aviso aos navegantes* Oscarito's character exaggerates the 'lisp' of Castillian Spanish when pronouncing 'Barcelona' and gives the clichéd exclamation 'olé'. In the same vein, in *Pistoleiro bossa nova* the barber in the town of Desespero just happens to be a heavily accented Italian, as is the TV station boss in *Vai, que é mole*, who predictably exclaims 'Mama mia!'[38] More than just a source of easy laughter, these jokes helped to make the equally marginalised Brazilians in the audience feel better about themselves and forget their inadequacies. As Davies argues, 'ethnic' jokes are not really about prejudice or ethnicity, but rather are a reflection of modern industrial society, in which two personality traits are valued above all others, namely the pursuit of advantage, and the ability to enjoy money. Thus, 'ethnic' jokes focus on the alleged stupidity and avarice of the target group to make those outside it appear 'normal'.[39]

Laughing together

Jokes for the initiated, and particularly saucy remarks, were directed at the adults in the audience, such as when in *Metido a bacana* two male characters are commenting on price rises and one of them comments: 'Até a banana subiu!' (Even bananas went up!) (There follows a lingering voyeuristic close-up of the shapely legs of a female carnival reveller, wearing fishnet stockings.) In addition, there are several examples of auto-citation or insider jokes in the *chanchada* tradition. In *Treze cadeiras*, Ivone, played by Renata Fronzi, goes into a shop and the shopkeeper asks her if she is Naná, a reference to the character she played in *Garotas e samba*, another film from Atlântida, released earlier in the same year. This inter-textual allusion is made explicit when the store owner adds that he recognises her from a film.[40] Also in *Treze cadeiras*, against his domineering wife's wishes, the same shopkeeper is listening to the radio because, he says, Zé Trindade is performing. He thinks Trindade is wonderful, whereas his wife says she cannot stand him. It is no coincidence that Trindade stars in this very *chanchada*. (He is also the protagonist of *Rico ri à toa*, in which he goes by his own forename, reinforcing the audience's familiarity with him). Vera Cruz used the same technique in their comedy *Sai da frente*, in which Isidoro (played by Mazzaropi) turns on the radio in his truck to hear the announcer say that Mazzaropi will be performing on air later that day. He declares, 'Esse não vale!' (He's no good!), but proceeds to mime the words of his own song being played on the radio.[41] Audiences could pick up on these inter-textual comic references and enjoy the sensation of being in on the joke and a member of a wider community. Similarly, they were encouraged to recognise the stars of the films, such as the accordionist Adelaide Chiozzo, who appears in many examples of the *chanchada*, such as *Aviso aos navegantes*, where she simply goes by her own forename. After a performance on the deck of the cruise ship in this film, another character reminds us who she is, saying 'Muito bem, Adelaide' (Well done, Adelaide), thus reinforcing the audience's sense of familiarity with the tradition and its stars. In the second-phase *chanchadas* of the 1950s the audience's familiarity with screen stars is self-consciously alluded to and taps into the star system created with the help of film magazines and personal appearances in stage shows, referred to in more detail in Chapter 3. This calculated fostering of stardom contrasts sharply with the approach of the *chanchadas* of the 1930s and early 1940s, which relied on the audience's prior knowledge of the stars of radio and popular music.

A comic crisis of masculinity

In the *chanchadas* of the 1950s masculine identity is presented, at best, as being under threat, and at worst as decidedly ambivalent and precarious in nature. Faced with the mounting demands of modern life, the male anti-heroes of these popular films tend to shy away from their patriarchal responsibilities in favour of handing over the reigns of domestic power to the ambitious, go-getting females of the 1950s. There are thus many instances of emasculated males and domineering fishwives in the *chanchada*, such as the two shopkeepers in *Treze cadeiras*, who bicker constantly. The husband tells his wife that she can beat him up, but not in front of their customers. When they are woken in the night by hammering on their front door it is the husband who cowers in fear and says it must be thieves. In *Esse milhão é meu* the fearsome Gertrudes will not even allow her husband Felismino, played by the diminutive Oscarito, to have the key to their wardrobe and thus controls his physical movements outside the home. Husbands are characteristically reluctant to assert their conjugal rights, and as the hen-pecked Zé of *Rico ri à toa* says, the only good thing about being rich is that 'Gente de bem dorme em quarto separado' (Well-off people sleep in separate bedrooms).

Stark comic contrasts are drawn between the feeble leading men of these films and traditional figures of masculinity and *machismo*. One only has to think of Oscarito's quivering sheriff in *Matar ou correr* (Kill or Run, 1954) and the courageous, broad-shouldered Gary Cooper of *High Noon* (1952), on which this parodic *chanchada* was based. Oscarito's physical presence, or lack of it, lent itself to comic parodies of masculinity, such as when he comes face to face with a muscular hunk at a poolside party in *A dupla do barulho*, or when in *Aviso aos navegantes* he is terrified of a skeleton. A similarly gawky weakling, wearing thick-rimmed spectacles, appears in *Colégio de brotos* alongside a macho football team, whose locker-room antics involve knocking his glasses off and declaring 'Futebol é para homem!' (Football is for men!) Ambivalent masculinity is articulated later in the same film, when Oscarito's character, Agapito, imitates a woman's voice. He then goes one step further by dressing as a woman when caught in a girls' dormitory at the university, borrowing a flower-print, low-back dress, high-heeled shoes, hat, necklace and earrings, an outfit that he then wears until the final scene. (Homosexuality is the target for a throwaway slur, earlier in this film, when the belligerent boss of a radio station reprimands one of his employees by calling him 'uma bicha' (a queer).

A playful undercurrent of homo-eroticism can be read into several examples of the *chanchada* tradition, which up-ends the implicit convention of the heterosexual male gaze, studied in more detail below. In *A dupla do barulho*, Oscarito's semi-autobiographical character Tonico readily embraces a male show business impresario, and later grabs the posterior of Tião (Grande Otelo) to help him into a bunk bed that the two of them share. Furthermore, the two actors kiss at the climax of the final shoot-out in *Matar ou correr*, totally undermining the macho posturing characteristic of the Western genre. In *Aviso aos navegantes* the villain, played by José Lewgoy, ends up in bed with Oscarito's character, mistaking him for his wife, and unwittingly tries to seduce him under the covers, while in *Pistoleiro bossa nova*, Grande Otelo's new comic sidekick, Ankito, ends up sitting in the black character's lap on a train journey. Such passing hints at a homo-erotic subtext conspire with the commonplace motif of transvestism in the *chanchada*, itself a mainstay of popular humour in the *teatro de revista*, to emphasise the fluid nature of gender identity. As Yvonne Tasker writes, 'comedies and musicals offer generic pleasures of excess, spectacle and the possibility of change/escape, a context within which an imagery of cross-dressing articulates the precarious persistence of sexual and racial binaries.'[42] Furthermore, the instability of gender boundaries in these films reflects the corrosion of traditional masculine identity and roles in the urban environment of the 1950s, particularly among the inarticulate, uprooted poor. Male authority and control were threatened by industrial society and the new freedoms enjoyed by women. Modern life and women had something in common: their otherness. By transforming themselves into women on screen, male anti-heroes deprived their female counterparts of their powerful alterity, symbolically asserting both male domination over women and man's place in modern, technological society.[43]

Imitation and parody of Hollywood paradigms

The 'Latino' motif: a Hollywood legacy

As illustrated in Chapter 2, the first Brazilian musicals were clearly inspired by their sophisticated Hollywood counterparts. This trend for recreating key cinematic motifs permeated the *chanchada* tradition throughout the 1950s, and was particularly apparent in the show numbers/dance sequences. It has been argued that the adopted sets, props and costumes, such as the feathers of the dancing girls' head-dresses, the top hats and tails worn by their male counterparts, and the sweeping staircases that often descended on to the stage, encapsulated a popular, metonymic interpretation of Hollywood's ostentation and glamour.[44] The costumes of the showgirls and the rather simplified choreography are clearly based on Hollywood templates, and it is the pastiched tourist's eye-view of Brazil/Latin America as depicted in countless 'south-of-the-border' US movies produced in Hollywood in the 1940s, which forms the basis of many of the cabaret shows in the *chanchadas*.[45]

In the third musical number of *Esse milhão é meu* black musicians dressed as African tribesmen play *atabaque* drums, as used in the Afro-Brazilian cult practice of *candomblé*, and dancing girls appear in a skimpy version of the *baiana* costume made famous by Carmen Miranda. Four male and four female dancers appear on the palm-fringed set, the women carrying baskets of tropical fruit, and then a Miranda look-alike takes centre stage, wielding a large spherical object. This interlude appears to take its cue from the beach-ball dance sequence in *The Gang's All Here* (1943), directed by Busby Berkeley and starring Miranda. It is a pale imitation of the extravagant kaleidoscope dance sequences of Berkeley's classic; in the Brazilian 'version' there are only four dancers and the choreography is limited to the showgirls lifting their legs in synchronised movements, caught in a spotlight in an effort to recreate the typical circular framing of the kaleidoscope effect. The opening sequence of Berkeley's 'Good Neighbour Policy' musical, a rendition of Ari Barroso's ultra-patriotic samba 'Aquarela do Brasil' (Watercolour of Brazil), is also echoed in the *chanchada Colégio de brotos*. A lone male singer, shrouded in darkness, performs a samba with the repeated refrain of 'Meu Brasil' (My Brazil), and he is then joined by dancing girls in stylised *baiana* costumes, just as Carmen Miranda in her tutti-frutti turban appears in the parallel scene in the Hollywood film.

Brazilian filmmakers looked to the country's Spanish-speaking neighbours for icons of a mythical *latinidad*. The first musical numbers of *Aviso aos navegantes* are set in Buenos Aires and resonate with Hollywood's 'Latino' motifs, with sets decorated with coconut palms, and black male musicians in frilly-sleeved shirts playing bongo drums, in an effort to re-create a generic 'tropics' in the temperate Argentine capital. The 'toreador' theme is taken up in this film in the form of a dream sequence in which Oscarito's character sings 'Soy un torero' (I'm a bullfighter) alongside female dancers in white lace mantillas and subsequently skimpy, mock bull-fighting outfits. He proudly states in the lyrics that he is 'um toureiro avacalhado, natural de Cascadura' (a sloppy bullfighter from Cascadura), a reference to a down-at-heel district of Rio. The citation of Hollywood movies is comically undermined by Oscarito's exaggerated lisp when speaking Spanish. Later, a male crooner on board the ship sings of his 'cubana' (Cuban woman), who is rhymed with the colloquial expression 'bacana' (cool), and the 'latino' motif reaches its crescendo when Oscarito, in drag, takes the place of a female rumba singer/dancer. He humorously invents lyrics about Niterói, the city across the bay from Rio and which understandably suffers by comparison with its glamorous neighbour, and rhymes 'rumbeira' (female rhumba performer) with 'Madureira', a down-market district in Rio's proletarian North Zone. Similarly, in Cinedistri's *Absolutamente certo!*, one of the television shows, which provide the central focus of the production numbers in the film, takes the form of a cabaret act which begins with a flamenco-style dance routine, followed by a vocal performance by three male crooners singing in Spanish. The influence of Hollywood musicals on this *chanchada* is even more apparent in the next section of this cabaret act, when male singers, complete with top hats and walking canes, sing in English to a big-band accompaniment, against a backdrop of skyscrapers. The show then conjures up stereotypical images of Paris and Venice, before returning to a cardboard Sugar Loaf

Mountain. Rio de Janeiro/Brazil are portrayed through the eyes of Hollywood, and the latter's stock motifs of 'Brazilian' identity once again overtly inform the way Brazilians depict themselves and their country on screen.

The male gaze

The female body is overtly displayed in the *chanchadas* of the 1950s, and these films clearly aimed to entice adult males into cinema theatres, along with their wives and children. In the opening scene of *Colégio de brotos*, for example, the audience is treated to lingering shots of partially clad young women waking from their slumber in a university dormitory, very reminiscent of a US sorority house, and every inch a heterosexual male fantasy. The prevalent male gaze is particularly apparent in the dance sequences of these films, in which the dancing girls display their ample thighs in leotard costumes and high heels, holding the look of the spectator and playing to and signifying male desire. These song-and-dance numbers clearly emulate the Hollywood norm of woman displayed as sexual object as the *leitmotif* of erotic spectacle.[46] The setting for such celebrations of the female form in the *chanchada* is usually the nightclub stage, but can sometimes be incongruous, such as when a showgirl on tour performs an impromptu dance for her fellow passengers in the aisle of a steam train in *Pistoleiro bossa nova*.[47]

The epitome of sexual temptation in the *chanchada* was the exotic foreign beauty, particularly the lascivious *latina*, a stereotype that the Brazilian film industry took from Hollywood.[48] It is no coincidence that in *Carnaval Atlântida* the respectable professor of Greek mythology, Xenofontes, is led to his moral downfall by a Cuban beauty tellingly named Lolita. Only moments after they meet, Oscarito's character is dancing to Latin rhythms and surrendering to the physical pleasures of carnival. It is perhaps surprising that these Brazilian musicals did not draw on the physical spectacle of the home-grown mulatto girl, who emerged as a symbol of the nation's hybrid identity and a sexual icon in the first decades of the twentieth century, as examined in more detail below. The *chanchada*, however, was permeated by an implicit racism, a subject that Robert Stam has analysed in depth, and which is dealt with later in this chapter.[49] It is no coincidence that the Cuban temptress who appears in *Carnaval Atlântida* is played by a white actress, and that when Grande Otelo's character says that he knows a *mulata* named Elena from a shantytown who would make an ideal Helen of Troy, the fictional director dismisses his suggestion by condescendingly explaining that he is looking for 'universal' beauty.[50]

The voyeuristic male gaze, although dominant in the *chanchada*, is comically undermined by the appearance of cross-dressed male characters, most commonly played by Oscarito. His seductive femmes fatales include the rumba singer/dancer in *Aviso aos navegantes*, a pastiche of the libidinous *latina*. The motif of transvestism is an obvious example of carnivalesque inversion, in which sexual instability is just another reflection of the temporary suspension of normality.[51] But drag scenes also serve to highlight the performative nature of gender, and to comically draw attention to Hollywood's manipulation of the female form on screen. As Annette Kuhn says, 'through the construction of sexually disguised male characters as objects of pleasurable looking, attention may be drawn to conventions of cinematic representation which are in ordinary circumstances so much taken-for-granted as to be invisible. Where the spectator is aware that the characters are, clothes notwithstanding, not really women, such self-referentiality heightens the comedy.'[52] The male identity crisis that these Brazilian films articulated, examined in more detail above, also conspired to debunk the all-knowing and all-powerful male gaze that nevertheless dominated the *chanchada* tradition in keeping with borrowed Hollywood conventions.

Brazil's *High Noon* and an epic adventure

While some *chanchadas* were content to occasionally mimic a stock element of Hollywood movies or even a well-known star, Atlântida's relationship with the North American film industry evolved in the 1950s, giving rise to sophisticated film parodies. The studio thus gave the *chanchada* genre a new comic twist, that would be further exploited by the *pornochanchadas* of the 1970s, as discussed in Chapter 6, not least in the Brazilian 'version' of *Jaws*, entitled *Bacalhau* (Codfish, 1976).

In 1954 Atlântida released two parodic *chanchadas*, *Matar ou correr* (Kill or Run), a self-confessed burlesque of *High Noon* (entitled *Matar ou morrer* – Kill or Die – in Brazil), and *Nem Sansão, nem Dalila* (Neither Samson, Nor Delilah), which satirised Cecil B. de Mille's biblical epic *Samson and Delilah* of 1949.[53] Both were directed by Carlos Manga, who admitted that his filmmaking career had always been heavily influenced by Hollywood, stating that, 'My cinematic training was totally American',[54] and yet voiced his resentment of the USA's cultural hegemony in Brazil. Manga's attitude to the target texts is ambivalent. As Dan Harries argues, 'Although parodic discourse typically engages with its familiar target text in a somewhat affectionate manner, it also demonstrates a certain degree of disdain towards its target.'[55] Like any example of parody, both of these Brazilian films hinge on blatant stylistic hybridity, and part of their success lies in the fact that they paradoxically acknowledge a debt of gratitude to the parodied style and admit to their own weaknesses, and yet poke fun at Hollywood and assert Brazil's autonomy at one and the same time. By keeping two distinct levels of discourse, one a faithful reproduction of the Western, the other an intrinsically Brazilian, clownish double-act, Carlos Manga expresses his admiration for Hollywood's craft (he saw *High Noon* many times), and at the same time subverts its message, revealing his resentment of the USA's domination of the Brazilian market.[56]

Matar ou correr is an example of sustained film parody, that is a film that operates within a parodic mode from start to finish.[57] It used extra-textual elements, namely promotional material, to situate the viewer into a parodic spectatorial mode and to indicate the target being parodied. Publicity for the film included the following description, which appeared in the film magazine *Revista Cinelândia*: 'In the film, our aim is to revisit, in a humorous way, the commonplaces of American Westerns . . . This is not a case of imitation, but rather of a parody of Wild West films.'[58] The negation inherent in the title of *Nem Sansão, nem Dalila* is a kind of disclaimer, tantamount to admitting that Brazil cannot compete with Hollywood and is restricted to producing low-budget, pale imitations. Comic self-deprecation permeates this film. The most striking example is the source of the Brazilian Samson's strength – a wig, in marked contrast to the luscious long hair of Victor Mature's Samson in the Hollywood original. The critic João Luiz Vieira describes this wig as a metaphor for the simulated strength of an imitative cinema in relation to the Hollywood superproduction, arguing that the primary intention of this kind of parody was not to criticise the target but to capitalise on its residual success.[59] The handsome, muscle-bound Victor Mature could not differ more from the slightly built, gauche Oscarito, who plays the Brazilian Samson. Like all *chanchadas*, *Nem Sansão, nem Dalila* was shot in black and white, with a limited budget for sets and costumes, providing an obvious contrast with the colourful, big-budget Hollywood epic.[60]

Hybrid texts and the mechanics of film parody
Generic hybrids like these two Brazilian films fit logically into the Bakhtinian category of the grotesque, formed through a process of hybridisation of binary opposites, particularly of high and low. Critics such as Robert Stam and João Luiz Vieira have studied these Brazilian parodies within a Bakhtinian frame, drawing on concepts such as the carnivalesque, dialogism and heteroglossia.[61] The work of Dan Harries on film parody is equally of interest in this context, as it provides a framework within which to analyse the mechanisms of film parody. As Harries argues, parody is characterised by the oscillation between similarity to and difference from a target, and it 'operates in terms of a system centred on "logical absurdity", with one dimension needed to ensure a logic and another for difference-creating absurdity'.[62] In general terms, film parodies employ similarity to and difference from the original film (the target, to use Harries's term) at the level of lexicon, syntax and style. Harries lists six primary techniques of film parody, the first of which is reiteration. All parodies must evoke or quote key elements such as the set, characters, costumes or iconography. Carlos Manga reproduces the Hollywood Western with striking authenticity in *Matar ou correr*, and the quality of the sets even led some Brazilian critics to accuse him of stealing a clip (the stage-coach scene) from

the Hollywood film *Calamity Jane* (1953). The iconography of the Western genre is reproduced, as are specific scenes or shots from *High Noon*, such as close-ups of characters' faces and the clock face as time draws closer to the villain's arrival, a shot of the villain when he has just arrived at the railroad station, and one of a woman crossing herself. Once familiarity with the target scene is registered, the lexical units (characters, costumes, props and so on) are rearranged to create an incongruous effect. For example, in this Brazilian parody, the final shoot-out scene is reiterated, but in true parodic tradition, it then extends to a logically absurd conclusion. (Oscarito, the sheriff is gripped with fear as the villain approaches, and yet manages to accidentally shoot him while fumbling to remove his gun from its holster. The extra-diegetic music inverts the expected style by contrasting 'authentic' Western motifs, representing the 'authentic' characters, with a comic-sounding clarinet melody, highly reminiscent of that associated with Laurel and Hardy, when the goofy sheriff is on screen.)

The dramatic opening musical number of *Nem Sansão, nem Dalila* is a good example of reiteration, in that it was a deliberate copy by Luiz Bonfá of that composed by Victor Young for De Mille's epic.[63] Unlike *Matar ou correr*, however, this Brazilian film is anything but a faithful replica of the original and takes very irreverent liberties with the classical Biblical epic. It takes only its basic premise from the Hollywood film. In fact, the action begins in a beauty salon in contemporary Rio. By a highly unlikely turn of events, a barber named Horácio, played by Oscarito, gains access to a time machine and travels to Gaza, the land of the Philistines, back in 1153 BC, where he takes on the identity of Samson after acquiring the magic wig. (It is only at this point that any similarity to De Mille's movie becomes apparent.) From then on the parody relies on the reiteration of sets, costumes and props.

The second key technique of film parody cited by Harries is that of inversion, whereby the lexicon, syntax or style are modified to create an opposite meaning for something in relation to its usage in the target film. Characters can be evoked but some of their traits can be inverted. In *Matar ou correr* the sheriff is a former con man played by Oscarito, described by João Luis Vieira as half-*cangaceiro* or bandit, half coward.[64] This yellow-bellied buffoon, who is terrified of the villains, frequently bursts into tears, and is even afraid of riding a horse, represents a blatant ironic contrast with the heroic Gary Cooper in *High Noon*. Grande Otelo plays an equally timid black cowboy. The casting of an Afro-Brazilian in this role adds a further dimension to the critical reworking of the Hollywood Western, in which black actors are conspicuous by their absence. What makes this Brazilian film so effective in critiquing the genre is the double-act of Oscarito and Grande Otelo. They behave like clowns, and are even explicitly referred to as 'palhaços' (clowns) by the villain of the piece, Jesse Gordon. They generate a sufficient difference from the source text to re-contextualise it, avoiding the film becoming just an exaggerated form of quotation.

Misdirection or a comic twist to the original plot is the third feature of film parody listed by Harries. A useful example is the ironic twist in the clock-face scene in *Matar ou correr*, in which the tension mounts as the arrival of the villain in town approaches (ironically he arrives at two o'clock not noon in Brazil, where punctuality is stereotypically disregarded). The striking of a clock (a rather comic-sounding one at that) is perfectly synchron-ised with the editing of a series of shots, such as of the railroad track on which the villain will arrive and of the tense faces of various characters. Just as in *High Noon* this marked precision editing accentuates the mounting tension.[65] This sequence is interrupted by a shot of the cowardly sheriff praying for help, and culminates with his attempts to postpone his fate by turning back the hands of the wall clock.[66] Misdirection can also take the form of a scene that looks like one from the target film but turns out to be a total fabrication, as is the case in *Nem Sansão, nem Dalila*, when Oscarito's character wakes up to reveal that the film's emulation of the Bibilical epic was nothing more than an extended dream sequence.

Both *Matar ou correr* and *Nem Sansão, nem Dalila* employ the parodic technique of literalisation, such as in the form of verbal or visual puns. The former is set in a frontier town called City Down (inevitably pronounced like the English 'sit down'), and the Afro-Brazilian cowboy is named Ciscocada (a comic play on the Portuguese word 'cocada' or coconut sweets and the Hollywood character the Cisco Kid). Literalisation also embraces self-reflexive elements that expose the constructedness of the parodic film and by extension that of the original, such as the Brazilian Samson's wig (Victor Mature may well have been wearing a wig but of course this was not made explicit).[67] In *Nem Sansão, nem Dalila* Horácio/Sansão arrives on the rural outskirts of Gaza, and thinking that he is still in 1950s Rio de Janeiro he declares that he must be in Jacarepaguá, on the fringes of the city but more tellingly the area used by the Atlântida studio for location shoots such as this one. This in-joke is reinforced when another character agrees with him, upon seeing the city of Gaza in the distance, which is obviously a film set, and thus he endorses this self-reflexive element.

Both of these Brazilian parodies incorporate extraneous material, another typical technique of film parody. In *Nem Sansão, nem Dalila* we see twentieth-century technology in 1153 BC in the form of an oversized, primitive telephone, telegrams written on large tablets of stone and large radio sets. (Exaggeration, such as of the size of objects is the final element of film parody identified by Harries.) Equally incongruous in a Biblical epic are the twentieth-century slang expressions and colloquialisms that Samson uses, much to the con-fusion of the other characters. Elements of realism are typically introduced into film parodies in order to disrupt the syntax, such as in *Nem Sansão, nem Dalila* when a dancing girl provocatively shows off her legs to Oscarito's Sansão and he shies away from her presumably malodorous feet.

Afro-Brazilian identity in the *chanchada*

Any analysis of the representation of Afro-Brazilians and their culture in popular film must naturally engage with the historical specificity of the Brazilian social and racial context. In the wake of the abolition of slavery in 1888 and the establishment of the First Republic (1889–1930), the Brazilian elite promoted the ideology of *branqueamento* or whitening, viewing Afro-Brazilians and their culture as primitive and barbaric. Drawing on wide-spread 'scientific' belief in the superiority of whites, the early Republic assumed that Brazil would gradually 'bleach out' its non-white element via miscegenation. After the First World War, however, a new attitude towards the Afro-Brazilian population emerged, championed by the writer-sociologist, Gilberto Freyre, whose seminal work, *The Masters and the Slaves* (1930) valorised the contribution of African slaves and their descendants to Brazilian social formation. This ideological shift was accompanied by the appropriation and commercialisation by the state of Afro-Brazilian urban culture, such as samba music, carnival groups, and *capoeira* martial arts circles. As Dain Borges writes, 'By making Afro-Brazilian practices more visible, less clandestine, it abated some of their connotations of polluting menace.'[68] The regime of Getúlio Vargas (1930–45), in particular, used Afro-Brazilian music and dance to bolster a new sense of national identity, diluting the symbolic force of black culture, which was increasingly assimilated into mainstream, 'white' society. The black and mixed-race population, however, continued to be discriminated against, marginalised and synonymous with the urban poor.

Robert Stam argues that *chanchadas* shockingly under-represented the black presence, in spite of their usual Rio de Janeiro setting and the Afro-Brazilian origins of the samba rhythm that featured in many of the musical sequences.[69] He compares the attitude of Brazilian filmmakers to that of their Hollywood counterparts, both of whom wanted to draw on black culture without dealing with the people who created it, and he points out the virtual absence of Afro-Brazilian women in major roles. *Chanchadas* tended to feature Afro-Brazilian performers only as bit-part actors or extras, such as the self-effacing office boy who is patronised by his white colleagues in the civil service in *O homem do sputnik*, and the two attractive mixed-race young women who study at the college in *Esse milhão é meu*. The notable exception that proved the rule was Grande Otelo, who usually starred as part of a double act, firstly with Oscarito and later with Ankito, and played the archetypal jovial, child-like black.

Although people of colour appear as musicians or dancers in the background of countless *chanchadas*, Stam argues that they are there to support the white stars and 'to visually "set off" the beauty and elegance of the white elite'.[70] The leading lady of Atlântida's musical comedies was more often than not the pale-skinned Eliana Macedo, described by Stam as 'Debbie Reynolds-like'.[71] Her casting is often ludicrous, such as in *Samba em Brasília*, where she plays a humble shantytown dweller well versed in *macumba*, who claims that she is a qualified *filha de santo* or priestess of this Afro-Brazilian religious practice. Macedo, whose 'star text' was established via her numerous appearances in leading roles on screen, where she often appeared in close-up, and in film magazines, served to establish a standard of attractiveness clearly based on Hollywood lines.

Stam also comments on the stage names of the few black actors who did appear in Brazilian films in the 1940s and 1950s, such as Chocolate, Blecaute (Blackout, who starred in *Carnaval Atlântida* and *Malandros em Quarta Dimensão* of 1954), Príncipe Pretinho (Little Black Prince) and Grande Otelo (Big Othello) himself, which call attention to their blackness and are 'evidence perhaps of a relatively unembarrassed color-consciousness or perhaps of objectification: they could not simply be seen as actors but rather only as *black* actors'.[72] The *chanchadas* of the 1950s give ample evidence of a tendency to caricature black identity. In *Aviso aos navegantes*, a Spanish-American woman refers to Grande Otelo's character as a 'negrito' (little black). Similarly, in *Vai, que é mole*, Grande Otelo's character is ironically named Brancura (whiteness). Brancura refers to his Afro-Brazilian girlfriend as a 'mulata sestrosa' (devious mulatto girl), reiterating a well-worn racial stereotype, discussed in more detail below, and she, in turn, describes him as 'pequenino, feio, preto, mas honesto' (little, ugly, black, but honest).

The *chanchada* largely overlooks the issue of racial inequality, save a few explicit token references, mentioned below, despite the fact that Afro-Brazilian music underpins the tradition. Instead these films focus on social inequalities based on class via the veneration of the ethos of *malandragem*. As Dyer argues, by implicitly addressing certain needs and inadequacies in society, entertainment effectively denies the legitimacy of others.[73] The subversion of racial stereotypes, as well as gender bending, did, however, form an important part of the carnivalesque inversions of the *chanchada*. In *A dupla do barulho*, for example, Grande Otelo whitens his face and dons a blonde wig to appear on a music hall stage as an ice skater (a parodic reference to the Norwegian figure skater and Hollywood star Sonja Henie). Although this film was partially based on the life stories of Oscarito and Grande Otelo, and focused on the prominence given to the former at the expense of the latter, the Afro-Brazilian protagonist tellingly becomes an alcoholic and falls from grace. For the most part the *chanchada* endorsed society's racist attitudes, sometimes by a throwaway comment in the script, but more obviously via the exclusion of Afro-Brazilian performers in lead roles. In *Quem roubou meu samba?* even a character with the racially inspired nick-name Blequinho (Little Black), who directs a samba school, is noticeably white-skinned. Typically of the *chanchada* tradition, Afro-Brazilian actors, particularly women, are conspicuous by their absence in this film, with the exception of the male lead role, which is all the more striking in a musical that is partially set in a shantytown.

Shantytown settings

Although most *chanchadas* were set in Rio de Janeiro, where the main producer, Atlântida was located, the shantytown or *favela*, where the majority of the Afro-Brazilian population of the then capital city resided, was rarely represented on screen. These films tended to be set in the up-market, affluent, beachfront districts of the city, particularly Copacabana. One exception to this rule was *Samba em Brasília*, in which the protagonist Teresinha, played by Eliana, lives in an idealised *morro*, where both black and white inhabitants live in harmony, and where there is a palpable sense of community spirit and an omnipresent diegetic *batucada*. When looking down on the affluent city below, one of the white residents of the shantytown articulates the superiority of the latter over the former, to an extra-diegetic musical backdrop of romantic strings: 'Aqui, Teresinha, nós estamos no alto. Olhe a cidade lá em baixo. Daqui em cima ela parece bonita. Mas lá em baixo, no meio daquela gente toda, dos edifícios, da fumaceira dos carros, no meio daquela gente falsa que pensa que com o dinheiro pode-se comprar tudo . . . A gente sente que a vida aqui no morro é muito melhor. Todo mundo se conhece. Todos se gostam.' (Here, Teresinha, we're on top of the world. Look at the city down there. From up here it looks pretty, but down there, in among all those people, those buildings, exhaust smoke, in the midst of all those false people who think you can buy anything with money . . . We know that life up here on the hill is much better. Everybody knows one another. Everyone likes each other.) A similar sense of community and solidarity exists in the shantytown where the taxi driver Zé resides in *Rico ri à toa*, and to where he longs to return after moving to the swanky district of Ipanema.

In the film *Treze cadeiras* the white comic anti-hero, played by Oscarito, finds himself in the shantytown of Salgueiro, real-life home of a famous samba school. The music in the following scene contrasts sharply with the typically stylised samba of the *chanchada* – it is the percussion-based, non-commercial *batucada* or *samba de morro* (literally, samba from the hillside), i.e. Afro-Brazilian samba that we hear in this scene. The unusual camera angles – detail shots of black hands beating rhythm on tambourines and small drums, and of feet in white shoes and trousers (the garb of the archetypal *malandro*) dancing samba – point to a fetishisation of the black body, more specifically of the clichéd idea of the innate musicality and rhythm of Afro-Brazilians.[74] It is no coincidence that the white clown played by Oscarito cannot dance. As an Afro-Brazilian asks him 'Que é que meu branco vem fazer aqui no morro?' (What are you doing here in the shantytown, white boy?) This sequence reveals the distance between the 'white' diegetic world of the *chanchada* and the predominantly Afro-Brazilian shantytown.

Another illustration of the exoticisation of black Brazil can be found in *O camelô da Rua Larga*, where one of the musical interludes in a nightclub centres on a white singer, dressed as a *baiana*, surrounded by a host of Afro-Brazilian *baianas* and musicians dressed as *malandros*. The frenzied, beguiling performance of the Afro-Brazilians on stage is drawn in stark contrast to the staid, sophisticated white screen audience. The black performers are as 'exotic' and alien to the screen spectators as the flamenco dancer, US cowgirl and belly dancer who feature earlier in this cabaret medley. Similarly, in *Rico ri à toa*, the shantytown is transformed into a stage set in an upscale nightclub, and although the backing singers and dancers are Afro-Brazilian, the lead singer is a fair-skinned beauty, who performs the song 'É samba' (It's Samba).

Afro-Brazilian culture

Afro-Brazilian religious practices are seen as fair game for farcical visual humour in popular films, such as in *Samba em Brasília*, when the pretentious socialite, Eugênia, played by Heloísa Helena, turns to *macumba* to help her get on to a 'best dressed' list in a society column. She is instructed by her very white-skinned maid (played by the archetypal girl-next-door, Eliana), a highly unlikely candidate to be well versed in this religious tradition and the more sinister practice of *quimbanda* or black magic. Eugênia comically performs a *despacho* or spell, which involves her smoking both cigars and a pipe, and drinking the cheap alcoholic beverage *cachaça*, much to her distaste. The kitchen staff join in the antics, and even the North Eastern cook, played by Nancy Wanderley, claims to be possessed by a *caboclo* or spirit.

Despite often forming part of the diegetic soundtrack of the *chanchada*, the lowly Afro-Brazilian origins of samba mean that it is scorned by the white elite characters in these films. In *Rico ri à toa*, for example, an aspiring social climber declares 'Nesta casa não quero saber de samba' (In this house I don't want to hear of samba). When the local samba school mistakenly arrives at her elegant mansion to rehearse, her high-society female guests are horrified by the music being played by the group and scold their husbands for dancing to it. A marked contrast is drawn between the 'respectable' elegiac ballad performed by the hostess and the irreverent music of carnival chaos, performed by black men who make the white ladies scream with fright.

The appearance of black faces on screen, albeit in peripheral roles for the most part, did, however, mirror the composition of popular audiences. In spite of the pigeon holing and latent racism of the depiction of black and mixed-race Brazilians in the *chanchada*, their mere inclusion in film, unheard of prior to the advent of sound when cinema had remained an elitist form, reflected the demographic focus of the medium by the 1950s. The representation of elements of Afro-Brazilian popular culture, however stylised and clichéd, also illustrated an attempt on the part of filmmakers to engage with their ethnically mixed, lower-class audiences.

The figures of the *mulata* and the *baiana*

A consideration of the ways in which Afro-Brazilian identity is represented in popular film from this era must inevitably focus on the gendered figures of the mixed-race *mulata* and the *baiana*. The *chanchada* rehashed the stereotype of the brazen, overtly sexual and gossipy young woman of mixed race, but she only ever appeared in bit parts and was never central to the plot. This clichéd representation of the Afro-Brazilian woman borrowed heavily from the '*mulata* temptress' myth as identified by Raymond Sayers in Brazilian narrative of the nineteenth century.[75] The lascivious *mulata* or *malandra* was an equally recurrent motif in the lyrics of popular song from the early twentieth century. The carnival hit of 1924, 'O casaco da mulata é de prestação' (The *Mulata*'s Coat was Bought on Tick), by Careca (Luiz Nunes Sampaio), for example, began: 'Ó mulata tão faceira / Não faz nada o dia inteiro / Passeia todos os dias / Com casado ou solteiro' (Oh *mulata* so devious / You do nothing all day / Every day you just hang around / With married or single guys).[76] The *mulata* has also been portrayed as a symbol of the Brazilian nation, an embodiment of the country's racially diverse population and history of miscegenation. The samba 'Leite com café' (Milk with Coffee), written by Noel Rosa and Hervé Cordovil in 1935, for example, begins: 'A morena lá do morro/ Cheia de beleza e graça/ Simboliza a nossa grande raça/ É cor de leite com café' (The dark girl from up there in the shantytown/ Full of beauty and charm/ Symbolises our great race/ She's the colour of milk with coffee). Given its close links with popular carnival music, it is not surprising that the *chanchada* reiterated the stock elements of this racial archetype.

In the film *Garotas e samba* a sassy, worldly-wise maid proudly shares her knowledge of men, much to the shock of her employer, the prudish owner of the aptly named Pensão Inocência (Innocence Guest House), played by the very white-skinned Zezé Macedo. Similarly, in *De vento em popa*, another sultry dark-skinned maid dances suggestively to the 'Latin' rhythms that she hears on the radio and shakes her posterior erotically (much to the delight of the character played by Oscarito). This mixed-race extra contrasts sharply with the prim, white, upper-class protagonist, in her thick-rimmed spectacles and frumpy dress. In another scene from *De vento em popa*, the white-skinned Sônia Mamede in blackface adopts the *mulata* persona in her rendition of the song 'Tem que rebolar' (You've Got to Wiggle). In *Samba em Brasília* a direct opposition is drawn between the good-natured, white-skinned Teresinha, played by Eliana, and an envious *mulata* named Ivete, played by little-known Carmen Montel, both of whom are competing for the key role of *porta-bandeira* or flag-bearer for their samba school. Not only does Ivete physically push Teresinha about, but she also proves to be treacherous, leaving her community in the lurch to go off to join another samba school at the last minute. In a rather tasteless carnivalesque inversion of the racist norms of society, this *mulata* says that a white girl should not fulfil the role of flag-bearer in the procession, thus incurring the wrath of her very dark-skinned mother, who exclaims: 'Nós não temos preconceito de cor' (We're not prejudiced about colour).

The most blatant indication of the structuring absence of the Afro-Brazilian woman in these popular films from the 1950s is the ubiquitous presence of the white-skinned *baiana*, who appears in countless musical numbers within the *chanchada*, maintaining a tradition established by the *teatro de revista*.[77] The origins of this costume lie with the Afro-Brazilian female street vendors of Salvador da Bahia and the priestesses of the religious practice of *candomblé*. It became a popular costume in carnival in the 1920s and 1930s, among both men and women, and in the late 1930s and 1940s the costume was appropriated by Carmen Miranda.[78] It was while wearing this *baiana* costume that Miranda was 'discovered' performing at the Urca casino by the US show-business impresario Lee Schubert in 1939. It was also the 'look' that became synonymous with the 'Brazilian Bombshell', as Carmen came to be known, on Broadway and later in Hollywood. In the context of the 'Good Neighbour Policy' towards the Latin American continent, Carmen starred in a host of Hollywood musicals in which she always wore a stylised *baiana* costume with its trademark fruit-laden turbans, frills, bracelets and earrings. Miranda's adaptation of the *baiana* personified not only Brazil but Latin America as a whole in Hollywood's eyes.[79] These images were projected back south of the border, and in Brazil Miranda's Hollywood style radically affected the way Brazilians visualised their own identity. Although the *baiana* persona was taken to the United States by Carmen Miranda in 1939, it was the exaggerated Broadway/Hollywood version of the outfit which reappeared in Brazil. The creations by Travis Banton worn by Carmen in *That Night in Rio* (1941), for example, made such an impact in the Brazilian press that organisers of the Rio carnival celebrations requested replicas from the Twentieth Century-Fox wardrobe department, that were used as the inspiration for the parade costumes in 1941.

4   Eliana Macedo (right, in a stylised *baiana* costume) and Grande Otelo in the *chanchada*, *Carnaval Atlântida* (1952).

In *Carnaval Atlântida* the ambivalent relationship between the *chanchada* and Afro-Brazilian identity, as well as the tradition's complex relationship with Hollywood, is underlined in the second musical number, which clearly borrows its *baiana*, played by the white Eliana Macedo, from Carmen Miranda's performances in the USA (see figure 4). Looking to Hollywood for emblematic motifs of national self-definition, the *chanchadas* re-worked the *baiana* persona, and just as Miranda had done in Hollywood, they whitened her skin. In Hollywood, her *baiana* persona was synonymous with tropical excess, fertility and the exotic, and the impact of her costume was heightened by glorious Technicolor. Back in Brazil, however, the Miranda clones in the low-budget, black and white *chanchadas* of the 1950s are decidedly lack-lustre. The *baiana* costume is pared down to its bare essentials and is a pale imitation of its Hollywood template. The celluloid white *baianas* of the *chanchada* sometimes attempt to reproduce Miranda's characteristic dance moves but they lack her vitality and exuberance. Most importantly, they are primarily dancers and often do not sing or communicate with the screen audience verbally at all (whereas Miranda's singing style, her vocal acrobatics and her exaggerated 'Latino' accent were her forte, and she could barely move in her platform shoes). The wannabes of the *chanchada* are a ghostly echo of the Hollywood star. Shari Roberts identifies the key elements of Miranda's 'star text' as follows. 'These elements centered on her look, especially her bright, multi-textured outfits, and on her voice – that is, her singing voice as pure sound as opposed to any message she communicated.'[80] These elements are totally lacking in the one-dimensional, monochrome *baianas* of the *chanchada*, who feature solely in the musical numbers, which acted as arti-ficial interruptions to the narrative proper. Thus, the *baianas* that appear on screen in Brazilian films from the 1950s are marked as synthetic constructs, totally separated from the 'reality' of the story line, and can therefore be interpreted as an ironic comment on Hollywood's falsification and homogen-isation of 'Latin' identity.

The *chanchadas* may use Miranda's star text to poke fun at the Hollywood clichés but the Carmen clones are not obviously parodic or self-deprecating. For this reason these recurrent images were scorned by Brazilian critics, for appearing to be simply mimetic. As Regina Paranhos Pereira writes, 'in films from the 1950s, for example, even the "baianas" and the "malandros" and their dance routines were slavishly copied from the worst foreign films.'[81]

In order to shed light on the cultural meaning of the white *baiana* figure in the *chanchada* Néstor García Canclini's work on intercultural hybridisation is particularly useful.[82] Although his work is based on contemporary Latin America, he admits that 'Hybridity has a long trajectory in Latin America.'[83] The *chanchada* is clearly an example of what Canclini calls a 'hybrid genre' in that it is a composite of Brazilian and US cultural traditions, and more

importantly is not simply an example of cultural imitation that can be attrib-
uted to dependency on the First-World, Hollywood model. Canclini argues
that hybridity is the ongoing condition of all cultures, which are involved in
continuous processes of 'transculturation'. The *chanchada* can be viewed as a
'transcultural medium', involved in a two-way movement of borrowing and
lending between Hollywood and the Brazilian film industry. In this respect,
the *chanchada* is an example of what Canclini calls 'impure genres' that have
expanded in Latin America upon contact with modernity (i.e. Hollywood).
The *baiana* clones of the *chanchadas* are the product of a multi-directional
cultural migration. To use Canclini's terms, the *baiana* persona was
'deterritorialised' upon her arrival in Hollywood with Carmen Miranda.
Canclini describes this process as 'the loss of the "natural" relation of culture
to geographical and social territories'.[84] Projected back to Brazil in Hollywood
movies, and subsequently re-appropriated by the *chanchadas* of the 1950s,
the white-skinned *baiana* is 'reterritorialised', in a process of 'certain relative,
partial territorial relocalizations of old and new symbolic productions.'[85] The
baiana that appears on screen in these Brazilian films in the 1950s has new
symbolic meaning. She is no longer merely a racial hybrid, who symbolises
Brazil's colonial past and imagined racial democracy, or just a stereotypical
embodiment of sexual licence. She is also an intercultural hybrid, whose
historical identity and memory in the Brazilian context are superseded by
the figure's re-working in Hollywood.

Innovation in the *chanchada*

According to Paulo Emílio Salles Gomes, the undeniable contribution made
by the high-brow, São Paulo-based Vera Cruz studio to raising the technical
and artistic standard of Brazilian cinema in the late 1940s and 1950s was to
prove a stimulus for the film industry in Rio and led to a certain renovation
of the *chanchada*, notably in Moacir Fenelon and Alinor Azevedo's *Tudo azul*
(All Blue, 1951).[86] This tale of a bored civil servant who dreams of becoming
a composer integrated its song and dance numbers via the device of the
Hollywood-inspired dream sequence, and incorporated shots of Rio's hillside
shantytowns, harking back to the realism of Humberto Mauro's acclaimed
Favela dos meus amores (Shantytown of My Loves, 1934).[87] Other films sought
to combine drama and comedy in authentic chronicles of daily life in the
city, such as *Agulha no palheiro* (Needle in the Haystack, 1953), the first
film made by the journalist and cinema critic, Alex Viany, and *Amei um
bicheiro* (I Loved a Crook, 1952), directed by the novice Jorge Ileli and
Paulo Wanderley. The following subsection will consider some of the more
successful attempts made in the 1950s to introduce innovations into the
chanchada tradition.

Intertextuality and citation

Watson Macedo's *A grande vedete* (1958) can be deemed to have pushed the frontiers of the *chanchada* in a new direction by taking its lead from Billy Wilder's 1950 film-noir classic, *Sunset Boulevard*. It centres on a reluctantly ageing vaudeville star, Jeanette, played by Dercy Gonçalves, who lives in the past and spends her time gazing at photographs of herself in her prime. It also stars Catalano as her loyal assistant, Ambrósio, who like Max Von Mayerling in the Hollywood movie, perpetuates her delusions by sending her flowers from fictitious fans. Like Norma Desmond in Wilder's film, Jeanette falls for the charms of a young writer, in this case the aspiring creator of theatre revues, Paulo, on whom she lavishes attention and gifts, exclaiming 'eu me sinto tão jovem' (I feel so young). Macedo combines his reworking of *Sunset Boulevard* with many of the stock conventions of the *chanchada*, such as musical and dance interludes and slapstick comedy, but it is undeniably an attempt to instil a more sophisticated, dramatic dimension in the tradition.

Cinedistri's *Quem roubou meu samba?* (Who Stole My Samba?, 1958), directed by José Carlos Burle, takes its cue not from a Hollywood film but from a national film drama, namely Nelson Pereira dos Santos's social-realist classic *Rio, Zona Norte* (Rio, North Zone, 1957). *Rio, Zona Norte* and *Quem roubou meu samba?* share the following characteristics: a black protagonist (unusual in the *chanchada*, with the notable exception of the roles played by Grande Otelo, who stars in *Rio, Zona Norte* but not in *Quem roubou meu samba?*, in which the lead role of Atanásio is played by Chuvisco); a plot that hinges on the practice of *falsa parceria* or fake songwriting partnerships within the realm of the popular music industry; the 'theft' of songs written by an illiterate, black *sambista* (samba performer and/or composer) from a shantytown, by two unscrupulous and exploitative white, middle-class men who work in the music business; scenes of auditions or rehearsals in recording studios; an attempt to deal with the issue of racism, although with strikingly contrasting levels of subtlety; parallel scenes, such as meetings between the *sambista* and record company representatives in a bar and scenes in a hospital; performances by the famous radio singer Ângela Maria; a shantytown setting (unusual for a *chanchada*); chase sequences through a *favela*; finally, and perhaps most strikingly, a black protagonist who suffers a head injury and appears in the final scenes with a bandaged head.

As one would expect, this *chanchada* trivialises some of the basic issues dealt with in *Rio, Zona Norte*: first, the head injury suffered by the protagonist (in *Quem roubou meu samba?* Atanásio is struck over the head by one of the record company scouts, which results in partial amnesia – he forgets all his songs, whereas in *Rio, Zona Norte* Espírito's injury proves fatal); second, the theft of the songs (in the *chanchada* this is a source of comedy – the clownish villain has to keep whistling Atanásio's song in order to remember it, since his attempts to record it were foiled); third, the hospital scenes, which are an excuse for slapstick comedy in the *Chanchada*; fourth, the chase scene, which is played for laughs, whereas in *Rio, Zona Norte* it results in tragedy. In *Quem roubou meu samba?* the fictional shantytown where the protagonist lives is a stage set and is called the Morro da Navalhada (Stabwound Hill), a rather offensive name that draws on clichéd associations between the largely Afro-Brazilian populations of such areas and violent crime. In sharp contrast to its name, however, the *morro* that the film depicts is highly ideal-ised and romanticised. The final scene is typical of the *chanchada* tradition – a celebration in carnival mood, where all is forgiven, tensions are smoothed over, and characters previously at odds form romantic couples. This totally undercuts any attempt to deal with social or racial issues, however light-heartedly, in the film. Everyone, including the nurses and doctors in the hospital, joins in the performance of Atanásio's samba, which he can now remember, and the rival record company bosses are still fighting over who owns the samba, their exploitation remaining unpunished.

Quem roubou meu samba? is not a conventional parody since it uses a recently released Brazilian film but does not seek to trade on its success at the box-office. In fact, having narrowly avoided not being distributed at all, *Rio, Zona Norte* proved to be a commercial failure, not managing to recover the two million *cruzeiros* invested in its production. It is also hard to imagine that the typical *chanchada* audience would have seen *Rio, Zona Norte*, and even if they had, the comic replica makes no attempt to mimic the former's title or to promote itself as a parodic re-working. This comedy simply borrows from the plot of dos Santos's classic but rather tastelessly trivialises the story for popular audiences. It is indicative of the efforts made to invest the *chanchada* tradition with more heavyweight concerns as the 1950s wore on and as the threat posed by television grew ever greater.

Popular film endeavoured to embrace its nascent competitor by giving television sets prominence as both an emblem of modernity and a means through which to integrate musical and dance numbers. Perhaps the best example of this is *Absolutamente certo!*, which centres on a television quiz show, based on the real-life programme 'O céu é o limite' (The Sky's the Limit) broadcast on TV Tupi. Directed by a former star of the Atlântida studio, Anselmo Duarte, this innovative film has been said to combine elements of the *chanchada* tradition and the neo-realist comedies of the Vera Cruz studio.[88] It brings together humour, a popular tale of daily life, and technical sophistication. Similarly, the camera in Cinedistri's *Samba em Brasília* takes the spectator through a television screen as a pretext for a musical/dance interlude.[89] Other more inventive *chanchadas* employed the television set as a device in the plot, such as those produced by Herbert Richers, which were filmed in the studios of TV Rio. In *Vai, que é mole* (Go On, It's Easy), directed by J. B. Tanko and produced by Herbert Richers in 1960, rehearsals for a TV show provide a suitable pretext for the inclusion of jiving routines and two rock-and-roll numbers, one performed by Ankito and the other by an Elvis Presley wannabe. Maristela's *Carnaval em lá maior* (Carnival in A-Major, 1955) drew on the collaboration of the TV Record station, and featured the latter's resident singers.[90]

Concluding remarks

Perhaps the most important contribution of the *chanchadas* of the 1950s was to render visible a social class within Brazil's socio-cultural landscape, and to champion the underdog, who succeeds in triumphing, through *malandragem*, over more powerful opponents, not least officials of the state, high society and even the representatives of foreign nations. Paulo Emílio Salles Gomes, who was instrumental in bringing about a re-evaluation of the cultural legacy of the *chanchada*, has convincingly argued that the mass enthusiasm for the marginalised characters of these films suggested a challenge on the part of the colonised against the coloniser. He writes:

> The young, popular audience that guaranteed the success of these films found in them re-elaborated and rejuvenated models that, although not without links to broad Western traditions, also emanated directly from a tenacious Brazilian heritage. To these relatively stable values, the films added ephemeral *carioca* features in the form of anecdotes and speech mannerisms, thought and behavior, a continuous flow that the *chanchada* crystallized even more effectively than caricature or variety theater.[91]

As João Luiz Vieira argues, 'It is as if Brazil, facing the traumatic double process of industrialization and urbanization, took advantage of the film medium to express a kind of elegiac regret for the imminent disappearance of the country's immediate, more rural, past.'[92] The stock types of the *chanchada*, he argues, are passive objects of destiny rather than active members of a self-aware working class, and are thus indicative of populist periods of the 1940s and 1950s.[93] The knowledge that the laughter provoked by Oscarito's antics was shared by audiences across the country also helped Brazilians to imagine a national community in the 1950s.

The decline in the popularity of the *chanchada* went hand in hand with the expansion of television, which became increasingly accessible as the 1950s drew to a close. The reception of the *chanchada* by the critics, who failed to appreciate the tradition's subversive carnivalesque dimension, also hastened its disappearance, as João Luiz Vieira argues: 'Mainstream journalistic criticism . . . became increasingly harsh towards the genre as the decade drew to a close. A more nationalistic ideology, extremely preoccupied with the country's internal and external image, could not tolerate its embarrassingly shoddy production values.'[94] Chapter 5 will consider how popular cinema survived in Brazil in the context of both the demise of the *chanchada* and the backlash against it from the art-house *cinema novo* movement of the 1960s.

Notes

1 Thomas E. Skidmore, *Politics in Brazil, 1930–1964: An Experiment in Democracy* (London and New York: Oxford University Press, 1967), p. 164.

2 Mário Audrá Jr, *Cinematográfica Maristela: Memórias de um Produtor* (São Paulo: Silver Hawk, 1997), p. 90.

3 *Ibid.*, pp. 132–3 (our translation).

4 Rosângela de Oliveira Dias, *O mundo como chanchada: cinema e imaginário das classes populares na década de 50* (Rio de Janeiro: Relume-Dumará, 1993), p. 34. Also quoted by Sérgio Augusto, *Este mundo é um pandeiro: a chanchada de Getúlio a JK* (São Paulo: Companhia das Letras, 1993), p. 138.

5 Quoted in Dias, *O mundo como chanchada*, p. 69 (our translation).

6 In 1950 28 per cent of adults over the age of twenty were illiterate in urban and suburban areas, and the figure rose to almost 68 per cent in the countryside. *Ibid.*, p. 35.

7 Richard Dyer, 'Entertainment and utopia', in Simon During (ed.), *The Cultural Studies Reader* (London and New York: Routledge, 1993), p. 273. Dyer argues that entertainment responds to real needs created by society, and that a sensibility of what utopia would feel like is achieved in the Hollywood musical by both overt representational signs, such as characterisation and plot, and, more importantly, non-representational signs, such as melody, rhythm and camera work. In the *chanchada* a utopian view of how society could be organised is most obviously conveyed via the motif of inversion within the plot, although the contradictions between the narrative and the musical numbers, the former predominantly representational and the latter predominantly non-representational, can often be seen to express an idealistic vision of Brazil's relationship with Hollywood and by extension the First World.

8 Similarly, in the *chanchada Um candango na Belacap* (A Migrant Worker in Rio, 1961) a woman feigns pregnancy to seek help in leaving Brazil's new capital to return to Rio de Janeiro.

9 Dyer argues that the ideals of entertainment, and more specifically of the Hollywood musical, imply wants that capitalism itself promises to meet. Dyer, 'Entertainment and utopia', p. 278. Elsewhere, Dyer studies the promotion of Hollywood stars as 'idols of consumption', who underpin the economic ideologies of their society. Richard Dyer, *Stars* (London: BFI Publishing, 1999), p. 42. In contrast, the *chanchada* mocked Hollywood's implicit ideological stance by the overt exaggeration of consumerism and material gain.

10 This film was released in April 1954, and Vargas committed suicide in August of that year.

11 Watson Macedo's *chanchada O petróleo é nosso* (The Oil is Ours, 1954) irreverently took its title from Vargas's nationalistic slogan employed to galvanise

opposition to the *entreguistas* or sell-outs, who supported the expansion of the operations of Standard Oil and Shell within Brazil.

12 Produced by the high-brow, São Paulo-based Vera Cruz studio, this comedy film incorporates many of the stock elements of the *chanchada*, such as musical interludes, acrobatic sequences and the theme of the hillbilly in the big city, combining them with aspects of melodrama. São Paulo's Maristela studios also adopted the *chanchada* formula in 1955, in *Carnaval em lá maior* (Carnival in A-Major), directed by Adhemar Gonzaga, featuring Renata Fronzi (the star of several Atlântida *chanchadas*) and Genésio Arruda (one of the stars of *O babão* (The Idiot) of 1931, see Chapter 1), playing a character called simply *caipira*. Maristela and TV Record collaborated on *Carnaval em lá maior*, clearly designed to follow in the *chanchada*'s footsteps, as reflected in the contract, which stipulated that it be ready to premiere in the run-up to carnival in order to promote the carnival songs that featured in it. The film starred many of the big names of the popular music scene of the 1940s and 1950s, such as the samba composer Ataúlfo Alves and the singer Araci de Almeida.

13 Augusto, *Este mundo é um pandeiro*, p. 170.

14 English words and imported brand names continue to be used in everyday language in Brazil as signs of modernity. In the context of 1950s Brazil, these comic swipes at the affected bourgeoisie from the perspective of the uprooted and disadvantaged masses are suggestive of the incomplete and ambiguous nature of the nation's encounter with modernity, which results in a particular type of alienation. See José de Souza Martins, 'The hesitations of the modern and the contradictions of modernity in Brazil', in Vivian Schelling (ed.), *Through the Kaleidoscope: The Experience of Modernity in Latin America* (London and New York: Verso, 2000).

15 There is a long-standing tradition of making fun of the names of famous stars in Hollywood film parodies. In 1922, for example, Stan Laurel starred as Rhubarb Vaselino in *Mud and Sand*, a spoof of Rudolph Valentino's *Blood and Sand* of the same year.

    Further echoing the theme of the superiority of the imported over the home-grown, in *A grande vedete* (The Great Star, 1958) Ambrósio promises Jeanette that her next show will have the finest set designs. At first he says that he will commission the famous Brazilian painter Portinari, but then goes one better and promises her the world-renowned Spaniard, Picasso.

16 It is significant that shortly after taking office in Cuba, Fidel Castro was invited to pay an official visit to Brazil.

17 His first name, common among the masses, also harks back to the eponymous protagonist of the silent precursor to the *chanchada*, *Nhô Anastácio chegou de viagem* (Mr Anastácio Arrived from a Trip, 1908).

    Oscarito's Mexican counterpart, Cantinflas, starred in a spoof of a Cold War thriller, *El señor fotógrafo* (The Photographer, 1952), in which he mistakenly kicks a dreaded Z-Bomb, thinking that it is a ball.

18 Blecaute's recording of 'Dona Cegonha' (Mrs Stork, Continental 16669) was one of the hit songs of the 1953 carnival in Rio. Written by Armando Cavalcanti and Klecius Caldas, the song deals with a well-worn theme, namely that of the decline in the birth rate: 'Ai! ai! ai! dona Cegonha / Saiu risonha / Pra trabalhar / Voltou

danada / Encabulada / Com a cegonha ninguém quer nada! (Ai! ai! ai!) Ela trabalhava noite e dia / Não encalhava mercadoria / Mas a carestia está medonha / Ninguém quer nada com a cegonha!' (Oh! oh! oh! Mrs Stork / She went out smiling / To work / She came back mad / Embarrassed / No one wants anything to do with Mrs Stork! (Oh! oh! oh!) She worked day and night / She doesn't let her goods pile up / But the prices are terribly high / No one wants anything to do with Mrs Stork!).

19 João Luiz Vieira, 'Hegemony and Resistance: Parody and Carnival in Brazilian Cinema', PhD dissertation, New York University, 1984.

20 *Conjuntura Econômica*, December 1955, p. 77. Quoted in Dias, *O mundo como chanchada*, p. 94.

21 Brazil's star system borrowed heavily from Hollywood's version, which relied on a 'success myth' based on several contradictory elements. Richard Dyer describes these as follows: 'that ordinariness is the hallmark of the star; that the system rewards talent and "specialness"; that luck, "breaks", which may happen to anyone typify the career of the star; and that hard work and professionalism are necessary for stardom'. Dyer, *Stars*, p. 42. While stardom holds all four things to be true, certain stars may exhibit only certain aspects. The stars of the *chanchada* were depicted as from non-privileged backgrounds, on the whole, having worked their way in to show business the hard way. An exception was the leading lady, Eliana Macedo, the niece of the Atlântida and subsequently independent director, Watson Macedo, whose 'star text' relied on her 'Hollywood' quality, but nonetheless emphasised her homeliness and sweet nature.

22 In 1938, in the *sertão* or arid hinterland of the state of Sergipe, the police ambushed and killed the bandit Lampião and his band of followers. Lampião's head, and that of his lover Maria Bonita, were displayed in an anthropological museum in Salvador da Bahia. *Maria Bonita* was the title of a theatrical revue staged in 1939.

23 In the late 1940s the *baião*, a new rhythm from the North East, was beginning to encroach on samba's popularity, and as Bryan McCann says, 'Rio seemed to be losing its stranglehold on the nation's musical attention.' Bryan McCann, 'The invention of tradition on Brazilian radio', in Robert M. Levine and John J. Crocitti (eds), *The Brazil Reader: History, Culture, Politics* (London: Latin America Bureau, 1999), p. 475. This new musical trend was picked up on in the *chanchadas* of the era. Luiz Gonzaga, an accordionist and singer from the state of Pernambuco in Brazil's North East recorded a song entitled 'Baião' in 1946, and the new genre was born. Gonzaga, who remains the figure most closely associated with this musical style, appeared in the 1948 *chanchada E o mundo se diverte* (And the World Has Fun), alongside Adelaide Chiozzo and the *caipira* country music duo Alvarenga e Ranchinho. *Vai, que é mole* (Go On, It's Easy, 1960) features a Luiz Gonzaga sound-alike, who sings in the *baião* style to an extra-diegetic accordion accompaniment and performs a comic dance. Furthermore, accordion music accompanies the opening titles of *Sai da frente* (Get Out of My Way, 1952), starring Mazzaropi.

24 In *Rico ri à toa* Zé Trindade's everyman character, Zé, is equally uncomfortable in a bank manager's office, where his overbearing wife chides him: 'Deixa de ser

ignorante, Zé' (Stop being so ignorant, Joe), no doubt reassuring cinema-goers about their own sense of unease in such settings. Zé is also unsure of the dress code for society functions, and dons a flat cap with his tuxedo.

25 The tower of Central Station, illuminated at night, appears in a stage set in *A grande vedete*, providing audiences with a familiar point of reference and reinforcing their sense of belonging.

26 Alan Dale, *Slapstick in American Movies* (Minneapolis and London: University of Minnesota Press, 2000), p. 14.

27 Dias, *O mundo como chanchada*, pp. 81–2.
    In 1939 the State held the so-called 'Semana de Trânsito' (Traffic Week) in Rio de Janeiro to train both drivers and pedestrians how to negotiate the city's streets.

28 There are notable similarities with Ari Barroso's well-known eulogistic samba classic, 'Aquarela do Brasil' (Watercolour of Brazil, 1939), which begins 'Brasil/ Meu Brasil brasileiro' (Brazil/ My Brazilian Brazil).

29 Similarly, Vera Cruz's *Sai da frente* begins with Mazzaropi's hillbilly character arriving in São Paulo in a clapped-out truck laden with rustic furniture and a barking dog, in sharp contrast to the city's palm tree-lined avenues and skyscrapers.

30 Dias, *O mundo como chanchada*, pp. 72–3.

31 Gastão Cruls refers to the 'Old Tunnel' linking Copacabana to down-town Rio, built in 1892, and the 'New Tunnel', built in 1904, which cut through the Morro da Babilônia hill, and which was augmented by a sister tunnel just before his book was published in 1949. Gastão Cruls, *Aparência do Rio de Janeiro* (Rio de Janeiro: José Olympio, 1949), p. 434.

32 Similarly, the lyrics of a musical number in *Metido a bacana* refer to the plans to build Brasília ('Dizem em voz corrente que em Goiás será a nova capital' – Everyone is saying that the new capital will be in Goiás state). *Pistoleiro bossa nova* merely takes its title from the latest musical trend to hit Brazil in the late 1950s (bossa nova – literally, new fashion), in a superficial nod to the zeitgeist. In the same vein, one of the villains of *Vai, que é mole* just so happens to declare: 'Vamos acabar com essa bossa nova de ladrões honestos!' (We're going to do away with this new fashion for honest thieves). The label became synonymous with the nation's modernity, with Kubitschek being referred to as the 'bossa nova president' and the cars that rolled off Brazilian production lines being called 'bossa nova cars'.

33 The nationality of this character is no coincidence, as discussed later in this chapter.

34 Similarly, in Charlie Chaplin's *Modern Times* (1936) the size of the machinery in the factories is dramatically exaggerated, such as the dynamos that tower above the workers, forming part of the comic critique of modernity and industrialisation. As in the *chanchada* tradition, this comedy film is premised on temporary social inversion, and unethical behaviour is routinely rewarded, in a direct challenge to the prevailing work ethic. See Mark Winokur, *American Laughter: Immigrants, Ethnicity and 1930s Hollywood Film Comedy* (New York: St Martin's Press, 1996).

35 The *pensão* or boarding house is a home-from-home in a menacing urban landscape, and an important site of transition in the *chanchada*. It acts as a safe house for naive girls who have just arrived in the city. In *Garotas e samba* the boarding

house even displays a sign saying 'Pensão Inocência/ Exclusivamente para solteiras/ Homens, não!' (Innocence Guest House/ Exclusively for spinsters/ No men!)

36 Similarly, in *Sai da frente* Mazzaropi has great difficulty in getting his truck to start. The vehicle then proceeds to backfire loudly, waking all his neighbours, spurting fumes and shaking uncontrollably.

37 Jerry Palmer, *Taking Humour Seriously* (London and New York: Routledge, 1994), pp. 61–2.

38 Verbal slapstick, such as hammed-up foreign accents, double entendres, vivid slang, malapropisms, mispronunciations and puns, can be interpreted as a legacy of physical clowning or knockabout, that popular cinema inherited from the circus. As Alan Dale writes in relation to Hollywood, but equally applicable to Brazilian popular film: 'In the talkies, the moviemakers instinctively developed verbal jokes in the manner of visual routines.' Dale, *Slapstick in American Movies*, p. 7.

39 Davies, C., 'Ethnic jokes, moral values and social boundaries', *British Journal of Sociology*, 33 (1982).

40 The audience is also invited to identify with the star-struck nature of this character, something that was encouraged by the proliferation of fanzines and cinema magazines.

41 As in the proto-*chanchadas* of the mid-1930s, the links between this cinematic tradition and the radio are made explicit.

42 Yvonne Tasker, *Working Girls: Gender and Sexuality in Popular Cinema* (London and New York: Routledge, 1998), p. 27.

43 Andreas Huyssen's essay 'The vamp and the machine: Fritz Lang's *Metropolis*' provides a useful analysis of the motif of the machine-woman. Huyssen examines the way in which in *Metropolis* (1927) the male vision assembles and disassembles woman's body, thus denying her identity and sexual power, and metaphorically representing man's exorcism of the fears of technology. Andreas Huyssen, *After the Great Divide: Modernism, Mass Culture and Postmodernism* (London: Macmillan, 1993).

44 Rudolf Piper, *Filmusical brasileiro e chanchada* (São Paulo: Global Editora, 1977), p. 61.

45 To more effectively implement the 'Good Neighbour Policy' towards Latin America the US government established the Office of the Coordinator of Inter-American Affairs (CIAA) in 1940. Headed by Nelson Rockefeller, the CIAA sponsored newsreels and documentaries for Latin American distribution and encouraged the Hollywood studios to make films with Latin American themes. Between 1939 and 1947, Hollywood films featuring Latin American stars, music, locations and stories flooded US and international markets. By 1943, for example, thirty films with Latin American themes or locales had been released and twenty-five more were in production, and by 1945, eighty-four films with Latin American subjects had been produced. Ana M. López, 'Are all Latins from Manhattan? Hollywood, ethnography and cultural colonialism', in John King, Ana M. López and Manuel Alvarado (eds), *Mediating Two Worlds: Cinematic Encounters in the Americas* (London: BFI Publishing, 1993), p. 70.

46 As Laura Mulvey writes in relation to classic Hollywood cinema: 'Traditionally, the woman displayed has functioned on two levels: as erotic object for the characters within the screen story, and as erotic object for the spectator within the auditorium, with a shifting tension between the looks on either side of the screen. For instance, the device of the show-girl allows the two looks to be unified technically without any apparent break in the diegesis. A woman performs within the narrative; the gaze of the spectator and that of the male characters in the film are neatly combined without breaking narrative verisimilitude.' Laura Mulvey, 'Visual pleasure and narrative cinema', *Visual and Other Pleasures* (London: Macmillan, 1993), p. 19.

47 It seems more than a coincidence that Billy Wilder's *Some Like it Hot*, that premiered in 1959, just a year before this parodic *chanchada*, should feature a strikingly similar scene.

48 Ana López examines Hollywood's celluloid manipulation of three female stars from Latin America, namely the Mexicans, Dolores Del Río and Lupe Vélez, and Carmen Miranda, who each represented different aspects of the exotic 'other' from the late 1920s to the mid-1940s. In the 1930s Vélez played the archetypal 'Latin' temptress with an insatiable sexual appetite, and embodied a potent ethnic 'otherness' that was too subversive for the climate of the 'Good Neighbour Policy' era. Whereas Vélez was by the late 1930s too 'Latin', Del Río's beauty and aloof indifference were not 'ethnic' enough, and it was Miranda, whose aggressive sexuality found its expression on screen only in gesture, innuendo and risqué comments, who became a non-derogatory and non-threatening symbol of *latinidad* in the 1940s. Ana M. López, 'Are all Latins from Manhattan?'.

49 Robert Stam, *Tropical Multiculturalism: A Comparative History of Race in Brazilian Cinema and Culture* (Durham and London: Duke University Press, 1997).

50 *Ibid.*, p. 98.

51 Chris Straayer has identified an entire genre of temporary transvestite films, and he attributes their enduring appeal to the way they allow audiences to cross social boundaries vicariously. Chris Straayer, 'Redressing the "natural": the temporary transvestite film', *Wide Angle*, 14 (January 1992).

52 Annette Kuhn, 'Sexual disguise and cinema', *The Power of the Image: Essays on Representation and Sexuality* (London and New York: Routledge, 1992), pp. 66–7.

53 Vera Cruz's comedy *Sai da frente* (1952) features a circus troupe, in which the strong man is called Samson and his girlfriend is Dalila. This film incorporated another intertextual reference to Hollywood in the form of an escaped gorilla (quite clearly a man in a fur suit – a classic case of parodic literalisation) who tries to capture a beautiful woman, in a clear 'aping' of *King Kong* (1933), starring Fay Wray.

54 Interview with Carlos Manga, by João Luiz Vieira, *Filme Cultura*, 41–2 (May 1983), 30 (our translation).

55 Dan Harries, *Film Parody* (London: BFI Publishing, 2000), p. 34.

56 The same can be said of the *chanchada Pistoleiro bossa nova*, another spoof Western in which Ankito teams up with Grande Otelo to up-end the genre.

57 Harries, *Film Parody*, p. 19.

58 *Revista Cinelândia*, 1952, p. 52 (our translation).

59 João Luiz Vieira, 'From *High Noon* to *Jaws*: Carnival and Parody in Brazilian Cinema', in Randal Johnson and Robert Stam (eds), *Brazilian Cinema* (New York: Columbia University Press, 1995), p. 257.

60 Jose Carlos Burle's *Carnaval Atlântida* parodies this entire genre rather than a specific film, and comically undermines the macro filmmaking conventions of the 'Hollywood style'. It sets out to ridicule Hollywood's big-budget excesses, and according to Sérgio Augusto the character of Cecílio B. de Milho (whose surname translates as corn or maize in Portuguese) is a caricature of Samuel Goldwyn rather than Milho's virtual namesake. Augusto, *Este mundo é um pandeiro*, p. 123.

61 See Robert Stam and João Luiz Vieira, 'Parody and marginality: the case of Brazilian cinema', *Framework*, 28 (1985).

62 Harries, *Film Parody*, p. 9.

63 Sérgio Augusto, 'A história de uma peruca que depôs Getúlio Vargas', *Folha de São Paulo*, 29 August 1984.

64 Vieira, 'From *High Noon* to *Jaws*', p. 256.

65 Film directors usually avoid regular cuts such as these, so here the technique is obviously used to deliberately reproduce the parallel section of the original film.

66 This scene can also be interpreted as the small man's rejection of conventional time in a reaction to the increasing technological control of the life of the individual, as depicted in *Modern Times* (1936), in which Charlie Chaplin's tramp is oppressed by industry and modern, urban society. One's own sense of time is all that matters to these champions of the masses, but ultimately the real, modernising world prevails, and you literally cannot turn the clock back.

67 The parody of the MGM logo, in which a mewing kitten replaces the growling lion, at the start of *O homem do sputnik*, was ahead of its time. In *The Fearless Vampire Killers (or Pardon Me, But Your Teeth Are in My Neck)* of 1967, the MGM lion morphs into a green cartoon vampire with blood-dripping fangs.

68 Dain Borges, 'The recognition of Afro-Brazilian symbols and ideas, 1890–1940', *Luso-Brazilian Review*, 32:2 (1995), pp. 70–1.

69 Stam, *Tropical Multiculturalism*, pp. 102–3.

70 *Ibid.*, p. 103.

71 *Ibid.*, p. 103.

72 *Ibid.*, p. 104.

73 Dyer, 'Entertainment and utopia', p. 278.

74 A close-up shot of black hands beating the samba rhythm on a series of drums also features in a scene from *Samba em Brasília*, that takes place at the rehearsal of the fictional 'Seu Matias' samba school.

75 Raymond Sayers, *The Negro in Brazilian Literature* (Denver: The Bell Press, 1956), p. 49. The Naturalist School depicted the dusky, sensual *mulata*; for example, Aluísio de Azevedo's novel *O cortiço* (The Tenement), published in 1890, has as one of its protagonists Rita Bahiana, a mulatto girl who is faithful to no one but who has almost bewitching power over men, whom she manipulates to her own ends. The '*Mulata* Myth' also embraces an element of danger; she poses a threat to the established order and harmony. In Coelho Neto's novel, *Turbilhão* (Whirlwind), published in 1906, we see the havoc caused by a mulatto woman's seduction of a white man, and the reader is implicitly warned against such contact.

76 Other examples include Noel Rosa's samba 'Mulata fuzarqueira' (Fun-loving *Mulata*) of 1931 and the 1948 carnival march 'A mulata é a tal' (The *Mulata* is the Greatest), by João de Barro and Antônio Almeida.

77 In the 1951 theatrical revue, *Eu quero sassaricá!* (I Wanna Fool Around) Oscarito appears in drag in the guise of a *baiana*.

78 It was first worn by Miranda on screen in Brazil in the film *Banana da terra* (Banana of the Land, 1939), see Chapter 2. The song 'O que é que a *baiana* tem?' that Carmen performed in this film and turned into a huge hit, introduced the Bahian word *balangandan* (metal ornamental amulets worn by *baianas*) into the Brazilian vocabulary. The term became synonymous with Carmen's screen/stage *baiana* in Brazil.

79 The image of the *baiana* as the quintessential embodiment of 'Latin' identity was central to Walt Disney's animated film *The Three Caballeros* (1945), which combines real people with cartoon characters, and in which the Brazilian cartoon parrot named Joe (Zé) Carioca takes the audience on a journey to Brazil. He appears with three identical parrots, all dressed in a stylised *baiana* costume. Aurora Miranda, Carmen's sister, dressed in the costume that her sibling made famous then performs the samba 'Os quindins de yayá' (Missy's Coconut Cakes) surrounded by an entourage of men dressed as roguish *malandros*.

80 Shari Roberts, ' "The Lady in the Tutti-Frutti Hat": Carmen Miranda, a spectacle of ethnicity', *Cinema Journal*, 32:3, p. 10.

   The *baiana* in the *chanchada* is clearly an aping of Miranda's Hollywood persona, however palely reproduced. Her over-the-top footwear and tutti-frutti headdresses are replaced by much less extravagant but none-the-less stylised costumes, and in many ways the *baianas* of the *chanchada* are more akin to the B-movie Miranda mimics in the USA, such as Maria Montez. Prior to its appropriation by Miranda, the *baiana* costume was an ethnic marker that signified Afro-Brazilian music, religion and tradition. The adoption of the costume by a white woman of European descent was thus groundbreaking.

81 Regina Paranhos Pereira, 'Introdução ao filme musical brasileiro', *Filme Cultura*, 6 (September 1967), p. 50 (our translation).

82 Néstor García Canclini, *Hybrid Cultures: Strategies for Entering and Leaving Modernity* (Minneapolis and London: University of Minnesota Press, 1995).

83 *Ibid.*, p. 241.

84 *Ibid.*, p. 229.

85 *Ibid.*, p. 229.

86 Paulo Emílio Salles Gomes, *Cinema brasileiro: uma trajetória no subdesenvolvimento* (Rio de Janeiro: Paz e Terra, 1986), pp. 75–6.

87 Hélio Nascimento, *Cinema brasileiro* (Porto Alegre: Mercado Aberto, 1981), pp. 33–4.

88 Augusto, *Este mundo é um pandeiro*, p. 142.

89 Directed by Watson Macedo, and released in 1960, this *chanchada* was deemed anachronistic by Sérgio Augusto, particularly in relation to Carlos Manga's productions from the end of the 1950s. *Ibid.*, p. 129.

90 Maristela's *Quem matou Anabela?* (Who Killed Anabela?, 1956), starring the music hall comedian, Procópio Ferreira and the star of *Alô. Alô. Carnaval!* (Hello, Hello,

Carnival!), Jaime Costa, also drew on the collaboration of TV Record, and the station was amply rewarded by featuring prominently in the film itself. This 'whodunnit' incorporated many elements of the *chanchada*, no doubt in an effort to broaden its appeal, such as a comic double act of detective and sidekick, a star-struck, sultry heroine who performs an extended dance routine and provides the customary 'flesh shots' of legs and cleavage, a clichéd attractive, untrustworthy *mulata* maid, and the performance of samba on the set of a shantytown in the television studios.

91 Paulo Emílio Salles Gomes quoted by Vieira, 'Hegemony and Resistance', p. 69. The turning point in the critical reception of the *chanchada* was the publication of Salles Gomes's *Cinema brasileiro: uma trajetória no subdesenvolvimento* in 1986.
92 Vieira, 'Hegemony and Resistance', p. 71.
93 *Ibid.*, p. 72.
94 *Ibid.*, p. 73.

5

The 1960s

Introduction

By the end of Juscelino Kubitschek's presidential term, the Brazilian economy had begun to slow down and the newly elected president, Jânio Quadros, was faced with the difficult task of continuing with the nation's modernisation programme, while at the same time keeping the needed flow of cash from foreign banks coming into the country. When the International Monetary Fund demanded the introduction of economic austerity measures, Quadros surprised the Left by giving in to these demands, such as the freezing of salaries. At the same time, however, he pursued an independent foreign policy, as witnessed in his support for the Cuban revolution. As a result, the Right gradually abandoned him and the Left did not have enough seats in Congress to give him and his policies the support that he needed. Quadros then took the surprising step of resigning, only eight months into his term of office, in the hope of being granted greater power by Congress. Unfortunately for him, his plan backfired and the government accepted his resignation. Quadros's vice-president, João Goulart, on an untimely trip abroad to socialist China, was prevented by military and conservative elements (with the support of the outgoing president himself) from assuming the presidency automatically and, instead, a parliamentary system was instated in the country, giving the president reduced powers. A universal plebiscite, encouraged by Goulart, returned Brazil to the presidential system in 1963, and Goulart was voted back into a position of real strength with the support of trades unions, progressive sectors of society, the working class and left-wing parties. Such support, along with his centre-left programme of limited land reform, redistribution of income, laws to protect the less well-off and nationalisation schemes, was enough to provoke a conspiracy among the military and right-wing politicians to overthrow the government. When troops surrounded Brasília in 1964 and Goulart fled to Uruguay, leaving the presidency vacant (there was, of course, no vice-president to take his place), the nation's military leaders carried out a coup and seized temporary control of government. General Humberto Castelo Branco was quickly elected by Congress.

Castelo Branco and other moderates within the military intended only to stay in power until the so-called radical elements of Brazilian society had been brought under control. But in 1967 Castelo Branco was replaced in power by General Arthur da Costa e Silva, the first in a line of extreme right-wing presidents that ushered in a period of oppression in 1968, referred to as 'the coup within the coup', which lasted until the mid-1970s and the so-called *abertura* or political opening-up.

It was, then, in the context of a very clear distinction between Left and Right that the 1960s got under way, and such distinctions would inflect discussions of culture, including popular culture, throughout the decade and beyond.

This chapter begins by considering the commercially successful cinematic adaptations of the work of two of Brazil's foremost playwrights of the twentieth century: Nelson Rodrigues and Dias Gomes, followed by a discussion of the popular pretensions of two significant *cinema novo* films, *Garota de Ipanema* (Girl from Ipanema, 1967) and *Macunaíma* (Macunaíma, 1969). It returns briefly to the work of Nelson Rodrigues with erstwhile *cinema novo* director Arnaldo Jabor's *Toda nudez será castigada* (*All Nudity Shall Be Punished*, 1973), a film from the early 1970s that enjoyed a certain amount of commercial success. The chapter ends with the work of Brazil's horror maestro, Zé do Caixão or Coffin Joe, whose early films made an impact at the box-office, despite, or perhaps because of, their suffering at the hands of the censors.

The legacy of the *chanchada* in the 1960s: Nelson Rodrigues and Dias Gomes on film

Nelson Rodrigues (1912–80) debuted on the Brazilian stage in 1941 with the play *A mulher sem pecado* (A Woman Without Sin), and by his death in 1980 he had written seventeen plays and countless serialised fictional works which were capable of doubling newspaper sales within a week. On the one hand some critics accused him of the worst excesses of disposable and exploitative culture: titillation, pornography, bad taste, poor writing, rehashing of material, melodrama, sexism, political conservatism and immorality. Others, however, considered him to have invented modern Brazilian theatre, with the staging in 1943 of the play *Vestido de noiva* (The Wedding Dress): a 'cinematographic' work that has strangely never been adapted for the big screen.[1] In an industry which has consistently laid its trust in literary adaptations, Brazilian cinema has unsurprisingly invested heavily in Nelson's work: a total of nineteen feature films have been released since 1952, based on his plays, novels and short stories, making him the most adapted Brazilian writer of all time, beating even the prolific and popular Jorge Amado.[2] Most of these films were critical or commercial successes.

Cinema rodrigueano got off to a disappointing start in the 1950s. The first adaptation of Nelson's work appeared in 1952, *Meu destino é pecar* (Bound for Sin), directed by the Mexican Manuel Pelufo for the Maristela Studios of São Paulo. The film disappeared without a trace on its release, and can therefore hardly be said to have contributed to the development of *cinema rodrigueano*. The film is now available on video (many more popular adaptations are still difficult to view in Brazil) and Nelson's fans can, despite the poor performances and direction, detect in the film a number of the thematic staples of the author's work: kitsch melodrama, dark forces colluding against supposedly pure characters, and a love triangle which ends in death. It was not until 1962 that an adaptation of his work would make an impact on the public and press. *Boca de Ouro* (Gold Mouth), based on the 1958 play of the same name, was directed by Nelson Pereira dos Santos, who took a break from filming his *cinema novo* masterpiece *Vidas secas* (Barren Lives, 1963) to accept an invitation from Nelson's brother-in-law, Jece Valadão to film him as the eponymous hero whom he had played on stage with resounding success. In the film Valadão plays Boca de Ouro, a *bicheiro* or gangster and illegal lottery organiser, from the suburbs of Rio de Janeiro, thus establishing the first prerequisite of the so-called *cinema rodrigueano*, and one shared with many a *chanchada*: a *carioca* setting, with characters and events taken from the popular lore of the city of Rio de Janeiro. Most of Nelson's subjects are from the *Zona Norte* or northern district of Rio, with its traditional way of life that is in sharp contrast to the more modern and wealthier southern beach-front districts. These characters are not slum-dwellers, but come from traditional families of Portuguese descent. They range from the working-class Zulmira of *A falecida* (The Deceased Woman, 1966),[3] who longs to rid herself of the stain of her poverty by dying quickly in order that she can be buried in style, to the wealthy businessman Herculano of *Toda nudez será castigada*, who wants for nothing but who is forced by his family's position to live a life of emotional frugality. Nelson's protagonists are never satisfied with their lot: in his fiction they rarely get what they want and the writer therefore uses them as a warning to those who seek to change the status quo. It is too easy, however, to read Nelson's work as reactionary and nothing else, despite what critics have maintained over the years. His work seems to seek out hypocrisy wherever it can be found in Brazilian society and hold it up to ridicule: the northern region of Rio with its stifling morality is revealed to be a hotbed of lust, deceit, adultery and incest.

As well as *Boca de Ouro*, in the 1960s two more films appeared which would establish a link between Nelson Rodrigues's filmic adaptations and popular culture. J. B. Tanko was a successful director by 1964 and prior to the release of *Asfalto selvagem* (Wild Asphalt) he had enjoyed success in the 1950s as a director of *chanchadas*. With the demise of the *chanchada* at the beginning of the 1960s, Tanko sought new directions, and chose to make two films based on one of Nelson's hugely popular newspaper serials.

As revealed in Chapter 4, in many *chanchada* films of the 1950s characters arrived in Rio de Janeiro from the countryside, were at first enamoured and then disillusioned by the modernity of urban life, and often returned to their traditional lifestyle at the end of the film. A similar confrontation between the archaic and the modern, as has already been mentioned, frequently appears in Nelson's work, and the popular flavour of his settings is also shared by the *chanchada*.[4] Tanko's contribution to *cinema rodrigueano* only exacerbated the belief that Nelson's adaptations were the inheritors of the *chanchada* tradition; a belief that would haunt directors of films based on Nelson's work for years to come. *Cinema rodrigueano* was quickly establishing itself as yet another commercial genre which, as many critics saw it, was pandering to the limited needs of the popular classes, but unlike the *chanchada* there was nothing wholesome about Nelson's fiction, and there was no uplifting message for viewers in the closing scenes. Characters were, for example, often debauched. The female protagonist of both *Asfalto selvagem* and Tanko's second film taken from the same source, *Engraçadinha depois dos trinta* (Engraçadinha in Her Thirties, 1966), like many characters in the *chanchada*, moved to Rio from another state, but in these films she embraces the social and sexual contradictions of the city, in what was perhaps a more genuine reflection of the confusion of the times, a confusion which had already been recognised by the military when they seized power in 1964, claiming that Brazil was on the brink of communist revolution. As a result of Tanko's and other adaptations released in the 1960s, J. P. de Carvalho's 1964 *Bonitinha mas ordinária* (Pretty But Wicked), for example, *cinema rodrigueano*, just like the fiction on which it was based, became (and for many continues to be) synonymous with critical outrage. This, as well as encouraging consumption of these films by a curious public, has only helped directors over the decades declare that they have a moral and political duty to film such material, as the critics themselves prove that there is still much work to be done to rid Brazilian society of its ingrained hypocrisy.[5]

J. B. Tanko was not the only *chanchada* veteran to turn his hand, in the 1960s, to adapting contemporary, popular stage plays for the big screen. Anselmo Duarte, a well-known *chanchada* actor and director, adapted and directed Dias Gomes's hit play *O pagador de promessas* (*The Given Word*) in 1962, achieving critical and box-office success.[6] The North Eastern setting and detailed discussions of poverty and oppression in the film link it inevitably to the first phase of the *cinema novo* movement that also appeared in

Brazil in the early 1960s. However, like the relative successes *Boca de Ouro* and *Os cafajestes* (*The Unscrupulous Ones*, 1962), considered *cinema novo* films, the film maintains a familiar linear narrative that popular audiences clearly appreciated, to the chagrin of many a more creative *cinemanovista* filmmaker hoping to inspire the masses to bring about the long-awaited revolution by, among other things, breaking with a so-called Hollywoodian narrative style.

O pagador de promessas has as its central character a simple peasant from rural Bahia, Zé do Burro, whose prize possession, his donkey, is one day struck by lightening. Zé makes a promise to God that, if his donkey recovers, he will carry a cross to a church in the state capital, Salvador, by way of thanks. The donkey duly recovers and Zé sets off for Salvador, but when he reaches the church steps, the priest refuses to let him in when he hears the nature of the promise, where it was made (in an *umbanda* temple) and to whom (Saint Barbara).[7] Various social types come and go as Zé stoically camps out on the church steps, and his interaction with these figures, and their expressions of popular religion and music, form the basis for much of the film's humour and social commentary.

Challenges to the *chanchada*: the *cinema novo*

Influenced by Italian neo-realism and the Brazilian left-wing regionalist literary movement of the 1930s and 1940s, the *auteurs* of the *cinema novo* movement sought to transform society by applying a new, critical and modernist vision of the nation, and to find a new cinematic language that better reflected Brazilian reality, as a challenge to what they considered the vacuous, derivative and industrially produced *chanchada* films that had dominated film production since the 1930s. Although the *cinema novo* did not inspire the Brazilian cinema-going public at the time, it did help to put Brazilian cinema on the world cinematic map and has helped to increase its international dissemination and popularity ever since.

The *cinema novo* arose initially as part of the cultural euphoria of Brazil's developmentalist period. One of the significant features of the period was a growth in state funding of culture. In 1961 GEICINE (Executive Group of the Cinema Industry) was set up to examine the film industry and increase exhibition, followed in 1966 by INC, the National Film Institute. The Institute, among other things, set compulsory screen quotas and offered production subsidies based on box-office success and for 'quality' films. Although *auteurs* such as Glauber Rocha and Nelson Pereira dos Santos were initially suspicious of such state intervention in the culture industry, most of these subsidies went to *cinema novo* films.[8] Faced with a market dominated by American films, and for a while untroubled by the country's military leaders in terms of censorship, *cinema novo*, then, increasingly turned to the state for protection, subsidies and production financing.

Illustrative of the first phase of *cinema novo* are the films of Nelson Pereira dos Santos (for example, *Vidas secas*), Ruy Guerra (*Os fuzis* (*The Guns*, 1963)), and Glauber Rocha (*Deus e o diabo na terra do sol* (*Black God, White Devil*, 1964)), the filmmaking approach and thematic choices of all of which can be summed up by Glauber Rocha's legendary definition: 'an aesthetics of hunger'.[9] To simplify considerably, these first-phase *cinema novo* films were visually characterised by a documentary quality, often achieved by the use of a hand-held camera, a preference for location shooting, and in particular in the poverty-stricken Brazilian *sertão* or backlands, the use of non-professional actors, and a refusal to deny on screen the precarious living conditions of the majority of Brazil's population. The first phase of films were made in black and white, using simple, stark scenery that vividly emphasised the harshness of the landscape of the Brazilian *sertão*. They dealt with the theme of the rural peasantry: the precariousness of their existence, their exploitation by landowners, the futile mysticism of their lives and the fact that their class consciousness was stifled by their fatalism and stoicism.

When the military seized power in Brazil in 1964, it was to an extent inevitable that such an openly revolutionary movement as *cinema novo* would eventually be quashed, especially after 1968 and the so-called 'coup within the coup', which brought in even greater censorship restrictions and persecution of left-wing intellectuals. By that time, a less utopian second phase of the movement had got under way, to be necessarily transformed after 1968 into the third and final phase, the 'tropicalist' or allegorical phase, of which Joaquim Pedro de Andrade's 1969 film *Macunaíma* is the best-known and most accessible example, and perhaps for that reason, it is one of the very few *cinema novo* films to have made a significant impact at the box-office.

Second-phase *cinema novo*: *Garota de Ipanema*

Despite the unprecedented critical success of early *cinema novo* films such as *Deus e o diabo na terra do sol* and *Vidas secas*, both at home and abroad, the movement's project inevitably started to come unstuck after 1964 and the military coup, even though there was only limited censorship of the arts before 1968 and the 'coup within the coup'. It was becoming clear at this time to many filmmakers associated with the movement that their preaching of a revolutionary utopia was both misguided, given the new political climate, and falling on deaf ears. As Carlos Estevam Martins put it, *cinema novo* filmmakers were trying to create a new language, and as a result, they ended up talking to themselves.[10] They recognised the irony in making so-called 'popular' films, to be viewed only by university students and art-house aficionados.

As a result, some *auteurs* began to move away from the so-called 'aesthetics of hunger' towards a filmmaking style and themes designed to attract the interest of the cinema-going public at large. Leon Hirzsman's *Garota de Ipanema* (Girl From Ipanema, 1967) is perhaps the most radical departure from the established *cinema novo* aesthetic at the time.

Garota de Ipanema was inspired by Tom Jobim and Vinícius de Moraes's classic *bossa nova* hit of the same name, and the suggestion for transforming the famous and very *carioca* song into a film came from Glauber Rocha himself. It was the first *cinema novo* film to be made in colour, and it dealt, in a deliberately light fashion, with the everyday life of a young, middle-class girl from one of the wealthy southern districts of Rio de Janeiro. The film follows her as she studies for the university entrance exam, goes to the beach with her friends at weekends, attends parties to celebrate Christmas, New Year and carnival, experiences boyfriend trouble and conflict with her parents, and so on. The fictional universe and narrative form are thus very different in this film from early *cinema novo* films. The glossy backdrop of Rio's bourgeois spaces, the inclusion of diegetic musical interludes, performed by well-known singers and composers such as Vinícius de Moraes himself, Chico Buarque and Nara Leão, and shots of Rio's carnival are more reminiscent of the *chanchada* than the politically charged and deliberately visually impoverished *cinema novo*.[11] Vinícius de Moraes, who was involved in the preparation of the film's script, said that he wanted to capture the precise moment when the girl from Ipanema was wanting to move on in her life, to start living, to spread her wings.[12] Like the real-life girl from Ipanema, Helô Pinheiro, who inspired Tom and Vinícius's song, the protagonist captures the mood of the times, comes of age and is fulfilled by being observed, in this case by the camera of a married photographer/cameraman with whom she enjoys a brief affair. Although a modern-day positive reading of *Garota de Ipanema* invariably struggles with the voyeuristic and rather sexist context of both the song and the film, the intended message at the time was one of personal freedom (an important message, given the context of dictatorship in which the film was made), of finding one's own way in life, and of the importance of never taking for granted the infinite possibilities afforded by Rio's bourgeois lifestyle.

With *Garota de Ipanema* Leon Hirzsman set out (but failed) to make a successful musical with the use of colour film, the best photographer available at the time (the Argentinean Ricardo Aronovich), pop music, high production values and just enough sensuality to still secure a decent exhibition certificate from the censors.[13] Nelson Motta wrote on the film's release that 'now the public knows that we can make colourful, beautiful, pleasant and luxurious films, like in foreign cinema, but with a much higher cultural level. For this reason *Garota de Ipanema* is a bad film, but an important one.'[14]

Cinema novo and *tropicalismo*: *Macunaíma*

With the strengthening of the military regime in 1968, many *cinema novo* directors were forced to abandon their filmmaking project, and in some cases, the country itself, as a result of severe political repression and increased censorship.[15] Those who stayed behind and continued to make films turned, necessarily, to a more allegorical approach, while maintaining their commitment to producing films that the public would want to pay money to see. The key to reaching the public at this time was, according to Fernão Ramos, via 'spectacle',[16] inspired by a new cultural movement that had appeared in 1967: Tropicalism. As it happens, *cinema novo*'s tropicalist project was a box-office failure, with the notable exception of one film: Joaquim Pedro de Andrade's *Macunaíma*, possibly the most vibrant, entertaining and challenging film to emerge in the 1960s in Brazil.[17]

Macunaíma is based on Mário de Andrade's 1933 classic modernist novel of the same name. In many ways it was a natural choice for adaptation, given the strong links that existed between the original modernist project, the *cinema novo* movement and Tropicalism. Brazilian modernists, from the 1920s onwards, 'attempted to democratise Brazilian art through a stance of cultural nationalism, rejecting a critical imitation of European models in favour of an interest in popular forms of expression and the culture of native Brazilian people'.[18] The similarities to the *cinema novo* project are clear to see in this definition. With regard to the tropicalists' debt to modernism, the key can be found in poet and playwright Oswald de Andrade's *Manifesto antropófago* (*Cannibalist Manifesto*, 1928), which 'advocated the creation of a genuine national culture through the consumption and critical re-elaboration of both national and foreign influences. Imported cultural influences were to be devoured, digested and reworked in terms of local conditions.'[19] Oswald took his inspiration from Brazilian Indians who, according to sixteenth-century travellers such as Jean de Léry and Hans Staden, devoured their enemies in order to gain strength from them. Rather than constantly doing battle against foreign influences (the old *cinema novo* ideology?), these influences could be consumed and transformed into something new and genuinely Brazilian. This is exactly what the tropicalists sought to do in the late 1960s.

Tropicalismo or *tropicália* is best known in Brazil in its musical context, with the release in 1968 of the seminal concept album *Tropicália ou panis et circenses*. A number of cutting-edge musicians contributed to the album, the most famous of whom were Gilberto Gil and Caetano Veloso. But Tropicalism infiltrated the other arts too. Robert Stam writes of a tropicalist trilogy: Glauber Rocha's film *Terra em transe* (*Land in Anguish*, 1967), José Celso's 1967 staging of Oswald de Andrade's 1933 play *O rei da Vela* (The Candle King) and the *Tropicália* album. His description of the trilogy serves as a useful definition of the movement:

5   Macunaíma (Grande Otelo, centre) and his brothers leave the rainforest to try their luck in São Paulo.

All three are centrifugal, dispersive texts that fracture the left-populist cultural consensus; they perform a kind of electroshock on dominant paradigms, excoriating both the reactionary Right and the populist Left. All three refuse the ideal of communicative transparency; rather, they favour a contradictory aesthetic that embraces a complex overlay of cultural meanings. All three texts share as well their nationalist cosmopolitanism, their debt to Oswald de Andrade, their references to carnival, their exaltation of bad taste, their fondness for inter-media cross-fertilisation, their penchant for allegory, their affection for shock images, and their refusal of any totalisation that would privilege a single voice/character/subject.[20]

In both the novel and film version of *Macunaíma*, the eternally lazy eponymous protagonist, born black (and later magically transformed into a white man) lives in the tropical forest with his family. Like many a poor peasant before him, he reaches the point where he can no longer survive in the countryside and is forced to try his luck in the big city, in this case São Paulo (see figure 5). While living there, he has a series of adventures, which revolve around his search for a lucky charm, the *muiraquitã* stone pendant. He eventually locates the stone and heads back home, where he dies in old age by jumping into a lake naked in pursuit of a beautiful woman, who turns out to be Uiara, a mythical and dangerous sea creature, who devours him.

In preparation for writing his novel, Mário de Andrade researched the myths and legends of Brazil's indigenous peoples, and incorporated many of them into his text. Joaquim Pedro de Andrade kept many of these in his film version, while omitting some and updating others. For example, there are numerous instances of cannibalism depicted in both the book and the film, ranging from the self-cannibalist Currupira, whom Macunaíma meets in the forest, after his mother tires of him and abandons him there, to the carnivalesque *feijoada* scene in São Paulo, in which the giant Pietro Pietra (transformed in the film into an Italian-Brazilian capitalist) throws guests into his swimming pool, filled with black beans, with the intention of devouring them.[21] Such cannibalistic references often have sexual connotations in the film. Many of the sexual romps depicted on screen involve biting, for example. In fact, a number of scenes in *Macunaíma* are reminiscent of the fledgling *pornochanchada* genre, to be discussed in detail in Chapter 6, particularly those that depict a bone-idle protagonist constantly on the lookout for a smutty, all-consuming kind of sex, referred to in *Macunaíma* via a euphemism, the verb *brincar* (to play), a common ploy in the *pornochanchada*. What is significant, however, is that sexual relations are inverted in *Macunaíma*, in that the women whom our hero comes across tend to be in charge in the bedroom, are often the sexual initiators, and make of Macunaíma their sex object. The film, then, goes some way to unmasking the myth of male dominance.[22]

In the film, cannibalism is synonymous with the exploitation of under-developed Brazil by the international capitalist system. 'Brazil devours its citizens through poverty and underdevelopment, its citizens devour Brazil, and Brazil, consequently, devours itself.'[23] The filmmaker therefore radicalises the ideology of the book, just like the *cinema novo* movement did with much of the ideology of the modernists. Both the opening and closing credits are accompanied by a patriotic tune by Heitor Villa-Lobos, whose lyrics glorify the heroes of Brazil. As Johnson argues, 'the film thus links immediately with the epic tradition, or more precisely, with the comic-epic tradition, as it proposes to deal with the problem of Brazil and the Brazilian hero.'[24] Johnson also points out that the film deals with a hero, but not the kind envisioned either by the dominant ideology, nor by opponents of the latter, thus fitting in neatly with Robert Stam's previously cited theory that the tropicalist project challenged dominant paradigms, on both the Left and Right.[25] In the novel, Macunaíma is both good and evil, courageous and cowardly, and capable and inept. According to Johnson, in Joaquim Pedro's film he only displays negative qualities.[26]

So why did Joaquim Pedro's highly politicised tropicalist feature film succeed at the box-office where other films failed? For a start, there are a number of features of the film that link it to the popular *chanchada* genre. For example, Macunaíma, until he is transformed into a white man, is played by Grande

Otelo, in one of his most highly regarded roles. Grande Otelo's performance is playful and borders at times on slapstick, as Mário de Andrade's original text dictates. He plays an indolent and naive character, prone to uttering the words 'Ai, que preguiça!' (Oh, I can't be bothered!), who cannot keep his eyes off his brother's girlfriend. He is, then, similar in many ways to the anti-heroes of the *chanchada*. In Mário de Andrade's novel, Macunaíma is blessed with magical gifts, but in the film he has no more powers than an ordinary man, and ultimately survives with a great deal of luck and by his own wits. The film's staging, performances and costumes are deliberately extravagant and theatrical, reminiscent of a carnivalesque aesthetic. As Johnson writes, 'The textual system of *Macunaíma* is one of the inversion, if not subversion, of established hierarchies, social mores, and, perhaps more importantly, spectator expectations.'[27] There are plenty of kitsch, bad-taste elements in the film, and much of the debauchery depicted is reminiscent of both *cinema rodrigueano* and the *pornochanchada*. For example, when Macunaíma's mother dies, a voiceover informs the viewers that our hero mourned heroically, while he is seen on screen discreetly fondling his brother's girlfriend's bottom.

Some of the many musical references in the film recall the *chanchada* and other popular films, for example the Brazilian version of a song used in a Busby Berkeley set from *Footlight Parade* (1933), which plays while a magic fountain turns Macunaíma white.[28] Later, a ludicrous and rather grotesque scene that involves Macunaíma dressed as a French woman trying to seduce the villain Pietro Pietra in order to steal the *muiraquitã* stone is played out to the sound of an Argentinian tango.[29] When the villain discovers that Macunaíma is a man, he is not deterred. As Johnson states, 'the entire episode is a tour de force of carnivalesque inversion and ambivalence',[30] and one cannot help but be reminded of the equally carnivalesque conclusion to the hit comedy film *Some Like it Hot* (1959).[31] A similar inversion of audience expectations takes place when the same villain later dies by falling into his own swimming pool filled with *feijoada* or black bean stew. Just before he goes under, he cries out: 'Falta sal!' (It needs salt!).[32]

Chanchada meets melodrama: *Toda nudez será castigada*

After Leon Hirzsman's intelligent but little-viewed adaptation of *A falecida* (*The Deceased Woman*) in 1966, in the early 1970s another *cinemanovista* director attempted to interpret Nelson Rodrigues's work for the big screen. Arnaldo Jabor, a name associated with the *cinema novo* movement in the 1960s,[33] was with *Toda nudez será castigada* and the less successful *O casamento* (*The Marriage*, 1975) the first cineaste to adapt Rodrigues's dramaturgy after the 'coup within the coup' of 1968, which heralded an era of violent political repression and censorship.

While *Toda nudez será castigada* was busy picking up prizes abroad, including a Silver Bear at the Berlin Film Festival for Darlene Gloria's performance as the prostitute Geni, it was banned by the censors at home.[34] The work quickly came to represent a challenge to the military regime. Nelson Rodrigues himself at the time was no longer frowned upon as a supporter of the military generals: despite his right-wing credentials, he had publicly protested against censorship of the arts. Also, in the early 1970s, critics were more open to the kitsch interpretation of urban reality at the heart of Nelson's work, partly as a result of the influence of the tropicalist movement in terms of a re-reading of Brazilian reality in the context of the dictatorship. An allegorical interpretation of the ills of society based on the debauched world of Nelson Rodrigues was now recognised by many as a legitimate subject to be tackled by Brazilian cinema.[35]

In *Toda nudez será castigada* wealthy businessman Herculano is in pious mourning over the death of his beloved wife. His son and sisters encourage his self-sacrificial existence, but his *malandro* brother, Patrício, tires of the dullness of the family home and fears that his brother is putting at risk the fortune which he happily lives off. He sets out to bring Herculano back to the land of the living by introducing him to his old flame, the prostitute and cabaret singer Geni. After a drunken evening together, both Geni and Herculano fall in love, but Herculano initially chastises himself for what he considers to be his immoral behaviour. He had sworn to Sérgio, his son that he would never be with another woman. He eventually gives in to his desires, but rather than making a decent woman of Geni, as she would wish (see figure 6), he shuts her up in his second home, and visits her occasionally, while he gradually plucks up the courage to confess to his son. His son, however, catches the two of them together, gets drunk and subsequently arrested, and is raped in a police cell by his Bolivian cellmate. Encouraged by Patrício, Sérgio sets out to destroy both his father and the latter's lover, by making the emotionally weak Geni fall in love with him. He then heads off for Europe with his Bolivian cellmate. Geni commits suicide, having left a tape recording for Herculano revealing all.

Jabor's great achievement in filming Nelson's work was that he was not afraid to handle the depraved characters and situations which the fiction invariably included, and he was able to use shocking scenes of depravity to challenge bourgeois hypocrisy; a courageous and fitting venture given the political climate of the times.[36] He was also the first director to comprehend that Nelson's work falls flat if it is toned down. Jabor recognised that an element of deliberately tacky melodrama emanated from much of the author's work, and the fact that such melodrama could sit comfortably alongside genuinely serious discussions was one feature that made him one of the most original and striking writers of his time. Randal Johnson describes the film in

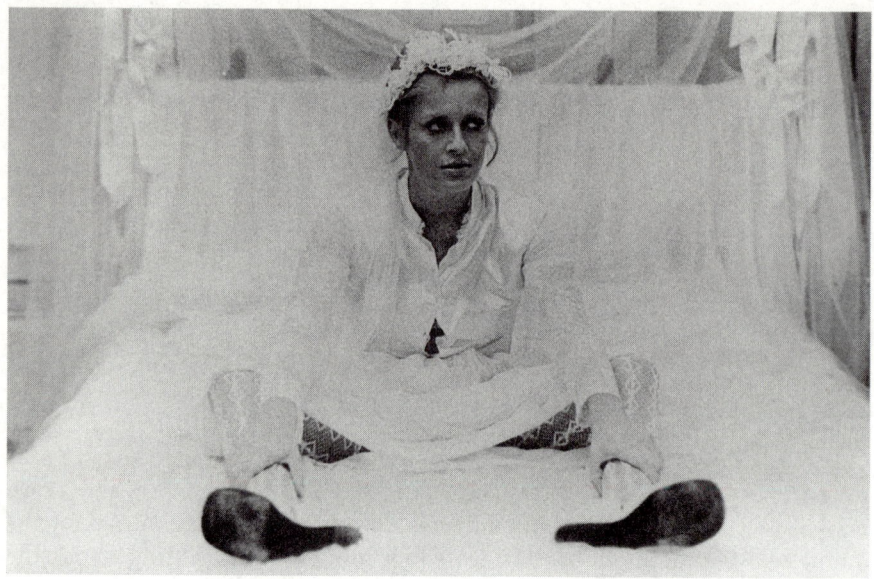

6 The prostitute Geni (Darlene Glória) dreams of a white wedding in *Toda nudez será castigada.*

the following terms: 'Combining elements of the melodrama of defeat and tragedy, *Toda nudez será castigada* is melodrama taken to the second degree, a melodrama which is a parody and a caricature of itself.'[37] Nelson Rodrigues (and those who adapted his work for the screen) were frequently accused of producing nothing more than the Brazilian equivalent of *dramalhões mexicanos*, or overblown Mexican melodramas, and until Jabor's adaptations were made, most critics had failed to appreciate this indispensable self-mocking and relief-providing element in his work.

Mojica Marins: Coffin Joe and Brazilian horror

José Mojica Marins was born, fittingly, on a Friday 13th in 1936 and brought up in a working-class, Spanish immigrant community in the city of São Paulo. Like many of the exponents of popular cinema in Brazil, his background was rooted in popular culture: both his grandfathers had been Spanish bullfighters, and his own father had been brought up in bullrings and circuses in Brazil. He spent a good part of his childhood living in a flat above a popular cinema where his father worked as a manager. Both the dramatic, dangerous and ostentatious side of bullfighting, and his close link with 1940s cinema would influence his films throughout his career. He started filming when he was a teenager, making little more than home movies with friends and no budget. As

Marins never learned to look after his money, and was constantly broke, even at the very height of his career his films are characterised by their very low budgets. In fact, it is a miracle that the films were ever made in the first place.

Marins's delusions of grandeur were evident even in the very early days of his filmmaking with his teenage friends, in the absurdly pompous titles that he gave to his home movies made with an 8-millimetre, and later, 16-millimetre camera, for example, *O juízo final* (Judgement Day, 1949) and *Encruzilhada da perdição* (Crossroads to Perdition, 1952). Marins first metamorphosed into Zé do Caixão, or Coffin Joe, as he is known in English translation, in 1963. He apparently dreamed one night of a horrific gravedigger dressed in a black cape, with long fingernails and wearing a top hat. He woke up the next morning, desperate to recreate the excitement, fear and dramatic tension of his dream. He decided to make his first horror film, and after abandoning his search to find a suitable leading man, Marins's alter ego, Zé do Caixão, was born.

Marins was arguably Brazil's finest exponent of 'popular' cinema, in that he did not rely on state funding for his films, nor did he have a wealthy family to fall back on financially when things went wrong. Instead, he made money and used free labour from his acting school and he often sold cheap pre-production shares in his movies in and around his neighbourhood, although admittedly few people ever saw a return on their investment. Marins was a great admirer of Amácio Mazzaropi who, as will be seen in Chapter 6, was for *paulista* audiences the most popular film performer and director. Marins was more interested in Mazzaropi's commercial success with the public at large, than the highbrow Rio-based *cinema novo* movement, for example. Despite this, the story goes that none other than Glauber Rocha was fascinated by Marins's early films, because of their deceptive simplicity, their shirking of the rules of filming and, perhaps more importantly, Marins's creative use of a shoe-string budget which offered a new take on Glauber's 'aesthetics of hunger'.[38] For example, in order to cut down on costs, in *À meia-noite levarei sua alma* (At Midnight I'll Take Your Soul, 1964) Marins famously used a 'live' grave in a graveyard in São Paulo to film one scene, just minutes before the real corpse arrived for burial.[39] In *Esta noite encarnarei no teu cadaver* (This Night I Will Possess Your Corpse, 1967) Marins included a stylised 12-minute colour sequence depicting Hell: despite the interesting effect of this sequence, his only motive for breaking with the black and white photography temporarily was that at the time he could not afford any more colour film.[40]

Marins has been described as Brazil's first genuinely multimedia performer, in that during his heyday in the 1960s, the character Zé do Caixão was associated with films, television programmes, radio presentations, gramophone records, advertising (soap, food, and so on), public appearances and, Marins's personal favourite, a range of horror comic books.[41] The extent to which

Marins was inspired in his filmmaking by horror comics is clear to see in his editing technique, use of close-ups, dialogue to camera, narration off-camera and the rather expressionist look of his films. The other original feature of Marins's filmmaking technique was best described by Rogério Sganzerla, one of many underground filmmakers from São Paulo's Boca do Lixo to admire Marins's work.[42] Sganzerla wrote that Marins had learned an important cinematic lesson: 'the more realist the atmosphere in which the absurd appears, the more absurd the result'.[43] There is therefore nothing tongue-in-cheek about what Marins places on the screen, despite contemporary audiences' relationship with his work.

Coffin Joe's first outing was in *À meia-noite levarei sua alma*. Set in an unnamed town in the interior of the state of São Paulo, the local gravedigger, Zé do Caixão, is obsessed with finding a woman who will give him the perfect son. First, he kills his barren wife Lenita by tying her up and letting loose on her body a poisonous spider.[44] Then he turns his attention to his best friend's fiancée, Terezinha. He drowns his best friend in a bathtub, and rapes Terezinha with a cry of: 'Você vai me dar o filho que sempre quis!' (You're going to give me the child I've always wanted!). Terezinha hangs herself as a result of the rape, and a gypsy rightly predicts that on All Souls Day, at midnight, the spirits of all the people Zé has killed will return to seek their revenge.

The film made a lasting impression on the public at the time because of one particularly blasphemous scene in which Coffin Joe tucks into a leg of lamb on Good Friday while laughing at an Easter procession passing by his house. Here was a director making, for the first time, a Brazilian horror film, with Brazilian concerns (the blasphemy scene would hardly have shocked Anglo-Saxon audiences as much) and a very Brazilian backdrop. For example, Coffin Joe established in this film his trademark cursing: audiences were delighted to be sent away with a curse of the ilk of 'Que você vague pela eternidade sentindo as dores de um leitão assado!' (May you wander through eternity feeling the pain of a roasted suckling pig!).[45] Also, Coffin Joe looks out for children and old people in his films, with a sentimentality that is perfectly acceptable to Brazilian audiences. Visually, Zé do Caixão is reminiscent of one of the deities from the popular Afro-Brazilian religion *candomblé*, Exú, who is often associated with the Christian devil. In fact Marins came up with Zé do Caixão's visual style when he borrowed a cape from a porter at his studio: the porter dabbled in *candomblé* and used the cape in his worship of Exú.[46]

Although the character Coffin Joe lived and worked in the small towns of the interior where Marins's films were set, he was not a man of the people like *chanchada* heroes tended to be, or Mazzaropi was in his films, for example. For a start, Joe had a distinctive, suave voice, with perfect diction, which contrasted on screen with the *caipira* accents of the townsfolk and helped to set him apart from the masses, whom he regularly ridiculed and victimised.[47] Those same masses who flocked to the cinema to see his films saw themselves being mocked on screen, but accepted this, as their mocker was immediately identified in the opening scenes of the films as evil through and through, and therefore in the wrong.

Coffin Joe's second cinematic outing, *Esta noite encarnarei no teu cadáver* (1967) picks up where the story line of his previous film left off. Having survived an attack by the spirits of those he had murdered in *À meia-noite levarei sua alma*, Joe continues both his search for the perfect woman to bear him a child, and his murderous ways. At the end of this film, he is drowned in a lake where he has dumped the bodies of his childbearing rejects. Marins had hoped to release his film as soon as it was ready in 1966, in order to make the most of the positive publicity and box-office success of *À meia-noite levarei sua alma*. The censors, however, had other ideas, and as was the case with all of Marins's feature films, lengthy negotiations had to take place between the producer and the censors, resulting in the film being severely cut, and even rewritten in parts by the censors themselves (and therefore re-edited later). For example, Coffin Joe in this film was obliged by the authorities to undergo a major personality transformation, being forced to recognise the existence and power of God at the end of the film and thus losing much of his carnivalesque grotesqueness. Influential film critics such as Salvyano Cavalcanti de Paiva were horrified by such interference in the creative process on the part of the censors, and Marins, who until then had taken such negotiation as a necessary evil of filmmaking, then saw the potential commercial advantage in declaring his outrage at such acts of censorship, and learned the important skill of using newspapers to express controversial views (and thus keep the censors forever on his back) as a way of promoting his own films.

The character Coffin Joe appeared in only four more fiction films between 1968 and 1983: *O estranho mundo de Zé do Caixão* (*The Strange World of Coffin Joe*, 1968); *Ritual dos sádicos* (renamed *O despertar da besta*) (*The Awakening of the* Beast, produced in 1969 but seized by the censor and not released until 1983); *O exorcismo negro* (*Black Exorcism of Coffin Joe*, 1974) and *Delírios de um anormal* (*Hallucinations of a Deranged Mind*, 1978).

With the 1968 'coup within the coup', Mojica Marins's problems with the authorities only worsened, so much so that he is said to be Brazil's most censored director. For example, he was threatened with imprisonment in 1969 if he attempted to release *O despertar da besta*.[48]

Although Marins, during interviews, tends to come across as taking himself and his *oeuvre* very seriously, his capacity to send himself up is clear from Zé do Caixão's final celluloid outing. In *Delírios de um anormal* Hamilton, a psychiatrist, suffers from paranoid hallucinations, fantasising that the horror film character Coffin Joe is trying to steal his wife, Tânia, in order (once again) to create the perfect child. Meanwhile Tânia, in an effort to aid her delusional husband, seeks the help of Hamilton's colleagues, who in turn seek the help of Mojica Marins himself. In the film, the director lives in a huge mansion and is attended to by blonde, uniformed maids: a far cry from the virtual penury that the real-life director was reportedly living in during the late 1970s and 1980s.

Like *O despertar da besta*, *Delírios de um anormal* makes use of footage from previous Coffin Joe movies, as befits the film's plot: Hamilton's paranoia has been sparked by his recollections of seeing the evil Zé do Caixão on the big screen. According to Luís Alberto Rocha Melo the film is no different from earlier Coffin Joe films in that the plot is thin and the bulk of the running time is taken up by the same orgy of gruesome images: 'Fancy tricks, puffs of smoke, bodies that appear and suddenly disappear, bottoms that turn into faces, masks and skulls that laugh, rats, snakes and spiders, amputated hands, tongues ripped out, blood and lots of screaming.'[49]

Meanwhile Mojica Marins continued, as he had always done, to make other, usually violent and sexually daring feature films (almost thirty in total between 1958 and 1986). In the 1970s and 1980s he followed the path of many an independent filmmaker in São Paulo in order to make ends meet and produced both soft- and hard-core porn films. In the 1970s these films included incursions into the world of the *pornochanchada*, for example, *A virgem e o machão* (The Virgin and the Macho Man, 1974, under the pseudonym of J. Avelar). In the 1980s, Marins achieved box-office success once again when he turned his attention to hard-core filmmaking, directing, for example, the notorious and hugely popular *24 horas de sexo ardente* (24 Hours of Hot Sex, 1985), in which Vânia Bournier played opposite a German shepherd dog named Jack and thus gave Brazilian cinema audiences their first experience of bestiality on screen. The film was followed up in 1987 with the even more energetic *48 horas de sexo alucinante* (48 Hours of Hallucinatory Sex).[50]

Coffin Joe entered a second phase of popularity in 1993 when Mike Vraney of Something Weird, a US distributor of horror videos, discovered his films and marketed them for an English-speaking audience. Admiration for his work from US directors and writers such as Tim Burton, Joe Dante and Stephen King has provoked an overdue reappraisal of his work by the press and public back home.

Concluding remarks

Inevitably, with the demise of the all-pervasive *chanchada* in the late 1950s and the intellectual legacy of the art-house *cinema novo* movement, the 1960s are not best remembered for the production of popular cinema. As a result, many of the films that the Brazilian population still made the effort to watch in cinema halls, despite the attraction of the new-fangled technology of tele-vision, have largely been ignored or forgotten.[51] This chapter has revealed, unsurprisingly, that a number of such commercially successful films incor-porated the themes and stylistic traditions of the *chanchada* genre. Even the *cinema novo auteurs*, keen after 1964 to engage more productively with their target audience, could not ignore the enormous impact these popular comedies had on the public imaginary. Despite right-wing military rule from 1964 onwards, the work of many of Brazil's avant-garde (and frankly unpopular) cineastes was supported by the state,[52] while films made by popular directors who were frowned upon by left-wing intellectuals, such as Mojica Marins and Mazzaropi, were not. As the next chapter will reveal, the potentially confusing relationship that the state maintained with cultural production (financing with one hand and censoring with the other) continued into the 1970s and beyond, as did the celluloid fascination with the style and themes of the old *chanchadas*.

Notes

1 *Vestido de noiva* was turned into a TV mini-series in the 1960s. It is a cinemato-graphic work in the sense that it uses three different temporal spaces on stage at the same time.

2 Jorge Amado (1912–2001) is one of Brazil's best-known and most widely translated writers. Film adaptations of his work include *Dona Flor e seus dois maridos* (*Dona Flor and Her Two Husbands*, 1976), discussed in Chapter 6, *Tenda dos Milagres* (*Tent of Miracles*, 1977), *Gabriela* (Gabriela, 1983) and *Tieta* (Tieta, 1996).

3 Directed by Leon Hirzsman, *A falecida* made little impact with the public and critics on its release. Only much later was its importance within the *cinema novo* movement recognised.

4 Characters are frequently placed in pool halls, at football matches, on buses, and so on.

5 The so-called 'depraved bourgeoisie' was also depicted at this time in Ruy Guerra's notorious *Os cafajestes* (*The Unscrupulous Ones*, 1962). The film, which dealt with the blackmail of bored rich girls carried out by a couple of *malandro* types (one of whom was played, once again, by Jece Valadão), included Brazil's first female full-frontal nudity shot, supplied by Norma Bengell. Leon Hirzsman's *Garota de Ipanema* (Girl From Ipanema, 1967), to be discussed later in this chapter, continued with the tradition, in part begun by the filmic adaptations of Nelson Rodrigues's work, of depicting a society on the brink of a sexual revolution. While *cinema rodrigueano* could boast a handful of minor successes in the 1960s, as a kind of legacy of the *chanchada*, popular comedian Amácio Mazzaropi starred in twelve straight hits in the 1960s, playing the indomitable country bumpkin, Jeca. Mazzaropi's films, which were likewise considered to be the inheritors of the *chanchada* tradition, also spanned the 1970s and will be discussed in detail in Chapter 6.

6 Dias Gomes was so displeased with the adaptation of his work that he asked for his name to be removed from the film credits. Despite his dissatisfaction with Anselmo Duarte's film, *O pagador de promessas* was the first and only Brazilian film to win the prestigious Palme d'Or at the Cannes Film Festival.

7 In the syncretic religion *umbanda*, with its blend of African, indigenous, spiritist and Catholic beliefs, Saint Barbara represents the African *orixá* or deity Iansã. Zé do Burro's mixing of Catholicism and syncretic religious practices is not uncommon in Brazil.

8 John King, *Magical Reels: A History of Cinema in Latin America* (London and New York: Verso, 1990), p. 112.

9 See Glauber Rocha, 'An aesthetic of hunger', reproduced in Randal Johnson and Robert Stam (eds), *Brazilian Cinema* (New York: Columbia University Press, 1995).

10 Carlos Estevam Martins, 'Artigo sobre aristocratas', in Maria Rita Galvão and Jean-Claude Bernardet (eds), *O nacional e o popular na cultura brasileira* (São Paulo: Brasiliense, 1983), p. 158.

11 Fernão Ramos likens the style of these musical interludes to modern music videos: 'Os novos rumos do cinema brasileiro (1955–1970)', in Fernão Ramos (ed.), *História do cinema brasileiro* (São Paulo: Art Editora, 1987), p. 372.

12 *Ibid.*, p. 371.

13 Helena Salem, *O navegador das estrelas* (Rio de Janeiro: Rocco, 1997), pp. 177–8.

14 Nelson Motta, *Última Hora*, 20 January 1968, quoted in *Ibid.*, p. 181 (our translation).

15 For example, director Joaquim Pedro de Andrade was in prison at the time of completion of *Macunaíma* for political reasons.

16 Ramos, 'Os novos rumos do cinema brasileiro', p. 356.

17 Mention should also be made here of Nelson Pereira dos Santos's 1971 tropicalist film *Como era gostoso meu francês* (*How Tasty Was My Little Frenchman*). Set in sixteenth-century Rio de Janeiro, the film depicts the capture and eventual eating of a soldier from an invading French army by a local Indian tribe. This later feature shares with *Macunaíma* a link with the aesthetic concept of cannibalism, use of allegory, bizarre comic juxtapositions and frequent nudity, and may well have made a greater impact at the box-office, had its release not been so hampered by the censors.

18 Randal Johnson, 'Cinema novo and cannibalism: *Macunaíma*' in Johnson and Stam (eds), Brazilian Cinema, p. 179.

19 Randal Johnson, introduction to Joaquim Pedro de Andrade, 'Cannibalism and self-cannibalism', in Johnson and Stam (eds), *Brazilian Cinema*, p. 82.

20 Robert Stam, 'Tropical detritus: *Terra em transe*, tropicália and the aesthetics of garbage', *Studies in Latin American Popular Culture*, 19 (2000), pp. 84–5.

21 The idea of the law of the hunt finds its most complete expression in this wedding party scene. 'There, high society meets and shapes its carnival – its moment of excess, of play and derangement – as a death pact, as an instance of literal anthropophagic realization, as a self-cannibalizing lottery, a rite through which a class radically commemorates its predatory vocation, Ismail Xavier, *Allegories of Underdevelopment: Aesthetics and Politics in Modern Brazilian Cinema* (Minneapolis: University of Minnesota Press, 1997), p. 143.

22 Pereira dos Santos's *Como era gostoso o meu francês* also depicts sexual initiation and dominance carried out by women. It is worth bearing in mind, however, that the portrayal of such sexual behaviour involved the nudity of some of the sexiest stars around at the time, for example Dina Sfat in *Macunaíma*.

23 Johnson, 'Cinema novo and cannibalism', p. 189. See Joaquim Pedro de Andrade, 'Cannibalism and self-cannibalism', pp. 82–3.

24 Johnson, 'Cinema novo and cannibalism', p. 183.

25 *Ibid.*, p. 184.

26 *Ibid.*, p. 181.

27 *Ibid.*, p. 182.

28 It is likely that in this scene Joaquim Pedro de Andrade was taking a tongue-in-cheek stand against cultural imperialism.

29 Many *chanchadas* also involved men dressed in drag for comic effect: see Chapter 4.

30 Johnson, 'Cinema novo and cannibalism', p. 188.

31 In the film Jack Lemmon is forced to dance tango with a man while disguised as a woman. When he reveals to his suitor in the final scene that he is in fact a man, he is told, 'Nobody's perfect!'.

32 The humour in this scene is reminiscent of Kenneth Williams's death cry of 'Frying tonight!' in the popular British comedy *Carry On Screaming* (1966).

33 Jabor made the important documentary *A opinião pública* (*Public Opinion*, 1967) and the disastrous attempt at Tropicalism in 1970, *Pindorama* (an indigenous name for Brazil), before achieving box-office success with his adaptations of the work of Nelson Rodrigues. He continued to make commercially successful and interesting films with the 1978 comedy *Tudo bem* (*Everything's Alright*) and the 1981 box-office smash starring Sônia Braga, *Eu te amo* (*I Love You*). As *Toda nudez será castigada* was made in the pre-*abertura* 1970s (before the period of political opening-up), we have included a discussion of the film in this chapter.

34 When the film was eventually released, the character of the police chief had been eliminated by the censors. Played by Hugo Carvana, the police chief was a parody of the Brazilian police force and a critique of its corruption: Randal Johnson, 'Nelson Rodrigues as filmed by Arnaldo Jabor', *Latin American Theatre Review* (Fall 1982), p. 22.

35 The film in some ways anticipated later *pornochanchadas* (see Chapter 6). For example, the character Patrício, somewhat the *malandro*, offers a kitsch take on all the overblown melodrama of film, with its 'large gestures, expressions of suffering and desperate tears' (our translation): José Carlos Avellar, *Cinema dilacerado* (Rio de Janeiro: Alhambra, 1986), p. 62.

36 Middle-class collusion with, or at least tolerance of, the dictatorship, particularly during the short-lived economic boom of 1968–72, was a source of much anger in left-wing circles at the time.

37 Johnson, 'Nelson Rodrigues as filmed by Arnaldo Jabor', p. 21. He continues: 'Both *Toda nudez será castigada* and *O casamento* are close enough to realism to make the spectator feel uncomfortable, and yet are exaggerated to such a degree as to create a critical consciousness in the spectator, causing him or her to question

not only the "story" transmitted, but also the form in which it is transmitted'. *Ibid.*, p. 27.

38 André Barcinski and Ivan Finotti, *Maldito: a vida e o cinema de José Mojica Marins, o Zé do Caixão* (São Paulo: Editora 34, 1998), p. 155.

39 *Ibid.*, p. 113.

40 Mentioned in an interview for the documentary film *World's Weirdest Movies: Coffin Joe*, Boum Productions, 2001.

41 Zé do Caixão even had the unlikely honour of having a Volkswagen car named after him, which enjoyed a (very) brief spell of popularity, especially among taxi-drivers, in the late 1960s.

42 The Boca do Lixo (Garbage Mouth) is a district in downtown São Paulo that gained its name due to the large number of prostitutes and pickpockets who frequented its streets. Foreign film distributors were attracted to the Boca from the 1920s, due it its cheap rent and proximity to major coach and railway stations. By the end of the 1950s a number of Brazilian producers were established in the district. Its most active period, in terms of production, was in the 1980s with the advent of hard-core: see Chapter 7.

43 Rogério Sganzerla, *Artes* (October 1967), quoted in Barcinski and Finotti, *Maldito*, p. 174 (our translation).

44 The fact that Mojica Marins's first wife was herself barren was the source of considerable tension within their marriage.

45 Barcinski and Finotti, *Maldito*, p. 107. Despite these features, Mojica Marins's horror films did still follow the European and US tradition of practically all-white casts, and on occasion the naked bodies of females were shot in such a way that they looked whiter than they really were.

46 www.jt.estadao.com.br/noticias/98/04/23/va4: consulted 1 May 2003.

47 Coffin Joe's voice was dubbed in all his films, because Mojica Marins himself had a speech impediment, like a number of other popular entertainers in Brazil. The director played on this impediment in *Delírios de um anormal*, in which he plays himself, but with perfect, confident speech.

48 Mojica Marins did not escape imprisonment altogether during the dictatorship: he was jailed for twenty-four hours and beaten in 1970 for allegedly having sex with an under-age girl: www.jt.estadao.com.br/noticias/98/04/23/va4 (*Hallucinations of a Deranged Mind*).

49 Luís Alberto Rocha Melo, 'Coffin Joe', *Jornal da tarde*, 4 July 2002 (our translation).

50 By the mid-1980s Mojica Marins was earning a living by performing in character as an M. C. for an amusement park. He had become a parody of himself, 'a kind of clown': *World's Weirdest Movies: Coffin Joe*.

51 For example, throughout the 1960s audiences flocked to see the so-called *cangaço* or Brazilian bandit series of films, starting with Carlos Coimbra's *A morte comanda o cangaço* (*The End of the Cangaceiros*, 1961). With the exception of some of Coimbra's work (see also, for example, *Lampião, o rei do cangaço* (Lampião, King of the Cangaceiros, 1964)) these films have largely disappeared from circulation.

52 *Macunaíma*, for example, was financed by the INC's co-production programme.

6

The 1970s

Introduction

The 1970s have witnessed a 'recarnivalisation' of Brazilian cinema, not only as a key trope orienting the film-makers' conception of their own production, but also as a means of renewing contact with the popular audience.[1]

Although democracy for Brazil was still a long way off in 1974, a moderate military president, General Ernesto Geisel, assumed power in that year, with the promise of gradually relaxing military control over the country. His presidency ushered in a period referred to as *abertura* or opening up, a kind of Brazilian *glasnost*. After the international oil crisis of 1973, the bottom had rapidly fallen out of Brazil's so-called economic miracle, which had guaranteed much of the dictatorship's support through the dark days of the 1968–72 period. Geisel was thus a compromise candidate, a general who could ensure that the military both oversaw and controlled any future return to democracy.

In terms of the number of Brazilian films made and their respective box-office success, the 1970s was one of the most important decades in the history of Brazilian cinema. This chapter will consider some of the reasons for this success, including the creation of a state film distribution agency, a sizeable increase in the national film quota, the proliferation of 'quota quickies' and a loosening of censorship restrictions.

The chapter is divided into two sections. The first section looks at three very popular cinematic sub-genres which provided a continuation of the *chanchada* tradition in Brazilian filmmaking: the films of Amácio Mazzaropi; those of the comedic quartet known as the Trapalhões; and the so-called *pornochanchada* series of films. The second part of the chapter concentrates on three of the biggest box-office successes of all time in Brazilian cinema: Carlos Diegues's *Xica da Silva* (*Xica*, 1976); Bruno Barreto's *Dona Flor e seus dois maridos* (*Dona Flor and Her Two Husbands*, 1976) and Neville D'Almeida's *A dama do lotação* (*Lady on the Bus*, 1978).

The *chanchada* legacy in popular film of the 1970s

The Brazilian Cantinflas: Amácio Mazzaropi

The *paulista* comedian Amácio Mazzaropi, forever associated in the Brazilian public imaginary with the country bumpkin character *Jeca*, starred in a total of thirty-two films between 1951 and his death in 1980. In 1958 he formed his own production company (PAM Filmes) and from then on he was responsible for the production and distribution of his films and the use of his image.[2] He even built his own studio in the grounds of his farm in the Paraíba valley in the state of São Paulo in the early 1970s.[3] Mazzaropi was a very astute businessman who from relatively early on in his performing career had been in charge of his own travelling theatre troupe, the Pavilhão Mazzaropi. He joined the radio in the late 1940s, and was quickly picked up by television from its inception in the early 1950s. The fact that he had worked the interior for many years before becoming a successful film star via radio and television meant that he had a good idea of what his audience wanted and how to make them laugh.[4]

All of Mazzaropi's films have a large number of features in common, the most striking of which is the *dramalhão* or element of sentimental drama, with its roots clearly embedded in popular theatre. The plots revolve around a battle between good and evil (good commonly being represented by a young couple in love and evil by the local landowner). The character Jeca, played by Mazzaropi in most of his films, almost loses his faith half way through the movies but is implicitly reconciled with God at the end as good is victorious over evil. As someone is invariably killed off midway, his films tend to include a funeral sequence as well as a wedding at the end, again, firmly rooting these films in popular cultural traditions.[5] Many films include a courtroom drama. Comedy is also very important, although surprisingly not as commonplace as the melodramatic elements. Comedy is supplied almost without exception by the Jeca character, who relies on visual humour (Jeca's gait, his clumsy, animal-like walk similar to that described by the character's original creator, Monteiro Lobato,[6] and his tatty garb, with the waistband of his trousers practically up round his armpits). Visually, then, Mazzaropi is very similar to his Mexican counterpart, Cantinflas, who starred as a *pelado* or country bumpkin in numerous films in the 1940s and 1950s.[7]

Comedy is also supplied by gags, which are inserted with little regard for the narrative.[8] There is plenty of lavatory humour in these films, for example the backward Jeca is often observed responding to a call of nature in a field. The humour throughout *Jecão . . . um fofoqueiro no céu* (Big Jeca . . . A Gossip in Heaven, 1977) was criticised by the press for being in rather poor taste, and jokes are often at the expense of Jeca's long-suffering wife, played in all films made between 1959 and 1978 by Geni Prado. The comedic and dramatic elements of the films are interspersed with musical interludes (invariably an old-fashioned *modinha* sung by Mazzaropi himself and at least one other musical sequence accompanied by dancing).[9] The way all these disparate elements are thrown together feels very much like the programme of the *teatro de revista*, or more specifically the *circo-teatro*. Watching a Mazzaropi film is like watching such a circus performance, complete with music, dance, melodrama with its hammy acting, wrestling in the form of an obligatory stylised fight sequence, and humour. The pace is surprisingly slow: 100 per cent concentration is not a requirement, as if to leave room for buying popcorn and exchanging opinions with other spectators.

While the plot and style of Mazzaropi's films have a deliberate timeless quality to them, they employ a number of techniques to situate the spectator in the present day. First of all, there are musical references to instantly recognisable soundtracks to Hollywood movies and hit television shows.[10] Secondly, there are references at the level of plot to contemporary culture, beginning with allusions to cinema and televisual genres, to be discussed later in this chapter. Other cultures familiar to the audience are brought in, including Japan (or rather the Japanese community in São Paulo) in *Meu Japão brasileiro* (My Brazilian Japan, 1964). Argentina and its trendy ski resort (*Um caipira em Bariloche* (A Caipira in Bariloche, 1973)) and Portugal (*Portugal minha saudade* (Longing for Portugal, 1973)). Common pastimes and customs are present in references to football (*O corintiano* (The Corinthians Supporter, 1966)), popular religions (the syncretic *macumba*, and spiritism, for example, in *O Jeca macumbeiro* (Jeca the Voodoo Practitioner, 1974), *Jeca e seu filho preto* (Jeca and His Black Son, 1978) and *Jeca e a égua milagrosa* (Jeca and the Miraculous Mare, 1980), superstitions (werewolves, fear of the dark, and so on, present in many of his films) and popular professions in the earlier films, for example truck driving, taxi driving, sausage selling, and so on.[11] Another unmistakable feature of the films is the Western-style setting where the bulk of the action takes place: supposedly a small town in the Paraíba Valley but visually closer to the High Chaparral.[12] In terms of attire, characters other than Mazzaropi look more like American cowboys (or at least Hollywood representations of American cowboys) than peasant folk in upstate São Paulo in the 1960s and 1970s. Characters fight by smashing bottles over each other's heads in saloons where the bartenders hide behind the bar for safety: evil and greedy landlords hire thugs to frighten women and children but get their come-uppance at the end: the only mode of transport seems to be horseback, and so on.

The archaic and the modern in Mazzaropi
In many of Mazzaropi's films generational differences are used to reveal a clash, experienced by much of Brazil's migrant population, between the

traditional, conservative values of the interior and the modernity of town and city life. The 1965 film *O puritano da Rua Augusta* (The Puritan from Augusta Street), for example, takes generational conflict as its main subject matter. In a later film, *Portugal minha saudade*, Mazzaropi plays a Portuguese immigrant (almost indistinguishable from his Jeca character, bar the pronounced, comic accent) who is rejected by his lawyer son. According to his daughter-in-law's middle-class family, Mazzaropi and his wife are a constant source of embarrassment and are holding back their own son's career prospects. Encouraged by his plotting mother-in-law, the son provokes his parents into moving out of his comfortable suburban home. For a while Mazzaropi, now tragically widowed in this ultimately humourless film, lives with his successful brother (his twin from whom he was separated at birth) in Lisbon. Despite the comfort of his brother's home and his sibling's kindness, Mazzaropi longs for his simple life in Brazil. By the end of the film Mazzaropi's good son shames his brother into recognising the error of his ways, and our hero returns with great pomp to kick the meddling mother-in-law out of his son's house with a cry of 'Rua!' (Get out!).

In his films Mazzaropi often expresses views that are at odds with national ideology, such as rejection of a proposed divorce law, one of the themes dealt with in *Jeca contra o capeta* (Jeca Versus the Devil, 1976),[13] or which are at least at odds with middle-class, urban, liberal ideology, such as the implicit condemnation of mixed-race marriage seen in *Jeca e seu filho preto* and of the poor who do not accept their station in life. Mazzaropi was the bane of many a left-wing film critic during the 1970s in particular, because of his undeniable conservatism. A well-known friend and supporter of many figures linked to the dictatorship (Presidents Médici and Figueiredo, to name just two), his films were understood as reinforcing both conservative moral values and the political and social status quo.[14] In his films landowners and local politicians are challenged for their exploitation and corruption, but they nearly always have a good son who helps save the day (for example, in *Meu Japão brasileiro*), so there is no suggestion that as a class they have anything to answer for. Individual priests may be pilloried (and frequently they are), but their belief system is not placed under any threat in these films, despite the space frequently afforded other popular religions. The popular courtroom drama scenes may poke fun at stuffy legal language, but they never seem to send up Brazil's notoriously slow and corrupt legal system.[15] Adultery is frowned upon in Mazzaropi's films, although it is often hinted at for comic effect, and so on.[16] Eva Bueno has argued that 'by acknowledging the existence of these films, as well as by watching them, the subaltern, displaced, disenfranchised *caipira*, crowded in *cortiços* – poor neighbourhoods – and slums around the industrial cities, effectively commits an act of insubordination against the official culture of the country, which ignores Jeca and what he represents.'[17] She quotes John

Fiske when stating that Mazzaropi's work embodies 'discursive resources by which people can articulate the meanings of their subordination, but not their acceptance of it'.[18] Mazzaropi could be interpreted as giving his disenfranchised audiences a voice, as he frequently uses phrases that spectators in cinemas reacted to positively. For example, in *Jeca e seu filho preto* he bemoans the fact the evil landowner further rips off his workers through the high cost of rent on his land.

Mazzaropi's relationship with his audience

Mazzaropi said of his screen persona that what made the *caipira* different from men in the city was lack of education and lack of language.[19] But that did not mean to say that the *caipiras* who made up a fair part of his audience were unintelligent. In his films Mazzaropi dealt with the trials of life using both innate perception and a simple, homespun philosophy, making it clear that life experience is just as important as book-learned knowledge. He further ingratiated himself with his displaced audience by including plenty of positive images of the interior (see, for example, *Meu Japão brasileiro*): 'Mazzaropi's films became, if not a link between these displaced Brazilians and their rural past, at least a window open to the idealisation of this past.'[20]

Furthermore, Mazzaropi's Jeca character is always portrayed as an integral part of a special community, for example when he appears dressed in traditional Japanese garb in *Meu Japão brasileiro*, or when in *Portugal minha saudade* he becomes homesick for his antiquated, hard life in Brazil when he is with his Portuguese family in Lisbon.

Paulo Emílio Salles Gomes famously wrote of Mazzaropi's work that it touches something archaic in all Brazilians. The static quality of his work – his constant use of repetition and commonplaces in his films – produced, in Salles Gomes's view, a kind of poetry.[21] Eva Bueno follows this line of thinking when analysing the impact of Jeca on the big screen: 'His presentation – non-official, extra-intellectual and not reclaimed by any established Brazilian intellectual group – reaches the screens untheorised and unmediated.'[22] Mazzaropi himself was the first to deny any ideological content in his films, and it is easy to see how such lack of 'mediation' and his denial of ideological content frustrated supporters of *cinema novo* in the 1960s and 1970s, for example.[23]

Importance is attached to speech in Mazzaropi's films, as apart from anything else his way of speaking is one of the main characteristics of the *caipira* character that he plays and one of the main sources of humour in his films. Like the earlier *chanchada* characters, 'Mazzaropi's work addresses a segment of the Brazilian public *in its own language*, and thus establishes a direct contact with the members of a culture from which he himself emerged.'[24] For example, in the 1964 film *O lamparina* (The Oil Lamp or Little Lampião), set in the

North East of Brazil, characters with distinct accents and spouting slang from different regions of Brazil are represented, along with some accents belonging to immigrant communities in Brazil. The difficulty that the characters have in understanding each other forms the basis of the humour in the film, and would doubtless have struck a chord with migrant workers in the audience.

According to Rowe and Schelling, the function of popular slang is to hold on to an awareness of the difference between the way things really are and the official version.[25] It is interesting to note, then, that like Cantinflas in Mexican popular cinema, Mazzaropi's form of speech is frequently pitched against forms of discourse considered superior. For example, courtroom scenes in his films not only serve to provide variety, dramatic tension and a moral and/or legal resolution to the plot, but they also offer the lead character the opportunity to contrast the clumsy, down-to-earth, popular speech of the *caipira* with that of the stuffy, erudite lawyers, by interrupting proceedings and telling the judge how it really is. In *Meu Japão brasileiro* Mazzaropi verbally attacks a prissy school teacher prone to quoting pretentious, romantic poetry. When she declares 'Afoga as minhas chamas' (Put out my flames) she is promptly chucked in a nearby creek.

The Brazilian Stooges: Os Trapalhões

Another popular film series of the 1970s starred the Trapalhões, or the morons, clumsy ones, scruffy ones (all of these are implied in their name in Portuguese), who were essentially a quartet of comedians, reminiscent of the Three Stooges, who dominated, and continue to make an impact on the national box-office listings in Brazil. No fewer than 14 of the 25 highest-grossing films released between 1970 and 1984 were from the Trapalhões series, the most successful of which, *Os trapalhões nas minas do rei Salomão* (The Trapalhões in King Solomon's Mines, 1977), was seen by almost seven million people by 1984. Renato Aragão (known as Didi in the group), the main player and owner of the production company which, like Mazzaropi's PAM Filmes, was responsible for the Trapalhões's cinematic output once the trademark characters were established in the public imaginary, hailed from the northern state of Ceará and reached cinema screens via television comedy. He is said to be the only producer in Brazil never to have lost money on a film.[26] Manfriedi (Dedé) Santana, the other founding member, had a background in the circus and *teatro de revista* in Rio de Janeiro. Together they made seven films,[27] before being joined in 1976 by another *carioca*, Antônio Carlos Bernardes Gomes (Mussum), who had made a name for himself first in a travelling musical troupe/circus and later on television as a good-humoured *sambista*. Mauro Gonçalves (Zacaria), a radio star from Minas Gerais, completed the quartet in 1978. The four made a remarkable twenty-one films together until the death of Zacaria in 1990.[28]

Although the Trapalhões films were ultimately produced for and aimed at children and teenagers, the viewing figures prove that part of the audience was made up of adults.[29] In terms of popular appeal the Trapalhões series of films works in similar ways to Mazzaropi's films: very strong evidence of the traditions of the *circo-teatro* (in terms of humour, sentimentality and the structure of the films) and references in film titles and plots to recent cinema and television successes. Once again football makes an appearance in the guise of Pelé (*Os trapalhões e o rei do futebol* (The Trapalhões and the King of Football, 1986), as well as *cangaço* (banditry), among other themes, which are often drawn from children's fiction.[30] Interludes with music and dance, often incorporating the latest teenage sensation (the pop bands Dominó and Grupo Polegar from the 1980s, for example), are a staple of these films. They are filled with nods to expressions of popular culture in vogue at the time, such as TV talent competitions (*Na onda do iê-iê-iê* (On the Wave of Rock 'n Roll), 1965), the Brazilian version of country and western music (*O casamento dos trapalhões* (The Marriage of the Trapalhões, 1988), and Beto Carrero's famous rodeo theme park in the South of Brazil (*Os trapalhões no reino da fantasia* (The Trapalhões in the Land of Make Believe), 1985). A frenetic pace, greater emphasis on clowning and humour in general and a didactic element are some of the features that distinguish the Trapalhões films from the Mazzaropi series. Renato Aragão described his films in the following way: 'Children want action and emotion. It's no use putting in a lot of dialogue, making things complicated, because kids make a lot of noise in the theatre and don't hear anything anyway.'[31] There are, then, plenty of sight gags and slapstick humour in the Trapalhões movies,[32] many of which seem to involve acrobatics and accidents with water. Renato has his own amusing visual catch phrases, borrowed from the TV series, such as running his index finger along his bottom lip to mean 'Leave it with me – I'll sort it.' Zacaria's wig-wearing and asexual campness along the lines of the characters played by Charles Hawtrey in Britain's *Carry On* comedy film series, also supplied humour in the films,[33] as did Mussum's facial gymnastics, reminiscent of Oscarito's. References to the nether regions are silly rather than erotic, but the odd joke that would be deemed inappropriate for children in Britain does slip through.[34]

The plots of these films are similar to the Jeca series: the Trapalhões play characters who start off as lowly and marginalised – they are often seen shovelling manure at the beginning of films to emphasise the point.[35] They are soon called upon to aid the forces of good, represented by young lovers, in overcoming evil in the form of a male figure of authority, and as would be expected from such a carnivalesque transformation into temporary heroes, the 'weapons' they use are typically lowly: lots of saucepans over the heads of villains, bug spray in their faces, and so on. A series of adventures and

7   Dedé, Didi and Mussum get down with the apes in *O trapalhão no planalto dos macacos.*

misfortunes befall them on the way, involving chase sequences which take up the bulk of the films' running time, but justice prevails in the end and they are rewarded for their efforts. The figures of evil in these films vary more than in the Jeca series: for example the police in *O trapalhão no planalto dos macacos* (The Trapalhão on the Plateau of the Apes, 1976, see figure 7), landowners in *O Casamento dos trapalhões* and *O cinderelo trapalhão* (The Cinderella Trapalhão, 1979), politicians in *Os heróis trapalhões* (The Hero Trapalhões, 1988), football club bosses in *Os trapalhões e o rei do futebol*, foreign businessmen in *Os trapalhões na Serra Pelada* (The Trapalhões in Serra Pelada, 1982), and so on. When political issues are tackled in these films (and Renato Aragão dealt increasingly with contemporary social themes in his films after 1982), discussion is limited to clear-cut, easy issues, such as the need for water in the North East, or that vote buying and the illicit sale of children for adoption abroad are wrong.

The relationship between the Trapalhões and television
Despite their domination of the cinema charts over the last thirty or so years, the Trapalhões are in fact best known in Brazil for their long-running television series of the same name. Having begun a successful TV career on TV Tupi, the gang made the unimaginably lucrative move to TV Globo in 1977, and

from then on, saturation advertising of the bi-annual release of their films was guaranteed. To give an idea of the extent of their exposure, by July 1983 Renato Aragão had starred in no fewer than 530 hours of weekly programmes on TV.[36] Saturation does seem to be the right word to use in the case of the Trapalhões: they simultaneously produced comic books, toys and even a children's clothing line, while making their television and film series. Many of the products they endorsed were advertised in their films and TV series, along with more traditional examples of product placement.[37]

With the might of TV Globo behind them, it is hard to imagine the Trapalhões' celluloid outings failing.[38] Promoted as children's cinema (the TV series was closer to the standard definition of light entertainment), the Trapalhões tapped into an important market in Brazil, allowing children to go and watch familiar faces and their antics, which had been previously rehearsed on television, without the interference of dubbing or subtitles. In the 1980s the Trapalhões could frequently rely on a supporting cast taken from the most successful national TV programmes, such as children's TV star and media mogul Xuxa (for example, *O trapalhão na arca de Noé*, *Os trapalhões e o mágico de Oroz* (The Trapalhões and the Wizard of Oroz, 1984) and *A Princesa Xuxa e os trapalhões* (Princess Xuxa and the Trapalhões, 1989)) and Gugu Liberato, already in the 1980s being groomed by Sílvio Santos to become the nation's most popular TV variety show presenter, along with the successful boy bands that he managed at the time (*Os fantasmas trapalhões* (The Ghostly Trapalhões, 1987), *O casamento dos trapalhões*, and so on). In one film, *O cangaceiro trapalhão* (The Bandit Trapalhão, 1983), producer Renato Aragão convinced two of TV Globo's soap authors to adapt their own successful mini-series for the troupe for the big screen. The Trapalhões paved the way for other TV Globo stars to make movies for a young Brazilian public in the 1980s and 1990s, such as Xuxa and Sérgio Mallandro.

Mussum made his last Trapalhões film in 1991 (he died of alcohol poisoning in 1994) and Renato Aragão and Dedé Santana made three more commercially successful movies together in the 1990s. Aragão continues to make popular television programmes and films based on his Trapalhão character to this day, with his latest outing as Didi being *O cupido trapalhão* (Cupid Trapalhão, 2003).

The *pornochanchada*

The popular film genre *pornochanchada*, as the name suggests, was said to have a number of the established characteristics of the *chanchada* (humour, plots commonly reliant on a clash between the archaic and modern in society and on mistaken identity, the glamorisation of Brazil's urban spaces, and so on), but all with added spice. The prefix *porno* is rather strong: these were pre-hard-core films that relied on suggestion rather than on sexual explicitness.

The occasional breast shot and distant glimpse of women's bodies in showers were usually the most that *pornochanchada* fans could expect. The reasons for the *pornochanchada's* popularity were three-fold: the inevitable censorship of more politically motivated films at the time, the fact that foreign porn was banned, and more significantly, compulsory screen quotas that resulted in exhibition groups producing their own films, the outcome of which were cheap, mass-produced soft-core porn films, many of which were partly financed by Embrafilme.[39]

For José Carlos Avellar, ironically the *pornochanchada* came into being as a result of censorship.[40] Avellar believes that it is more than a coincidence that censorship and the *pornochanchada* both appeared in the first few months of 1969. Censorship, for Avellar, also influenced the style of the *pornochanchada*: 'Censorship, the violent language of power, could do nothing against those who used the same methods. Censorship did not alter a language that in its own conception was censored and disarticulated.'[41]

Evidence of this self-censorship (a kind of *coitus interruptus*, in the words of Randal Johnson and Robert Stam[42]) and disarticulation can be found in the fact that films rarely delivered on the promise of sex and nudity, and in the omission of rude words from the film soundtrack but which can clearly be read on the lips of actors. For example, in the provocatively titled *As secretárias . . . que fazem de tudo* (Secretaries . . . Who Do It All, 1975), in point of fact, the said secretaries do next to nothing, other than wiggle their bottoms, and they even get married at the end of the film. Self-censorship can also be seen in the large number of euphemisms and double entendres in the film scripts and film titles. For example, the verb *dar* literally means 'to give' in Portuguese, but it can also suggest penetration, 'giving it out' or offering sex. The innuendo frequently crops up in the titles of *pornochanchadas*, for example *Cada um dá o que tem* (Each One Gives Whatever They Can, 1975) and *Eu dou o que ela gosta* (I Give Her What She Likes, 1975).[43] The word *boa*, the feminine form of the adjective 'good', also implies both good-looking and good in bed, as suggested in the 1973 film *Como é boa nossa empregada* (How Good Our Maid Is).

The *pornochanchada* was also influenced by the episodic Italian sex comedies, such as those starring Lando Buzzanca, which were commercially successful (and thus an interesting genre to imitate) both in Europe and in Brazil at the time. The episodic nature of these Italian films, copied in most cases in their Brazilian counterparts, made them cheaper and quicker to produce than feature-length films with a single plot line, and narratively less challenging for inexperienced writers. In the early days of the *pornochanchada*, these films were copied wholesale, such as Dino Risi's *Sessomatto* (*How Funny Can Sex Be?*, 1973), which was transformed in Brazil into *Com as calças na mão* (With His Pants in His Hands, 1975). Although many of the best-known *pornochanchadas*, including the first ever example, *Os Paqueras* (The Flirts, 1969), were made and set in Rio, the genre is closely associated with the city of São Paulo, and more specifically the district called the Boca do Lixo ('Mouth of Garbage'), the most prolific centre of film production in Brazil of all time, where most *pornochanchadas* were produced. To give an idea of the district's prominence in terms of popular Brazilian cinema, around 700 *pornochanchadas* were produced there during the genre's lifetime. During the 1970s and early '80s, the Boca do Lixo was responsible for around sixty of the ninety Brazilian films produced annually.[44]

The *pornochanchada* typically dealt, in a good-humoured way, with the issue of sex (and how to get some/more of it), using stock characters, many of whom were familiar to audiences from bawdier examples of the *teatro de revista* and the circus.[45] These types included the womaniser, the virgin (male and female), the homosexual, the impotent old man, the old prostitute, the frustrated widow, the randy maid, the repressed secretary, and so on. The early films marked a return of the *carioca* tradition of popular urban comedies (these had, as we know, practically disappeared with the growth of television) and gave expression to a new wave of permissiveness in (sophisticated, urban) Brazilian society. When the first *pornochanchada* film, *Os paqueras*, was released to popular acclaim, critics and the audience were said to have felt that they had seen something different from the usual comedies of the time, because of the film's irreverence in dealing with social relationships. The two main characters in the film are an older, wealthy womaniser and his young follower, a work-shy, middle-class dropout. An example of the irreverent treatment afforded marital relationships in the film can be found in an important scene in which the womaniser is caught in the act with another woman by her husband and the police. En route to the police station, the husband is booed by gathering crowds while the old seducer is carried through the streets by a rejoicing throng. As a result of the success of the film, the word *paquera* (flirting) started to be used almost indiscriminately in film titles, and helped to crystallise one of the principal elements of the *pornochanchada*: the element of voyeurism.

This voyeurism is often articulated literally in these films, with the act of peering through telescopes, spy-holes, over walls and round corners, all carried out, on behalf of eager audiences, by the camera itself. For example, in the episodic *Como é boa nossa empregada*, the plot line of the first part of the film revolves around a young lad's attempt to spy on his maid using a series of contraptions that supply the film's humour. His attempts to see her naked during the course of the film are ultimately frustrated. In *A superfêmea* (Superwoman, 1973), during a test for a photo shoot involving a large number of women, an advertising executive inspects one of them, tellingly and for no good reason, through a telescope. And in the *Jaws* (1975) parody *Bacalhau*

(Codfish, 1975) a policeman using a monocular to search for a deadly beast that is terrorising the coastline shouts 'Que monstruosidade!' (What a monstrosity!), while the camera, peering as if through the monocular, reveals he is in fact checking out a young woman's backside. Snatched glances are typical of the furtive kind of behaviour displayed by male characters in many *pornochanchadas*. Such furtiveness is often alluded to only in film titles: for example in the 1975 film, *O roubo das calcinhas* (The Theft of the Panties), the supposed subject hardly enters the film.

The new wave of permissiveness alluded to earlier inevitably brought with it clashes between different generations in Brazilian urban society, and the issue of the generation gap is dealt with in many *pornochanchadas*. *Os paqueras* itself pitches the young anti-hero against his stuffy, bourgeois family. In the third part of *Como é boa nossa empregada* an aggressive, authoritarian father dominates his family, and is seen as being out of place in the chilled-out 1970s. In *Essa gostosa brincadeira a dois* (This Tasty Game For Two, 1974) a young couple are thwarted by their elders in their plan to move in together. What tends to happen in films that deal with the generation gap is that the older generation are happily indulging in all sorts of peccadilloes while chastising their offspring for their liberal take on relationships. Such hypocrisy is one of the comedic staples of the *pornochanchada*, as is the younger family members' use of *malandragem* to outwit their parents or take their revenge.

Another common feature of the *pornochanchada* is the presence of pivotal characters from the interior, and their trials during a (frequently temporary) visit to the big city. For example, in *Cada um dá o que tem*, the seducer arrives in the city having just worked for six months on the Trans-Amazonian Highway. In *Nos tempos da vaselina* (In The Days of Vaseline, 1979), the young protagonist arrives at Rio's busy bus station from a small town upstate (the suggestively titled Macacú)[46] and immediately has his luggage stolen. A taxi driver then takes him to Ipanema in a roundabout way, giving him en route a carnivalesque explanation of the history of the city,[47] and kicks him out of the car when his money has run out. Film producers' fascination with places in the interior of the states of Rio and São Paulo continued throughout the life of the *pornochanchada*. In *Bem-dotado: o homem de Itu* (Well-endowed: The Man from Itu, 1977) a young lad from the interior is invited to work in the home of a rich woman in the city. The town of Itu is renowned in Brazil for containing bigger than average flora and fauna. Needless to say, the rich hostess soon finds out that nature has blessed her houseguest in a similar way.

In another typical storyline, in *Como é boa nossa empregada*, an innocent young girl from Campos (also in the interior of the state of Rio de Janeiro) arrives in Rio city looking for work as a maid in a decent home, and quickly becomes the object of lust of the men of the house. Like the stock *chanchada* heroes, in the *pornochanchada* characters from the sticks are portrayed as gullible and naive alongside their *carioca* and *paulista* counterparts, but by the end of the film, they have usually 'come of age' through an (admittedly superficial) exploration of their repressed sexuality.

The depiction of sexuality in the pornochanchada

There has been a consensus of opinion over the years that the depiction of sexuality in the *pornochanchada* was unmistakably conservative and sexist. The *pornochanchada* is conservative in that sexually liberated characters are usually either punished or, more frequently, married off by the end of the film. Critics fail to take into account, however, that such moralising may well have been inspired by fears of the censors, as if supplying a conservative ending could make up for sexual daring earlier on in the films. It is worth bearing in mind that sexuality, no matter how conservative, repressed and commodified, had never been systematically discussed on screen in Brazil before then. And besides, any kind of confirmation of the status quo was never going to be tolerated by a left-wing press during a military dictatorship, so the *pornochanchada* was doomed to be either condemned or ignored by critics at the time. For example, according to Salles Gomes, while the *chanchada* mocked conventional social relations, the *pornochanchada* endorsed them.[48] Likewise, the only mocking going on in the *pornochanchada*, in Jean-Claude Bernardet's view, was of elderly, ugly and gay people who wanted a sex life like anyone else.[49]

Jean-Claude Bernardet has also argued that many of the sexual themes of these films spoke to aspects of the Brazilian male psyche at the time, such as machismo and fear of castration. Hence the presence of the homosexual character in these films: laughing at these modern-day court jesters proved the audience's masculinity and exorcised their sexual insecurity and fear of impotence.[50]

Many of the features that are highly characteristic of Brazilian sexual life are dealt with in the *pornochanchada*, for example the complex relationship that white, middle-class men have with maids and other subaltern females, commonly of mixed race, such as secretaries and nannies. Although nowadays considered a luxury, given their increased wages and fairer working hours, in the 1970s even most lower-middle-class families could afford a live-in (and frequently exploited) maid, the majority of whom were mixed-race or black migrant workers. It was common practice for young men to lose their virginity to such women, very much in the tradition of master–slave relations and the stereotype of the seductive charms of the *mulata* described, for example, by sociologist Gilberto Freyre.[51] The maid usually represents a different race and class to her boss, and thus the whole notion of furtive, naughty sex, one of the lynch pins of the *pornochanchada*, could successfully be explored through her (see figure 8). There was never any question in these films of the

8 Juciléa Telles as the archetypal sexy mixed-race maid in *Uma mulata para todos* (1975).

inappropriateness of such relationships. For example, in the second part of *Como é boa nossa empregada*, a teenage lad is taken to a psychologist (another popular and particularly randy character in these films) because of his fixation on maids. The psychologist tells him that his behaviour is not that unusual and that he has an inferiority complex because of the state of Brazilian society. As a cure, he suggests to the lad's mother that she take him to see a high-class prostitute (the inference clearly being that, in the scheme of things, prostitutes are a step up from racially marked maids).

Another feature of Brazilian sexual life that is dealt with, albeit in a more veiled way, is the issue of sodomy. Although sodomy is a more openly popular sexual practice in Brazil than, say, in some Anglo-Saxon societies, where it is strongly associated with homosexuality, in the *pornochanchada* the threat of homosexual, rather than heterosexual sodomy often appears in the form of a visual gag. Camera positions (which eventually pull back to reveal innocent scenarios) frequently hint at anal penetration. We clearly get the impression of homosexual activity in one scene involving the psychologist and the teenager in *Como é boa nossa empregada*, and on at least three occasions the camera hints at it again, in *Nos tempos da vaselina*. For example, in one scene, the protagonist is lying face down on the bed and, in a common enough visual joke involving heterosexual couples, his cousin can be seen moving behind him in what looks like a penetrating motion. When the camera pulls back we discover that the cousin is merely putting cream on the other's sunburnt back.[52] As these scenes have no bearing on the plot of the films in question, they seem to be merely an opportunity to include some near-the-knuckle depictions of sexuality without the censors picking up on them (after all, how many examples of bad editing must the censors have sat though when assessing these films?). Sodomy, like sex with subaltern females and homosexual desire, is equated with dirtiness and smut. As José Carlos Avellar summed up succinctly in an article entitled 'Gross National Product', the goal of the *pornochanchada* was not to be erotic or pornographic, but lewd, smutty and dirty.[53] He cites as an example of this a scene from *Cada um dá o que tem* where a short-sighted seminary student sniffs the bed sheets to see if a woman had been in his bed, or if it was a wet dream.

Watching pornochanchada

Avellar's previously mentioned views on the carnivalesque defiance of the *pornochanchada* audience in the light of the dictatorship are worth pursuing in greater depth, in the context of our discussion on sexuality in these films. Avellar argues that: 'The spectator . . . would go to the cinema to take part in a kind of plot, to conspire against the established order, to conspire against conversations in broad daylight, made up of irrelevant subjects, or using words that he could not even understand.'[54]

In the darkness of the cinema, the established order, as depicted by the government propaganda films that preceded all feature films at the time, could be freely derided.[55] These advertisements for the dictatorship were shot frequently in soft focus, with smooth, paternalistic voiceovers, echoing messages such as 'Meu Brasil, eu amo você' (My Brazil, I love you) and they dealt with themes like hygiene, health and work with the objective of improving living conditions and galvanising the work force. Also, they sought to strengthen 'the national character with regard to love for work and patriotism, and to maintain the support and patience of the masses'.[56] *Pornochanchadas*, by contrast, were bad mannered, sluttish, utterly stupid, and promoted individualism and a rejection of the work ethic.[57] Avellar thus concludes that it is possible that audiences started going to see these films because they knew they were bad – when you cannot deal rationally with your own reality, you (in good Bakhtinian fashion) turn to the absurd.[58] Avellar cites as an example of this Mozael Silveira's 1975 film *Secas e Molhadas* (Dried Up and Moist).[59] The critic explains that the film is shoddily produced and plays on its poor quality to attract the public. Perhaps, he argues, it is an unconscious act of revenge on the official publicity that depicted Brazil as a supernation, with, among other jewels in the crown, the Trans-Amazonian Highway, Maracanã, the largest football stadium in the world 'and other such things, equally gigantic, but far removed from the experience of the spectator of *pornochanchada*. The film is badly made: if this has been done deliberately or if it is as a result of lack of money and the creative incapacity of the director, is of no consequence. What is for certain is that the *pornochanchada* plays with this idea.'[60]

Parody in popular films of the 1970s

Just as the *chanchada* had done before them in the 1950s, a number of films starring Mazzaropi, the Trapalhões and from the *pornochanchada* genre cashed in on the popularity of foreign box-office successes, either through mimicking titles or through attempting more elaborately constructed parodies of the originals. Parody in Brazilian film has been extensively researched by João Luis Vieira and Robert Stam, who describe it in the following terms: 'By parody . . . we refer to a reflexive mode of discourse which renders explicit the processes of intertextuality through distortion, exaggeration, or elaboration of a pre-existing text or body of texts.'[61]

For these authors, parody has a special role in the context of asymmetrical arrangements of power, such as those frequently encountered in Brazilian society: 'By appropriating an existing discourse but introducing into it an orientation oblique, or even diametrically opposing it to that of the original, parody is especially well-suited to the needs of the oppressed and the powerless, precisely because it *assumes* the force of the dominant discourse, only to deploy that force, through a kind of artistic jujitsu, *against* domination.'[62]

While Mazzaropi's borrowings from Hollywood and elsewhere tended to be limited to passing references, such as incidental music or set pieces, some of his films were at least partly re-workings of hit movies of the time: *Jeca contra o capeta* was very loosely based on the high-grossing *Exorcist* (1973), while *Uma pistola para Djeca* (A Pistol For Djeca, 1970) and *O grande xerife* (The Great Sheriff, 1971) self-consciously imitated the so-called *bangue-bangues* or Westerns of both Hollywood and the Italian film industry. Imitations included those of home-grown popular cinematic genres such as *cangaço* or banditry in the North East, the Brazilian equivalent of the Western (*O Lamparina*), *pornochanchada* (*A banda das velhas virgens* (The Gang of Old Virgins, 1979)), and soap operas (*Betão Ronca Ferro*, 1970, Mazzaropi's version of the very popular TV Globo soap opera *Beto Rockefeller*). The Trapalhões were particularly fond of parodying Hollywood blockbusters, for example *Planet of the Apes* (*O trapalhão no planalto dos macacos*, 1976),[63] *Star Wars* (*Os trapalhões na guerra dos planetas* (The Trapalhões In the Battle of the Planets, 1978)), *Oliver* (*Os vagabundos trapalhões* (The Homeless Trapalhões, 1982)), *Seven Brides for Seven Brothers* (*O casamento dos trapalhões*), and Indiana Jones, Rambo, and Superman (*Os heróis trapalhões*). In fact, at least thirteen films starring the Trapalhões have been re-workings of Hollywood movies and US television series.

In a memorable scene from *Jeca contra o capeta*, Mazzaropi's wife is in bed, seemingly possessed by the Devil. The bed starts to move up and down and only some time afterwards is it revealed that a large dog has been hiding underneath. Mazzaropi retorts: 'Isso me lembra um filme que vi outro dia: *O eletricista*' (That reminds me of a film I saw the other day: The 'Electricist').[64] As well as *Jeca contra o capeta*, references to *The Exorcist* can be found in the *pornochanchadas Pesadelo sexual de um virgem* (Sexual Nightmare of a Virgin, 1976) and *O exorcista de mulheres* (The Exorcist of Women, 1974). Hong Kong martial arts films partly inspired *As massagistas profissionais* (The Professional Masseuses, 1976) and *Kung Fu contra as bonecas* (*Kung Fu Against the Dolls*, 1975).

In the case of *Nos tempos da vaselina* the tenuous link with *Grease* (1978) (entitled *Nos tempos da brilhantina* (In the Days of Brylcreem) in Brazil) is found in the *caipira* protagonist's gullibility and 'squareness' alongside the sophisticated teenagers that he meets in Rio de Janeiro. The plot is moved on by references to disco dancing, thus picking up on another Hollywood box-office hit, *Saturday Night Fever* (1977). The word 'Vaseline' has obviously been used for its phonetic similarity to *brilhantina*, along with its useful sexual connotations. It has little to do with the film's plot: the protagonist's cousin has a pot of Vaseline and when some of it goes missing he mistakenly believes that the protagonist is making use of it when sleeping with the former's girlfriend.

9   Everyone's after the sexual healing of Carlos Imperial in *A banana mecânica* (1974).

Another *pornochanchada* to play with the title of a well-known foreign film is *A banana mecânica* (The Mechanical Banana, 1974), which takes its inspiration from the Brazilian title of *A Clockwork Orange* (1971), *A laranja mecânica* or 'mechanical orange'. By simply swapping one fruit for another, more sexually suggestive one, director Braz Chediak was able to tap into the interest surrounding the release and censorship of the original film with very little effort. *A banana mecânica* is a good-natured sexual romp and thus has little in common with Kubrick's ultra-violent and politically charged movie. The aversion therapy story line of the original is maintained in the vaguest possible way in the Brazilian film through the presence of psychoanalyst Dr Ferrão (played by Carlos Imperial), whose usual line of work involves giving sexual advice to attractive women, while at the same time seducing them. One day he is set a more difficult challenge: Paulo Frederico is the effeminate son of a wealthy family, and Dr Ferrão sets about transforming him into a stud through psychoanalysis (see figure 9).

One film to mimic, rather than parody, a US blockbuster was *Costinha e o King Mong* (Costinha and King Mong, 1977), inspired by the *King Kong* re-make of 1976. It was a clear example of the 'parasitic strategy' referred to by Vieira and Stam in the context of filmic parodies. It was simultaneously released in Brazil with the Hollywood version, and the poster was designed in such as way as to trick potential audiences for the American movie into seeing the wrong film. In addition, the Brazilian version was deliberately aimed at children, taking advantage of the fourteen-and-over certificate limitations imposed on the American film, and it adhered, rather humourlessly, to the general plot of the original.[65]

Clearly, then, differing degrees of parody/citation/mimicry/referencing were used in popular movies in the 1970s. One film from the era, however, can be said to have shadowed its original more closely, and with the more specific intention of debunking the values it represented: *Bacalhau*. A number of devices are employed to ensure that the audience is kept aware of the fact that *Bacalhau* is the Brazilian answer to *Jaws*. The poster mimics the Hollywood film's poster, in showing a lone woman swimming in the sea and being hunted by a large fish. In keeping with the *pornochanchada* tradition the woman is smiling cheekily at the viewer of the poster and her bikini top has fallen off. In the same way that posters advertising foreign films in Brazil highlight the original title of films in English underneath their titles in Portuguese, the word *Bacs* appears in brackets underneath the title, as if *bacs* means *bacalhau* in English. The word *bacalhau* in Brazil has two strong connotations: first, it is associated with the Portuguese community, salted cod being the national dish of Portugal, and secondly, it is pejoratively associated, through its strong smell, with aroused sexuality in women. Props used in the film are deliberately kitsch and cheap looking, such as the rubber skeleton washed up on the beach at the beginning of the film. In a humorous scene, the label 'Made in Ribeirão Preto' can clearly be seen on the side of the model used to represent the codfish in the sea.[66] Even the film's editing has a pronounced clumsiness to it, which suggests that it has been done on purpose. The stock types of the *pornochanchada* are present in *Bacalhau*. These include the 'gay fool', whose camp screams when he encounters a skeleton on the beach are confused with the sound of a police siren; the attractive young women who are keen to be 'eaten' by the codfish; and the predatory male (a lazy politician who seems to spend most of his time in bed).

Bacalhau is therefore set up from the start as being a low budget, badly made and debased version of *Jaws*, and therein lies its carnivalesque humour. Vieira and Stam write that: '*Bacalhau* highlights the discrepancies between parody and original in a self-destructive manner, not as a weapon against domination. In a vicious circle, both author and public share and stimulate an attitude of self-contempt based on the alleged Brazilian incompetence in imitation.'[67] They continue: 'amused but feeling cheated, the public responds (to the shark) with ambiguous laughter . . . rather than question spectatorial identification with the foreign model, *Bacalhau* fosters uncritical admiration'.[68]

It is not clear, however, how seeing proof of Brazil's celluloid failure compared to the dominant Hollywood model results in 'ritual self-degradation'
on the part of the audience.[69] It seems, instead, that films such as *Bacalhau*
offer an otherwise alienated film audience a cosy, knowing feeling of complicity when faced with a hegemonic model, be it a Hollywood blockbuster
or a government propaganda film. And besides, as has been seen in the case
of the *pornochanchada* audience, the self-contempt referred to by Vieira and
Stam can arguably be seen as a form of resistance, given the context of the
nationalist discourse of the dictatorship.

Furthermore, self-contempt suggests an identification on the part of the
viewer with the characters in the film, but the social types being pilloried in
this film are predominantly the Portuguese, the Americans and the Brazilian
authorities. In order to catch the codfish, a Portuguese oceanographer is
sent for: he arrives from Lisbon in a tea chest posted to the policeman's
house. He has the comedy accent used by many a Portuguese character in
popular cinema and theatre, his dress sense is ludicrous (he wears a wetsuit
with a collar and tie on over the top) and he conforms to stereotype further
by showing an interest in dark-skinned Brazilian women. In order to catch
the codfish in the final hunt scene, the oceanographer uses broken pieces of
records by the famous Portuguese *fado* singer Amália Rodrigues as bait.

As a number of the individuals in *Bacalhau* are based on original characters
from *Jaws*, the audience's understanding is that the film is ridiculing the
stock types of Hollywood blockbusters, as much as the incompetent Brazilian
authorities.[70] For example, the policemen first appear wearing Bermuda shorts,
Stetsons and striped knee socks, in what has to be a parody of the unsophisticated dress sense of small-town America.[71] The constant references to the
filmmaking process in *Bacalhau* also serve to remind the audience just how
nonsensical, despite its high entertainment factor, the whole notion of *Jaws*
the film really is (see figure 10).

The legacy of the *chanchada* in popular comedies of the 1970s

Mazzaropi in the 1960s and 1970s, the Trapalhões in the 1970s and 1980s,
and the *pornochanchada* in the 1970s in many ways continued with the
chanchada comic tradition in Brazilian cinema. For example, the *trapalhão*
Renato Aragão, who once said that he had learned his comic trade from
watching the *chanchada* star Oscarito over and over again,[72] is very reminiscent of the stock *chanchada* hero. Both he and Mazzaropi starred in *chanchadas*
early on in their careers,[73] and likewise, many *pornochanchadas* incorporated
the actors of the *chanchada* era, for example José Lewgoy in *Os paqueras*,
A viúva virgem (The Virgin Widow, 1972) and *Um soutien para papai* (A Bra
For Daddy, 1975), and Zezé Macedo in *As mulheres que fazem diferente*
(Women Who Do It Differently, 1974), *Oh! Que delícia de patrão!* (Oh! What

10   Publicity still for *Bacalhau* (1975).

a Tasty Boss!, 1974) and *Com as calças na mão* (With His Pants in his Hands, 1975). Many of the stars associated with these films, like their *chanchada* counterparts, learned their trade in the *teatro de revista*, the circus and the radio.[74] Many Trapalhões movies were directed by J. B. Tanko, a well-known *chanchada* director. The inclusion in the group of the character Mussum, who was given his trademark nickname by none other than Grande Otelo, suggests a recognition of the importance of the *carioca malandro* element in popular comedy films, as established by the *chanchadas*, and as developed further by *carioca pornochanchadas*. All the main characters from the Mazzaropi and Trapalhões series represent the marginalised poor, just as Grande Otelo, Oscarito and Ankito had done before them. Mazzaropi's Jeca continued with the *chanchada*'s tradition of appealing to an audience partly made up of the displaced rural migrants in the big cities and ennobling the archaic, conservative traditions of those from the interior. As in many *chanchadas* from the 1950s, Mazzaropi's films often include clashes between the rural and the urban, between peasants and the middle classes, and between traditional values and materialism, through which the poor in the audience could view their own lives more positively.

   Like the *chanchada*, the Mazzaropi and Trapalhões films and the *pornochanchada* were mass-produced and stuck to safe and acceptable formulae, incorporating many elements from the popular circus and the *teatro de revista*. Like the *chanchada* in the 1930s and 1940s, released to coincide with carnival, the first two series were associated with certain dates: Mazzaropi aimed to premiere his films on the same date (25 January: the anniversary of São Paulo) and in the same place (the Art-Palácio cinema in the centre of the city) every year, while the Trapalhões films were released bi-annually to coincide with school holidays.

A number of plot devices typical of the *chanchada* genre are drawn on in Trapalhões films, for example the reliance on mistaken identities to effect an inversion of social hierarchies for comic effect, quirks of fate which bring good luck to the heroes, and, although to a much lesser extent, the use of foreign filmic models to joke about the inferior national copy. As an example of this, in the Trapalhões version of *The Incredible Hulk* (*O incrível monstro trapalhão* (The Incredible Monster Trapalhão, 1980), Renato Aragão's character is transformed into a *super-jegue* (*jegue* signifying a kind of mule strongly associated with Brazil's backward, rural past). Mistaken identities are also frequently played on in the *pornochanchada*. For example, in the third part of *Como é boa nossa empregada*, a husband asks a friend to take his maid out, who is waiting for him in his car, because he has just spotted his wife in town. The maid (who is black but who could easily be confused with his white wife as she is wearing a blonde wig!) meanwhile gets bored and wanders off, while the wife spots her husband's car and climbs in. The friend then mistakenly takes the protagonist's wife off for an afternoon of love-making. In the first part of *Oh, que delícia de patrão!* the boss falls ill and is replaced, in typical *chanchada* fashion, by a car mechanic look-alike.

As in both the *chanchadas* and the Mazzaropi series, the Trapalhões team also used plenty of slang and colloquialisms in their films, and the character Mussum spoke an invented language, adding the suffix 'is' onto the ends of words. Arguing the case for an inversion of hierarchies here, as has been argued elsewhere, is problematic, however, as the language seems to be aimed specifically at children and worked only really on this level. Inversions of hierarchies take place at the level of plot, but as the heroes tend to make good through luck or with the aid of magic, it is hard to see any elements of the challenge to the status quo that is present in a number of *chanchadas*.[75] The best that one could argue is that the Trapalhões' attitude to life and behaviour at times bordered on *malandragem*, exemplified in the character Mussum's relationship in these films with alcohol. The counter-culture of *malandragem*, as previously discussed, is a significant feature of the *chanchada*, and the *pornochanchada* too, for that matter. Hierarchical inversions are also present in the story lines of many *pornochanchadas*, one of the most popular being domestic servants who exert power over their employers in the bedroom, but these films inevitably ended with a return to the status quo, not to mention the implicit power the male spectator would feel when viewing women in such bedroom scenes. They do, however, like the *chanchada*, offer an ironic and critical vision of the elite as seen from below, particularly with regard to the issues of sexual repression and hypocrisy.

In terms of spectatorship, there are clear similarities, as has been seen, between the *chanchada* audience and Mazzaropi's faithful fans, but the *pornochanchada* audience also enjoyed a secret intimacy with the films they watched, similar to the experience of regular viewers of the *chanchada*. As José Carlos Avellar has put it: 'There is an easy complicity between the spectator and the irreverent world [of the *pornochanchada*], very probably because he finds relief from the tensions of day-to-day life in this special reality: [in the cinema], he has no material problems, no duty to the person beside him or with society, nor anyone to tell him how to behave.'[76]

Abertura and Embrafilme: comedy and *pornochique*

Film critic Jean-Claude Bernardet wrote in 1979 that one of the strategies of Geisel's government had been to co-opt intellectuals, in order to defuse opposition.[77] Within this context it is interesting to see the extent to which one-time radical cineastes continued, after 1968, to depend on the state for support in their filmmaking projects. For example, the co-production scheme of the National Cinema Institute (INC), that filmmakers such as Joaquim Pedro de Andrade had found useful (see Chapter 5), was replaced in 1973 by a similar scheme run by a new government agency, Embrafilme (Brazilian Film Enterprise). Embrafilme, which had been set up in 1969, began as a state distribution agency, but started producing films in 1973. During the directorship of film producer Roberto Farias (1974–79) the organisation's budget rose from 600,000 to eight million dollars. Embrafilme was responsible for the distribution of over 30 per cent of Brazilian films in the 1970s, and for between 25 and 50 per cent of annual film production. As a result, the market share of Brazilian cinema increased from 15 per cent in 1974 to more than 30 per cent in 1980, while the number of spectators of Brazilian films doubled.[78] Three films, *Xica da Silva*, *Dona Flor e seus dois maridos*, and *A dama do lotação*, each partly financed and/or distributed by Embrafilme in the mid-1970s, set box-offices alight, and have been quoted ever since as proof of the success of Embrafilme and the importance of state intervention in the national cinema industry. During the dictatorship, cineastes such as Carlos Diegues, Bruno Barreto and Neville D'Almeida, directors of the three films to be analysed in this section, were happy to support a cultural agency of the government, in exchange for that agency's backing against a greater enemy: an invading foreign cinema.

By the mid-1970s, occasionally actors and directors associated with mainstream cinema and television would wander into the territory of erotic comedy, usually in an attempt to tap into the huge commercial success that the *pornochanchada* was enjoying at the time.[79] With their big budgets, famous actresses and catwalk models, and high production values, films such as *Xica da Silva*, *Dona Flor e seus dois maridos*, and *A dama do lotação* created a cleaned-up version of the *pornochanchada*, as Jean-Claude Bernardet has put it.[80] They tended to rely on the nudity (or promise of nudity) of the leading actresses, especially if the public was used to seeing the latter in more 'respectable' roles in TV soap operas, for example. Thus the element of transgression in these films is clear from the outset and even in the choice of actress for the leading role. It was arguably this element of transgression that attracted viewers to the cinema as much as the promise of nudity associated with such films.

Xica da Silva

Xica da Silva (*Xica*, 1976), starring black actress Zezé Motta, is based on the story of the real-life eighteenth-century slave woman from Minas Gerais who became the lover of and was granted her freedom by a wealthy diamond merchant, João Fernandes, a representative of the Portuguese crown in Brazil. Her boundless sexual energy, extravagance and outrageous behaviour made her the talk of the colony, so much so that Portugal eventually insisted on João Fernandes's return, resulting in Xica's rapid fall from grace.

Many critics have argued that *Xica da Silva* merely serves to reinforce the myth of the Afro-Brazilian as a predominantly sexual being. As Peter Rist put it, the portrayal of Xica on screen could be seen as distinctive carnivalesque Brazilianness, or as reeking of Africana stereotype.[81] Others have argued that slave women had their bodies to barter with and little else at the time and Xica is portrayed in the film as mostly in control of hers.[82] One of the significant lines in the film, oft-repeated by the men who come in contact with her sexually is: 'Não, Xica, não . . . !' (No, Xica, no . . . !). She is seen as initiating a sexual act of which her various partners are fearful. A lack of revolutionary dimension is what critics also found hard to stomach in the film,[83] particularly one directed by Carlos Diegues, still strongly associated with the *cinema novo* movement, who had made in 1963 *Ganga Zumba*, a film about a *quilombo* or maroon slave community, and therefore very specifically about black resistance in Brazil. What is ironic, then, is the information that has recently come to light about Xica's life, which contrasts with her depiction in the film.[84] Xica had fourteen children with João Fernandes and her four eldest sons accompanied their father back to Portugal. Her daughters married well into local high society. Xica herself joined various lay religious orders and was buried in a space reserved for whites. And that was twenty years after João Fernandes had returned to Portugal.

Randal Johnson has identified a series of carnivalesque elements in the film, and has discussed its Bakhtinian hierarchical inversions in detail.[85] The film was in fact based on the winning entry of Salgueiro samba school for the 1963 Rio carnival, and the notion of spectacle was foremost in director Diegues's mind during filming.[86] Zezé Motta brings to the screen the colourful and camp performative excess that is reminiscent of both the Rio carnival and the roles played by Carmen Miranda in Hollywood.[87] The use of archetypes (the lascivious black slave woman, for example) is typical of a carnivalesque interpretation. The fact that Xica uses her sexual prowess to rise in power is somehow more acceptable when viewed in the carnivalesque terms of the material bodily principle. Robert Stam reports that Lelia Gonzales, a leading spokesperson for both feminism and black liberation, dismissed the attack on *Xica da Silva* as puritanical, arguing that it was in some ways a very black film, a hymn to the vitality of black culture.[88] It can be argued that a worse stereotype would be to depict slaves as morose and downtrodden. Also, what other Brazilian film has a black woman playing the lead role? *Uma mulata para todos* (A Mulata For Everyone), a *pornochanchada* released the year before, starred Julciléa Telles playing a young girl up from the sticks who stereotypically becomes a prostitute. It is hard to remember any examples of black females in lead roles since, even including the *pornochanchadas*.[89]

Diegues remarked later in an interview with Sílvia Oroz that his film had struck a chord with the cinema-going public in Brazil because it depicted 'the victory of the *malandro* over the hero'.[90] It seems, then, that the inversion of societal norms played out by Xica, and how it was celebrated by the spectators, who brought a 'party atmosphere' to cinema halls, revealed the important message of resistance contained in the film, confirming in part the observations made by José Carlos Avellar on the *pornochanchada*.

In *Xica da Silva* Diegues privileges 'food, sex, music and dance': the elements of Brazilian culture most associated with the nation's African heritage. Diegues's views, then, on the contribution of the African to Brazilian culture are not that far removed from Gilberto Freyre's outdated and frankly paternalistic notions.[91] Diegues wrote of his film: 'The film shows how a segment of Brazilian society, the Afro-Brazilians, socially oppressed and politically defeated, can be culturally victorious, something that certain leftist intellectuals fail to comprehend.'[92]

According to most contemporary commentators, including Robert Stam, this concentration on the notion of cultural victory represents the main weakness of the film: any privileging of the cultural power of blacks in Brazil detracts from the fact that they continue to be ultimately politically powerless.[93] But elsewhere Stam writes that it is wrong to look for positive images in films that belong to a carnivalesque genre, favouring what Mikhail Bakhtin calls 'grotesque realism': 'Satirical and parodic films, in the same way, may also be less concerned with constructing positive images than with challenging the stereotypical expectations an audience may bring to a film.'[94]

11   Vadinho (José Wilker, centre) in *baiana* costume, shortly before he drops dead in *Dona Flor e seus dois maridos* (1976).

Regardless of where one falls in this debate, it is clear that carnivalesque depictions of Afro-Brazilian culture regularly make for box-office and TV success in Brazil. For example, a similar privileging of the cultural legacies of African slaves and their descendants can be seen in *Dona Flor e seus dois maridos*.

Dona Flor e seus dois maridos

In the same year as the premiere of *Xica*, Bruno Barreto released the hugely popular film based on Jorge Amado's novel from 1966, that was set in Salvador in the 1940s.[95] *Dona Flor e seus dois maridos* (*Dona Flor and Her Two Husbands*, 1976) still holds the record for the largest number of spectators for a national film.[96] In the film Sônia Braga plays Flor, a lower middle-class woman who longs for the return of her dead *malandro* husband, Vadinho, who collapsed during carnival after a short and over-indulgent life (see figure 11). Her second husband, decent, honest and hard working, cannot offer her the intense sexual gratification of her late husband. She therefore consults a *macumba* priestess and Vadinho returns, visible only to her, so that she can enjoy the best of what both men have to offer her. Over ten million spectators in Brazil went to see this film on its release.

The film's link with carnival, inversion, transgression and Afro-Brazilian culture is established from the beginning, when Vadinho appears dressed as a *baiana* at a street carnival, dances with a *mulata* and then drops dead. It is therefore carnival that generates the situation that forms the focus of the plot: the death of Vadinho. The tale is set in Salvador, Brazil's most Afro-Brazilian city. Although José Wilker's representation of Vadinho is faithful to the novel in that he is blond and white, he is clearly identified in the film with black culture, particularly when contrasted with Flor's second husband, the staid and conservative pharmacist Teodoro. João José Reis argues that it would have made no sense to make Vadinho black or dark-skinned, because this would merely have served to reinforce black stereotypes. Making Vadinho a white, blond, and nominally petit-bourgeois *malandro* in Brazil's blackest city would hit the government where it hurt in terms of the transgressive element he represented.[97] Flor, too, is associated with Afro-Brazilian culture in the sense that she is a cookery teacher, invariably preparing Afro-Bahian cuisine. The shadow of Gilberto Freyre can clearly be seen in her association of food with sex, for example in the memorable scene where she prepares *moqueca de siri-mole* (a kind of crab stew) to remind her of her love-making with Vadinho: *siri*, in Bahia, being slang for the female sexual organ.[98] Sônia Braga, who played not only Flor but a number of Jorge Amado's Bahian heroines in the cinema and on television, is a mixed-race *morena*. The screen *morena*, of which Braga is the most celebrated example, is sensual, dark-skinned, with long wavy hair and European features. Flor's colour is emphasised when she is naked. Therefore, in the scenes in which she makes love to Vadinho, she appears much darker-skinned than when she is with her second husband (she has sex with him beneath the bedclothes), which returns us once again to the cliché of the lascivious dark-skinned Brazilian woman. Braga said of herself: 'I am a typical Brazilian. I have a typical Brazilian bottom, typical Brazilian colouring, even a bit Africanish, and a typical Brazilian style.'[99] Gilberto Freyre himself described her as 'the perfect example of a Brazilian woman' and Jorge Amado defined his character Flor as being of mixed-race, with Indian blood.[100] Given the general absence of people of colour from TV and cinema screens in Brazil, the *morena* frequently fills the role assumed by the *mulata* in other art forms. On the one hand Sônia Braga was criticised in some quarters for being too white to play one of Amado's heroines. On the other, her 'whiteness' did not prevent her from playing the lead in films with titles such as *A moreninha* (Little Dark Girl, 1970) and *Mestiça, a escrava indomável* (The Indomitable Mixed-race Slave, 1973) earlier in her career.

A dama do lotação

The final film to be discussed in this chapter is *A dama do lotação* (*Lady on the Bus*), released in 1978 and directed by Neville D'Almeida. Based on an eponymous short story by Nelson Rodrigues, it is considered to be the second most successful Brazilian film of all time. The film also stars Sônia Braga, who plays Solange, a sexually frustrated and recently married woman, incapable of making love to her husband, who finds solace on Rio's busy buses, picking up strangers, like a *carioca Belle de Jour*. In her quest for sexual satisfaction, she also beds her father-in-law and her husband's best friend. On discovering his wife's philandering, the husband Carlos retreats to his bed and remains there, in a kind of living death, while his wife both dutifully assumes the role of nurse by night, and continues her sexual sojourns by day. Sônia Braga here is playing a white upper-middle-class housewife, but race and sexuality are still relevant in the film, as revealed in one scene in particular. The scene in question appears to be a clear parody of a scene from Luis Buñuel's *Belle de Jour* (1967), where the main character Séverine indulges in a sexual act with another man underneath the table where her husband and a female friend are also sitting, in a ski lodge (the two couples are on a skiing holiday at the time). Similarly, in D'Almeida's film, an erotic game of footsie takes place between Solange and her husband's best friend, Assunção as they and their respective partners watch a saucy *mulata* dance show in Rio's legendary Oba Oba nightclub.

One striking difference between the two scenes is that in D'Almeida's film the spectator is placed in the privileged position of observing what is going on underneath the table. It is clear that events take place in real time in the Brazilian film, but that is not the case in *Belle de Jour*: so Brazilian sexuality is acted out while in France it is imagined. The other contrast is the setting: on the one hand snow-capped, icy mountains in an exclusive ski resort in *Belle de Jour* and on the other Rio de Janeiro's Oba Oba night-club with its half-naked mulatto women in *A dama do lotação*.

So, in *A dama do lotação* once again the *mulata* is presented as a seductress, a sexual initiator, having loose morals and enjoying sex: the direct opposite of the virginal, frigid, white wife, which Solange is supposed to be. The *mulatas* also remind us of the extended family of colonial Brazilian society. Gilberto Freyre's views on the extended family of masters and slaves (and by extension landowners and indentured workers and patrons and servants), and how they influenced the nation's social and sexual practices, were well known at the time of this film's release and were widely believed to be true.[101] But seeing the *mulatas* perform for a largely white, privileged audience strips them of any real power to represent the desires and sexual liberation which women in 1970s Brazil were increasingly expressing, or any kind of notion of the inversion of hierarchy represented by carnival, for example, found in *Xica da Silva* and *Dona Flor e seus dois maridos*. They merely reinforce the traditional notions of the wife/whore dichotomy that date back to colonial times. Just as in colonial times, each woman has her own space and her own function. Rio de Janeiro is a very sensuous city, but despite the images of chaos, and of freedom captured by Neville's camera, in terms of sex, there is an order of sorts. Solange takes strangers to open spaces, but her father-in-law and husband's best friend are taken to a motel. Her seductions are deliberately monotonous to view, as if she was not daring to deviate from a well-laid plan of sorts. The *mulata* dancers present an open show of sexuality that contrasted with the hidden sexuality of what is taking place beneath the table, indicative of two different worlds, and reminding us of the extent to which Solange has been taught to believe that sex was shameful and dirty.

Pornochique and national identity

With regard to their portrayal of sexuality, these three highly successful films from the 1970s share as their driving force the sexual voraciousness of the three leading ladies. Xica goes dizzy when she is aroused and then makes grown men holler in a mixture of agony and ecstasy by carrying out an unnamed act with them off screen. Flor is a pseudo-necrophiliac bigamist who summons her husband back from the grave to make love to her. Solange is a stunningly attractive nymphomaniac (and pseudo-necrophiliac too, since her husband is playing dead at the end of the film) who has sex with filthy, repulsive strangers in broad daylight. All three films clearly involve exaggerated scenarios that are either grotesque or ludicrous, or both, and they would have been viewed as such by the audience. Hence the element of carnivalesque spectacle in all of them. Xica, Flor and Solange subvert the patriarchal order in the sense that they destroy the myth of conservative family values so dear to the heart of the dictatorship.

There is an expression of (albeit very tentative) female resistance in all three films, considering how each returns to its starting point with the female leads in strengthened positions in terms of their relationships. Xica is at the beck and call of her young master at the beginning of the film. By the end she is reunited with the same young master (now a revolutionary in hiding), but she is now a free woman and is seen to control their relationship. Flor had been downtrodden by and submissive to her husband before his death. Faithful to Jorge Amado's unsurprisingly sexist text, the screen Vadinho on one occasion beats his wife up and steals her earnings, only to have the couple reunited in their lovemaking later. By the end of the film Vadinho both returns to his widowed wife and stays at her behest. Solange at the beginning of *A dama do lotação* is raped by her husband on her wedding night, and yet by the end of the film she is cuckolding the dying man.

In terms of the issue of national identity in 1970s Brazil, what is highly relevant to these three films is the importance placed on the notion of syncretism in the *Política Nacional de Cultura*, the National Cultural Policy developed by the dictatorship in the first half of the 1970s with the aid of a number of cultural producers, including cineastes.[102] This policy, which signalled an attempt to industrialise cultural production, as was taking place

in other countries at the time, favoured popular culture and a positive historical re-examination of the development of the nation from the point of view of
hybridity. Filmmaker Nelson Pereira dos Santos appeared to echo one of the
features of the National Cultural Policy when he wrote the following words:
'Gilberto Freyre has taught us that there are two cultures in Brazil: one that is
imported, an imitation of Western culture, and another, natural, spontaneous
one, with deeper roots, which is repressed.'[103]

The three films in question both affirm the existence of these two cultures
and offer examples of how the spontaneous, repressed element that Nelson
Pereira dos Santos refers to, can be set free. Furthermore, *Xica da Silva* and
Dona Flor e seus dois maridos appear to promote the notion of synthesis
between the two cultures as the key to the nation's development. *Xica da
Silva* is filled with examples of synthesis: in music, the use of colour and the
interaction of the black and white characters of the film. In the film Portugal
and Africa meet in Minas Gerais, the site of Brazil's failed eighteenth-century
independence movement, the *Inconfidência*, and therefore forever associated
with the birthplace of the Brazilian nation. Xica's joining of forces at the end
of the film with José, a young, white prototype *inconfidente* or freedom fighter,
allegorically offers an alternative way forward for the nation living under the
shadow of dictatorship, a seeming mixture of *jeitinho* and an element of
(resigned but undefeated) revolutionary spirit. In *Dona Flor e seus dois maridos*
Vadinho represents syncretism in the film: he is described as a *filho de Exú*[104]
and thus serves as a link between two worlds, or the two cultures of petit-
bourgeois Bahia. Flor, a Bahian *morena* and thus a national symbol of the
blending of two cultures, craves modernity and progress, associated with
Salvador's white middle class in the film, but not if it means sacrificing her
own passion and spontaneity, associated here with Bahia's African heritage.
In contrast, *A dama do lotação* does not offer any such easy solutions in
terms of national progress, as Solange's 'arrangement' remains unresolved at
the end of the film.

Xica ends up as neither a submissive slave nor the mistress of an aristocrat
but somewhere in between, in that she joins forces with a young (white)
revolutionary. Dona Flor keeps both husbands rather than settle for one, and
Solange keeps the husband she loves as well as an array of bus passengers.
According to Roberto DaMatta, this third way or middle path most aptly
expresses the dynamics of Brazilian culture.[105]

Concluding remarks

There can be no disputing the fact that the 1970s represent a high point in
the production and distribution of Brazilian films. On average seventy national
films were released per year during the first half of the decade, almost twice

as many as during the second half of the 1960s.[106] This figure rose again in the second half of the 1970s, peaking at 104 in 1979. The number of spectators paying to see national films also rose considerably over the decade, with over fifty million tickets sold per year on average from 1975 onwards. The number of days that Brazilian cinema halls were obliged to show Brazilian films increased from sixty-three days in 1969 to 112 days in 1975.[107] While the box-office charts at the time were dominated by the Trapalhões movies, as well as the 'big three' Embrafilme productions considered above, the importance of the *pornochanchada* has to be recognised in terms of the sheer increase in production and general viewing figures, much to the dismay of many working within the industry at the time.

Consider, for example, a document released by the *Conselho Federal de Cinema* (Federal Cinema Council) on the National Culture Policy on 4 January 1976, which summarily dismissed the *pornochanchada* because it 'uneducated' the public.[108] It was the only cultural expression to be condemned in the document. The year before, Embrafilme president Roberto Farias had said that his organisation would no longer financially support the production of such films, but would continue to distribute them.[109] The government preferred patriotic films that recouped in an epic format Brazil's past, such as Carlos Coimbra's popular historical costume drama *Independência ou morte* (*Independence or Death*, 1972), which portrayed Emperor Pedro I's battle for and declaration of independence as above all a brave and nationalist gesture.[110] There were therefore few figures within the industry, beyond the Boca do Lixo, that were prepared to support the production of these 'quota quickies', and with the gradual loosening of censorship restrictions and the arrival of hardcore from the United States, many *pornochanchada* directors left the industry or simply gave up the battle for respectability and turned their attention, in the 1980s, to the production of a much more culturally and socially destructive kind of film: *sexo explícito* or Brazilian hard-core pornography.

Evidence of the sustained influence of the *chanchada* genre on popular cinema in the 1970s has been clear to see in many of the films discussed in this chapter. Furthermore, Ely Azeredo observed as early as 1969 that the *jeitinho* factor ('that untranslatable *carioca* virtue that sustained in both inglorious and more heroic phases the Brazilian film industry') was rising sharply in the context of Brazilian cinema.[111] Likewise, the presence of this informal, occasionally illicit, clever and potentially transgressive way of getting round, parodying or debunking bureaucracy, authority, formality and the status quo is evident in the popular films under discussion. By contrast, in the late 1970s and 1980s, with greater freedom from censorship, many popular cineastes turn to more serious genres (violent thrillers, for example), often in what are token gestures towards acknowledging Brazil's recent politically troubled and violent past.

Notes

1 João Luiz Vieira and Robert Stam, 'Parody and marginality: the case of Brazilian cinema', *Framework*, 28 (1985), p. 24.
2 Nuno César Abreu, 'Anotações sobre Mazzaropi, o Jeca que não era Tatu', *Filme Cultura*, 40 (August/October 1982), p. 38.
3 PAM filmes survived on a hand-to-mouth economy when it first started. Mazzaropi even bought used and broken machines from the bankrupt Vera Cruz studios: Eva Bueno, 'The adventures of Jeca Tatu: class, culture and nation in Mazzaropi's films', *Studies in Latin American Popular Culture*, 18 (1999), p. 42.
4 Mazzaropi stopped his tireless touring of the interior and performing on television after he became famous, in order to protect his image. His approach to ensuring the longevity of his stardom was, then, very different from the saturation techniques employed on behalf of the Atlântida stars of the 1940s and 1950s, for example, or later performers such as the Trapalhões and Xuxa.
5 Weddings and funerals have long been stock features of Brazilian folkloric plays and songs, for example.
6 Jeca Tatu, created in 1918, was backward-looking, lazy and sickly. A more positive version appeared in 1924 in the *Almanaque Fontoura*.
7 For more information on Cantinflas, see Jeffrey M. Pilcher, *Cantinflas and the Chaos of Mexican Modernity* (Wilmington: Scholarly Resources Books, 2001).
8 Take, for example, the joke on the subject of trapped wind during a funeral scene in *Jeca e seu filho preto* (Jeca and His Black Son, 1978).
9 One of the roots of modern popular music in Brazil, the *modinha* enjoyed success in the nineteenth century. Based on the arias of European opera, it came to symbolise a blending of high and low art, or a reinvention of erudite music for the masses.
10 As an example, in only two films the following signature tunes can be identified: *The Addams Family*, Sergio Leone film soundtracks and Western TV series, classical Hollywood drama, the horror film of the 1940s, the musicals *Oliver!* and *South Pacific*, and the perennial comedy series *Laurel and Hardy* and *Tom and Jerry*.
11 *Sai da frente* (Get Out of The Way, 1952); *Chofer de praça* (Taxi Driver, 1958) and *O vendedor de lingüiça* (The Sausage Seller, 1962) respectively.
12 Although the rural settings used in Mazzaropi's films are clearly exaggerated, it is worth bearing in mind that many small towns in the Paraíba Valley were still 'one-horse towns' in the 1960s and 1970s.
13 In this film, divorce is bizarrely equated with taking whatever woman you like.
14 Playwright Nelson Rodrigues and his cinematic adaptations suffered a similar fate at the hands of the left-wing press. See Chapter 5.
15 Likewise, the country bumpkin played by Cantinflas used his down-to-earth language skills to send up the legal profession in *Ahí está el detalle* (That's the Point, 1940): see Carmelo Esterrich and Angel M. Santiago-Reyes, 'From the *carpa* to the screen: the masks of Cantinflas', *Studies in Latin American Popular Culture*, 17 (1998).

16 For example, in *Jeca e seu filho preto* Mazzaropi is placed in a trance and inadvertently gets into bed with another woman, while in *Meu Japão brasileiro* Mazzaropi's screen wife overhears a schoolteacher quoting a love poem to her husband and mistakenly believes he is having an affair.

17 Bueno, 'The adventures of Jeca Tatu', p. 47.

18 John Fiske, *Reading the Popular* (Boston: Unwin Hyman, 1989), p. 135, quoted in Bueno, 'The adventures of Jeca Tatu', p. 48.

19 In *Folhetim da Folha de São Paulo*, 2 July 1978, quoted in Abreu, 'Anotaões sobre Mazzaropi', p. 39.

20 Bueno, 'The adventures of Jeca Tatu', p. 41.

21 Quoted in Abreu, 'Anotaões sobre Mazzaropi', p. 41.

22 Bueno, 'The adventures of Jeca Tatu', p. 49.

23 Mazzaropi similarly had little respect for the filmmaking approach of the *cinema novo* group: 'You can't make films without money. It's stupid to talk the way they all do – work of art, a camera in the hand – that's for fools. It's amateur, it's a joke.'. Quoted in 'Nunca fui chupim do governo', *Valeparaibano*, 16 September 1979 (our translation).

24 Bueno, 'The adventures of Jeca Tatu', p. 39.

25 William Rowe and Vivian Schelling, *Memory and Modernity: Popular Culture in Latin America* (London and New York: Verso, 1991) p. 164.

26 'O palhaço do Brasil', *Veja*, 13 July 1983.

27 *Na onda do iê-iê-iê* (On the Wave of Rock 'n' Roll, 1965); *O adorável trapalhão* (The Adorable Trapalhão, 1966); *A ilha dos paqueras* (The Island of Flirting, 1968); *Ali Babá e os 40 ladrões* (Ali Baba and the 40 Thieves, 1972); *Aladim e a lâmpada maravilhosa* (Aladdin and the Magic Lamp, 1973); *Robin Hood, o trapalhão da floresta* (Robin Hood, the Trapalhão of the Forest, 1973); *O trapalhão na ilha do tesouro* (The Trapalhão on Treasure Island, 1974); *Simbad, o marujo trapalhão* (Sinbad the Sailor Trapalhão, 1975).

28 The group temporarily split in 1983 due to artistic differences, and that year two Trapalhões movies were released simultaneously: Renato Aragão's *O trapalhão na arca de Noé* (The Trapalhão on Noah's Ark) and *Atrapalhando a suate* (Getting in the Way of the Swat Team). Renato Aragão's film drew larger crowds: his budget was twice as big and Dedé, Mussum and Zacaria were not allowed to use the Trapalhões trademark name – in *Atrapalhando a suate* they went by the name of the Trapalhaços: 'Guerra de estrelas', *Isto é*, 14 December 1983.

29 The average number of spectators for a Trapalhões film in the 1970s and 1980s was around four million. See the statistics gathered by Fatimarlei Lunardelli in *Ô psit! O cinema popular dos Trapalhões* (Porto Alegre: Artes e Ofícios, 1996), pp. 130–57.

30 The first films that Renato Aragão and Dedé Santana made together were based on works of children's fiction, moving on to loose parodies of Hollywood block-busters, and then turning their attention to social themes.

31 'Renato Aragão quer também o mercado externo', *Jornal do Brasil*, 26 June 1980, translated by and quoted in Randal Johnson, 'Popular Cinema in Brazil', *Studies in Latin American Popular Culture*, 3 (1984), p. 90.

32 It is interesting to note this, as Renato, Mussum (and Zacaria to a lesser extent) were said to have had speech problems.

33 The characters played by Zacaria (a homosexual), were understood to be weak in a tender and affectionate way, for example, in *O casamento dos trapalhões*, when the heroes are married off at the end of the film, Zacaria is carried in the arms of his bride. Jokes referring to homosexuality (in a roundabout way) as a rule are not aimed at the characters played by him. Zacaria was said to be the children's favourite, and his private life did not affect his relationship with his young audience.

34 For example, in *O casamento dos trapalhões*, Renato Aragão cracks a masturbation joke when he asks Dedé if he has confused a cow with a bull at milking time.

35 Unlike their more recent cinematic outings, and those of other children's entertainers such as Xuxa, the Trapalhões films, particularly in the 1970s, were often surreal and anarchic, and lacking a linear narrative.

36 'O palhaço do Brasil'.

37 Take, for example, their consistent plugging of Itapimirim coach travel in their films. Product placement was and continues to be a very common and acceptable practice on Brazilian television, and in the 1970s film producers (such as those of many a *pornochanchada*) increasingly used it too.

38 It must be borne in mind that in Brazil national television series, especially those shown on TV Globo, are often more popular than foreign series. As a result, the television audience's relationship with the national product is very different from the cinema audience's relationship to national films. For example, twenty-seven million people regularly tuned in to the Trapalhões TV series at its height of popularity: 'O palhaço do Brasil'.

39 For example, Paris Filmes, a film importer and distributor (and therefore with little or no filmmaking experience), set up a production side to its business in 1976, aiming to produce six films per year, as a result of the raising of quotas for national films to 112 days per year: 'E depois da pornochanchada?', *Veja*, 7 January 1976.

40 José Carlos Avellar, 'Teoria da relatividade', *Anos 70: cinema* (Rio de Janeiro: Europa Empresa Gráfica Editora, 1979), p. 70. In contrast, José Mário Ortiz Ramos argues that censorship has been overly blamed for shaping Brazilian cultural production at the time: 'O cinema brasileiro contemporâneo (1970–1987)' in Fernão Ramos (ed.), *História do cinema brasileiro* (São Paulo: Arte Editora, 1987), p. 401.

41 Avellar, 'Teoria da relatividade', p. 67 (our translation).

42 Randal Johnson and Robert Stam, 'The shape of Brazilian film history', in Randal Johnson and Robert Stam (eds) *Brazilian Cinema* (New York: Columbia University Press, 1995), p. 40.

43 Tag lines often reinforced the innuendo of film titles, such as the tag line for *Eu dou o que ela gosta* (I Give Her What She Likes, 1975): 'e o que ela gosta não é mole!', which roughly translates as: 'And what she likes isn't for softies!' The tantalising titles used by *pornochanchadas* were not new to the popular cultural scene in Brazil: the *teatro de revista* had been making use of double entendres and titillation in revue names for decades.

44 For more information, see Nuno César Abreu, 'Boca do Lixo', in Fernão Ramos and Luiz Felipe Miranda (eds), *Enciclopédia do cinema brasileiro* (São Paulo: Editora Senac, 2000), p. 59.

45 Paulo Emílio Salles Gomes points out that in Brazil the circus was family entertainment but was full of lewd jokes and behaviour hidden behind double entendres: 'Within the *pornochanchada* we find all the traditions of popular Brazilian entertainment, and people who are shocked by such things have no idea of what went on in a certain area of our popular culture.' Quoted in Maria Rita Kehl, 'Entrevista com Paulo Emílio Salles Gomes', *Movimento* , 19 January 1976 (our translation).

46 *Cu* is slang in Portuguese for anus: a favourite in the word play frequently used by the *pornochanchada*. For example, one of the characters from martial arts spoof *As massagistas profissionais* (The Professional Masseuses, 1976) is called Fung Ku.

47 It is interesting to note here that Robert Stam describes one of the aesthetic features of Brazilian carnival as the relaying of 'contradictory forms of historical representation': 'Tropical detritus: *Terra em Transe*, tropicália and the aesthetics of garbage', *Studies in Latin American Popular Culture*, 19 (2000), p. 87.

48 Quoted in Kehl, 'Entrevista com Paulo Emílio Salles Gomes'.

49 Jean-Claude Bernardet, 'A pornô-moral', *Movimento*, 7 July 1975.

50 Jean-Claude Bernardet, 'Nós, invasores', *Movimento*, 22 December 1976. A number of *pornochanchadas* portray parents living in fear of having a homosexual son: see for example the second part of *Como é boa nossa empregada*. The *chanchada* similarly depicted a crisis of masculinity: see Chapter 3.

51 First published in 1933, this is one of the main issues dealt with by Freyre's *The Masters and the Slaves: A Study in the Development of Brazilian Civilization*, translated by Samuel Putman (New York and London: Knopf, 1956).

52 The use of the word 'Vaseline' in the film's title comes with its own suggestive significance in this respect.

53 José Carlos Avellar, 'Produto nacional bruto', unsourced clipping, MAM archive, Rio de Janeiro, 16 August 1975.

54 Avellar, 'Teoria da relatividade', pp. 84–5 (our translation).

55 For a description of the reaction to government-sponsored short films during the 1930s, see Chapter 1.

56 Avellar, 'Teoria da relatividade', p. 75 (our translation).

57 *Ibid.*, p. 70.

58 *Ibid.*, p. 77.

59 The title *Secas e molhadas* is a play on words on 'Secos e Molhados', the name given to general stores, or shops that sold everything ('dry and wet goods'), traditionally found in small towns in the interior of the country. By changing the gender of the adjectives, the title appears to refer to the state of sexual arousal of women.

60 Avellar, 'Teoria da relatividade', p. 81 (our translation).

61 Vieira and Stam, 'Parody and marginality', p. 21.

62 *Ibid.*, pp. 21–2.

63 In the title, the word 'planet' has been swapped with *planalto*, literally meaning plateau, but figuratively used to refer to the seat of government in Brasília. Far from setting up an amusing parody of national politics, the Trapalhões seem to have chosen the word for its phonetic similarity to the original, and to explain why Renato Aragão and the gang do not leave Earth during the course of the film.

64 In the *Grease/Saturday Night Fever* spoof *Nos tempos da vaselina* the protagonist declares, after a successful night's disco dancing, 'Sabe, isso me lembra tanto um filme americano' (You know, this is so like an American film). There are also plenty of references in *Bacalhau* to the film being a parody.

65 Vieira and Stam, 'Parody and marginality', p. 36.

66 Ribeirão Preto is a typical city of the São Paulo hinterland (and therefore nowhere near the Brazilian coast), which was still associated in the 1970s, to a certain extent, with the kind of *caipirismo* depicted in the films of Mazzaropi.

67 Vieira and Stam, 'Parody and marginality', p. 35.

68 *Ibid.*

69 Robert Stam, João Luíz Vieira and Ismail Xavier, 'The shape of Brazilian cinema in the postmodern age', in Johnson and Stam, *Brazilian Cinema*, p. 398.

70 See Vieira and Stam, 'Parody and marginality', pp. 33–4, for more information on the references to original characters in *Bacalhau*.

71 That is not to say that Brazil's more popular classes survive intact in this parody: in one scene, for example, the clever codfish is able to saw through the boat sent out to catch it because the passengers are busy drumming out a *batucada* rhythm on deck with their hands.

72 Lunardelli, *Ô, psit!*, p. 60.

73 Aragão starred in *Dois na lona* (Two on the Canvas) in 1967, while Mazzaropi made for the Vera Cruz studios the *chanchadas Sai da frente* (Get Out of The Way, 1952), *Nadando em dinheiro* (Rolling in Money, 1952) and *Candinho* (Little Candide, 1953).

74 Salles Gomes, however, claims that the *chanchada* filmmakers learnt their story-telling trade through radio theatre. The *pornochanchada* makers, by contrast, did not know how to tell a story. As a result, it became easy to make feature films in Brazil and the public was growing used to seeing badly told stories on screen: quoted in Kehl, 'Entrevista com Paulo Emílio Salles Gomes'.

75 It is worth noting an interesting difference between the outcome of the average Trapalhões film and the *chanchada*: Renato Aragão and the gang start out poor, but usually end up very rich, with no suggestion that the life they have left behind is to be returned to or missed. They are never rewarded with cash, as this would be too obvious: they are often given jewels or bars of gold.

76 José Carlos Avellar, 'Animal doméstico', *Jornal do Brasil*, 31 May 1973.

77 Jean-Claude Bernardet, 'A new actor: the State', *Framework*, no. 28 (1985), p. 19, quoted in John King, *Magical Reels: A History of Cinema in Latin America* (London and New York: Verso, 1990), p. 116. Randal Johnson, in a comment to the author, pointed out that the process of co-optation started much earlier.

78 King, *Magical Reels*, pp. 115–16. See also Chapter 6 of Randal Johnson, *The Film Industry in Brazil: Culture and the State* (Pittsburgh: University of Pittsburgh Press, 1987).

79 The soft- and later hard-core porn producer and actor David Cardoso commented that the *pornochanchada* was responsible for forming the audience that put *Dona Flor* in the record books: 'Luz, cama, ação!', *Revista domingo do Jornal do Brasil*, 3 May 1998.

80 Jean-Claude Bernardet, 'Uma pornô grã-fina para a classe média', *Última hora*, (São Paulo, 29 April 1978). In this article, Bernardet also alludes to such films as *pornochanchadas de luxo*, or luxury *pornochanchadas*.

81 In Timothy Bernard and Peter Rist (eds), *South American Cinema: A Critical Filmography (1915–1994)* (Austin: University of Texas Press, 1998), p. 179.

82 See, for example, Robert Stam, *Tropical Multiculturalism: A Comparative History of Race in Brazilian Cinema and Culture* (Durham and London: Duke University Press, 1997), p. 294.

83 See some of the comments in Various, 'Xica da Silva, genial? racista? digno de Oscar? abacaxi?', *Opinião*, 15 October 1976.

84 Interview with Junia Ferreira Furtado in the newspaper *Estado de Minas*, 14 September 1998, quoted in Mariza de Carvalho Soares, 'As três faces de Xica', in Mariza de Carvalho Soares and Jorge Ferreira (eds), *A história vai ao cinema: vinte filmes brasileiros comentados por historiadores* (Rio de Janeiro: Record, 2001), p. 56.

85 Randal Johnson, 'Carnivalesque celebration in *Xica da Silva*', in Johnson and Stam (eds), *Brazilian Cinema*, pp. 216–24.

86 Carlos Diegues's 1984 film *Quilombo* was also based on a *samba-enredo* or carnival parade theme.

87 See Chapter 2. For more information on Carmen Miranda's star text, see Ana López, 'Are all Latins from Manhattan? Hollywood, ethnography and cultural colonialism', in John King, Ana López and Manuel Alvarado (eds), *Mediating Two Worlds: Cinematic Encounters in the Americas* (London: British Film Institute, 1993), pp. 67–80.

88 Robert Stam, 'Slow fade to Afro: the black presence in Brazilian cinema', *Film Quarterly*, 36, 2 (Winter 1982–83), p. 29.

89 See Chapter 3 for a discussion of the structuring absence of Afro-Brazilian women in the *chanchada*.

90 Silvia Oroz, *Carlos Diegues*: os films que não filmei (Rio de Janeiro, 1984), p. 130 (our translation).

91 See, for example, Section 2 of *The Masters and the Slaves*.

92 Oroz., *Carlos Diegues*, p. 128 (our translation).

93 Stam, *Tropical Multiculturalism*, p. 296.

94 Robert Stam and Louise Spence, 'Colonialism, racism and representation: an introduction', *Screen*, 24, 6 (1983).

95 Jorge Amado, *Dona Flor And Her Two Husbands*, translated by Harriet de Onis (London: Serpent's Tail, 1986).

96 *Cinejornal* 6 (Rio de Janeiro: Embrafilme, 1986). See also Maria do Rosário Caetano, 'As maiores bilheterias do cinema nacional', *Revista de cinema* (www.revistadecinema.com.br), (accessed April 2002), for an alternative interpretation of Brazil's box-office top fifty, which still places *Dona Flor* at number one. The massive television advertising campaign behind the film clearly did it no harm.

97   João José Reis, '*Dona Flor e seus dois maridos*: viagem a um mundo que muda',
     Soares and Ferreira (eds), *A história vai ao cinema*, p. 26. Vadinho is, despite this
     argument, one in a long line of white *malandros* to grace the Brazilian big screen
     over the years.
98   *Ibid.*, p. 22.
99   In film press notes (microfiche on Sônia Braga, BFI, London).
100 *Ibid.*; quoted in 'Dona Flor e seus dois maridos', *Filme Cultura*, 33 (May 1979),
     p. 110.
101 See Freyre, *The Masters and the Slaves*.
102 Randal Johnson describes the policy thus: 'The document says explicitly that the
     state role includes support of spontaneous cultural production and in no way
     implies that the state has the right to direct such production or to impede in any
     way freedom of cultural or artistic creation . . . It formulates a desire to construct
     a harmonious "national identity" on a symbolic level based on respect for regional
     and cultural diversity and the preservation of the nation's cultural and historical
     patrimony': 'The rise and fall of Brazilian cinema, 1960–1990', in Johnson and
     Stam, *Brazilian Cinema*, p. 384. For more information on the National Cultural
     Policy, see Renato Ortiz, *Cultura brasileira e identidade nacional* (São Paulo:
     Brasiliense, 1999), pp. 79–126 and José Mário Ortiz Ramos, *Cinema, estado e
     lutas culturais: anos 50/60/70* (Rio de Janeiro: Paz e Terra, 1983), pp. 113–58.
103 Quoted in Ortiz Ramos, *Cinema, estado e lutas culturais*, p. 130 (our translation).
104 The deity with whom Vadinho most identifies in *candomblé* is Exú, simultan-
     eously a trickster, door opener and messenger: hence his association with both
     the world of the gods and humans.
105 Quoted in Reis, 'Dona Flor e seus dois maridos', p. 23.
106 Ortiz Ramos, *Cinema, Estado e lutas culturais*, p. 136.
107 Ortiz Ramos, 'O cinema brasiliero contemporâneo', p. 410.
108 'Veredas na tela', *Movimento*, 19 January 1976. Elsewhere in the official document,
     ironically, it is stated that it is inappropriate to impose cultural conceptions and
     ideas on society, as this would represent a curtailment of freedom typical of
     totalitarian regimes.
109 *Ibid.* The article rightly observes that 'supporting such official positions against
     the *pornochanchada* is tantamount to establishing a precedent against any type of
     cultural production that displeases culturally dominant groups' (our translation).
110 The notion of promoting 'historical' cinema had been discussed by the Ministry
     of Education and Culture (MEC) in 1971–72 and had come back into vogue
     at Embrafilme in 1975, precisely at a time when the success of and tacit support
     for the *pornochanchada* was beginning to irritate the government and left-wing
     cultural producers alike.
111 Ely Azeredo, 'O fenômeno dos "paqueras"', *Jornal do Brasil*, 7 March 1969 (our
     translation).

7

The 1980s

Introduction

At the beginning of the 1980s many of the elements that both benefited and influenced Brazilian cinema in the second half of the 1970s continued to be present, such as favourable quotas[1] and greater freedom for filmmakers afforded by *abertura* or the process of political opening up. As the dictatorship drew to an end (a civilian president was indirectly elected in 1984 and direct presidential elections were held in 1989), a more positive note could be detected in a number of films from the first half of the decade.[2] Inevitably, however, the world economic slump, and in particular the Mexican crisis of 1982, along with the rampant inflation that overtook Brazil as a result of this and of the complicated re-democratisation programme, hit the domestic film industry hard and the positive impact of the financial support supplied by Embrafilme, the state production and distribution company, was severely missed. Although Embrafilme was not abolished until 1990, its role in the film industry had been steadily reduced throughout the previous decade. For example, in 1979 Carlos Diegues's *Bye bye Brasil* (*Bye Bye Brazil*) was the last film to benefit from a low-interest loan from Embrafilme, and between January and July 1980, forty-five national films were released, only eighteen of which were distributed by this organisation.[3] The bulk of the rest of national production in the decade was made up of hard-core porn, produced and distributed independently from São Paulo's Boca do Lixo or red-light district.

A number of commercially successful films will be considered in this chapter, ranging from Diegues's *Bye bye Brasil* and Ruy Guerra's *Ópera do malandro* (*Malandro*, 1985), as examples of the new approach of veteran *cinema novo* filmmakers to depicting popular culture and making popular cinema, to examples of the ever-popular *cinema rodrigueano* in the 1980s, and the so-called '*abertura* naturalism' films. Finally, mention will be made of the impact of the consolidation of the hard-core porn genre on Brazilian culture and society.

Cinema novo, utopia and popular culture

Many of the films that have been examined so far in this study, the *chanchada*, the films of Mazzaropi, those of the Trapalhões and Coffin Joe, and the *pornochanchada*, are about as far removed as is possible from classic 1960s *cinema novo*, the films that Brazil is best known for on an international art-house stage. But as was witnessed in its Tropicalist phase in the late 1960s and early 1970s, the *cinema novo* project did aspire to a dialogue with the Brazilian public. *Cinema novo* director Carlos Diegues's *Bye bye Brasil* (1979, but exhibited in 1980), coming in the wake of his immensely popular *Xica da Silva* (*Xica*, 1976), confirmed the director as the most successful of the *cinema novo* group at producing this desired dialogue with the public. A commercial success both at home and abroad, the film lends itself to analysis in the context of this study, as it synthesises better than any other film both many of the aspects of popular culture and some of the theoretical concerns regarding what constituted popular culture in Brazil in the late 1970s and early 1980s.

Bye bye Brasil

The film opens with the Caravana Rolidei[4] arriving in Piranhas, a small town somewhere in the *sertão* of Alagoas. It is typical of many small circuses or *circos mambembes* that worked their way round the interior of the country, packing everything up every couple of days into the back of an old lorry in search of the next village free from roof aerials, where television's all-consuming presence was not yet felt. The circus troupe is made up of the ringmaster, magician and fortune-teller Lorde Cigano, played by José Wilker, the rumba dancer, magician's assistant and part-time prostitute Salomé, played by Betty Faria, and the deaf-mute strongman and fire-eater Andorinha. Director Diegues's inspiration for his depiction of the circus came from his childhood in Maceió in the North East of Brazil. Lorde Cigano, the *rumbeira* Salomé and the Caravana Rolidei were all based on real life, as was Zé da Luz, the travelling film projectionist the troupe meet later on in the film. All were common sights in the small towns of the interior and suburbs of cities on the coast. While José Wilker and Betty Faria were well-known film and soap actors, Príncipe Nabor, who plays Andorinha the deaf-mute, was discovered in a circus in the suburbs of Rio de Janeiro. The character was not originally down to play a deaf-mute. The script had to be adapted when it was discovered that, just like the dubbed José Mojica Marins in the Coffin Joe films, Príncipe Nabor had a speech impediment. This was his only film, as he returned immediately to his old life in the circus when filming was complete.

Among the spectacles on offer to the packed audience in Piranhas, Lorde Cigana fulfils what he declares to be every Brazilian's dream. Not 'muita fartura e progresso' (plenty of everything and progress), as suggested by the town prefect. Instead he makes it snow, just like in Old Europe (desiccated coconut falls from the roof), while 'I'm Dreaming of a White Christmas' plays in the background.

The troupe are later joined by an accordion player Ciço, played by the well-known singer Fábio Junior, and his heavily pregnant wife Dasdô, who seemingly are luckier than most in that they are able to convince the troupe to take them away from a life of hopelessness in the *sertão*, despite Lorde Cigano's protestations that they already own a record player.

The scene in which Ciço announces to his father that he is to leave is clearly a pastiche of many an early *cinema novo* film, both in its subject matter (poor *retirante* or migrant worker of few words dramatically leaves the *sertão* in the direction of the sea) and in its style, with its baroque atmosphere and its sociological distance (for which *cinemanovistas* were later criticised), apparent even in the literal distance the scene is shot at.[5]

Ciço's accordion playing provides the soundtrack to the troupe's and the spectators' journey through the *sertão*. First of all, following in the footsteps of many a *retirante* before them, they head towards the coast, but Maceió has left the simple pleasures of the circus behind, symbolised by the constant traffic jams and roof-top television aerials as far as the eye can see. Heading back into the *sertão*, they reach a small town and, unluckily for them, the 'prefeitinho de merda' (the crappy little mayor), rather than building the usual bridge leading to nowhere (as a symbol of his ineffectuality) has installed a television set in the public square where people sit and stare transfixed, watching TV Globo's super-soap *Dancin' Days*. After performing a promotional magic trick and blowing up the TV set, the troupe are asked to leave town.

At the next small town the townspeople are busy praying for rain. During the troupe's show Lorde Cigano exploits the desperation of his audience with his mind-reading and fortune-telling skills. When an emotional old woman asks where her family are now, Cigano is suddenly inspired and remembers a tale a lorry driver told him towards the beginning of the film about a new town called Altamira in the backlands of Pará state, where everyone was heading, as it was the centre of the construction of the new Trans-Amazonian highway. The link between popular mysticism, the myriad myths of El Dorado to have featured down the centuries in Brazilian culture, and national ambition, is cleverly forged in this scene.

According to the logic of the military dictatorship, the ludicrously ambitious construction of this highway was the symbol *par excellence* of modernity and national integration, the idea being that it would open up the Amazon, integrate the isolated Northern region with the rest of the country and interrupt the outpouring of migrant labour to the South. In reality, as is made clear in the film, the task of uniting the country was rapidly being carried out by the modern media[6] and most of the military's badly planned and environmentally damaging highway was swallowed back up by the forest.

On the way to Altamira the circus troupe give a lift to a group of Indians who listen to transistor radios, ask after the president of Brazil, drink coke and are fascinated by aeroplanes. Unfortunately, the travellers arrive at their destination seven or eight years too late: the highway has already been built, 'modernity' has reached Altamira, which has become a kind of trading post in human labour, airlifting potential workers to jobs in dodgy paper factories with shifty multinational connections. Cigano turns down the offer of a job, declaring: 'Mal sei ler e escrever. Parar mim, papel é para embrulhar pão e limpar a bunda' (I can barely read and write. For me, paper is for wrapping up bread and wiping my arse). He gambles all his money, as well as the Caravana Rolidei itself, on Andorinha's arm-wrestling ability, and loses. The one thing the troupe has left to offer the predominantly male, adult, displaced population are the sexual services of Salomé.

The group then splits: the Indians take work (ironically returning to the forest in order to be underpaid to chop it down), Andorinha disappears, and despite his unrequited love for Salomé, Ciço is convinced to accompany his wife and child to Brasília. When Salomé and Cigano visit them a few years later, Ciço is still playing the accordion, now the owner of a *forró* or North Eastern accordion music club, where he and his wife, surrounded by television sets on stage, entertain the *candangos*, Brasília's migrant workforce. Ciço resists the call to join them in their new venture (they are still searching for new frontiers – this time in Rondônia, yet another government-aided boom region about to collapse), and stays where he clearly has a future.

The city of Brasília can be thought of in the film as just one more El Dorado. Inaugurated in 1960, it was a city fated to exist since the days of discovery, according to Christian and Indian myths, and had been planned since the early days of the Empire:

> This complex mythical and religious tradition interacted with the latent millenarianism of Brazilian culture, shaping the expectations with which the project of the New Capital was received ... Brasília would be the 'third bank', the bridge between the undesirable past and a still impalpable future, the materialisation of the impossible.[7]

The two couples represent two different survival strategies that are culturally creative rather than destructive and reveal Brazil's cultural diversity. In the end Ciço and Dasdô find a way to retain their North Eastern cultural identity and to return to their own community.[8] Salomé and Cigano too have found a way to stay true to their cultural origins: they not only get the Caravana Rolidei back on the road, but it is a newer, more modern, flashier and internationalised *caravana*, symbolised by its excess of neon (even Salomé has neon lights flashing in her now blonde hair), its television sets, Frank Sinatra's English version of Ari Barroso's 'Aquarela do Brasil' ('Brazil') blasting out of the loudspeakers and the *caravana*'s corrected spelling: no longer spelt R-O-L-I-D-E-I, it now ends with a Y, as they think it should in English.

Although both couples are given hope at the end of the film, it is clear where the director's sympathies really lie,[9] if we bear in mind that Salomé had to prostitute herself for so long in order for the troupe to carry on in the circus trade. By contrast Ciço, Dasdô and their little daughter form a whole-some, stable family unit. The *caravana* has been internationalised, while Ciço makes his living playing 'authentic' Brazilian music.[10] Despite this, and despite the seemingly negative title of the film, the overall message is a positive one:

> *Bye bye Brasil* seems to reject the notion that there exists somehow a pure, untainted 'Brazilian' culture . . . Brazilian culture, rather, is a mixture of elements from diverse sources, both foreign and domestic . . . *Bye bye Brasil* thus rightly proposes a salutary form of cultural anthropophagy in which the origin of cultural elements is less important than the way they are assimilated and re-elaborated.[11]

In *Bye bye Brasil* the archaic and the modern are still, miraculously, managing to co-exist and they are doing this because, like popular culture, they are constantly adapting to the rapidly changing Brazilian environment. According to Diegues, the film is about a country that is coming to an end in order to make way for another that has just begun, a fitting message for a time of political transition.[12]

A estrada da vida

A year later, another veteran *cinemanovista* Nelson Pereira dos Santos achieved commercial success with a similar kind of road movie featuring popular characters: *A estrada da vida* (*Highway of Life*, 1980). In the film Dos Santos continues his examination of Brazilian popular culture, having dealt with popular religions, with differing degrees of success, in the previous decade in *O amuleto de Ogum* (*The Amulet of Ogum*, 1974) and *Tenda dos milagres* (*Tent of Miracles*, 1977). *O amuleto de Ogum*, a box-office success, was the first film to deal with the subject of *umbanda*, a popular syncretic religion of African origin based predominantly in and around Rio de Janeiro. In it Gabriel, a North Eastern youth arrives in the poor suburbs of Rio de Janeiro and becomes a henchman for a local *bicheiro* or illegal lottery organiser. Gabriel is protected by both an amulet and by an *umbanda* ceremony previously carried out on him in which his body was made immune to all harm.[13] The Rio setting, the popular *carioca* figures that crop up in the film and the storyline of a naive young man who can seemingly come from nowhere and turn things around to his own advantage are, of course, reminiscent of the *chanchada* tradition of Brazilian cinema. Its release coincided with Nelson Pereira dos Santos's so-called 'manifesto' on popular culture, initially distributed on the art-house cinema circuit, in which he encouraged filmmakers temporarily to set their ideologies to one side and objectively film 'the people' and their popular customs and forms of entertainment, in order to win the support of those same 'people' for national cinema.[14]

In *A estrada da vida* José Rico and Milionário, a popular *dupla sertaneja* or country-music duo, play themselves in what is ultimately a semi-autobiographical film, depicting their lowly beginnings and complicated rise to fame and fortune. The film offers spectators a greater utopian sense of energy and community than Diegues's film, as portrayed in the musical sequences and happy ending, but at same time it does show the poverty, inequality, alienation of work and duplicity of everyday life under a capitalist regime.[15] The duo move to São Paulo to seek their fame and fortune, and after performing in a down-market circus in the outskirts of the city, they are forced to take work on a construction site, where most migrant workers ended up in the 1970s and early 1980s. Unlike the sense of alienation described in Ruy Guerra's 1976 film set on a construction site, *A queda* (*The Fall*), *A estrada da vida* emphasises the solidarity of the marginalised population through the shared experience of work and music.

Música sertaneja or the Brazilian equivalent of country and western, was and continues to be frowned upon by Brazil's urban bourgeoisie for being trite and Americanised, a pale imitation of traditional backlands music, such as the tunes that formed the creative soundtrack of many an early *cinema novo* film. It is perhaps for this reason that Dos Santos's film received little positive criticism in the press at the time of its release. The public, however, supported the film: *A estrada da vida* was viewed by over one million spectators in 1981.[16]

As well as tapping into the popularity of *sertaneja* music, *A estrada da vida* to an extent built on the success of the films of Mazzaropi, as did two surprise hits from the 1970s that were set in the interior of São Paulo: Moreira Filho's *O menino da porteira* (The Porter's Lad, 1976) and *Mágoa de boiadeiro* (A Cowhand's Suffering, 1977). There are also a number of similarities between *A estrada da vida* and the *chanchada* genre. Like the *chanchada* and the films starring Mazzaropi, Dos Santos affectionately portrays the migration of poor Brazilians from the interior to the city. The plot and innocent humour of the film are also reminiscent of the *chanchadas* starring the likes of Grande Otelo and Oscarito, as are the slapstick style of humour, the playing with different linguistic registers and the importance of music in the film.

Ópera do malandro

Dos Santos was not the only *cinema novo* filmmaker to deal at this time with the changing political landscape through the genre of the musical. In 1985 Ruy Guerra released *Ópera do malandro* (*Malandro*) with some commercial success (it was the highest-grossing domestic film of 1986). *Ópera do malandro*, the stage musical, was written by Chico Buarque de Hollanda, a well-known and respected singer-songwriter since the 1960s, and was first performed in 1978. It is based loosely on Bertholt Brecht's *Threepenny Opera* of 1928, which in turn was based on the eighteenth-century English comic work, *Beggar's Opera* by John Gay.[17] The film was adapted for the screen by Guerra and Buarque and was a radical change of style for the cineaste in that it was shot in stylised studio interiors with lush orchestration, and it revealed a kind of affection for the Hollywood musical model from which the film takes some of its inspiration.[18]

The stage musical and film version are set in Rio de Janeiro's bohemian district of Lapa in the 1940s. The *malandro* of the title, Max Overseas, played by Edson Celulari (following in the long tradition of white *malandros* portrayed on the big screen in Brazil), is a petty criminal and pimp, and true to type, he is a sharp dresser, smooth talker, and symbolises the blurring of boundaries in Brazilian society at the time, slipping as he does in and out of high society and the underworld. Having ditched his on-off prostitute girlfriend, Margot, played by popular North Eastern singer Elba Ramalho, he joins forces with Ludmilla (Cláudia Ohana), the ruthless young daughter of the local cabaret owner, and sets up a successful 'import/export business', dealing in smuggled goods.

The backdrop to the action is the brink of the Second World War, as Brazil decides on whether to support the Allies or the Axis powers. Thus, the diplomatic 'slipperiness' of the Vargas government is echoed in the wheeling and dealing of the title character. Since coming to power in 1930s, and especially after the establishment of his New State in 1937 President Vargas had introduced a large number of labour laws, but there simply was not enough work to go round. The marginalised population, also symbolised by the figure of the *malandro*, thus grew significantly. The parallels between the transitional time of the end of Vargas's *Estado Novo* and that of the post-1964 dictatorship are clear to see in both the musical and film versions. While both versions are critical of the exploitative and dishonest aspects of *malandragem*, there are echoes, particularly in Guerra's film, of the delight in many of the aesthetic qualities of the *malandro* that can be found in the *chanchada* films: his style of walking, talking, singing and dancing, and his blatant disregard for the rules.

Ruy Guerra's choice of genre, the musical, is an interesting one, given that it is so bound up with both Hollywood culture and that of the *chanchada*, two of the main targets that the original *cinema novo* movement was set up to attack. The fact that Guerra could make a movie with 'self-flaunting MGM-style artifice'[19] reveals the extent to which the infamous anti-capitalist 'ideological patrols' of the 1960s and early 1970s had been dismantled.[20] Guerra stated that he made *Ópera do malandro* in order to 'rediscover the pleasure of making films'.[21]

That is not to say that the director made a movie that is indistinguishable from the Hollywood model, bar the language. *Ópera do malandro* does not look or sound like the classic American musical. For a start, the segues into the musical numbers in the film are deliberately clumsy, and as was the case of the *chanchadas*, in which the music and dance sequences were simply pauses in the narrative, there is often little connection between the plot and the songs (some numbers are too long for the action they are supposed to be illustrating, for example). The intended effect of this is that, rather than producing a badly made musical, the director draws attention to the techniques of filmmaking itself, in order to debunk the myth of both the *malandro* and of the possibility of a genuine 'happy ending' in the real world:

> To suggest that *Ópera do Malandro* is a dubbing of the American musical, and to cut off the conversation at this point, gives a false idea of the film, that actually provides, in a form familiar to the average viewer, a conversation and at the same time a critique of this way of conversing.[22]

Nelson Rodrigues on screen in the 1980s

With Rodrigues' death in 1980, and the resounding success of the filmic adaptation of *A dama do lotação* (*Lady on the Bus*, 1978), the first half of the 1980s saw considerable interest in the controversial playwright, with the release of five adaptations of his work for the big screen. The most successful of these were two remakes: Bruno Barreto's *O beijo no asfalto* (*The Kiss*, 1980) and Braz Chediak's *Bonitinha mas ordinária* (Pretty But Wicked, 1981).

In the play and film version of *O beijo no asfalto*, the action begins when a man is knocked down by a bus in Rio de Janeiro, and as he lies dying, he asks a passer-by, Arandir, for a kiss. Arandir, moved by the dying man's request, responds. A reporter, desperate for a story and knowing that 'pederastia faz vender jornal pra burro' (homosexuality sells papers like hot cakes), colludes with an unscrupulous detective and invents a homosexual scandal in broad daylight, which later develops into an accusation of murder. The entire city, Arandir's wife included, start to believe the fabricated tale. Only his sister-in-law defends him, and sees in her own father's promotion of the fiction a jealousy of his other daughter provoked by unnatural feelings of love for her. She is wrong, however, and the homosexual of the play is the father, secretly in love with Arandir, whom he kills at the end.

According to Nelson, the play was written in twenty-one days towards the end of 1960. It was inspired by the true story of a reporter from *O Globo* newspaper, Pereira Rego, who had been knocked down by a bus in Rio. The reporter, as he lay dying, asked a passer-by, who had knelt down to help him, for a kiss. The passer-by, as it happened, was a young woman. Nelson rewrote the ending of this true story to increase the dramatic effect. At the end of the play, he ironically uses a gay man to carry out the 'necessary' exercise of patriarchal justice, and therein lies his own attack on sexual hypocrisy and stereotypes of masculinity. Of course, far from writing his first politically correct play, what Nelson really had in mind when preparing *O beijo no asfalto* was an attack on those whose rigid political ideologies had forced him into isolation in artistic circles. These so-called 'ideological patrols' were, as he saw it, hypocritical, in that while he was labelled retrograde, he was the only author in the early 1960s to be producing sufficiently socially challenging material, and the only author in Brazil to be censored.[23] The similarities to Franz Kafka's *The Trial* are surely more than coincidental.[24]

In Barreto's film version, Arandir is not portrayed as being clearly innocent of accusations of homosexuality. Barreto plants the seeds of doubt partly in his choice of actor to play the part of Arandir. By 1980 Ney Latorraca would have been known to most film and television audiences as gay, despite frequently playing straight roles. Latorraca's interpretation, at times, borders on camp, particularly in the scenes where he is revealed as being more sensitive than the average man. This is the only evidence that the spectators have to go on in this mystery; those who are swayed by it discover to their horror that the father-in-law Tarcísio Meira, that icon of manliness and one of TV Globo's principal *galãs* or heartthrobs at the time, is the homosexual of the piece. The seeds are therefore sown to increase the dramatic impact of the denouement, and to reinforce the notion of collective participation in the witch-hunt.

The director takes this idea of unanimity one stage further by allowing the story of the homosexual scandal to transcend the newspaper offices and infiltrate the visual media. A TV journalist carries out a *vox pop*, posing the question: 'Você daria o beijo?' (Would you have kissed him?). Amid the almost expected negative responses appears a soundbite from the textbook feminist/psychoanalyst/left-wing intellectual (Nelson Rodrigues's nemesis?), and the contrast between her measured and sensible response and that of the public at large could not be more marked. This is a key moment in Barreto's film. He seems to want to emphasise this gap between the ideal that intellectuals and cultural commentators in Brazil work towards, or to put it another way, the official version of the nation (an intellectually mature and tolerant one, with no torture), and the other version, symbolised by the people who crop up in Barreto's film as previously mentioned (such as the man selling sugar-cane juice).

One of the most striking segments of Barreto's film is the harrowing and sexually graphic assault on Arandir's wife carried out by the journalist. In the scene, which happens offstage in the play, Selminha is forced to lift her skirt and remove her underwear in front of the journalist (with the detective looking on in the background), while the journalist's fist and cigar are alternately placed between her legs. One respected film critic bizarrely pointed to the tasteful eroticism of the scene, apparently incapable of distinguishing between it and an earlier scene where we see the sister Dália, played by the pin-up of the moment, Lídia Brondi, taking a shower.[25] And surely that is the point that Barreto is trying to make here. His film is dotted with the clichés of the *pornochanchada* (which, of course, would normally have been played for laughs as well as titillation): for example, the young and beautiful girl unwittingly observed taking a shower, young and beautiful girl undressing to seduce sexually frustrated man, young girl losing her underwear. The film appears to be stating that the real effect of *pornochanchada*, rather than getting Brazilians to watch national cinema after the demise of the *chanchada*, as the same critic suggests, is that from then on any kind of nudity, regardless of the context, would be interpreted as being there on purpose to excite the audience. *Pornochanchada* (and the dictatorship's tacit approval of it), at least in the first half of the 1970s, confirmed that it was acceptable to be a voyeur. And this is exactly what the spectators are in the aforementioned sexual assault scene. The camera angle is such that it views for the audience as if they were participating in the act, mirroring the detective's colluding gaze.

There is little doubt that the displays of nudity (regardless of the context) by Cristiane Torloni and Lídia Brondi provided one of the film's main attractions at the box office. Just as many directors of Rodrigues' work had done before and would do after him, Barreto both condemns and enjoys the benefits of the exploitation of female bodies, in the wake of the officially sanctioned ascendancy of the *pornochanchada*.

In *Bonitinha mas ordinária* a millionaire's daughter, Maria Cecília, is gang-raped by five black men, and her father sets to finding her a husband as soon as possible among his lowly clerks. The willing suitor would be offered the added incentive of a cheque for marrying the beautiful but soiled Maria Cecília. Edgar, the clerk in question, is in love with Rita, who unbeknown to him is living a double life. Instead of surviving on the honest wage of a school teacher, her noble desire to support her sisters and mother has forced her into prostitution. Edgar successfully does battle with the egotism and greed that surround him and threaten to make him lose sight of his real beliefs. In the end he makes the right choice, as it is revealed that his sympathy for Maria Cecília's plight had been ill-founded, and that she herself had, in her desire for sexual fulfilment, organised the rape. She, and not Rita, is the 'pretty but wicked' of the title.

In *Bonitinha mas ordinária* director Braz Chediak continued with the use, established successfully in the 1970s by Arnaldo Jabor, of both an 'aesthetic of bad taste', as a vehicle to depicting, as one critic put it, the 'tortured, morbid and debauched universe of Nelson Rodrigues',[26] and of an element of tongue-in-cheek kitsch, reminiscent of the *pornochanchada*. For example, the lead role of the sluttish Maria Cecília is played by popular soap actress and girl-next-door Lucélia Santos, and the unbelievable happy ending of the film is closer to the world of *telenovelas* where Santos originated.[27] Lucélia Santos also starred in similar roles in two more adaptations of Rodrigues' work released in the same year (1981): *Engraçadinha* and the notorious *Álbum de família* (Family Album). Braz Chediak's second adaptation of Nelson Rodrigues' work, *Álbum de família* was based on a play that had been banned for twenty-three years. If the original would have made for difficult viewing for the faint-hearted, a film version that deliberately added in scenes such as the rape of a pregnant woman and explicit self-abuse with a candlestick were bound to provoke a strong reaction. A portrait of Nelson's most decadent family, the film shocked all but the most hardened of Brazil's critics.

For critics and audiences who, in the light of *abertura* yearned for a break with the past in cultural as well as political terms, these adaptations of Rodrigues' work offended on two counts: they were based on the work of Brazil's most adapted writer; and their voyeuristic and explicit (simulated) sex scenes meant that for many they were indistinguishable from the pornographic films being produced *en masse* at the time in the Boca do Lixo in São Paulo.

The style of the large number of nominally political films that were released in Brazil in the late 1970s and early 1980s, including *O beijo no asfalto*,[28] has been described as '*abertura* naturalism':[29]

> The new films were frankly entertainment-oriented, favoring action-filled plots accompanied by a modicum of redeeming social value . . . Naturalism becomes part of a seductive strategy associating cinematic spectacle with authenticity and even audacity in presenting the raw data of everyday life.[30]

Within this group of films, one from 1977, *Lúcio Flávio, passageiro da agonia* (Lucio Flavio) by Argentine-born director Hector Babenco, stands out, given its surprise success at the box-office. Based on the life of the counter-cultural hero of the title, the film starred the lead of many a *pornochanchada*, Reginaldo Faria,[31] in the role of the true-life middle-class drop-out and inhabitant of the Rio underworld. Over five million people saw the film on its release, making it one of the most successful Brazilian films of all time. Babenco followed up his debut hit with an even grittier and more critical observation of post-*abertura* society in *Pixote, a lei do mais fraco* (Pixote, 1981), which deals with the tragic lives of Brazil's abandoned street children.[32] Such films, although criticised for their alleged use of violence to increase their commercial appeal, undoubtedly helped to push back the barriers of censorship and make way for freer political discussion on screen.

Hard-core porn

The boundaries of censorship were also being challenged from another angle in the 1980s. The process of moving from light-hearted, smutty, innuendo-ridden *pornochanchada* films to hard-core was a relatively rapid one in Brazil, following similar patterns to be found in many other countries. Around the beginning of the 1980s, the humour was gradually removed from the *pornochanchada* and what Randal Johnson has described as intermediate films, with simulated sexual activity woven into serious dramas, proved popular for a couple of years, until the censors permitted the release of sexually explicit material.[33] For example, one and a half million spectators went to see David Cardoso's *A noite das taras* (Night of Perversion, 1980).[34] The film was said to contain everything considered to be the sexual preferences of Brazilians. These preferences included sodomy, talking dirty, men lubricating their penises with spit, and so on.[35] Like Ody Fraga's *Fome de sexo* (Hunger for Sex, 1981), these were 'protopornôs' in that they used simulated sex scenes. By 1984 Cardoso, along with a number of other directors who had enjoyed success during both the *pornochanchada* and intermediate phases, would be making easy money filming and often starring in hard-core porn films.

The first hard-core film to be given an exhibition certificate in Brazil was Italian-born director Rafaelle Rossi's *Coisas eróticas* (Erotic Things, 1982). The year before the Board of Censors had approved the setting-up of special theatres for showing more explicit material, such as Nagisa Oshima's *Ai no corrida* (*In the Realm of the Senses*, 1976) and Tinto Brass and Bob Guccione's *Caligula* (1979). Rossi took three weeks to make *Coisas eróticas*, with the intention of limiting its exhibition to these new theatres. In the end he did not need to, as his film was granted a certificate for general release by the censors.[36]

With the release of *Coisas eróticas* the floodgates opened and by 1983, of the sixty-one films produced in São Paulo, half were sexually explicit. In 1984, of the 105 national films produced and shown in São Paulo, sixty-nine were hard-core, and in 1988, of the top-grossing 100 Brazilian films, only twenty were not pornographic.[37] By the end of the decade some 500 hard-core films had been produced in Brazil,[38] and they fought for space at downtown cinemas alongside US hard-core. The 'genre' therefore completely dominated national cinema in the 1980s, so much so that it would not be an exaggeration to claim that domestic cinema became synonymous with hard-core at this time.[39]

The social impact of hard-core could be seen in city centres, which practically became no-go areas, as cinemas, hitherto attended by 'decent citizens' and families, resorted to showing pornography to stay open at a time of economic crisis, turning once respectable neighbourhoods into zones of prostitution and vice.[40] At the end of February 1985, of the fifty-three cinema halls in the centre of São Paulo, forty-four were showing explicit sex films.[41] In city centres, films would be freely advertised both day and night, by large, graphic posters and salacious announcements over loud speakers. For example, on the poster for Roberto Fedegoso's (pseudonym for David Cardoso) *Viciado em c* . . . (Addicted to A . . . , 1985) the missing noun (*cu* or anus) is supplied by a drawing of a woman's curvy buttocks. The tag line reads: 'There's never been anything like it! Animals, men, women and queers in a real orgy!'[42] Such commercial use of censorship was common to hard-core films, as was the trick of imitating the titles of successful foreign films, for example Gerard Dominó's *A b . . . profunda* (Deep P . . . , 1984), the missing noun being *buceta* or pussy, whose title drew on the success of Gerard Damiano's porn classic *Deep Throat* (1972).[43]

Within the industry itself the family atmosphere that, according to *pornochanchada* stars, existed in the Boca do Lixo in the 1970s was replaced by one of seediness and exploitation, as many actresses were forced to give up their careers and were replaced by prostitutes, who earned for one film what they would be paid for an overnight trick.[44] With the box-office success of hard-core, pressure was placed on mainstream producers and directors of adult-oriented movies to include plenty of scenes of nudity and sexual activity in their films. Such pressure can clearly be seen, for example, in Ruy Guerra's *Kuarup* (1989), based on the novel of the same name by Antônio Callado, a minor hit on its release (Kuarup is the Amazonian Indian Day of the Dead).

By the end of the 1980s film production in the Boca do Lixo, where most hard-core films were made, had ceased. Economic crisis, the constant struggles with the censors and local government, and competition from hard-core video from the USA meant that even the production of cheap hard-core films was no longer viable. Only a handful of 'porno' cinemas remain in downtown areas, catering for a specialist audience, far from the days when four million Brazilians paid to see *Coisas eróticas*.

Concluding remarks

With the shrinking of the internal market,[45] provoked by the impoverishment of the lower-middle-class audience, the closing of cinema halls, and the growing popularity of television and home video,[46] national film production was practically non-existent by the end of the 1980s. Unlike other national cinemas, also fighting for survival at a time of economic crisis, Brazilian cinema could not rely on television to supply an additional source of income, because as a rule there has never been any integration between the two media.[47] The only exception to this at the time was the successful crossover of popular children's television entertainers to the big screen, such as the Trapalhões (see Chapter 6), Sérgio Mallandro (*As aventuras de Sérgio Mallandro* (The Adventures of Sérgio Mallandro, 1985) and Xuxa (*Superxuxa contra o baixo astral* (Superxuxa Against the Blues, 1989)).

State support for the industry, for example in the shape of Embrafilme, which had played a significant role in its success in the 1970s, had practically disappeared by the end of the 1980s. According to Ipojuca Pontes, one of Embrafilme's sharpest critics, the organisation was plagued by clientelism, and was in financial crisis because of unpaid debts, the fortunes it paid to keep its burgeoning bureaucracy going, and because of the number of producers who could not repay their loans because their films were such huge flops.[48] As Randal Johnson observes:

> Since the State assumed the lion's share of the financial risk involved in film production, many directors and producers tended to be less concerned with keeping costs down and, at least to some extent, with public acceptance of their films. This problem was compounded by the political favoritism or clientelism that came to characterize the selection process.[49]

Embrafilme was reorganised after 1987, but it still tended to support individual films rather than the industry as a whole.[50] It was viewed with increasing scepticism by the public and by many within the film industry itself. Without financial assistance, making movies was becoming an impossibly expensive business at that time of crisis. According to CONCINE (the Executive Group of the Cinema Industry), the average film cost 500,000 US dollars to make, and would therefore need to be seen by an audience of just under two million to break even. In 1988 only two films, both starring the Trapalhões, reached that level, revealing the extent to which the legacy of the *chanchada* lived on at the Brazilian box-office.[51]

Notes

1 In 1982, for example, national cinema enjoyed a 36 per cent share of the internal market: Robert Stam, João Luiz Vieira and Ismail Xavier, 'The shape of Brazilian cinema in the postmodern age', in Randal Johnson and Robert Stam (eds), *Brazilian Cinema* (New York: Columbia University Press, 1995), p. 391. In 1984 the quota was set at 140 days: Randal Johnson, 'Popular cinema in Brazil', *Studies in Latin American Popular Culture*, 3 (1984), p. 92.

2 As a result of re-democratisation in the 1980s, patriotism was back in style in Brazilian society: Stam, Vieira and Xavier, 'The shape of Brazilian cinema in the postmodern age', p. 428.

3 Ipojuca Pontes, *Cinema cativo: reflexões sobre a miséria do cinema nacional* (São Paulo: EMW Editores, 1987), p. 22.

4 The caravan phonetically spells out the English word 'holiday'. The spelling proves, to borrow the famous phrase from Paulo Emílio Salles Gomes, Brazilians' creative incapacity for copying: Stam, Vieira and Xavier, 'The shape of Brazilian cinema', p. 422.

5 Randal Johnson points out that the trajectory of the caravan recalls stylistic developments within *cinema novo* itself: 'Film, television and traditional folk culture in *Bye Bye Brasil*', *Journal of Popular Culture*, 18:1 (1984), p. 124.

6 Since 1962 the national government had been planning to link up Brazil via telephones, telex and televisual systems. Such a project of national integration was dear to the heart of the dictatorship, on the grounds that it would improve national security: Stam, Vieira and Xavier, 'The shape of Brazilian cinema', p. 390. Brazil's communications were linked up by satellite in 1969.

7 Nicolau Sevcenko, 'Peregrinations, visions and the city: from Canudos to Brasília the backlands become the city and the city becomes the backlands', in Vivian Schelling (ed.), *Through the Kaleidoscope: The Experience of Modernity in Latin America* (London and New York: Verso, 2000), pp. 101–2.

8 The character Ciço 'represents an essentially conservative ideology based on tradition and the permanence of values': Johnson, 'Film, television and traditional folk culture in *Bye bye Brasil*', p. 130.

9 Randal Johnson suggests that Diegues is also sympathetic towards Lorde Cigano, going as far as to consider him to be the director's alter-ego: 'an urban artist who has travelled the long roads of Brazil in search of the perfect audience and the optimum form of spectacle', *Ibid.*, p. 131.

10 The advertising for Ciço's show is drawn from the traditional wood carving of the Brazilian interior, while Cigano's is set in neon: *Ibid.*, p. 130.

11 *Ibid.*, p. 131.

12 From the pressbook of *Bye Bye Brasil*, quoted in *Ibid.*, p. 121. José Carlos Avellar writes that the idea of bidding farewell to the country contained in the film is relevant for much of the cinema of 1980s: 'Backwards blindness: Brazilian cinema of the 1980s', in Ann Marie Stock (ed.), *Framing Latin American Cinema: Contemporary Critical Perspectives* (Minneapolis: University of Minnesota Press, 1997), p. 28.

13 This ceremony is known as *corpo fechado* – literally 'closed body'. The director commented that his portrayal of religion in the film was well received within the *umbanda* community: see Randal Johnson's interview with Nelson Pereira dos Santos in 'Toward a popular cinema', in Julianne Burton (ed.), *Cinema and Social Change in Latin America: Conversations With Filmmakers* (Austin: University of Texas Press, 1986).

14 For more information, see *Ibid. Tenda dos milagres*, based on Jorge Amado's novel of the same name, tackled the issue of another popular religion, *candomblé*, but failed to engage with a popular audience.

15 Darlene J. Sadlier, 'Entretenimento e solidariedade: uma releitura da *Estrada da vida*', *Revista Fronteiras*, 4:1 (2002), p. 59.

16 José Mário Ortiz Ramos, 'O cinema brasileiro contemporâneo (1970–1987)' in Fernão Ramos (ed.), *História do cinema brasileiro* (São Paulo: Art Editora, 1987), p. 444.

17 With music by Kurt Weill, it was Brecht's most popular work. John Gay wrote *Beggar's Opera* to satirise the aristocracy of the time by pointing out similarities between them and the rogues who made up his list of characters, while Brecht's targets were the middle classes.

18 Stam, Vieira and Xavier, 'The shape of Brazilian cinema', p. 471.

19 *Ibid.*, p. 397.

20 The expression *patrulhas ideológicas*, a favourite of filmmaker Carlos Diegues, referred to the refusal of left-wing artists and critics of the 1960s and 1970s to accept artistic endeavour that did not have as its main focus an attack on capitalism and North American imperialism. These 'patrols' frustratingly left no room for artistic manoeuvre and represented the kind of unanimous voice of which Nelson Rodrigues, for example, was highly critical. Ruy Guerra himself was not entirely dissociated from these 'patrols' in the 1970s in that he stated that it was inappropriate to use popular cinema to show the people *em festa* or at play: see Randal Johnson and Robert Stam, 'The shape of Brazilian film history', in Johnson and Stam (eds), *Brazilian Cinema*, p. 49.

21 Quoted in Avellar, 'Backwards blindness', p. 33.

22 *Ibid.*, p. 32.

23 Ruy Castro, *O anjo pornográfico: a vida de Nelson Rodrigues* (São Paulo: Companhia das Letras, 1992), p. 321.

24 The kiss of the title triggers a journey of self-discovery, similar to K's in *The Trial*, where Arandir discovers the real meaning of his relationship with his wife, his sister-in-law, his colleagues, his father-in-law, and so on.

25 José Carlos Oliveira, 'Um beijo bem dado', *Jornal do Brasil*, 27 March 1981.

26 Valério de Andrade, *O Globo*, 27 January 1981 (our translation).

27 Rogério Bitarelli, *Ibid.*

28 Through its subject matter: the persecution of those who have done nothing wrong, and the quick acceptance by society in general of a reality constructed by the media.

29 Quoted in Ortiz Ramos, 'O cinema brasileiro contemporâneo', p. 441. *Abertura* naturalism films are those that deal with sex and violence and repressed political experience of the last two decades of dictatorship: Stam, Vieira and Xavier, 'The shape of Brazilian cinema', p. 412.

30 *Ibid.*

31 Reginaldo Faria also starred in and wrote *Para frente, Brasil* (Forward, Brasil, 1982), a commercially successful film dealing with the dark days of the dictatorship. It too was criticised for turning themes such as torture, imprisonment and the struggle for political liberation into a source of entertainment.

32 For a detailed analysis of both films, see Randal Johnson, 'The *romance-reportagem* and the cinema: Babenco's *Lúcio Flávio* and *Pixote*', *Luso-Brazilian Review*, 24:2 (1987). Babenco enjoyed further international success with the critically acclaimed *O beijo da mulher aranha* (*Kiss of the Spiderwoman*, 1985), based on the novel of the same name by Argentinean Manuel Puig, which included an Oscar-winning performance by William Hurt. He has recently topped the box-office charts of the so-called *retomada* or Brazilian cinema renaissance post-1995 with *Carandiru* (2003), in which he returns to the gritty subject of Brazil's violent penal system.

33 Randal Johnson, 'Popular cinema in Brazil', p. 92.

34 José Mário Ortiz Ramos, 'Sexualidades em construção (Cinema Pornô)', *Folha de São Paulo*, 4 September 1983.

35 *Ibid.* The same can be said for early hard-core movies, but these gradually became more fantasy-based, for example, the infamous cycle of films involving horses.

While the *pornochanchada* tended to concentrate on breast shots, hardcore was more phallocentric: Ortiz Ramos, 'O cinema brasileiro contemporâneo', p. 439.

36 Paulo Sérgio Markun suggests that Rossi was granted an exhibition certificate by underhand means: 'Cartazes de filmes eróticos causam polêmica', *Folha de São Paulo*, 3 March 1985. Despite the relaxing of censorship laws in the 1980s, hard-core films experienced constant problems with the censors: according to one industry union official, occasionally a large number of films would be apprehended and later liberated in one go. Exhibitors would then screen them all at the same time, in case they were apprehended again. In an interesting turn of phrase, given the context, he is quoted as saying that exhibitors adopted a policy of horizontal rather than vertical exploitation: *Ibid.*

37 Randal Johnson, 'The rise and fall of Brazilian cinema, 1960–1990', in Johnson and Stam (eds), *Brazilian Cinema*, p. 384.

38 Nuno César Abreu, 'Boca do Lixo', in Fernão Ramos and Luiz Felipe Miranda (eds), *Enciclopédia do cinema brasileiro* (São Paulo: Editora Senac, 2000), p. 59.

39 The hostility of elite journalists further exacerbated the crisis in the film industry: Stam, Vieira and Xavier, 'The shape of Brazilian cinema', p. 390. This hostility is likely to have been aroused by the dominance of hard-core.

40 For example, the downtown district of Rio de Janeiro known as Cinelândia, where smart cinema halls existed comfortably alongside the more high-brow Municipal Theatre, National Library and Fine Arts Museum, was practically transformed into a second red-light district by the plethora of cinemas showing hard-core films in the 1980s. As a result of this transformation, the district became out of bounds for many *cariocas* seeking evening entertainment.

41 Markun, 'Cartazes de filmes eróticos causam polêmica'.

42 Our translation.

43 In this film Gerard Dominó (real name Álvaro Moya) imitates the name of the director of *Deep Throat*: Nuno César Abreu, 'Pornochanchada', in Ramos and Miranda (eds), *Enciclopédia do cinema brasileiro*, p. 433. Such imitation of nomenclature was also a way to avoid any distinction in the minds of spectators of hard-core pornography between foreign films and the national product.

44 Johnson, 'Popular cinema in Brazil', p. 92. Raphael Rossi was notorious within the industry for not paying actors and actresses at all: *Ibid.*

45 In 1978 there were almost sixty-two million spectators for Brazilian films. This figure had dropped to just under twenty-four million by 1988: Johnson, 'The rise and fall of Brazilian Cinema', p. 365.

46 Stam, Vieira and Xavier, 'The shape of Brazilian cinema', pp. 389–90.

47 Johnson, 'The rise and fall of Brazilian cinema', p. 366.

48 Pontes, *Cinema Cativo*, pp. 22–3. Pontes is also critical of Embrafilme's wasteful project to promote Brazilian cinema abroad, seemingly forgetting that that was the organisation's original remit when it was first set up: *Ibid.*, p. 48.

49 Johnson, 'The rise and fall of Brazilian cinema', p. 374.

50 *Ibid.*, p. 376.

51 *Ibid.*, p. 375. The films were *O casamento dos Trapalhões* (The Marriage of the Trapalhões, 1988) and *Os heróis Trapalhões* (The Hero Trapalhões, 1988).

8

The 1990s

Introduction

In 1991 Brazil's first elected president in almost three decades, Fernando Collor de Mello (shortly afterwards impeached on corruption charges), dealt a fatal blow to the languishing Brazilian film industry when he abolished all state support for the arts, including Embrafilme and the useful Sarney Law, which had offered businesses tax incentives in exchange for investment in national cinema. A major part of Collor's economic modernisation programme involved reducing the role of the state in the economy, and in this respect, the culture industry was treated the same as any other industry. In 1990 only thirteen films had been produced in Brazil, a considerable drop since the industry's heyday of the mid- to late 1970s, when the average number of Brazilian films in exhibition in any one year was around ninety. But with the loss of state support, this figure dropped even further to three, four and seven national films in 1992, 1993 and 1994 respectively.[1] It was around 1995 that national cinema would re-emerge with some optimism: the 1993 Audio-visual Law had started to make an impact on production by then and helped foster the *retomada* or renaissance of Brazilian cinema. The Audio-visual Law, like the Sarney Law of the 1980s, gives businesses a reduction on their tax bill in return for investing in audio-visual projects. The law is designed to encourage filmmakers and producers to rely less on the state for financial support and to foster productive relationships with the private sector:

> This is not simply a neo-liberal imposition of market imperatives on a sector that has never had to survive based on success in the market alone. Rather . . . government policy seeks to help films reach some sort of accommodation with the marketplace through a combination of direct private (and indirect public) investments. The policy measure has proven to be a highly attractive one and has resulted in a dramatic increase in the amount of production financing available and in the current resurgence of Brazilian cinema.[2]

A further law allowing foreign film distributors to invest up to 70 per cent of their taxes in Brazilian film also proved useful, with Columbia, Warner and Sony taking up this opportunity.[3] The biggest investors in Brazilian cinema are companies owned by the state or with mixed ownership, such as state banks and Petrobrás, Brazil's petroleum company.[4]

Defining the *retomada*

The first easily identifiable trend in films produced in Brazil since around 1995 is an international flavour. This can be seen, for example, in the number of foreign actors and characters cropping up in national films. The following long list is far from exhaustive, but does give some idea of just how common this phenomenon has been. The title character of what is considered to be the first film of the *retomada*, *Carlota Joaquina, princesa do Brazil* (*Carlota Joaquina, Brazilian Princess*, 1995), is Spanish and the film is narrated by a Scotsman. In the Oscar-nominated *O quatrilho* from 1995 Fábio Barreto deals with the lives of an Italian immigrant community in the South of Brazil at the turn of the last century (the *quatrilho* of the title is a type of card game). In brother Bruno Barreto's also Oscar-nominated 1997 feature, *O que é isso, companheiro?* (*Four Days in September*) Alan Arkin plays the US ambassador, kidnapped and eventually released by a group of young revolutionaries fighting to overthrow the dictatorship in Brazil in the late 1960s. In another hostage drama, Murilo Salles' *Como nascem os anjos* (*How Angels Are Born*) from 1996, a group of street children hold to ransom an American family who are on holiday in Brazil. Brazil's Middle Eastern immigrant community is represented by the character Benjamim Abraão in Paulo Caldas and Lirio Ferreira's *Baile perfumado* (*Perfumed Ball*, 1997), the true-life journalist who travelled through the backlands and eventually found and filmed the famous bandit Lampião and his gang. The difficulties of Brazil's Italian and German communities during the Second World War are mentioned, albeit in passing, in Buza Ferraz and Luiz Carlos Lacerda's *For all: o trampolim da vitória* (*For All: The Springboard to Victory*, 1997). Andrew McCarthy and Natasha Henstridge played an American couple living in the North Eastern state of Ceará in the 1930s in Fábio Barreto's *Bela Donna* (*White Dunes*, 1998). Elliot Gould starred in Lucas Amberg's *Sonho no caroço dum abacate* (*Avocado Seed*, 1999), and Anthony Quinn, one of the most 'multinational' of Hollywood's veteran actors, took on the role of the head of an Italian immigrant family in Ricardo Bravo's *Oriundi* from 2000. Also in 2000 Bruno Barreto directed wife Amy Irving in *Bossa nova* and veteran cineaste Ana Carolina returned with *Amélia*, a film that tells the tale of the trip to Brazil in 1905 of actress Sarah Bernhardt (played by French actress Béatrice Agenin). Finally, for the time being at any rate, is Tizuka Yamasaki's *Gaijin II*, a sequel to her film of 1980, based on the experiences of Brazil's large Japanese community at the turn of the last century.[5]

The presence of foreign actors in Brazilian films could easily be explained by concern for breaking into the international market and by the larger budgets currently available to producers. But it also hints at a desire to reveal the cosmopolitan side to the country. Despite its size, Brazil's borders appear restrictive to its filmmakers: thus the need to bring in an external element (be that a foreign visitor or an immigrant community within Brazil) to shed a different light on Brazilian culture. One negative effect of this is that spectators occasionally form the impression that the Brazilian filmmakers observe their material in much the same way that, at best, a well-informed foreign spectator might do. Budget limitations mean that foreign actors are rarely hand-picked for what they could bring to a certain role. Some films even appear to be destined more for foreign consumption than for the domestic market, despite the fact that few are ever distributed widely outside of Brazil. And many feel more like extended commercials for regional tourist boards. In the words of Brazilian film scholar André Parente: 'It is as if we can only see who we are through the eyes of the foreigner.'[6]

This tendency to bring in a foreigner's eye-view inevitably affects the choice of material used by directors and scriptwriters. For example, many of the films in question are set in the nineteenth or early twentieth centuries, when immigration was still in full flow and these communities were still very different from their hosts (in terms of language, social codes, politics, and so on). It is precisely their 'otherness' and their capacity to observe Brazil as outsiders that interests the filmmaker, rather than their condition of immigrant or future Brazilian. Take *Carlota Joaquina, princesa do Brazil*, for example, analysed in more detail below, which was said to have kick-started the mid-1990s boom. What better vehicle for revealing the outsider's view of Brazil than the Portuguese royal family, who arrived in Rio de Janeiro in 1808, fleeing from Napoleon's armies, and set up court there, thus provoking the political and cultural changes which would eventually bring about Brazil's independence in 1822.[7]

Two other trends that characterise Brazilian cinema since the *retomada*, which are worthy of further detailed study, given their search for greater dialogue with the public and the box-office returns such a dialogue can bring, are the resurgence of the theme and topography of the *sertão*, and the revisiting of the era and format of the *chanchada*, which together constitute both a homage to and critical reworking of Brazil's celluloid past.

The *sertão* on screen

One of the most significant of Brazil's regional identities to have impacted on its national culture is that of the *sertão*, or the Brazilian backlands, and more specifically, the underdeveloped interior of the North East of the country. Both the land and its people were often the focus of literature and other arts in the twentieth century, and what seems to fascinate writers, artists and filmmakers is the extent to which the *sertão* can be used to represent, in the words of Nicolau Sevcenko, 'the itinerant, unstable and fluid order which characterises the most extensive and profound dimensions of Brazilian society'.[8] Backlanders or *sertanejos* are traditionally understood to be stoic, passionate people, given to mysticism. The landscape they inhabit is rugged, forcing many to pursue a nomadic existence, and the difficulty in surviving in an environment so prone to vicious droughts, where successive central governments have been slow to invest any money, has proved an irresistible metaphor for the nation's Third-World woes.

As discussed in Chapters 3 and 4, from the 1940s onwards, migrant populations of North Easterners (*nordestinos*) began arriving in huge numbers in Southern cities such as Rio de Janeiro and São Paulo in search of work. *Nordestinos* who have settled in the South are proud of their North Eastern traditions and maintain strong community ties in their adopted cities. They have historically suffered extreme prejudice at the hands of their Southern neighbours, and continue to do so, because of their marked accents, style of speech and looks, as well as their supposed social conservatism. Since the days of the War of Canudos, the *sertão* has been portrayed as a site of the archaic, contrasting strongly with the modernist project of the coastal regions. The Canudos conflict, which took place at the end of the nineteenth century, involved national troops, and a messianic community headed by one-time priest Antônio Conselheiro, which refused to recognise the rule of the new Republican government. The troops were defeated on two occasions by the wily backlanders, before mercilessly wiping the community out. The army's initial defeat had been seen as an affront to the fledgling Republic, and symptomatic of Brazil's racial, cultural and economic backwardness, to be eradicated at all costs.

The hills of Rio de Janeiro, and the shantytowns with which they have become synonymous, are known as *favelas* thanks to the same soldiers who returned from the expeditions to Canudos. They brought this place name with them from the hinterland of the state of Bahia. Also known as *morros* (literally 'hills'), the shantytowns of Rio were inhabited at the beginning of the twentieth century by former African slaves and their descendants, who had moved to the capital city from the North Eastern plantations in search of work after Abolition in 1888. Initially this migrant population had settled near to the port, where they sought casual work, but they were subsequently expelled from the inner city during the capital's savage urbanisation, known as the *bota-abaixo* or 'knocking down', at the turn of the century. From the 1940s onwards the population of Rio's hillside shantytowns has been swelled

by waves of North Eastern migrants fleeing drought, prompting Lúcia Nagib
to write that 'the Brazilian North East is concentrated in the Rio hills' and
that therefore the *sertão* and the *favela* are in many ways two sides to the
same coin.[9] North Eastern culture has frequently been depicted by the cultural elite as being a purer or more authentic and therefore more significant
form of popular culture than that found along the coastal regions, following
similar patterns to those found in other Latin American cultures. In the
words of Jean Franco, 'the very conservatism of rural communities which
made them living links with the past also meant that they became an important source for high culture in its search for the expression of Latin American
originality.'[10]

Guerra de Canudos

Sérgio Rezende's *Guerra de Canudos* (*Battle of Canudos*, 1997) is a big-budget,
two-and-a-half-hour-long epic that was released to coincide with the centenary of the defeat of the Canudos community. Rezende's intentions are clear
from the outset: to produce a film version of the Canudos affair worthy of its
importance in terms of Brazilian cultural history, and to use the vehicle of
cinema in order to bring the history of Canudos to a wider audience. One
way in which he does this is by investing in a well-known cast. Antônio is
played by José Wilker, who has had his fair share of roles in popular films
(*Dona Flor e seus dois maridos* (*Dona Flor and Her Two Husbands*, 1976),
Xica da Silva (*Xica*, 1976), *Bye bye Brasil* (*Bye Bye Brazil*, 1979), as well as
being a successful soap opera star. Other stars of the film include Cláudia
Abreu (also a popular soap star) and Marieta Severo, who had delighted
audiences in the title role in *Carlota Joaquina, princesa do Brazil*. Rezende's
wide audience was guaranteed when TV Globo bought the film shortly after
its cinema release, and screened it over a week as a mini-series. It could
therefore arguably be the most watched Brazilian film ever.

In the film, Rezende picks out seemingly at random a fictional group
of individuals who are caught up in events, rather than filming from the
point of view of Antônio Conselheiro or the Brazilian army. He focuses on
the experiences of one impoverished family who are forced to join Antônio's
band. Zé Lucena and Penha are a simple farming couple with three children.
When their land is ravaged by drought, they are forced to sell their few
remaining emaciated cattle to a local political chief for a pittance. Having
spent part of the money (paid up front) on a photograph of the two daughters,
the family's cattle are commandeered by a government official in lieu of
taxes, thus leaving them with no choice but to join Antônio's followers, who
happen to be passing by their humble home. The film makes clear that the
father of the family joins Antônio first and foremost because of his genuine
faith, while his wife follows this charismatic leader because of her outrage at

losing everything to the official. The eldest child, who sees Antônio as little more than a madman, refuses to accompany her family, and ends up turning to prostitution, and she is later found selling her favours in the army camps at Canudos. We are thus given three clear reasons as to why people went to the settlement: religious fervour, political outrage and economic necessity.

The key to situating Canudos in its historical context is a journalist, who is first seen taking the photograph of the two daughters at the beginning of the film, who later becomes one of the elder daughter's customers, and who then hears about Canudos and sets off to report on events and sell his story back home in the South. The journalist is evidently loosely based on Euclides da Cunha, who had been sent to the North East by a Southern newspaper to report on the national campaign. Despite belittling the backlanders in cultural and in particular in racial terms, he revealed a deep admiration for their efforts in his book *Os sertões* (*Rebellion in the Backlands*, 1902). He also articulated a certain horror at the bungling of the state and vindictive army officers involved in the fourth expedition, which would finally raze Canudos to the ground.

Furthermore, the journalist had notably introduced the new-fangled technology of photography to the family's community, and the photograph of the two daughters symbolises in the film both a meeting of two worlds (the modern photograph with its archaic subjects), and the notion of progress. Luiza, the prostitute daughter asks the journalist if he can do anything to save her now-faded photo (the only link she has with her family). He is unable to use his modern technology to preserve the image (of her old way of life), and thus the photo heralds the arrival of a new era in a land that up to then seemed to be untouched by the passing of time.

The daughter's prostitution is a clever (albeit clichéd) ploy to remind the audience of the lack of alternatives open to the backlanders. Shots constantly switch from the construction of the Canudos settlement (the building of a church to symbolise faith and morality, for example) to the brothel where she works, and thus images of co-operation and equality are drawn in opposition to the exploitative and lonely nature of her new life. One of her first customers is the political chief who had cheated her family.

However, Luiza is not portrayed as the archetypal innocent thrown into the exploitative world of the sex trade. After all, she makes the decision not to go with her family and Conselheiro, and thus forges her own destiny. She marries a young man who is called upon to join the troops, and she accompanies him through choice. A young army officer from a wealthy Southern family falls in love with her, but to his confusion, when her husband is killed, she returns to prostitution. He tells her that he could be with a clean, perfumed young lady in Rio de Janeiro, but he seems fascinated by her difference from the stiff, artificial and cold women of his acquaintance back home. Both Luiza's father and lover are killed, and she and her sister are two of the few survivors of the massacre. The journalist also survives, and his material, which is damning of the war effort, is censored. As the general leads the surviving troops away from Canudos, the journalist declares that he is a disgrace to the army. The closing shot is of the two sisters leaving Canudos, and heading off to find their future elsewhere.

The real strength of *Guerra de Canudos*, both aesthetically and as a faithful account of historical events, lies in the battle scenes, in which the well-disciplined backlanders fight with courage and strategic prowess. Their knowledge of and identification with their inhospitable land gives them the edge over the poorly trained enemy, in what in many ways was a textbook 'people's war'. Their inspired leadership stood in contrast to the incompetence of the army generals despatched from Rio to sort out the rebellion. Zé Lucena, one of the last remaining backlanders, defends his bunker for almost thirty minutes of the film, emphasising the tenacity and conviction of Canudos's citizens.

In *Guerra de Canudos* the main actors are white, Southern (or at least Southern-based) soap actors, and as such are decidedly unconvincing in their roles as the long-suffering, North Eastern mixed-race poor. They also struggle with the required regional accent. It is worth bearing in mind, however, that in his film Rezende had clearly gone for the so-called *padrão global*, or the 'Global' standard of production: the glossy production values associated with the Globo network, and in particular its soap operas and mini-series. Had he not, it is unlikely that his film would have made it to primetime television. Ivana Bentes compares a number of contemporary films which have a backdrop of the *sertão* to the classics of *cinema novo* and notes that, while *cinema novo* refused to express 'the intolerable in the middle of a beautiful landscape', or to glamorise poverty, films such as *Guerra de Canudos* use 'classic language and cinematography [to] transform the *sertão* into a garden or an exotic museum, to be "rescued" by spectacle'.[11] She continues: 'We move from the "aesthetics" to the "cosmetics" of hunger, from the idea-in-mind and the camera-in-hand . . . to the Steadicam, a camera that surfs on reality, a sign of a narrative that values the beauty and the quality of the image.'[12] In response to Bentes's criticisms, the producer of *Guerra de Canudos* stated that: 'The challenge was to fulfil what I consider to be the most complex ambition of all those who produce and make films in Brazil: to reveal the country to Brazilians and to gain their support for national cinema. But perhaps this is not what a certain so-called elite considers relevant.'[13] *Guerra de Canudos* is thus promoted as following one of the original objectives of the *cinema novo* movement, which was to show the true face of Brazil,[14] while at the same time making aesthetic choices designed specifically to attract a public that held great faith in its national television.

The War of Canudos temporarily brought together two very different societies. The survival of the prostitute daughter enables Rezende to end the film on a positive note, suggesting through her that something good came of this meeting of two worlds, and that she was able to cut a path through them, gaining from both and dominated by neither. By way of contrast, as the army retreats, it is clear that they have gained nothing from the experience.

At no point are we shown shots of the South of Brazil, which gives the various expeditions the aura of an invading, foreign army. This is compounded by the fact that Rezende avoids framing the battle as one of conflicting ideals, as little mention is made of Conselheiro's creed, or of the political goals of the national government at that time. The battle here is between what Rezende considers to be the *real* Brazil and its polar opposite.

Central do Brasil

Marcos Bernstein first began to develop the script of *Central do Brasil* (*Central Station*, 1998) when his outline project was successfully submitted to and sponsored by Robert Redford's Sundance Institute in 1996. The film was directed by Walter Salles, who had notably honed his directing skills in documentary making and television advertising (the latter being an industry within which Brazil is internationally respected in technical and creative terms). Salles took his completed film to Berlin in 1998 and returned home with a Golden Bear for his efforts, subsequently winning a BAFTA and Oscar nomination for best foreign film.

In *Central do Brasil* Fernanda Montenegro, whose performance earned her a well-deserved Silver Bear at Berlin, as well as an Oscar nomination in the Best Actress category, plays Dora, a retired school teacher who survives financially by working in a train station writing letters for the illiterate public. One of her customers is a North Eastern woman, Ana, who has a nine-year-old son Josué, played by Vinícius de Oliveira. Just like the ill-fated young star of Hector Babenco's 1981 film *Pixote: a lei do mais fraco* (*Pixote*), Vinícius was not an actor before joining the cast of *Central do Brasil*.[15] He was famously discovered shining shoes in Santos Dumont airport in Rio and beat thousands of child actors to win the part.

Dora's existence is clearly precarious. School teachers in Brazil are notoriously badly paid, and as a spinster, she would have no family to support her in her old age. Her situation would have been compounded by the backdrop of recession and unemployment provoked by the Collor government, suggested, albeit subtly, in the film. She happily gives back-handers to Pedrão, a security guard, for her pitch on the concourse of the train station. The same friendly security guard will later shoot dead a young thief who has stolen a cheap transistor radio from a stall. This sequence, which some spectators found exaggerated and rather clichéd, brings Dora and Josué together. After having a letter written to her drunken ex-husband in the North East, whom Vinícius is keen to meet, Ana is knocked down and killed by a bus, leaving the child alone and destitute. Pedrão then enlists Dora's help in preparing the boy 'for adoption in Europe', and she takes a cut of the earnings of the sale.

Having taken the (endearing) child home for the evening, Dora then delivers him to the security guard's associates. When her neighbour Irene finds out, she tells Dora that the boy will be killed and his vital organs sold (another exaggeration and alarmist stereotype?). Dora manages to rescue the boy, and they set off together on their journey to the North East to find his father.

The film's title in Portuguese refers to the main train station in the centre of Rio de Janeiro, which serves the city's sprawling suburbs, filled with migrant workers, most of whom have come from the North and North East of the country. However, the title could also be interpreted as meaning the central part, or heartland of Brazil, and this seems to be what Walter Salles is aiming at in the film as a whole: a journey to the heart of the nation, once again to the *real* Brazil. But unlike depictions of the *sertão* in *cinema novo* films, the *real* Brazil is not an ugly, poor and violent one. Brazil's negative features are ultimately left behind in the city. Even the image of abandoned children is sanitised, certainly compared to those in the film *Pixote*. The journey in *Central do Brasil* is one of discovery for both Dora and Josué, and of self-discovery too. Because of her circumstances, Dora is at first a heartless and selfish woman, who is quick to turn a blind eye to the evils of society around her. She naively hands over her young charge, when he is obviously too old to be a suitable candidate for adoption. During the journey she under-goes a gradual transformation, provoked by the adventure itself, and by the increasingly strong bond that she forms with Josué. She is forced to recon-sider her basic and convenient assumptions about the nature of things, and the long, empty roads ahead seem to mirror the emptiness of her existence.

Dora's previous naiveté is paralleled in that of Brazil's middle classes. One solution frequently put forward, for example, for the problem of street chil-dren is to create more state-run orphanages and correction centres, despite the fact that Brazil's *Febens* (Foundations for the Well-being of Minors) have the reputation of being very dangerous places indeed for any young child. Similarly, government housing schemes aimed at removing slum-dwellers from their *favelas* and placing them in apartment blocks are erroneously assumed to be improving standards of living.[16] Such policies seem popular because they remove the offending elements of society from the view of the middle classes, and thus allow them to be forgotten.

When Dora first sets off on her journey, she only intends to take Josué part of the way (and out of her view), but circumstances force her to stay with him to the end. Josué, after a couple of false starts, finds his family (his two half-brothers) in a new urban development in an unnamed town in the

North East. The father, however, is still missing. Salles's depiction of Josué's family in the film is clearly allegorical: it offers hope for the Brazilian people and their culture in a society that is post-dictatorship, post-Collor and post-collapse of the film industry.

Josué's two brothers have different attitudes to the absent father. The elder loves and respects him, despite everything, and is confident that he will one day return. He is thus encouraged to work hard at building up the small family business. The younger brother is embittered by his father's departure, and seems determined to forget him and move on. The film leaves the question of the father open, as we do not ever meet him. The father thus symbolises many things: the old way of life in the North East; the future, and perhaps more poignantly, the nation itself.[17]

In *Central do Brasil* Walter Salles offers an alternative, admittedly romanticised and idealistic view of Brazilian society. A conservative message of the importance of family values is clearly espoused at the end of the film, and the *sertão* is once again idealised as a site of purity and authenticity: a strong sense of community still exists in the region and therefore such values can still be found there. *Central do Brasil* paints a positive picture of life in one of the poorest regions on earth. In doing so it struck a chord with the cinema-going public in Brazil and beyond, making it one of the most successful films in recent years, despite competing at home with the Hollywood blockbuster *Titanic* (1998).[18]

But crowds were not just drawn to the film for its happy ending. Vinícius de Oliveira's performance is heart-warming, and his involvement in promoting the film both at home and abroad did it no harm. The photography is of a high quality, bringing to the screen the beauty of a region that is little known to Brazil's predominantly coastal population. Brazil's television audiences had to an extent been prepared for the glossy and positive depictions of rural Brazil seen in the successful *retomada* films by a number of popular soap operas, for example the now extinct Manchete TV's blockbuster soap *Pantanal*, set in the beautiful wetlands of Brazil's mid-West, and *O salvador da pátria* (The Saviour of the Nation), set in the North East. In *Central do Brasil* the vast, open spaces of the *sertão* contrast with the bustle and dehumanisation of the city.[19] Deborah Shaw points to one thoughtful scene in particular to highlight this: after Josué's mother is killed, he is filmed seated in the railway station, and the camera angle is such that the passers-by behind him appear headless.[20]

In the film, individual North Easterners, both in their home region and in the Rio train station, are treated with a rare dignity, and their culture is not seen as exotic or anachronistic. Salles achieves this by using a documentary style to open his film, with North Easterners speaking and looking straight to camera in the train station, who, it then transpires, are writing home with

Dora's help. The first customer seen dictating a letter to Dora is Socorro Nobre, the focus of Salles's documentary short film of the same name from 1995.[21] Equally, the religiosity of the masses is depicted, rather than commented on, in Salles's film, which is filled with fascinating examples of the rich North Eastern traditions of popular Catholicism. These include the sequence featuring the Virgin Mary of the Candlelight parade, in which photographer Walter Carvalho effectively used the natural light from the millions of candles of this authentic pilgrimage. Salles described the celebration as bringing 'the possibility of a ray of light in the darkness which in a way is emblematic of cinema itself',[22] marking a clear difference between the depiction of popular Catholicism in his film and the old *cinema novo* way of seeing religion as the opium of the people. The depiction of Brazilian culture in the film is aimed in the first instance at a national, rather than international audience, evident from the fact that it does not feel in any way stylised. More importantly, the conclusion of the film sees Josué's new community firmly inserted into mainstream culture and society in Brazil, as it is one with which cinema-goers could comfortably identify.

With this in mind, there are two ways of reacting to *Central do Brasil*. Some might balk at the suggestion of the absorption of North Eastern society into the mainstream, labelling Walter Salles' work politically naive and destructive of popular North Eastern culture. One might even suggest that Vinícius' return to the North East is tantamount to repatriation, or at best the removal of the 'social problem' from view. It could also be argued, however, that like any good ad man Salles knows how to sell an idea, regardless of how trite and 'dumbed down' it might seem. The idea of *Central do Brasil* is that it is worth investing in the North East, when investments are supported by co-operation, good administration and continuity.

Eu, tu, eles

Appearing in the wake of the success of *Central do Brasil*, *Eu, tu, eles* (*Me, You, Them*, 2000) confirmed the fascination held by audiences, including international audiences, for tales from the Brazilian *sertão*. Like *Guerra de Canudos*, the film is set entirely in the backlands and here no reference whatsoever is made to urban, coastal life in Brazil. The film's remit is thus not to set up a comparison with the kind of existence experienced by most Brazilian cinema-goers: it simply tells the story, based loosely on fact, of a rural worker who lived with three men as if they were all her husbands. The real-life polygamist, Maria Marlene da Silva Sabóia, had appeared on TV Globo's popular human interest series *Fantástico* in 1995, watched by a young director, Andrucha Waddington, who immediately set about transforming the tale into a feature film.

The film has a very different take on life in the *sertão* from *Guerra de Canudos* and *Central do Brasil*, for example, which reveals the wealth of styles and approaches to social issues that have come to characterise the films of the *retomada*. The film's pace is slow and there is little plot or action to speak of (note the absence of violence and archetypal baddies, which we see in early *cinema novo* films and in *Guerra de Canudos* and *Central do Brasil*). The whole picture is beautifully filmed and edited and it is impossible not to feel sympathy (note: sympathy, rather than pity) for all the characters involved in the story.

Like many contemporary films, both in Brazil and beyond, the film concentrates on the personal details of people's lives. As a result, as in *Central do Brasil*, more space is afforded the depiction of popular culture. The food, music and dance of the region are highlighted in the film, as is the importance of the radio for remote communities, working practices and equipment (for example, the fact that newly recruited workers in the sugar plantations supply their own tools), and so on. Like many a popular film and play before it, *Eu, tu, eles* includes a marriage and a funeral sequence, along with more than one trip to the local bar on *forró* music night. The diegetic and extra-diegetic music in the film is, without exception, North Eastern.[23] *Eu, tu, eles* has a different approach to the filmic story-telling commonly seen in films set in the *sertão* in that it is a wholly secular tale. There is no discussion of religion in the film, with no religious parades or festivals included for good measure, either for their spirituality or as an entertaining aspect of popular culture of the North East (unlike the previous two films discussed in this section).[24] As Lúcia Nagib has written:

> The filmmakers of today, who are much less ambitious than their predecessors of the Cinema Novo . . . seem to be simply observing and recording a people who are usually excluded from the high cultural media, letting them express themselves in their own way. In the process, the old desire to denounce gives way to a respectful attitude towards popular culture, an attitude that is not political, but *politically correct*.[25]

In *Eu, tu, eles* the polygamist Darlene's first and legitimate husband, Osias, is a lazy rogue, and after marrying him she quickly becomes a drudge, doing the housework and working long shifts in the sugar-cane fields while he lies in a hammock all day long listening to his transistor radio. Much of the film's humour is supplied by Osias, played by veteran film and soap opera actor Lima Duarte: jokes are premised on his own *malandragem* and how he defends it, as well as his comments on the differences between the sexes, and the fact that he is cuckolded throughout the film. Darlene first gives birth to a black baby (obviously not fathered by her husband), then to a son with blond hair and blue eyes, bearing a striking resemblance to Osias's cousin Zezinho (Stênio Garcia), who has moved into their home and ultimately becomes Darlene's second, more tender and supportive, 'husband'. Both these older men are no competition, however, for Ciro (Luís Carlos Vasconcelos), a younger, fitter and better-looking sugar-cane worker who lodges in their home. Darlene therefore displays a modern kind of female *malandragem*, which involves a clear inversion of traditional gender roles.

It is interesting to compare the portrayal of the female leads of *Central do Brasil* and *Eu, tu, eles*. Both women are unusual in the context of Brazilian visual media, which are filled with Manichean characterisations of woman-hood. Dora in *Central do Brasil* is a rather cold and heartless character for most of the film, but audiences are still expected to empathise with her. Darlene in *Eu, tu, eles* is a very sympathetic character but one who gives her eldest son away and experiences no crisis of conscience when she betrays her various partners.[26] Darlene is a sexually honest woman played by the plump, homely and middle-aged actress Regina Casé: a far cry from the 'bombshell' Sônia Braga and her portrayal of Brazilian cinema's other famous bigamist from the 1970s: Dona Flor. Casé was described by the director, Andrucha Waddington, as a typical Brazilian woman whom he had in mind for the role from the start of the project, unconsciously echoing the words of Jorge Amado and Gilberto Freyre when describing the ultra-sensual Braga in her roles in 1970s cinema.[27] The depiction of womanhood in *Eu, tu, eles* is, as a result, less conservative than in *Central do Brasil*, in which Dora is gradually brought in line and 'feminised', for the better, the audience is led to understand.[28]

The message of *Eu, tu, eles* is much simpler than that of *Central do Brasil*: that poor women in the North East of Brazil have similar aspirations to their middle-class counterparts in the South (and in cinema audiences) – they just have a different way of fulfilling these aspirations. Thus, the film's premise – that everyone has the right to find happiness, at whatever cost – could not be more different from the ideology of the *cinema novo* movement. Inevitably, a similar accusation to that levelled against *Guerra de Canudos* by Ivana Bentes of resorting to a 'cosmetics' of poverty has been made against *Eu, tu, eles*. For a start, despite the brave choice of leading lady, the film uses safe, TV Globo soap actors (Lima Duarte and Stênio Garcia in the roles of husbands number one and two) and the ubiquitous *nordestino* pin-up Luís Carlos Vasconcelos as husband number three.[29] Interestingly, it is Walter Salles who comes to the rescue of Waddington's film in the face of accusations of glamorising the *sertão* through its photography, by asking why people from different social classes have to be filmed differently – why is it, he asks, that poor people and poverty should always be shot in grainy black and white?[30]

Nostalgia and revisiting the *chanchada* in the 1990s

The *retomada* gave rise to a variety of films, ranging from a musical comedy (*For all: o trampolim da vitória*, 1998) to a historical comedy drama (*Carlota*

Joaquina, Princesa do Brazil, 1995) that actively engaged with the legacies of the *chanchada* tradition. The latter half of the 1990s similarly bore witness to a renewed interest in nostalgia for the so-called 'Golden Age' of Brazilian popular music in the 1930s and early 1940s, in the form of Helena Solberg's *Carmen Miranda: Bananas is My Business* (1995), that recounted the life story of radio and screen legend Carmen Miranda, and Rogério Sganzerla's *Tudo é Brasil* (All is Brazil, 1998), which was inspired by the presence of Orson Welles in Rio de Janeiro in 1942, as the USA's 'cultural ambassador' to Latin America.[31]

For all: o trampolim da vitória

Set in the town of Natal, in the Northern state of Rio Grande do Norte, in 1943, the action of *For all* centres on Parnamirim Field, a real-life American military base, where fifteen thousand US servicemen were stationed after President Getúlio Vargas declared war on the Axis powers. Directed by Buza Ferraz and Luiz Carlos Lacerda, the film focuses primarily on the impact that the presence of the First-World foreigners has on the lives, desires and aspirations of the forty thousand local people. In accordance with its historical setting, *For all* consciously cites recognisable aspects of the 'war-time entertainment musicals' produced in Hollywood during the war years and beyond, such as big-band show numbers by the likes of Tommy Dorsey and his orchestra.

For all more importantly pays tribute to home-grown cinematic traditions, drawing much of its inspiration from the archetypal *chanchada* in terms of characterisation and plot. As Luiz Carlos Lacerda said in interview: '*For all* is clearly influenced by the *chanchadas* that I saw when I was a child.' The comic protagonist, Sandoval, a good-hearted, camp clown, bears more than just a passing physical resemblance to Oscarito, the anti-hero of countless *chanchadas* of the 1940s and 1950s (see figure 12). As Lacerda explained, 'Sandoval was an explicit homage to Oscarito.'[32] They share a puny, anti-macho physique and wide-eyed naivety, and like Oscarito's alter-ego, the uneducated hillbilly bewildered by his abrupt encounter with urban Brazil, Sandoval is bowled over by his exposure to the exotic world of show business at the military base. As in the *chanchada* tradition, Sandoval represents the disadvantaged man in the street, who manages to worm his way into a seductive, alien environment via an act of *malandragem* (he claims that he can speak English, which subsequently proves not to be the case in farcical circumstances, in order to secure a job at the base as a cleaner). The humour of this character stems from his facial expressions and his clumsy attempts to better himself, and in both respects he has much in common with the typical anti-heroes with which Oscarito became synonymous. Like Oscarito's characters, Sandoval uses everyday vernacular and slang in his speech and

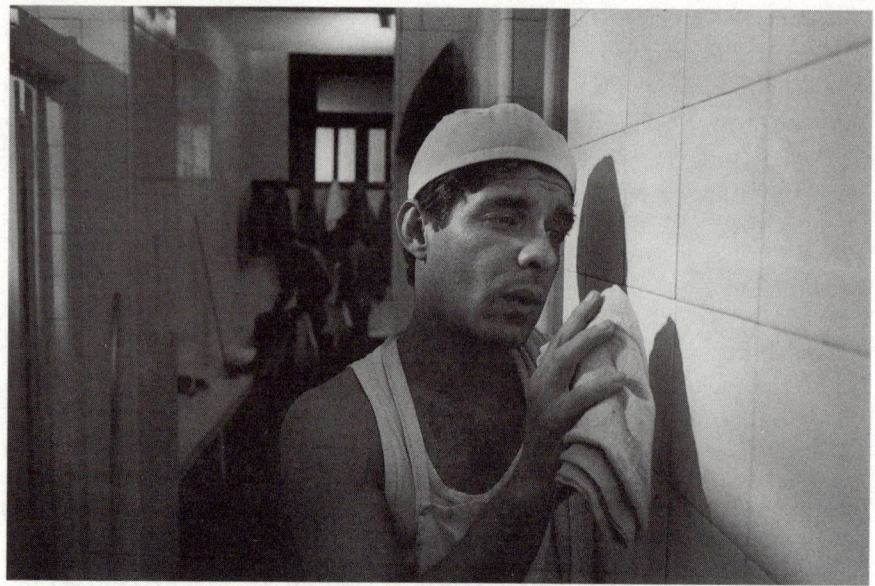

12   Luiz Carlos Tourinho in the role of Sandoval in *For all: o trampolim da vitória* (1998).

struggles with alien linguistic forms, more specifically English. In an attempt to imitate the speech of the American airmen, he comically transforms the expletive 'Oh, shit!' into the popular North Eastern colloquialism 'Oxente!', an expression of surprise or disdain.

As in the *chanchada*, the tropes of *malandragem* and *jeitinho* run through *For all*, as the Brazilian characters attempt to improve their lot in life by exploiting the presence of American troops with dollars to spend. The immoral barber, Senhor Bola, lures young local women into prostitution, for example. (In true *chanchada* style he is the villain of the piece, who is defeated by the handsome hero, Miguel, who succeeds in buying his sweetheart, Jucilene out of a life of vice.) Similarly turning the unforeseen circumstances to their advantage, a young black boy, Severino, polishes up his English as well as the soldiers' boots for profit (boots that are crafted by the local cobbler as an equally profitable sideline), and the love-struck João Marreco gains employment at the base as a Portuguese teacher.

For all, in line with the unwritten conventions of the *chanchada* tradition, combines themes such as *malandragem* with a romantic sub-plot, in the form of the tragically short-lived love affair between local beauty Iracema and broad-shouldered American airman, Lt Robert Collins, complete with musical interludes. In the words of Luiz Carlos Lacerda, 'As in the *chanchada*, the musical numbers in *For all*, if you look closely, are a parody, mocking US musicals. The dancers mess up their steps and their movements are out of synch. It is an example of cultural cannibalism. It is not imitation, but neither is it a criticism of foreign cinema or the culture that the latter represents.'[33] Early in the film, the camera cuts to two female singers in uniform who are dancing and obviously miming to the well-known 'Beer Barrel Polka', sung by the Andrews Sisters. This song then becomes the background music for scenes at the base, which are spoken in English. Although the two women are miming to a record being played on a jukebox, this instance of lip-sync, together with Sandoval's sudden spouting of fluent English when he is introduced on stage to his idol, Jay Francis, are significant because they act as a kind of distancing effect which serves to critique the clichés of the musical genre. The climax of *For all* is a quintessential *chanchada* finale, in which the North Eastern musical style, *forró* replaces the earlier Hollywood-style big-band numbers. It is set at a dance at the base, to which both locals and military personnel have been invited. As an officer informs Sandoval, 'It's for all.' This musical finale fondly evokes the community spirit and optimism of the *chanchada*, as previous differences are overcome, and tensions are smoothed over, as characters previously at odds dance together, and both the diegetic and extra-diegetic audience of the show are encouraged to participate in the carnivalesque celebration. Our unlikely hero, the closet homosexual, Sandoval, is paired up with his heroine, the glamorous star, Jay Francis, in a classic example of inversion worthy of any Atlântida *chanchada*.

Carlota Joaquina, princesa do Brazil

Carla Camurati's comic spin on the life story of the Spanish wife of prince Dom João of Portugal, who fled to the colony of Brazil in 1808 to escape the invading forces of Napoleon, recalls various key features of the *chanchada* tradition. The opening section of this surreal historical comedy, which is told like a fairytale, centres on the carnivalesque exuberance of the Spanish court and is characterised by an aesthetic of baroque excess. The overtly stylised visuals and high-camp quality of the sets, costumes and make-up, together with the emphasis on diegetic flamenco music and communal frivolity, are subsequently drawn into sharp contrast with the dour relative austerity of the Portuguese court. This clash of cultures, a common motif in the *chanchada*, is drawn into focus when the spirited young Carlota and her lady-in-waiting perform a flamenco dance for Dom João's mother, the mad Queen Maria.

The mockery of the Portuguese (a natural target as Brazil's former colonial power) in the form of their staid behaviour and insipid diet continues throughout the film. (The *chanchada* similarly made fun of the legendary stupidity, instantly recognisable accent, and often the avarice of the Portuguese immigrant community in Brazil, maintaining a tradition of ethnic jokes established by the *teatro de revista*.) Dom João is depicted as an effeminised buffoon, who is afraid of thunder and is repeatedly cuckolded by his Spanish wife. The film's narrator also describes him as 'notoriously tight-fisted'. His exaggerated accent and pedantic way of speaking are emphasised for comic effect, and it is no coincidence that a more humble Portuguese family who have settled in Brazil, and who willingly give up their home for the newly arrived royalty, are seen alongside their donkey, literally 'burro' in Portuguese, a word that also means stupid.[34]

Carlota Joaquina, princesa do Brazil brings together a host of other elements which Brazilian audiences of a certain generation would associate with the *chanchada*. These include characters that pay tribute to the stock protagonists of the latter tradition; firstly, Carlota herself, a domineering, foul-mouthed fishwife (in spite of her status) in the style of countless anti-heroines played by the likes of Dercy Gonçalves and Zezé Macedo; secondly, Carlota's page, a black clown, who constantly sports an inane grin and is treated with racist condescension by his mistress, and thus has much in common with the down-trodden characters played by Grande Otelo; finally, the infantile, gauche and idle Dom João, with his comic facial expressions, owes much to Oscarito's screen persona. The film also persistently makes fun of the elite, many of whom are the most unlikely and undeserving recipients of aristocratic titles, and uses slapstick and toilet humour to do so. During the trans-Atlantic crossing, for example, members of the court indecorously vomit overboard. Dom João, in particular, is a figure of ridicule, who while sleeping during a hunting expedition, fires his gun unwittingly and a large bird crashes into his lap, and when king, relieves himself in front of his entourage and daughter and breaks wind noisily.

In the style of an archetypal *chanchada*, *Carlota Joaquina, princesa do Brazil* incorporates the Afro-Brazilian population and their culture, in the form of minor characters and extras,[35] a brief glimpse of *capoeira* street fighting, and a soundtrack that features instruments such as the berimbau, with which this martial art/dance form is closely associated. As in the earlier cinematic tradition, 'Afro-Brazil' provides an 'exotic' backdrop for the film, which centres on the lives of the white elite. Furthermore, the steamy sex scenes between Carlota and her black lover Fernando are played out to the extra-diegetic melody of the very famous popular song 'Tico-Tico no fubá' (Tico-Tico Bird in the Cornmeal), recorded by Carmen Miranda in 1945, and which she performed in the Hollywood film *Copacabana* in 1947. Forced to bandage her head to combat an epidemic of lice during the ocean crossing to Brazil (a comic interlude that harks back to the outbreak of fleas that makes people dance frenetically in the *chanchada Carnaval Atlântida* (Atlântida Carnival, 1952)), Carlota transforms the turban into a fashionable headdress. Combined

with her rococo décolleté costumes and eye-catching jewellery, this look is a virtual homage to the apocryphal *baianas* who re-worked Carmen Miranda's screen persona in popular film from the 1940s and 1950s.

Carmen Miranda: Bananas Is My Business

Helena Solberg's film, *Carmen Miranda: Bananas Is My Business* is a well-executed intersection of documentary footage and fictional narration referring to the life of Carmen Miranda, the star of Brazilian radio and popular film musicals in the 1930s. The film is symptomatic of a renewed interest in the star as a Brazilian cultural phenomenon, and equally of a desire to return on screen to an age when notions of national identity, however stylised and often risible, were brought to the fore. *Carmen Miranda: Bananas Is My Business* focuses on the manipulation of Miranda's screen persona in the Hollywood movies in which she starred in the 1940s and 1950s, particularly within the context of the 'Good Neighbour Policy'. It also examines the polemical status of the self-styled 'Brazilian Bombshell' in Brazil. Her success in the international arena as the epitome of 'Latino' identity hinged on her acquiescence in diluting samba for the Anglo-Saxon palate in particular, and for this reason she has remained a controversial figure for Brazilians. Against a backdrop of newsreel footage of crowds in the streets of Rio de Janeiro when Miranda's body was taken back there in 1955, Solberg, as narrator, says:

> After she left for the United States in 1939 her relationship with us Brazilians became kind of complicated, really complicated. Some people resented her for leaving us with all her fruits on her head. There was even some gossip that she was a tool of US imperialism. But for most of the people, those who filled the streets to bid her farewell, there was never any doubt about their love for her.

Hollywood's portrayal of Carmen Miranda after she was 'discovered' in the Urca casino in Rio by the American show business impresario Lee Schubert, is of particular fascination to Solberg. As she says in the opening narrative voice-over: 'I always wonder what gets lost when you are seen through the eyes of a foreigner.' For American audiences she was to remain the archetypal *latina* bimbo (who, in her first interview in the USA famously claimed to know only the following words of English: 'money' and 'men'). When she returned to Brazil some eighteen months after her departure for the United States, the Vargas regime's DIP (Press and Propaganda Department) held an official reception in her honour, and the masses clamoured to greet her. This warm welcome could not have differed more from the frosty reception that she received from the elite audience at her homecoming show at the Urca casino, which had been organised by Brazil's first lady, Darcy Vargas. Carmen soon returned to the USA and to a contract with Twentieth Century-Fox, and her immense popularity ensured that she was the studio's greatest asset. Consequently, Twentieth Century-Fox insisted that she played stereotypical roles in identikit musicals, which reproduced the image of the exaggerated and caricatured *latina*.

Fragmented identity is the predominant organising principal in *Carmen Miranda: Bananas Is My Business*. As David William Foster writes:

> The opening and closing scenes of the documentary are of her collapsing on the floor, holding a hand mirror, which shatters into innumerable shards as it hits the floor – a sign of how Miranda had, at the time of her death, hit bottom, living a persona that no longer had any personal or sociocultural coherence.[36]

In spite of her desire to play more varied roles, Carmen was prevented from doing so by the studios. Solberg comments on her poignant attempts to reaffirm her own Brazilian identity, often by merely speaking a few words of Portuguese in a film, and by poking fun at her poor English. Solberg also focuses on the racial paradox of Carmen's screen image; her outfits and the music she danced to (samba) were symbols of black Brazil, and yet she was the daughter of white Portuguese immigrants. Furthermore, the issue of gender identity and construction of the feminine is explored in this film, which features the female impersonator Erik Barreto, who plays Miranda in several fictional re-enactments, such as in the opening and closing scenes, and in the recreation of her arrival in New York in 1939. Miranda's Hollywood star text relied on extravagant costumes that revealed a bare midriff, tropical excess in the form of fruit-laden turbans, high platform shoes and make-up that exaggerated her lips, and ultimately she became a caricature of both 'Latinness' and the feminine. As David William Foster argues, this screen image thus came to occupy 'a gender no man's land: Miranda appears to be a woman playing a man playing a woman.'[37] This is underscored by the choice of a transvestite to play the role of Miranda in Solberg's film, which also echoes a recurrent motif of the *chanchada*, that of the carnivalesque inversion of gender via male characters appearing in drag. Like the *chanchadas* of the 1940 and 1950s, Solberg's film considers what it means to be Brazilian, and it helps audiences to appreciate how cultural identities may be forged through a complex dialogue between expectations, perceptions and realities.[38]

Popular music in 1990s film

Two films made by the acclaimed director Carlos Diegues, one of the leading members of the *cinema novo* generation, could not differ more from the 'aesthetic of hunger' and art-house appeal of the films associated with that avant-garde cinematic movement. Both *Veja esta canção* (*Rio's Love Songs*, 1994) and *Orfeu* (Orpheus, 1999) rely heavily on contemporary, commercialised popular music in their soundtracks and story lines, thus appealing to a wide audience and providing a ready-made marketing strategy (as well as perhaps unconsciously echoing the *chanchada* tradition).

Although associated with the *retomada*, *Veja esta canção* was made before the introduction of the Audio-visual Law and thus relied on funding from São Paulo's TV Cultura television company and the Banco Nacional bank.[39] This low-budget film, made in just four weeks, explicitly uses popular music as its source of inspiration, more specifically the lyrics of four contemporary songs, each composed by a renowned singer-songwriter. As the director has said, 'the film is a homage to Brazilian popular music, that I love so much and that is so important to Brazil and to all Brazilians.'[40] The first of the four unrelated love stories that make up the film and each depict a different social milieu within the city of Rio, takes its title from Jorge Ben Jor's song, 'Pisada de Elefante' (Elephant's Footstep). This song forms a recurrent part of the diegetic soundtrack as accompaniment to the stage performance of an erotic dancer. The lyrics directly contribute to the somewhat clichéd depiction of this sexually liberated mixed-race beauty by describing her as 'vaidosa, maliciosa, perigosa' (vain, malicious, dangerous), echoing the stereotypical portrayal of mulatto women that can be traced through the *chanchada* tradition and beyond.[41] The second tale shares its name and theme with the song 'Drão' by Gilberto Gil, that happens to be the song that the two protagonists associate with their relationship and which ultimately reunites these two estranged lovers. The soundtrack also includes diegetic percussion-based carnival samba, performed at a rehearsal of a samba school or neighbourhood carnival association, a rhythm and setting which made its appearance in the *chanchada*.[42] A composition by Caetano Veloso, Gilberto Gil's artistic partner in the creation of the avant-garde Tropicalist movement in popular music in the late 1960s, lends its title to the third story, 'Você é linda' (You are Beautiful). The young mixed-race heroine, who lives on the street and is forced into prostitution, escapes her reality by listening on a stolen personal stereo to a tape of Veloso singing this song. The latter also provides the extra-diegetic accompaniment to a montage sequence of scenes of Rio's carnival, again harking back to the *chanchada*'s perennial theme, one of which features Veloso himself on a parade float. Like the other three tales but to a greater extent, this section of the film owes much to the visual techniques of the music video industry, and plays up to Rio's trite image as a haven of sexual licence. The final story similarly deals with prostitution and sex, and takes its title and theme tune from Chico Buarque's 'Samba do grande amor' (Samba of the Great Love Affair).

In spite of the obvious links between the *chanchada* and *Veja esta canção*, it is unlikely that Carlos Diegues was consciously inspired by the tradition. As he has said in interview:

As far as Brazilian cinema is concerned, the *chanchada* was the cinema of my childhood and adolescence, a tradition that has had a great impact on Brazilian film. But, in spite of my affection for those films, I have never tried to emulate the *chanchadas*, because they were parodies of American cinema, and I never like parodies, I have never been interested in them, as I consider them to be a perverse means for showing love for one's enemy.[43]

Nevertheless, *Veja esta canção*, in terms of the use of diegetic contemporary popular music, the carnival setting of one of the episodes, its depiction of typical characters from all rungs of *carioca* society, and its interaction with another medium (in this case the television as opposed to the radio), perhaps unwittingly follows in the footsteps of the *chanchada* tradition. More obviously, perhaps, the film uses well-known contemporary songs and their famous artists, together with a televisual aesthetic, in a quest for widespread appeal and dissemination. This tactic is understandable given that the project was commenced before the Audio-visual Law improved the economic conditions for filmmaking in Brazil. As late as 1999, however, Diegues expressed his concerns over the future viability of producing feature films: 'I am very afraid, I see clouds on the horizon as the current cycle comes to an end. If nothing else is done, the current experience, economically made possible by the advent of the [Audio-visual] law, could soon come to an end due to the lack of the necessary conditions.'[44] This concern may well partially explain Diegues's decision to cast a musician with 'street cred[ibility]', a large fan base among Brazil's youth, and a face made instantly recognisable by his exposure on television, in the title role of his film, *Orfeu*, by far the most popular Brazilian film at the box-office in 1999.

Orfeu reworks the play *Orfeu da Conceição* by poet and songwriter Vinícius de Moraes, written in 1953 and first staged in 1956. It seeks to remedy the questionable interpretation of this play made by French director Marcel Camus in his film *Orfeu negro* (*Black Orpheus*, 1958), the winner of the Palme D'Or in Cannes and the Oscar for best foreign film in 1959. Camus's acclaimed film was responsible for popularising Brazil and its popular music, more specifically bossa nova, throughout the world, but was criticised in Brazil for its romanticised depiction of the black inhabitants of Rio de Janeiro's shantytowns. Diegues, known for his championing of the black cause in his work, recalls his reaction to *Black Orpheus* in the press release of his remake:

I saw with great disappointment the film *Black Orpheus*, a French production directed by Marcel Camus, based on *Orfeu da Conceição*. Despite his sincere fascination for the human and geographic landscape of Rio de Janeiro, and although he even showed a certain tenderness for what he was shooting, the film gave an exotic and tourist view which betrayed the meaning of the play and completely abandoned its fundamental qualities. I truly felt myself personally insulted, and from then on I began to dream about the film which became our present *Orfeu*.[45]

In his play, de Moraes sought to universalise black music, allowing Brazilian music to transcend its popular associations with carnival lasciviousness and Afro-Brazilian religious ceremonies, by drawing on the Orphic myth of the charming power of music. In Camus's film the spectacle of Rio's carnival celebrations, against the stunning backdrop of the city's topography, is accompanied by rhythmic drumming, that takes over the soundtrack again and again. As Robert Stam writes, 'it was [also] *Black Orpheus*, more than any other film, that introduced both samba and bossa nova to the world. More accurately, the success of *Black Orpheus* opened doors for the newborn bossa nova, the "modern samba" that the film's soundtrack juxtaposes with traditional samba.'[46]

Popular music is equally central to Diegues's *Orfeu*, in which the title role is played by Tony Garrido, the pin-up lead singer of successful reggae band Cidade Negra (Black City) and part-time television presenter (his credits include the Brazilian version of *Fame Academy*, *Fama*, produced by Globo Television in 2003).[47] In the film Garrido plays a samba composer for the local samba school (the fictitious Unidos da Carioca). The vibrant images of the school participating in Rio's annual carnival parade were achieved by placing the chief actors in the real-life 1998 musical entry of Unidos do Viradouro, a Niterói-based samba school, who used famous singer-song-writer, Caetano Veloso's *samba-enredo* or themed carnival samba, specially prepared for the film, for that year's competition.[48] In the film when a police-man enters the shantytown where he encounters Orfeu, he sings the chorus of this *samba-enredo*, which Orfeu has composed for the coming celebra-tions. The lyrics of this song venerate the black origins of samba, carnival and the *favelas* or shantytowns of Rio. The musical backdrop to the *favela* portrayed in *Orfeu* is rap music rather than samba, however, played to accompany the local radio announcements that blast out of loudspeakers on every corner. In this the film recognises that nowadays most young working-class people listen to hip-hop and other forms of Brazilian urban music rather than samba. The soundtrack to *Orfeu* thus includes bossa nova and rap, and samba is often only heard on the run-up to and during carnival. Even Orfeu's composition for the carnival parade daringly incorporates a rap halfway through, performed in the film by Orfeu himself and written by popular rapper Gabriel o Pensador. Diegues thus brings the tale of Orpheus right up to date with his use of contemporary urban music, contributing to the film's striking realism. As Lúcia Nagib writes:

Orfeu's plot develops in a purpose-built *favela*, so that none of the sordid or picturesque details that exist in reality are forgotten. There are the labyrinthine stairs, the filthy trash deposits, and also the pirate radio station with its loud-speakers dotted everywhere, reporting the *favela* news in the flexible and creative local language in rap/funk rhythm. There are the scruffy bars where samba players get together (and the film does not fail to pay homage to such celebrities as Nelson Sargento) and the small evangelist temples for those who wish to flee from alcohol and corrupting pleasures of music.[49]

Diegues's reworking of the Orpheus myth also pays homage to the *chanchada* tradition in a metacinematic detail. While the heroine of the film, Eurydice is trying on her carnival costume, a television screen in the same room shows a scene from the well-known *chanchada*, *Carnaval Atlântida* (Atlântida Carnival, 1952), in which the black comic actor Grande Otelo, dressed in a toga, dances at a carnival ball with Helen of Troy. Diegues thus pays tribute not only to this intrinsic element of Brazilian popular culture, but equally to the contribution of blacks to the latter. Nagib argues that this detail also recalls Grande Otelo's portrayal of another talented samba com-poser in Nelson Pereira dos Santos's film, *Rio, Zona Norte* (Rio, North Zone, 1957), 'an Orphic character whose songs are stolen and appropriated by whites from the affluent districts of Rio'.[50] In contrast, Diegues's Orfeu of the late 1990s is a successful, wealthy composer, whose name is widely recognised and respected by all sections of society.

Concluding remarks

At the beginning of the 1990s the demise of the Brazilian film industry seemed certain. By 1995 its fortunes seemed to have been saved by the intervention of the state and a return to popular filmmaking. In 2003, with an economic crisis looming, a brand-new government and the end in sight of the beneficial Audiovisual Law, it was not clear whether the valuable state promotion and sponsorship of cinema, or the boom in interesting filmmaking, world last. It is worth remembering that while by the late 1990s a healthy thirty-five to forty films were being made each year in Brazil, few of these gained more than a limited art-house release. Within the current context of uncertainty, there appears to be a consensus of opinion for the first time among Brazilian filmmakers on the need to make their product more commercially viable.

This need for commercial viability has inevitably led Brazil's film critics and cultural old guard to level criticisms at many successful young directors and producers, and the debate continues on how to reconcile artistic originality and integrity with the laws of the marketplace. Commercial viability, as has been discussed in this chapter, has encouraged many filmmakers to turn to the popular cinematic styles and tropes of the past. Others have relied on the continued success of national television programmes and contemporary popular music, for example, to create films starring popular performers from both domains. There is equally a trend for films produced partly by production companies linked to television channels.[51]

The success of the *retomada* is also partially due to a number of talented individuals who have been involved in various projects over the last few years, lending the renaissance, despite its variety of themes and styles, its own look and language. Walter Salles, for example, directed four critically acclaimed feature films between 1995 and 2001, as well as producing, among other notable films, one of the biggest national box-office successes of the twenty-first century so far: *Cidade de Deus* (*City of God*, 2002). Salles has worked closely with the very talented cinematographer Walter Carvalho, who also photographed the comedy *Pequeno dicionário amoroso* (*Little Book of Love*, 1997), set in Rio de Janeiro, along with Karim Ainouz's critically acclaimed *Lavoura arcaica* (*To the Left of the Father*, 2001) and *Madame Satã* (2002).[52] Marcos Bernstein, who scripted *Oriundi*, *O xangô de Baker Street*, *Terra Estrangeira* (*Foreign Land*, 1995) and *Central do Brasil*, has helped to raise the profile of the scriptwriter within the industry in Brazil.[53]

Brazilian cinema in the 1990s, and continuing into the first few years of the twenty-first century, has been, if anything, eclectic, as filmmakers battle to place on the screen as many different representations of Brazilian national identity as they possibly can. As one of the directors of *For All* said in interview: 'Democracy has arrived on Brazilian cinema screens in the form of the depiction of the thousand and one aspects that a culture like ours should have. Films made in Brazil today reflect this multiplicity, this complexity, these thousand different tongues, these thousand different faces, which form on a map the continent we call Brazil.'[54]

Notes

1 *Brazil 1994–2002: The Era of the Real* (Brasília: SECOM, 2002), p. 133.
2 Randal Johnson, 'From the ashes? Brazilian cinema in the 1990s', unpublished article.
3 *Ibid*. John King, *Magical Reels: A History of Cinema in Latin America* (London: Verso, 2000), p. 272, cited in Deborah Shaw, 'National identity and the family: *Pixote* by Hector Babenco and *Central Station* by Walter Salles', *Contemporary Latin American Cinema: Ten Key Films* (New York, London: Continuum, 2003).
4 In order to contextualise the significance of such state support for filmmaking in Brazil, the 2002 blockbuster *Cidade de Deus* (*City of God*) had a budget of 8.2 million reais (around £2,000,000 at the time) and only 15 per cent of that budget came from Laws of Incentive.
5 Other examples of this trend include *Jenipapo* (*The Interview*, Monique Gardenberg, 1995), *Terra estrangeira* (*Foreign Land*, Walter Salles and Daniela Thomas, 1995) and *Hans Staden* (Luís Alberto Pereira, 1999). A significant number of films use multilingual dialogue, such as *For all: o trampolim da vitória* (English

and Portuguese), *Carlota Joaquina, Princesa do Brazil* (Portuguese, Spanish and English), *O que é isso, companheiro?* and *O xangô de Baker Street* (*Xango of Baker Street*, 1999) (Portuguese and English).

6 André Parente, 'Reflexão sobre a arte simulada', *Jornal do Brasil*, Caderno B, 28 May 1998 (our translation).

7 See Stephanie Dennison, 'A meeting of two worlds: recent trends in Brazilian cinema', *Tesserae*, 6:2 (2000).

8 Nicolau Sevcenko, 'Peregrinations, visions and the city: from Canudos to Brasília, the backlands become the city and the city becomes the backlands', in Vivian Schelling (ed.), *Through the Kaleidoscope: The Experience of Modernity in Latin America* (London and New York: Verso, 2000), p. 76.

9 Lúcia Nagib, 'Death on the beach: the recycled utopia of *Midnight*', in Lúcia Nagib (ed.), *Brazilian Cinema: A Renaissance* (London: I. B. Taurus, 2003). The three films set in the *sertão* to be discussed in this chapter were chosen because of their commercial success. There are many other interesting films with the *sertão* as backdrop from the *retomada*, such as those dealing with banditry: for example, the aforementioned *Baile perfumado*, *Corisco e Dadá* (Corisco and Dadá, Rosemberg Cariry, 1996) and Aníbal Massaini Neto's 1997 remake of Lima Barreto's 1953 classic *O cangaceiro* (*The Bandit*). The *retomada* has also witnessed the production of a number of films dealing with the subject of the *favela*. Due to constraints of space and their lack of commercial impact, these films will not be analysed in this chapter. For more information on them, see Lúcia Nagib, 'The New Cinema meets *Cinema Novo*: new trends in Brazilian cinema', *Framework*, 42 (Summer 2000), www.frameworkonline.com/42ln.htm.

10 Jean Franco, 'What's in a name? Popular culture theories and their limitations', *Studies in Latin American Popular Culture*, 1 (1982), p. 8.

11 Ivana Bentes, 'The *sertão* and the *favela* in contemporary Brazilian film', in João Luiz Vieira (ed.), *Cinema Novo and Beyond* (New York: Museum of Modern Art, 1998), p. 114.

12 *Ibid.*

13 Mariza Leão, 'Condenados em nome do Glauber?', *Jornal do Brasil*, 10 July 2001

14 Johnson, 'From the ashes?'.

15 The lead actor of *Pixote*, Fernando Ramos da Silva, later returned to a life of crime, and he and his brother were shot dead by the police in São Paulo. He is the subject of José Joffily's 1996 film *Quem matou Pixote?* (*Who Killed Pixote?*) For a comparison of *Pixote: a lei do mais fraco* and *Central do Brasil*, see Shaw, 'National identity and the family'.

16 Consider, for example, the notorious Cidade de Deus housing scheme, depicted in the 2002 film of the same name.

17 It is difficult not to notice the Christian symbolism in names used in the film, for example the name of the town in Pernambuco where Josué finds his family (Bom Jesus do Norte – literally Good Jesus of the North), and the biblical names of Josué (Joseph) and the members of his (carpenter) family.

18 According to director Walter Salles, more than seven million people worldwide went to see *Central do Brasil* at the cinema: quoted in 'Walter Salles sem cortes' www.criticos.com.br (accessed May 2002).

19 Walter Carvalho made a point of shooting the countryside and city differently in the film, emphasising the vibran beauty of the former in contrast with the gloomy grime of the latter. Filming was carried out, among other places, in the *cinema novo* favourites of Milagres and Vitória da Conquista: 'a movie lover's "tourism" in the same Glauberian *sertão*': Nagib, 'The new cinema meets *cinema novo*'.

20 Shaw, 'National identity and the family'. This sequence is in contrast to the 'talking heads' that appear at the beginning of the film: Dora's customers are seeking to make contact with the backlands through their letters and are thus shot in a sympathetic, individualised way.

21 *Socorro Nobre* (*Life Somewhere Else*, 1995) deals with the correspondence which took place between the female prisoner of the title and Polish artist Frans Krajcberg, who had given up life in Europe and moved to the backlands of Bahia.

22 Quoted in James, 1999, p. 14, in Shaw, 'National identity and the family'.

23 The soundtrack famously topped the charts before the film was released and included re-workings of North Eastern standards by Luis Gonzaga, such as 'Asa branca' (White Wing), performed by Gilberto Gil.

24 The only church to appear in the film is significantly half-built.

25 Lúcia Nagib, 'The New Cinema meets *Cinema Novo*'.

26 The anonymous father of Darlene's first child is a *coronel*, a social type very much associated with the semi-feudal traditions of the Brazilian North East. Taking his name from titles in local militia, a *coronel* is ultimately a landed gent to whom the local peasantry owe political, as well as social allegiance. It is common practice in many poorer communities in Brazil for mothers to hand over illegitimate children fathered by such men, in order to offer their offspring greater opportunities.

27 Marcelo Janot, 'Do sertão para o mundo', *Revista Programa do Jornal do Brasil*, 18 August 2000. Regina Casé is a household name in Brazil through her humorous and irreverent popular Globo documentary series such as *Brasil Legal* (Cool Brazil) and *Movuca* (Mess), in which she reveals amusing and poignant sides to life in Brazil, always showing the greatest respect in her interactions with the public.

28 See Shaw, 'National identity and the family'.

29 Vasconcelos played Lampião in *Perfumed Ball*, a *favela* inhabitant in Walter Salles's *O primeiro dia* (*Midnight*, 1999) and starred in Salles's backlands-set *Abril despedaçado* (*Behind the Sun*, 2000).

30 'Walter Salles sem cortes'. Carlos Diegues made a similar observation in relation to filming *Bye bye Brasil* (*Bye Bye Brazil*, 1979): Robert Stam, João Luiz Vieira and Ismail Xavier, 'The shape of Brazilian cinema in the postmodern age', in Randal Johnson and Robert Stam (eds), *Brazilian Cinema* (New York: Columbia University Press, 1995), p. 423.

31 Although an art-house film and not a box-office success, *Tudo é Brasil* is worthy of mention in the context of this trend towards recouping elements of Brazilian popular culture from the heyday of the 1930s and 1940s. Drawing on clips of archive footage, re-photographed images, excerpts from other films, snapshots and graphic designs of the era, Sganzerla's film, the product of a four-year labour of love editing together news clips, takes up where Orson Welles's ill-fated and unfinished documentary about Brazil, *It's All True* left off, and centres on the

sentimental and clichéd radio broadcasts made by the 'cultural ambassador' to Latin America from Rio's Urca casino back to the USA in 1942. Part of a trilogy inspired by Welles's sojourn in Brazil, which also includes *Nem tudo é verdade* (*It's Not Quite All True*, 1986) and *A linguagem de Orson Welles* (*Welles's Language*, 1990), Sganzerla's work is a very personal and poetic art film rather than a classically informative documentary, and relies on a complex circular structure. The film explores the manipulation of cultural stereotypes, and offers contemporary audiences a reassuring reminder of an era when issues of identity were openly articulated, and images of *brasilidade*, however ideologically inflected, manufactured and often derisory, were easily recognisable and readily devoured. By featuring the testimonies of home-grown stars of the Brazilian screen, such as Grande Otelo and Carmen Miranda, *Tudo é Brasil* fondly evokes a bygone age, when popular culture could more than hold its own in the face of foreign incursions. In the same spirit, Júlio Bressane's *O mandarim* (The Mandarin, 1995) recounts the life story of the 'Golden Age' samba crooner, Mário Reis within the context of Rio's burgeoning popular music scene of the 1920s and 1930s. Largely shot in the luxurious Copacabana Palace Hotel, where Reis lived for many years, and which rose to iconic status in the Atlântida *chanchadas* of the late 1940s and 1950s, *O mandarim* stars the leading lights of contemporary Brazilian popular music, such as Caetano Veloso, Gal Costa, Chico Buarque de Holanda, and Gilberto Gil, who plays the legendary mixed-race popular composer, Sinhô. The film's soundtrack nostalgically recreates classics by the likes of the samba composers Noel Rosa and Ismael Silva, and reconstructs performances by the iconic Carmen Miranda. More recently, Karim Ainouz's *Madame Satã* (2001), inspired by the life of João Francisco dos Santos (1900–76), legendary Afro-Brazilian *malandro* turned transvestite cabaret artist, is set in 1932 in Lapa, Rio's then red-light and earthy nightlife district. The film evokes the spirit and decadence of the early 1930s, when the music industry was beginning to take shape and boost creativity, not least through its emblematic soundtrack, that features hit sambas from that era written by Noel Rosa and Ismael Silva.

32 Interview with Luiz Carlos Lacerda by Lisa Shaw, 14 December 2002 (our translation). Lacerda's father, João Tinoco de Freitas produced the *chanchada Balança, mas não cai!* (Sways but Doesn't Fall Over!, 1953).

33 *Ibid.*

34 In the *chanchada*, *O homem do sputnik* (Sputnik Man, 1959), a simple Portuguese character is similarly seen riding his donkey in the opening and closing scenes, and he acknowledges the ethnic stereotype: 'E depois nós é quem somos os burros' (And then they go and call us asses).

35 The exception is Fernando, Carlota's handsome black lover, whose body and sexuality are foregrounded in the film, in keeping with the *chanchada*'s stereotypical depiction of the lascivious mulatto woman.

36 David William Foster, *Gender and Society in Contemporary Brazilian Cinema* (Austin: University of Texas Press, 1999), pp. 105–6.

37 *Ibid.*, p. 109.

38 Joan M. West and Dennis West, 'Carmen Miranda: Bananas is My Business', *Cineaste*, 22:1, 1996, pp. 41–3.

39 Diegues has subsequently been involved in talks with TV Cultura and GNT, Globo's cable and satellite network, with a view to basing a television series of approximately fifteen episodes on this film. Carlos (Cacá) Diegues, interview in Lúcia Nagib (ed.), *O cinema da retomada: depoimentos de 90 cineastas dos anos 90* (São Paulo: Editora 34, 2002), p. 181.
40 Diegues, *O cinema da retomada*, p. 180 (our translation).
41 See Chapter 4.
42 See, for example, *Quem roubou meu samba?* (Who Stole My Samba?), *Treze cadeiras* (Thirteen Chairs) and *Samba em Brasília* (Samba in Brasília), all discussed in Chapter 4.
43 Diegues, *O cinema da retomada*, p. 177 (our translation).
   Indeed, Diegues attacked what he saw as the *chanchada*'s stereotypical depiction of Brazil as a land of tropical excess in his *cinema novo* film, *Os herdeiros* (The Heirs, 1969), part of the so-called Tropicalist phase of the movement, described by Johnson and Stam as follows: 'a movement that . . . emphasized the grotesque, bad taste, *kitsch*, and gaudy colors. It played aggressively with certain myths, especially the notion of Brazil as a tropical paradise characterized by colorful exuberance and tutti-frutti hats à la Carmen Miranda.' Randal Johnson and Robert Stam, 'The Shape of Brazilian Film History', in Johnson and Stam (eds), *Brazilian Cinema*, pp. 38–9.
44 Diegues, *O cinema da retomada*, p. 179 (our translation).
45 Quoted in Lúcia Nagib, 'Black Orpheus in color', *Framework: The Journal of Cinema and Media*, 44:1, Spring 2003, p. 94.
46 Stam, *Tropical Multiculturalism*, p. 177.
47 *Orfeu* aimed at box-office success by adhering to what is often described as the '*padrão global de qualidade*', the glossy production values associated with Globo Television, one of the world's biggest exporters of soap operas. The movie was co-produced by Globo Filmes, the film production wing of the Globo media empire. The acting style is straight from the Globo soap opera textbook, as are many of the actors in the film, such as Patrícia França who plays Eurydice.
48 The hit single from the film, 'Sou você' (I am You), was composed by Caetano Veloso and performed by Tony Garrido.
49 Nagib, 'Black Orpheus in color', p. 101.
50 *Ibid.*, p. 100.
51 Television performers who have enjoyed box-office success in the 1990s include Renato Aragão of the Trapalhões (see Chapter 6), and Xuxa Meneghel, children's entertainer and media phenomenon: *Lua de cristal* (Crystal Moon, 1990); *Xuxa Popstar* (2000); *Xuxa e os duendes* (Xuxa and the Elves, 2001) and *Xuxa e os duendes II: o caminho das fadas* (Xuxa and the Elves II: the Road to the Fairies, 2002). Popular chat show host (and erstwhile *chanchada* actor) Jô Soares scored a hit with the adaptation of his comedy novel *O xangô de Baker Street*. Singers and musicians who have crossed over into film acting include Tony Garrido of the band Cidade Negra (*Orfeu*) and Paulo Miklos of the band Titãs, and rapper Sabotage in *O invasor* (The Trespasser, 2001). As well as *Eu, tu, eles*, another recent film to tap into the popularity of North Eastern music is *Baile perfumado*, whose soundtrack was performed by Chico Science e Nação Zumbi and Fred Zero Quatro,

exponents of 'mangue (swamp) beat' – an exciting mixture of traditional North
Eastern sounds with heavy rock and techno music. Co-productions made with
television companies include *Veja esta canção* with TV Cultura. All of the top
ten most successful films of the *retomada*, and many from the top fifty, had the
participation of Globo Filmes: *Filme B*, Edição Especial (November 2002), cited
in Randal Johnson, 'TV Globo, the MPA and contemporary Brazilian cinema', in
Lisa Shaw and Stephanie Dennison (eds), *Latin American Cinema: Modernity,
Gender and National Identity* (Jefferson: McFarland, forthcoming in 2004).
52 Carvalho also directed the intelligent 2001 documentary *Janela da alma* (Window
of the Soul).
53 Among a group of significant scriptwriters is Fernando Bonassi, who as well as
writing the novel upon which Tata Amaral based her critically acclaimed 1996
film *Um céu de estrelas* (*A Starry Sky*), was the scriptwriter on Beto Brant's *Os
matadores* (*Belly Up*) of 1997 and Hector Babenco's *Carandiru* (2003), the most
successful film of the *retomada* within the domestic market.
54 Email interview with Luiz Carlos Lacerda by Lisa Shaw, 14 December 2002.

Conclusion

In this study we have established the multiple roots of commercially successful cinema in Brazilian popular culture, such as the *teatro de revista*, the circus and carnival. We have identified a number of key elements that link popular Brazilian cinema through the decades since the advent of sound. Popular film in Brazil has historically been characterised by a city-countryside dialectic, to give just one example. The physiognomy of the city and the dualities of everyday existence, particularly the opposition between the rural world and urban modernity, were key elements of the *chanchada*, in particular. The *chanchada*, from its inception in the 1930s, harked back to a pre-industrial era, rejecting modernity and urbanisation in favour of the nostalgic assertion of traditional values of friendship, camaraderie, neighbourliness and a community lifestyle typical of rural regions or the poor suburbs of the big cities of the South. This tradition continued in the films of Amácio Mazzaropi in particular in the 1960s and 1970s. In popular film the precarious and fragmented nature of everyday life for the poor is mirrored in the constant interplay between fantasy and reality, carnival interludes and the daily grind.

The unlikely heroes of popular film have traditionally taken their inspiration from the pervasive ethos of *malandragem*. The male leads epitomised by the characters played by Oscarito and the stars of many a popular comedy from the 1970s, for example, refused to assume a fixed position within the social hierarchy, preferring a precarious existence of living by their wits. Like the *teatro de revista*, the *chanchada* focused on the question of what it meant to be an inhabitant of Brazil's urban spaces. The physical appearance and facial expressions of stars like Oscarito, Zé Trindade, Grande Otelo and the Trapalhões permitted them to each become the synecdoche of large swathes of an ethnically diverse population. They all came to embody national identity, and even more affluent Brazilians could enjoy the victories of these underdog characters, whose physical appearance implicitly mocked the extremes of masculine posturing.

In his article on the *teatro de revista*, Antônio Herculano Lopes argues that the vision of the 'national', as articulated by this cultural medium, was essentially restricted to Rio de Janeiro, federal capital and emblem of civilisation in the tropics.[1] Artur Azevedo's theatrical works, in particular, featured the city as their main protagonist, and by extension the *carioca* came to represent an archetypal Brazilian. The description that Herculano Lopes gives of this caricature could equally be applied to the protagonists of countless *chanchadas*: '*malandro*, sensual, musical, armed with humour and *jeitinho*, preaching a lifestyle of idleness and resisting any form of established order as a survival strategy'.[2] It is true to say that Rio de Janeiro takes centre stage in the *chanchadas* produced there, and that just as São Paulo could not compete with its rival city in terms of music hall, nor could it in relation to popular film, despite the later importance of São Paulo's Boca do Lixo in terms of production, since the city of Rio came to synthesise urban identity for the masses. In both popular theatre and film the stock types of the urban landscape consolidated the self-image of the *carioca* by making fun of the 'other', whether Portuguese, French or a hillbilly, and bolstered their sense of self by venerating the figures of the *malandro*, the *mulata*, and the *zé-povinho* or everyman figure.

The search for national identity is central to any national cinema, and both real-life locations and the contradictions of life become key reference points. The *chanchada* is often referred to as the only truly Brazilian genre, and there is little doubt about the inescapable 'Brazilianness' of this popular tradition. Humour is central to this sense of 'Brazilianness'. As Jerry Palmer writes:

> To share something like a joke or a metaphor, something whose presence in a culture is by no means predetermined, and which is not shared by others, no doubt creates an even greater degree of intimacy, especially if those who do not share it are the butt of it as well as not understanding what is going on . . . Thus what we see occur at the border established by the divide between comprehension and its opposite is a process of inclusion and exclusion with respect to some section or dimension of the social order.[3]

In Brazilian cinema since the *retomada*, as we have seen, the search for a definition of the nation through cinema continues. It is interesting to note that, as Brazil enters what appears to be a new, post-*retomada* phase of filmmaking in the new millennium, the two most successful films at the box-office, *Cidade de Deus* (*City of God*, 2002) and *Carandiru* (2003), share little of the good-humoured, light-hearted spirit that nearly all of Brazil's earlier top-grossing films share. What they do share with many of the films discussed in this study, however, is a determination to debunk the officially espoused myth of Brazil as an orderly, mature, 'First-World' nation. Instead these two films describe a country that the millions of Brazilians who went to see them experience: one of chaos, one of battling against fate in a kind of parallel world filled with fast-talking, street-wise citizens, and a determination to keep on the move, no matter how tough the going gets.

Notes

1 Antônio Herculano Lopes, 'O teatro de revista e a identidade carioca', in Antônio Herculano Lopes (ed.), *Entre Europa e África: a invenção do carioca* (Rio de Janeiro: Topbooks/Edições Casa de Rui Barbosa, 2000), p. 22.
2 *Ibid.* (our translation).
3 Jerry Palmer, *Taking Humour Seriously* (London and New York: Routledge: 1994), p. 153.

Filmography

This filmography provides a list of all films cited in this book, together with a translation of their title. Production details are given only when these are referred to in the main text because of their particular relevance. Where Brazilian films have been exhibited abroad under a translated title, the latter is given in italics. Definite and indefinite articles (*um, uma, o, a, os* or *as* in Portuguese) have been ignored in the alphabetical ordering of films.

16-0-60 (*Sixteen-oh-sixty*), 1995, Vinícius Mainardi.
24 horas de sexo ardente (24 Hours of Explicit Sex), 1985, José Mojica Marins.
48 horas de sexo alucinante (48 Hours of Hallucinatory Sex), 1987, José Mojica Marins.
À meia-noite levarei sua alma (*At Midnight I'll Take Your Soul*), 1964, José Mojica Marins.
Abacaxi azul (Blue Pineapple), 1944, Wallace Downey, Sonofilmes.
Abril despedaçado (*Behind the Sun*), 2000, Walter Salles.
Absolutamente certo! (Absolutely Right!), 1957, Anselmo Duarte, Cinedistri.
Acabaram-se os otários (No More Suckers), 1929, Luiz de Barros.
O adorável trapalhão (The Adorable Trapalhão), 1966, J. B. Tanko.
Agulha no palheiro (Needle in the Haystack), 1953, Alex Viany, Flama.
Ahí está el detalle (That's the Point), 1940, Juan Bustillo Ovo.
Ai no corrida (*In the Realm of the Senses*), 1976, Nagisa Oshima.
Aladim e a lâmpada maravilhosa (Aladdin and the Magic Lamp), 1973, J. B. Tanko, J. B. Tanko Filmes.
Álbum de Família (Family Album), 1981, Bráz Chediak.
Ali Babá e os 40 ladrões (Ali Baba and the 40 Thieves), 1972, Victor Lima.
Alô, alô, Brasil! (Hello, Hello, Brazil!), 1935, Wallace Downey, João de Barro and Alberto Ribeiro, Waldow Filmes.
Alô. Alô. Carnaval! (Hello, Hello, Carnival!), 1936, Adhemar Gonzaga, Cinédia-Waldow.
Amei um bicheiro (I Loved a Crook), 1952, Jorge Ileli and Paulo Wanderley, Atlântida.
Amélia, 2000, Ana Carolina.
O amuleto de Ogum (*The Amulet of Ogum*), 1974, Nelson Pereira dos Santos.
Argila (Clay), 1940, Humberto Mauro, Brasil Vita Filme.

Aruanã, 1938, Líbero Luxardo, Cinédia.

Asfalto Selvagem (Wild Asphalt), 1964, J. B. Tanko.

Atrapalhando a Suate (Getting in the Way of the Swat Team), 1983, Dedé Santana and Victor Lustosa.

Augusto Anibal quer casar! (Augusto Anibal Wants a Wife!), 1923, Luiz de Barros.

As aventuras de Sérgio Mallandro (The Adventures of Sérgio Mallandro), 1985, Erasto Filho.

Aviso aos navegantes (Calling All Sailors), 1950, Watson Macedo, Atlântida.

O babão (The Idiot), 1931, Luiz de Barros.

Bacalhau (Codfish), 1976, Adriano Stuart.

Baile perfumado (*Perfumed Ball*), 1997, Paulo Caldas and Lirio Ferreira.

Balança, mas não cai! (Sways but Doesn't Fall Over!), 1953, Paulo Wanderley.

Banana da terra (Banana of the Land), 1939, Rui Costa, Sonofilmes.

A banana mecânica (A Clockwork Banana), 1974, Bráz Chediak.

A banda das velhas virgins (The Gang of Old Virgins), 1979, Amácio Mazzaropi and Pio Zamuner, PAM Filmes

Barnabé, tu és meu (Civil Servant, You're Mine), 1951, José Carlos Burle, Atlântida.

Barro Humano (Human Mud), 1928, Adhemar Gonzaga, Cinearte and Benedetti Filmes.

O beijo da mulher aranha (*Kiss of the Spiderwoman*), 1985, Hector Babenco.

O beijo no asfalto (*The Kiss*), 1980, Bruno Barreto.

Bela Donna (*White Dunes*), 1998, Fábio Barreto.

Belle de Jour, 1967, Luis Buñuel.

Bem-dotado: O homem de Itu (Well-endowed: The Man from Itu), 1977, José Miziara.

Berlim na Batucada (Berlin to the Samba Beat), 1944, Luiz de Barros, Cinédia.

Betão Ronca Ferro (Big Beto Snorts Iron), 1970, Pio Zamuner, PAM Filmes

Blood and Sand, 1922, Fred Niblo and Dorothy Arzner.

Boca de Ouro (Gold Mouth), 1962, Nelson Pereira dos Santos.

Bonequinha de seda (Little Silk Doll), 1936, Oduvaldo Vianna, Cinédia.

Bonitinha mas ordinária (Pretty But Wicked), 1964, J. P. de Carvalho.

Bonitinha mas ordinária (Pretty But Wicked), 1981, Bráz Chediak.

Bossa Nova, 2000, Bruno Barreto.

Broadway Melody, 1929, Harry Beaumont, MGM.

A b . . . profunda (Deep P . . .), 1984, Gerard Dominó.

Bye bye Brasil (*Bye Bye Brazil*), 1979, Carlos Diegues.

O caçula do barulho (The Topsy-Turvy Kid), 1949, Riccardo Freda, Atlântida.

Cada um dá o que tem (Each One Gives Whatever They Can), 1975, John Herbert, Adriano Stuart, Sílvio de Abreu.

Os cafajestes (*The Unscrupulous Ones*), 1962, Ruy Guerra.

Caídos do céu (Fallen from the Sky), 1946, Luiz de Barros, Cinédia,

Um caipira em Bariloche (A Caipira in Bariloche), 1973, Amácio Mazzaropi and Pio Zamuner, PAM Filmes.

Calamity Jane, 1953, David Butler, Warner Bros.

Caligula, 1979, Tinto Brass and Bob Guccione.

O camelô da rua Larga (The Street Vendor of Larga Street), 1958, Renato Restier, Cinedistri.

Um candango na Belacap (A Migrant Worker in Rio), 1961, Roberto Farias, Herbert Richers.

O cangaceiro (*The Bandit*), 1953, Lima Barreto.

O cangaceiro (*The Bandit*), 1997, Aníbal Massaini Neto.

O cangaceiro trapalhão (*The Bandit Trapalhão*), Daniel Filho, 1983, Renato Aragão Produções.

Carandiru, 2003, Hector Babenco.

Carioca maravilhosa (Marvellous Girl from Rio), 1935, Luiz de Barros, Cinédia and Régia Film.

Carlota Joaquina, princesa do Brazil (Carlota Joaquina, Princess of Brazil), 1995, Carla Camurati.

Carmen Miranda: Bananas Is My Business, 1995, Helena Solberg.

Carnaval Atlântida (Atlântida Carnival), 1952, José Carlos Burle, Atlântida.

O carnaval cantado de 1933 no Rio de Janeiro (The 1933 Rio de Janeiro Carnival in Song), 1933, Léo Marten and Fausto Muniz.

Carnaval em lá maior (Carnival in A-Major), 1955, Adhemar Gonzaga, Maristela-Emissoras Unidas.

Carnaval no fogo (Carnival on Fire), 1949, Watson Macedo, Atlântida.

O casamento (*The Marriage*), 1975, Arnaldo Jabor.

O casamento dos trapalhões (The Marriage of the Trapalhões), 1988, José Alvarenga Jr, Renato Aragão Produções.

Central do Brasil (*Central Station*), 1998, Walter Salles.

Um céu de estrelas (*A Starry Sky*), 1996, Tata Amaral.

Cidade de Deus (*City of God*), 2002, Fernando Meirelles and Kátia Lund.

Cidade-mulher (City-Woman), 1936, Humberto Mauro, Brasil Vita Filme.

O cinderelo trapalhão (The Cinderella Trapalhão), 1979, Adriano Stuart, Renato Aragão Produções.

A Clockwork Orange, 1971, Stanley Kubrick.

Coisas eróticas (Erotic Things), 1982, Rafaelle Rossi.

Coisas nossas (Our Things), 1931, Wallace Downey, Byington & Cia.

Colégio de brotos (College of Chicks), 1956, Carlos Manga, Atlântida.

Com as calças na mão (With His Pants in His Hands), 1975, Carlo Mossy.

Como é boa nossa empregada (How Good Our Maid Is), 1973, Ismar Porto, Víctor di Mello.

Como nascem os anjos (How Angels Are Born), 1996, Murilo Salles.

Copacabana, 1947, Alfred E. Green, United Artists.

Coração materno (Maternal Heart), 1951, Gilda de Abreu.

Corações sem piloto (Hearts without a Driver), 1944, Luiz de Barros, Cinédia.

O corintiano (The Corinthians Supporter), 1966, Milton Amaral, PAM Filmes.

Corisco e Dadá (Corisco and Dadá), 1966, Rosemberg Cariry.

O cortiço (The Tenement), 1945, Luiz de Barros, Cinédia.

Costinha e o King Mong (Costinha and King Mong), 1977, Alcino Diniz.

O cupido trapalhão (Cupid Trapalhão), 2003, Paulo Aragão, Renato Aragão Produções.

A dama do lotação (*Lady on the Bus*), 1978, Neville D'Almeida.

Deep Throat, 1972, Gerard Damiano.

Delírios de um anormal (*Hallucinations of a Deranged Mind*), 1978, José Mojica Marins.

O descobrimento do Brasil (The Discovery of Brazil), 1937, Humberto Mauro, Cinédia.

Deus e o diabo na terra do sol (*Black God, White Devil*), 1964, Glauber Rocha.

De vento em popa (Wind in the Sails), 1957, Carlos Manga, Atlântida.

Dona Flor e seus dois maridos (*Dona Flor and Her Two Husbands*), 1976, Bruno Barreto.

A dupla do barulho (The Terrible Twosome), 1953, Carlos Manga, Atlântida.

O ébrio (The Drunkard), 1946, Gilda de Abreu, Cinédia.

É com este que eu vou (I'll Go with This One), 1948, José Carlos Burle, Atlântida.

Encruzilhada da perdição (Crossroads to Perdition), 1952, José Mojica Marins.

E o circo chegou (And the Circus Arrived), 1940, Luiz de Barros, Marli Filme.

Engraçadinha (Engraçadinha), 1981, Haroldo Marinho Barbosa.

Engraçadinha Depois dos Trinta (Engraçadinha in Her Thirties), 1966, J. B. Tanko.

E o mundo se diverte (And the World Has Fun), 1948, Watson Macedo, Atlântida.

É proibido sonhar (Dreaming is Forbidden), 1943, Moacir Fenelon, Atlântida.

Essa gostosa brincadeira a dois (This Tasty Game For Two), 1974, Víctor de Mello.

Esse milhão é meu (That Million is Mine), 1958, Carlos Manga, Atlântida.

Está com tudo (You've Got It All), 1953, Luiz de Barros.

Esta é fina! (She's a Good One!), 1948, Luiz de Barros.

Esta noite encarnarei no teu cadaver (This Night I Will Possess Your Corpse), 1967, José Mojica Marins.

Este mundo é um pandeiro (This World Is a Tambourine), 1946, Watson Macedo, Atlântida.

A estrada da Vida (*Highway of Life*), 1980, Nelson Pereira dos Santos.

O estranho mundo de Zé do Caixão (*The Strange World of Coffin Joe*), 1968, José Mojica Marins.

Estudantes (Students), 1935, Wallace Downey, Waldow-Cinédia.

Eu dou o que ela gosta (I Give Her What She Likes), 1975, Bráz Chediak.

Eu quero é movimento (What I Want Is Action), 1949, Luiz de Barros.

Eu te amo (*I Love You*), 1978, Arnaldo Jabor.

Eu, tu, eles (*Me, You, Them*), 2000, Andrucha Waddington.

O exorcismo negro (*Black Exorcism of Coffin Joe*), 1974, José Mojica Marins.

The Exorcist, 1973, William Friedkin.

O exorcista de mulheres (The Exorcist of Women), 1974, Tony Vieira.

A falecida (The Deceased Woman), 1966, Leon Hirzsman.

Os fantasmas trapalhões (The Ghostly Trapalhões), 1987, J. B. Tanko, Renato Aragão Produções.

Favela dos meus amores (Shantytown of My Loves), 1934, Humberto Mauro, Brasil Vita Filme.

The Fearless Vampire Killers (or Pardon Me, But Your Teeth Are in My Neck), 1967, Roman Polanski.

Flying Down to Rio, 1933, Thornton Freeland, RKO.

Fogo na canjica (Fire in the Soup), 1947, Luiz de Barros.

Fome de sexo (Hunger for Sex), 1981, Ody Fraga.

Footlight Parade, 1933, Lloyd Bacon.

For all: o trampolim da vitória (*For All: The Springboard to Victory*), 1998, Luiz Carlos Lacerda and Buza Ferraz.

Os fuzis (*The Guns*), 1963, Ruy Guerra.

Gaijin II, 2004, Tizuka Yamasaki.

Ganga bruta (Brutal Gang), 1933, Humberto Mauro, Cinédia.

Ganga Zumba (Ganga Zumba), 1963, Carlos Diegues.

The Gang's All Here, 1943, Busby Berkeley, Twentieth Century-Fox.

Garota de Ipanema (Girl from Ipanema), 1967, Leon Hirzsman.

Garotas e samba (Girls and Samba), 1957, Carlos Manga, Atlântida.

Goldiggers of 1933, 1933, Mervyn LeRoy.

Gone with the Wind, 1939, Victor Fleming and George Cukor.

A grande vedete (The Great Star), 1958, Watson Macedo, Cinedistri.

O grande xerife (The Great Sheriff), 1971, Pio Zamuner, PAM Filmes.

Grease, 1978, Randal Kleiser.

Guerra de Canudos (*Battle of Canudos*), 1997, Sérgio Rezende.

Hans Staden (Hans Staden), 1999, Luís Alberto Pereira.

Os herdeiros (The Heirs), 1970, Carlos Diegues.

Os heróis trapalhões (The Hero Trapalhões), 1988, José Alvarenga Jr, Renato Aragão Produções.

High Noon, 1952, Fred Zinnemann.

Histórias que nossas babás não contavam (Stories Our Nannies Never Told Us), 1979, Oswaldo de Oliveira.

O homem do sputnik (Sputnik Man), 1959, Carlos Manga, Atlântida.

How to Marry a Millionaire, 1953, Jean Negulesco, Twentieth Century-Fox.

A ilha dos paqueras (The Island of Flirting), 1968, Fauzi Mansur.

Independência ou morte (*Independence or Death*), 1972, Carlos Coimbra.

Inconfidência mineira (Conspiracy in Minas Gerais), 1948, Carmen Santos, Brasil Vita Filme.

O incrível monstro trapalhão (The Incredible Monster Trapalhão), 1980, Adriano Stuart, Renato Aragão Produções.

O invasor (*The Trespasser*), 2001, Beto Brant.

It's All True (unfinished version), 1942, Orson Welles.

Janela da alma (Window of the Soul), 2001, Walter Carvalho.

Jaws, 1976, Steven Spielberg.

The Jazz Singer, 1927, Alan Crosland.

Jeca contra o capeta (Jeca Versus the Devil), 1976, Amácio Mazzaropi and Pio Zamuner, PAM Filmes.

Jeca e a égua milagrosa (Jeca and the Miraculous Mare), 1980, Amácio Mazzaropi and Pio Zamuner, PAM Filmes.

Jeca e seu filho preto (Jeca and His Black Son), 1978, Pio Zamuner, PAM Filmes.

O Jeca macumbeiro (Jeca the Voodoo Practitioner), 1974, Amácio Mazzaropi and Pio Zamuner, PAM Filmes.

Jecão ... um fofoqueiro no céu (Big Jeca ... A Gossip in Heaven), 1977, Amácio Mazzaropi and Pio Zamuner, PAM Filmes.

Jenipapo (*The Interview*), 1995, Monique Gardenberg.

João Ninguém (Johnny Nobody), 1937, Mesquitinha, Sonofilmes.

Joujoux e balangandans (Knick-knacks and Trinkets), 1939, Amadeu Castelaneta, Hammann Filme.

O juízo final (Judgement Day), 1949, José Mojica Marins.

King Kong, 1933, Merian C. Cooper and Ernest B. Schoedsack.

King Kong, 1976, John Guillermin.

Kuarup (Kuarup), 1989, Ruy Guerra.

Kung Fu contra as bonecas (Kung Fu Against the Dolls), 1975, Adriano Staurt.

O lamparina (The Oil Lamp or Little Lampião), 1964, Glauco Mirko Laurelli, PAM Filmes.

Laranja da China (Orange from China), 1940, Rui Costa, Sonofilmes.

Lavoura arcaica (*To the Left of the Father*), 2001, Karim Ainouz.

A linguagem de Orson Welles (*Welles's Language*), 1990, Rogério Sganzerla.

Lovely to Look At, 1952, Mervyn LeRoy and Vincente Minnelli.

Lua de cristal (Crystal Moon), 1990, Tizuka Yamazaki.

Lúcio Flávio, passageiro da agonia (*Lucio Flavio*), 1977, Hector Babenco.

Macunaíma (Macunaíma), 1969, Joaquim Pedro de Andrade.

Madame Satã (Madame Satã), 2002, Karim Ainouz.

Mágoa de boiadeiro (A Cowhand's Suffering), 1977, Moreira Filho.

O malandro e a granfina (The Spiv and the Lady), 1947, Luiz de Barros, Brasil Vita Filme.

Malandros em quarta dimensão (Malandros in the Fourth Dimension), 1954, Luiz de Barros, Atlântida.

O mandarim (The Mandarin), 1995, Júlio Bressane.

Maridinho de luxo (Upmarket Hubbie), 1938, Luiz de Barros, Cinédia.

As massagistas profissionais (The Professional Masseuses), 1976, Carlo Mossy.

Os matadores (*Belly Up*), 1997, Beto Brant.

Matar ou correr (Kill or Run), 1954, Carlos Manga, Atlântida.

O menino da porteira (The Porter's Lad), 1976, Moreira Filho.

Mestiça, a escrava indomável (The Indomitable Mixed-Race Slave), 1973, Lenita Perroy.

Metido a bacana (A Cut Above the Rest), 1957, J. B. Tanko, Herbert Richers-Cinedistri.

Meu destino é pecar (Bound for Sin), 1952, Manuel Pelufo, Maristela.

Meu Japão brasileiro (My Brazilian Japan), 1964, Glauco Mirko Laurelli, PAM Filmes.

Minervina vem aí (Here Comes Minervina), 1959, Eurides Ramos, Cinedistri.

Modern Times, 1936, Charles Chaplin.

Moleque Tião (Street Kid Tião), 1943, José Carlos Burle, Atlântida.

A Moreninha (Little Dark Girl), 1970, Glauco Mirko Laurelli.

Mud and Sand, 1922, Gilbert Pratt.

Uma mulata para todos (A Mulata For Everyone), 1975, Roberto Machado.

As mulheres que fazem diferente (Women Who Do It Differently), 1974, director unknown.

Na onda do iê-iê-iê (On the Wave of Rock 'n' Roll), 1965, Aurélio Teixeira.

Não adianta chorar (It's No Good Crying), 1945, Watson Macedo, Atlântida.

Nem Sansão, nem Dalila (Neither Samson, Nor Delilah), 1954, Carlos Manga, Atlântida.

Nem tudo é verdade (*It's Not Quite All True*), 1986, Rogério Sganzerla.

Nhô Anastácio chegou de viagem (Mr Anastácio Arrived From a Trip), 1908, Julio Ferrez.

A noite das taras (Night of Perversion), 1980, David Cardoso.

Nos tempos da vaselina (In The Days of Vaseline), 1979, José Miziara.

Oh! Que delícia de patrão! (Oh! What a Tasty Boss!), 1974, Alberto Pieralisi.

Ópera do malandro (*Malandro*), 1985, Ruy Guerra.

A opinião pública (*Public Opinion*), 1967, Arnaldo Jabor.

O que é isso, companheiro? (*Four Days in September*), 1997, Bruno Barreto.

Orfeu (Orpheus), 1999, Carlos Diegues.

Orfeu negro (*Black Orpheus*), 1959, Marcel Camus.

Oriundi (Oriundi), 2000, Ricardo Bravo.

O pagador de promessas (*The Given Word*), 1962, Anselmo Duarte.

The Pagan, 1929, W. S. Van Dyke.

Para frente, Brasil! (Forward, Brazil!), 1982, Roberto Farias.

Paz e amor (Peace and Love), 1910, Alberto Botelho and Alberto Moreira.

Pequeno dicionário amoroso (*Little Book of Love*), 1997, Sandra Werneck.

Os Paqueras (The Flirts), 1969, Reginaldo Faria.

Pesadelo sexual de um virgem (Sexual Nightmare of a Virgin), 1976, Roberto Mauro.

O petróleo é nosso (The Oil is Hours), 1954, Watson Macedo.

Pif-Paf (Card Game), 1945, Adhemar Gonzaga and Luiz de Barros, Cinédia.

Pindorama (Pindorama), 1970, Arnaldo Jabor.

Pinguinho de gente (Tiny Tot), 1949, Gilda de Abreu, Cinédia.

Pintando o sete (Painting the Town Red), 1959, Carlos Manga, Atlântida.

Uma pistola para Djeca (A Pistol For Djeca), 1970, Ary Fernandes, PAM Filmes.

Pistoleiro bossa nova (Bossa Nova Gunman), 1960, Victor Lima, Herbert Richers.

Pixote: a lei do mais fraco (*Pixote*), 1981, Hector Babenco.

Planet of the Apes, 1968, Franklin J. Schaffner.

Portugal minha saudade (Longing for Portugal), 1973, Amácio Mazzaropi and Pio Zamuner, PAM Filmes.

Prá lá de boa (Top Notch), 1949, Luiz de Barros.

O primeiro dia (*Midnight*), 1999, Walter Salles.

A princesa Xuxa e os trapalhões (Princess Xuxa and the Trapalhões), 1989, José Alvarenga Jr, Renato Aragão Produções.

Pureza (Purity), 1940, Chianca de Garcia, Cinédia.

O puritano da Rua Augusta (The Puritan from Augusta Street), 1965, Amácio Mazzaropi, PAM Filmes.

O quatrilho, 1995, Fábio Barreto.

A queda (*The Fall*), 1976, Ruy Guerra.

Quem matou Anabela? (Who Killed Anabela?), 1956, Dezsö Ákos Hamza, Maristela.

Quem matou Pixote? (*Who Killed Pixote?*), 1996, José Joffily.

Quem roubou meu samba? (Who Stole My Samba?), 1958, José Carlos Burle, Cinedistri.

Quilombo (Runaway Slave Camp), 1984, Carlos Diegues.

O rei do samba (King of Samba), 1952, Luiz de Barros, Brasil Vita Filme.

Rico ri à toa (The Rich Can Afford to Laugh), 1957, Roberto Farias, Brasil Vita Filme.

Rio, Zona Norte (Rio, North Zone), 1957, Nelson Pereira dos Santos.

Ritual dos sádicos (renamed *O despertar da besta*) (*The Awakening of the Beast*), 1969, José Mojica Marins.

Robin Hood, o trapalhão da floresta (Robin Hood, the Trapalhão of the Forest), 1973, J. B. Tanko, J. B. Tanko Filmes.

Romeo y Julieta (Romeo and Juliet), 1943, Miguel M. Delgado.

O roubo das calcinhas (The Theft of the Panties), 1975, Bráz Chediak.

Rube and Mandy at Coney Island, 1903, Edwin S. Porter.

Sai da frente (Get Out of the Way), 1952, Abílio Pereira de Almeida, Vera Cruz.

Sai de baixo (Look Out!), 1956, J. B. Tanko, Herbert Richers.

Salário mínimo (Minimum Wage), 1971, Adhemar Gonzaga, Cinédia.

Os saltimbancos trapalhões (The Acrobatic Trapalhões), 1981, J. B. Tanko, Renato Aragão Produções.

Saludos Amigos, 1943, Walt Disney, RKO-Disney.

O samba da vida (The Samba of Life), 1937, Luiz de Barros, Cinédia.

Samba em Berlim (Samba in Berlin), 1943, Luiz de Barros, Cinédia.

Samba em Brasília (Samba in Brasília), 1960, Watson Macedo, Cinedistri.

Samson and Delilah, 1949, Cecil B. de Mille, Paramount.

Saturday Night Fever, 1977, John Badham.

Secas e Molhadas (Dried Up and Moist), 1975, Mozael Silveira.

As secretárias . . . que fazem de tudo (Secretaries . . . Who Do It All), 1975, Alberto Pieralisi.

El señor fotógrafo (The Photographer), 1952, Miguel M. Delgado.

Sessomatto (*How Funny Can Sex Be?*), 1973, Dino Risi.

Simbad, o marujo trapalhão (Sinbad the Sailor Trapalhão), 1975, J. B. Tanko, J. B. Tanko Filmes.

Socorro Nobre (*Life Somewhere Else*), 1995, Walter Salles.

Some Like it Hot, 1959, Billy Wilder.

Sonho no caroço dum abacate (*Avocado Seed*), 1999, Lucas Amberg.

Um soutien para papai (A Bra For Daddy), 1975, Carlos Alberto de Souza Barros.

Star Wars, 1977, George Lucas.

Sunset Boulevard, 1950, Billy Wilder.

A superfêmea (Superwoman), 1973, Aníbal Massaini Neto.

Superxuxa contra o baixo astral (Superxuxa Against the Blues), 1989, Anna Penido and David Sonnenschein.

Tenda dos milagres (*Tent of Miracles*), 1977, Nelson Pereira dos Santos.

Tererê não resolve (Chatting Gets You Nowhere), 1938, Luiz de Barros, Cinédia.

Terra em transe (*Land in Anguish*), 1967, Glauber Rocha.

Terra estrangeira (*Foreign Land*), 1995, Walter Salles and Daniela Thomas.

That Night in Rio, 1941, Irving Cummings, Twentieth Century-Fox.

The Three Caballeros, 1945, Walt Disney, RKO-Disney.

Tico-Tico no fubá (Tico-Tico Bird in the Corn Meal), 1952, Adolfo Celi, Vera Cruz.

Titanic, 1997, James Cameron.

Toda nudez será castigada (*All Nudity Shall Be Punished*), 1973, Arnaldo Jabor.

O trapalhão na arca de Noé (The Trapalhão on Noah's Ark), 1983, Antônio Rangel, Renato Aragão Produções.

O trapalhão na ilha do tesouro (The Trapalhão on Treasure Island), 1974, J. B. Tanko, J. B. Tanko Filmes.

O trapalhão no planalto dos macacos (The Trapalhão on the Plateau of the Apes), 1976, J. B. Tanko, J. B. Tanko Filmes.

Os trapalhões e o mágico de Oroz (The Trapalhões and the Wizard of Oroz), 1984, Dedé Santana and Victor Lustosa, Renato Aragão Produções.

Os trapalhões e o rei do futebol (The Trapalhões and the King of Football), 1986, Carlos Manga, Renato Aragão Produções.

Os trapalhões na guerra dos planetas (The Trapalhões In the Battle of the Planets), 1978, Adriano Stuart, Renato Aragão Produções.

Os trapalhões na Serra Pelada (The Trapalhões in Serra Pelada), 1982, J. B. Tanko, Renato Aragão Produções.

Os trapalhões nas minas do rei Salomão (The Trapalhões in King Solomon's Mines), 1977, J. B. Tanko, J. B. Tanko Filmes.

Os trapalhões no reino da fantasia (The Trapalhões in the Land of Make Believe), 1985, Dedé Santana, Renato Aragão Produções.

Treze cadeiras (Thirteen Chairs), 1957, Francisco Eichhorn, Atlântida.

Tristezas não pagam dívidas (Sadness Won't Pay Your Debts), 1944, José Carlos Burle and Rui Costa, Atlântida.

Tudo azul (All Blue), 1951, Moacir Fenelon, Flama.

Tudo é Brasil (*All is Brazil*), 1997, Rogério Sganzerla.

Os vagabundos trapalhões (The Homeless Trapalhões), 1982, J. B. Tanko, Renato Aragão Produções.

Vai, que é mole (Go On, It's Easy), 1960, J. B. Tanko, Herbert Richers.

Vai trabalhar, vagabundo (Go and Get a Job, You Lout), 1973, Hugo Carvana.

Veja esta canção (*Rio's Love Songs*), 1994, Carlos Diegues.

Viciado em c . . . (Addicted to A . . .), 1985, Roberto Fedegoso.

Vidas secas (*Barren Lives*), 1963, Nelson Pereira dos Santos.

A virgem e o machão (The Virgin and the Macho Man), 1974, J. Avelar.

A viúva virgem (The Virgin Widow), 1972, Pedro Carlos Rovai.

A voz do carnaval (The Voice of Carnival), 1933, Adhemar Gonzaga and Humberto Mauro, Cinédia.

O xangô de Baker Street (*Xango from Baker Street*), 1999, Miguel Faria Jr.

Xica da Silva (*Xica*), 1976, Carlos Diegues.

Xuxa e os duendes (*Xuxa and the Elves*), 2001, Rogério Gomes and Paulo Sérgio de Almeida.

Xuxa e os duendes II: o caminho das fadas (*Xuxa and the Elves II: the Road to the Fairies*), 2002, Tizuka Yamasaki.

Xuxa Popstar, 2000, Tizuka Yamasaki and Paulo Sérgio de Almeida.

Select bibliography

Abreu, Nuno César, 'Anotações sobre Mazzaropi, o Jeca que não era Tatu', *Filme Cultura*: 40 (August/October 1982).

Augusto, Sérgio, *Este mundo é um pandeiro: a chanchada de Getúlio a JK* (São Paulo: Companhia das Letras, 1993).

Avellar, José Carlos, 'Teoria da relatividade', *Anos 70: cinema* (Rio de Janeiro: Europa Empresa Gráfica Editora, 1979).

Barcinski, André and Ivan Finotti, *Maldito: a vida e o cinema de José Mojica Marins, o Zé do Caixão* (São Paulo: Editora 34, 1998).

Bentes, Ivana, 'The *sertão* and the *favela* in contemporary Brazilian film', in João Luiz Vieira (ed.), *Cinema Novo and Beyond* (New York: Museum of Modern Art, 1998).

Bueno, Eva, 'The adventures of Jeca Tatu: class, culture and nation in Mazzaropi's films', *Studies in Latin American Popular Culture*, 18 (1999).

Catani, Afrânio M. and José I. de Melo Souza, *A chanchada no cinema brasileiro* (São Paulo: Brasiliense, 1983).

Dias, Rosângela de Oliveira, *O mundo como chanchada: cinema e imaginário das classes populares na década de 50* (Rio de Janeiro: Relume-Dumará, 1993).

Foster, David William, *Gender and Society in Contemporary Brazilian Cinema* (Austin: University of Texas Press, 1999).

Gomes, Paulo Emílio Salles, *Cinema brasileiro: uma trajetória no subdesenvolvimento* (Rio de Janeiro: Paz e Terra, 1986).

Gonzaga, Alice, *50 anos de Cinédia* (Rio de Janeiro: Record, 1987).

Johnson, Randal, *The Film Industry in Brazil: Culture and the State* (Pittsburgh: University of Pittsburgh Press, 1987).

Johnson, Randal, 'Film, television and traditional folk culture in *Bye bye Brasil*', *Journal of Popular Culture*, 18:1 (1984).

Johnson, Randal, 'Nelson Rodrigues as filmed by Arnaldo Jabor', *Latin American Theatre Review* (Fall 1982).

Johnson, Randal, 'Popular Cinema in Brazil', *Studies in Latin American Popular Culture*, 3 (1984).

Johnson, Randal, and Robert Stam (eds), *Brazilian Cinema* (New York: Columbia University Press, 1995).

King, John, *Magical Reels: A History of Cinema in Latin America* (London and New York: Verso, 1990).

López, Ana M., 'Are all Latins from Manhattan? Hollywood, ethnography and cultural colonialism', in John King, Ana M. López and Manuel Alvarado (eds), *Mediating Two Worlds: Cinematic Encounters in the Americas* (London: BFI Publishing, 1993).

Lunardelli, Fatimarlei, *Ô psit! O cinema popular dos Trapalhões* (Porto Alegre: Artes e Ofícios, 1996).

Nagib, Lúcia, *O cinema da retomada: depoimentos de 90 cineastas dos anos 90* (São Paulo: Editora 34, 2002).

Nagib, Lúcia, 'Black Orpheus in color', *Framework: The Journal of Cinema and Media*, 44: 1 (Spring 2003).

Nagib, Lúcia, 'The New Cinema meets *Cinema Novo*: new trends in Brazilian cinema', *Framework: The Journal of Cinema and Media*, 42 (Summer 2000), www.frameworkonline.com/42ln.htm.

Ortiz, Renato, *Cultura brasileira e identidade nacional* (São Paulo: Brasiliense, 1999)

Piper, Rudolf, *Filmusical brasileiro e chanchada* (São Paulo: Global Editora, 1977).

Ramos, Fernão (ed.), *História do cinema brasileiro* (São Paulo: Arte Editora, 1987).

Ramos, Fernão and Luiz Felipe Miranda (eds), *Enciclopédia do cinema brasileiro* (São Paulo: SENAC, 2000).

Ramos, José Mário Ortiz, *Cinema, estado e lutas culturais: anos 50/60/70* (Rio de Janeiro: Paz e Terra, 1983).

Rowe, William and Vivian Schelling, *Memory and Modernity: Popular Culture in Latin America* (London and New York: Verso, 1991).

Schelling, Vivian (ed.), *Through the Kaleidoscope: The Experience of Modernity in Latin America* (London and New York: Verso, 2000).

Schnitman, Jorge A., *Film Industries in Latin America: Dependency and Development* (Norwood, NJ: Ablex, 1984).

Shaw, Deborah, 'National identity and the family: *Pixote* by Hector Babenco and *Central Station* by Walter Salles', in *Contemporary Latin American Cinema: Ten Key Films* (New York: London: Continuum, 2003).

Soares, Mariza de Carvalho and Jorge Ferreira (eds), *A história vai ao cinema: vinte filmes brasileiros comentados por historiadores* (Rio de Janeiro: Record, 2001).

Stam, Robert, *Tropical Multiculturalism: A Comparative History of Race in Brazilian Cinema and Culture* (Durham, NC and London: Duke University Press, 1997).

Stam, Robert and João Luiz Vieira, 'Parody and Marginality: The Case of Brazilian Cinema', *Framework: The Journal of Cinema and Media*, 28 (1985).

Viany, Alex, *Introdução ao cinema brasileiro* (Rio de Janeiro: Revan, 1993).

West, Joan M. and Dennis West, 'Carmen Miranda: Bananas is My Business', *Cineaste*, 22: 1, 1996.

Xavier, Ismail, *Allegories of Underdevelopment: Aesthetics and Politics in Modern Brazilian Cinema* (Minneapolis: University of Minnesota Press, 1997).

Xavier, Ismail, 'O sonho da indústria: a criação de imagem em *Cinearte*', in *Sétima arte: um culto moderno* (São Paulo: Perspectiva – Secretaria da Cultura, Ciência e Tecnologia do Estado de São Paulo, 1978).

Index